CW00418105

INDIA'S FREEDOM REASSESSED

The Legacy of the Desais and Patels of Gujarat

Dr Chittaranjan Dadubhai Desai

Book Guild Publishing
Sussex, England

First published in Great Britain in 2007 by
The Book Guild Ltd
Pavilion View
19 New Road
Brighton BN1 1UF

Copyright © Dr Chittaranjan Dadubhai Desai 2007

The right of Dr Chittaranjan Dadubhai Desai to be identified as the author of this work has been asserted by him in accordance with the Copyright, Designs and Patents Act 1988.

All rights reserved. No part of this publication may be reproduced, transmitted, or stored in a retrieval system, in any form or by any means, without permission in writing from the publisher, nor be otherwise circulated in any form of binding or cover other than that in which it is published and without a similar condition being imposed on the subsequent purchaser.

Typesetting in Times by
Keyboard Services, Luton, Bedfordshire

Printed in Great Britain by
CPI Antony Rowe

A catalogue record for this book is available from
The British Library

ISBN 978 1 84624 012 6

Dedicated to the Memory of
Vithalbhai, Vallabhbhai, Dadubhai
Who Twice Rescued the Indian National Congress
From Terminal Decline
and
Brought Forward the Independence of India
By Many, Many Years

CONTENTS

Part One: HISTORY

Part Two: STRUGGLE and INDEPENDENCE

Part Three: MAJOR CHARACTERS

APPENDICES

LIST OF MAPS AND TABLES

Maps

Tables

LIST OF PHOTOGRAPHS

PARTIAL FAMILY TREE OF THE DESAIS

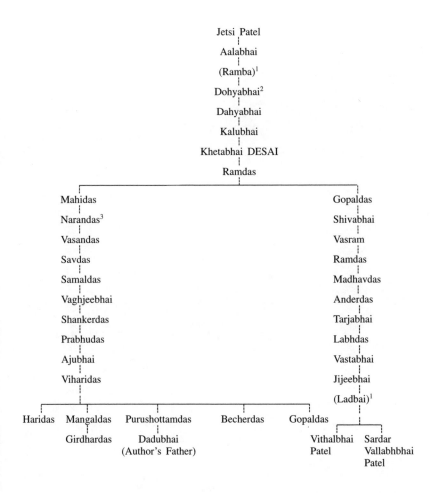

- Jetsi Patel
  - Aalabhai
    - (Ramba)[1]
      - Dohyabhai[2]
        - Dahyabhai
          - Kalubhai
            - Khetabhai DESAI
              - Ramdas
                - Mahidas
                  - Narandas[3]
                    - Vasandas
                      - Savdas
                        - Samaldas
                          - Vaghjeebhai
                            - Shankerdas
                              - Prabhudas
                                - Ajubhai
                                  - Viharidas
                                    - Haridas
                                    - Mangaldas
                                      - Girdhardas
                                    - Purushottamdas
                                      - Dadubhai (Author's Father)
                                    - Becherdas
                                    - Gopaldas
                - Gopaldas
                  - Shivabhai
                    - Vasram
                      - Ramdas
                        - Madhavdas
                          - Anderdas
                            - Tarjabhai
                              - Labhdas
                                - Vastabhai
                                  - Jijeebhai
                                    - (Ladbai)[1]
                                      - Vithalbhai Patel
                                      - Sardar Vallabhbhai Patel

[1] As customary, only male descendants are shown – except Ramba Patel who married Rajabhai and Ladbai Desai who married Zaverbhai Patel.
[2] In 1429 arrived in Nadiad and founded the DESAI dynasty.
[3] In 1636 the title and position of DESAI was reaffirmed

FOREWORD

I am happy to recommend Dr Desai's historical account of the Indian campaign for freedom. It sheds new light on the popular campaign of *Satyagraha* on the role of Pandit Nehru and of Mahatma Gandhi.

From the Indian point of view, the process of attaining independence had two great failures. The first was the deterioration in the relations between the Hindu majority and the Muslim population which led to partition. Many Indian historians still feel that might have been avoided.

The second failure was economic. The three great Asian economies are those of India, China and Japan. After 1945, under American occupation and then as an independent country, Japan followed a free market system on the United States model. From the victory of the Chinese Communist Party in 1948, China followed the Marxist-Leninist model until the reforms of Deng Xiao Ping which started in 1979. From Independence in 1947, India followed the social democratic policies which were adopted by the Congress Party under the influences of the Nehru family.

Japan's economic results were by far the most favourable and Japan still has much the highest income per head. In the Mao period, China's results were much the worst, but since the 1979 reforms, which established the free market in China, the Chinese economy has grown faster than Japan or India.

It was not until 1991 that the Indian economic reforms were introduced, and they had the same effect as the American inspired free market reforms in Japan, or the Deng Xiao Ping reforms, which were themselves the results of complete disillusionment with the stagnation of the Russian Soviet model. Since 1991, the Indian economy has grown at an accelerating rate.

Dr Desai's book is written from the point of view of the distinguished Desai family of Gujarat, which made a great contribution to the history of Indian independence.

William Rees-Mogg
12 July 2006

PREFACE

While writing a history one must be careful not to invent 'facts', but equally one must not suppress relevant truths. We have a responsibility to present historical facts in general and to criticise any politico-ideological abuse of history by vested interests. The point from which the historian must start is absolutely central, distinguishing between established facts and invented fiction, between those historical statements which are based on evidence and subject to scrutiny and those which are not. Often historians review other publications on their subject and, while doing so, either inadvertently or deliberately omit or ignore some facts which do not fit into what they are constructing. It is my endeavour to put the matter straight on some aspects of Indian history and to give credit to those who deserve credit.

In the long period of India's fight for freedom, the Government of India declared many organisations and actions of individuals to be illegal, and as such these were suppressed. During that time evidence of some events was lost or destroyed. Dadubhai's Haveli was twice searched and ransacked by the authorities, both times taking away sackfuls of papers. Some evidence and certain facts never saw the light of day or were concealed because the historians of the time did not want them to be brought forward. Once India became independent and a ruling hierarchy had been installed, only the facts and evidence showing that hierarchy in a favourable light (plus related unsubstantiated events and actions) were considered relevant. All other events and happenings, however real and true as well as formidably effective they might have been, were ignored and excluded from publications or publicity.

We all know that nobody can suppress the truth forever – 'Truth always wins' (Satya Mew Jayate). It is my good fortune that providence has favoured me to reveal such truth; the truth which for over 75 years has remained suppressed and ignored. Here are two examples of such omissions. The real effectiveness of the Indian National Congress was the result of its ability to organise civil disobedience in the form of mass movements. Initially only two movements were large enough to affect the British rulers: Bardoli Satyagraha and Dharasana (salt) Satyagraha. Both of these were carried out in Gujarat by the people of Gujarat alone. Throughout the life of the Indian National Congress, up to 1930, only these two movements, which were not only the largest so far but also the ones of which the Government took note, gave the Congress recognition as the main enemy of British rule. But for these two movements, the Government was never going to recognise the Congress as an effective All-India opponent. To the historians who wrote the history of Congress, however, their hero was Pandit Jawaharlal Nehru, although he had not taken any real or substantial part in either of these movements. Moreover, they took place in Gujarat, a small province which had only eleven members in the Parliament compared to over 80 members from Uttar Pradesh, the province of the ruling clan of Nehrus and Nehru-Gandhis. So they could ignore Gujarat and its achievements as Gujarat had little voice in the New Delhi Parliament.

Immediately following the Bardoli Satyagraha, the Viceroy wrote a long letter to the Governors of all the principal provinces warning of the serious nature of that movement and that they should guard against such a movement being started in their provinces. Bardoli Satyagraha in 1928 and Dharasana Salt Satyagraha in 1930 were the very movements which forced the British government to recognise the Congress and Gandhi as the All-India motive force which one day could replace them. These two movements gave teeth to the Congress and if they had not come into being, one wonders where the Indian National Congress would have been in the story of India's struggle for freedom.

Almost immediately after the Dharasana Salt Satyagraha, the British government gave in and the Gandhi-Irwin Pact was signed in March 1931. This was the first meaningful official contact ever with the Congress; before that the British were not ready to recognise the power of the Congress. The letters that passed between Vithalbhai Patel and Lord Irwin the Viceroy (who later, as Lord Halifax, became Britain's Foreign Secretary) prove that point. In 1930, after Bardoli and during the course of the salt satyagraha of Dharasana, Vithalbhai, in his capacity as President of the Viceroy's Legislative Assembly, told the Viceroy that in the final analysis he would have to deal with Gandhi and the Congress if he wanted a peaceful settlement.

The backbone and the real power base of Mahatma Gandhi lay in Gujarat and that too was concentrated in the Patidar community of Kaira District and Bardoli Taluka. In both places resided the Patidars who had descended from the same roots. In June 1930, a dispirited revenue officer wrote:

> The Patidar community, which is taking a prominent part in this movement in the Kaira District, is known for its intelligence and organisational capacity. Their unity is almost proverbial. They are capable of accomplishing anything on earth, whether good or bad. It is this community which is leading the no-tax campaign and it would be no wonder if they succeeded in this move as their resourcefulness and tenacity are really very wonderful.

Since verbal science has no final end, since life is short, and obstacles impede, let central facts be picked and firmly fixed as swans extract the milk from water mixed. (THE PANCHATANTRA)

Where history has been abused, we have a responsibility to criticise such actions. This was so throughout the Nehru/Gandhi rule over nearly half a century. When, in the 1950s and 1960s, massive transformations in the mode of production and financing took place throughout the entire industrial world, the Nehru dynasty stuck to the rigid regime of the Planning Commission, closed the Indian economy to the outside world, and forcibly allocated resources in a manner which worked against future prosperity and an improved standard of living. The net result was that India was left behind while others, less well endowed, prospered. The Nehru dynasty's slogan, Garibi Hathao (down with poverty) was a hollow one, as the regime itself did nothing to improve the lot of the poor. India's poverty remained at over 50 per cent from the 1950s through to the 60s, 70s and 1980s, which crushed three successive generations of the poor under the steamroller of the Udyog Bhavan (the Citadel of Bureaucracy). Inauguration of layers of bureaucracy led to the introduction and increase of corruption. There is a clear link between levels of bureaucracy and levels of corruption. Worse still, brilliant graduates in engineering, science and literature migrated to the UK, to the USA and other industrial countries to escape unemployment in India. Nehru's five year plans were unable to employ them, and his restrictive licensing policies did not allow them to start their own ventures in India. Frustrated as they were, they migrated overseas. The reign of the Nehru dynasty saw the greatest migration of Indian talent abroad. This was one of the great crimes of Nehru – the flight of talent which India lost forever. These talented migrants now belatedly support the growing economy of India. Suffice it to say that remittances from abroad and the investments by overseas Indians into India are now counted in billions of dollars every year. Mistrust of the business community and reluctance to encourage youth to take part in politics led to a gradual decline in political thought and standards of politicians in India.

Only after the controls were lifted, in 1991, and India entered the free market economy for the first time since independence did poverty start to decline: to 36 per cent by 1994, 29 per cent by 2000 and estimated to be 25 per cent today. In fact, Nehru and his descendants knew that the ignorant poor gave them votes and, poverty being their ally, they were happy to allow it to remain as such. As William Rees-Mogg once stated: 'The Soviet Union ultimately failed because the economy allocated resources without information of demand and prices that only the free market can give.' India went the 'Soviet Union way' on account of the same market failure. In short, the Nehru dynasty was the scourge and curse of India.

I make no apology about writing, and incorporating in the text, the whole history of the Desais of Nadiad. Desais were always in the forefront of social and political upheaval in Kaira District and broadly in Gujarat; either it was war or flood disaster or famine or Government atrocities. They co-operated with the regime only up to a point. Once they saw injustice they were always up in arms. At the moment I am writing there are thousands of Desais, Patels and their descendants in Britain, the United States and the rest of the industrial world as well as in Africa and Far and Middle East. This is their story along with the story of India's struggle for freedom.

Vallabhbhai, Vithalbhai and Dadubhai, as well as the other Desais and Patels mentioned in the following pages, were all Patidars. Gandhiji annexed this community and accomplished miracles with their help and their faith in him. One can now say that in his final steps in promoting Jawaharlal Nehru, he betrayed the Patidars' trust in him, and indeed that of all India. Pandit Nehru had a good tongue and was able to address both mass meetings and small gatherings effectively; but he had neither the inclination for, nor the experience of, organising a mass movement and taking it to success. He never ventured to experience the rough and tumble of real rural life of hardship at the poverty level. He never shared the food and drink with villagers in their earthenware pots and cups. He never slept in huts and shacks alongside the villagers. In contrast to Vithalbhai, Vallabhbhai and Dadubhai who did all that at great personal inconvenience and hardship. The heart and soul of India resides in the villages and he however knew how to exploit them by suitable, bombastic slogans, which were spoken but were never meant to be acted upon.

With these words, I leave it to the readers to decide for themselves.

ACKNOWLEDGEMENTS

I am deeply grateful to the very helpful staff of the India Office at Blackfriars' Bridge and the British Library at Euston Road in London. Their assistance was invaluable in the search for documents of historical interest. These documents form the basis of this book.

David Hardiman's book on his experiences in the Kheda District was very useful; I have included a number of quotations from his work and I am indebted for the information his book provides.

The accounts of India gaining its freedom by the late Subhas Chandra Bose and by the late Maulana Azad were also a great help. Their books contained many pertinent facts and explained their thinking at that time.

I must also express my gratitude to my late wife, Sarojben, for her many years of support.

Finally I must thank my good friend John L. Cox for his help and advice. This book would not have been possible without his assistance.

Part One

HISTORY

1

INTRODUCTION: THE TOWN OF NADIAD

Years of political struggle led up to independence for India. This is the story of that struggle from the perspective of one Indian family, the Desais of Nadiad, and revelations about their involvement. They had originally settled in the Gujarati town of Nadiad, but now have branches scattered about the world.

Nadiad lies about 25 miles East of the coast of the Arabian Sea, situated at a latitude of 22°44' North and a longitude of 73°00' East. It is a station on the Bombay to Ahmedabad broad gauge railway line. At the beginning of the seventeenth century (1612) Nadiad was a large town where people made indigo.[1] In 1638 its houses were good and it had some cotton and indigo manufactures.[2] In 1666 it was a place of middle size where much cotton was processed.[3] In 1775 it was one of the prettiest cities in Gujarat, nearly three miles round with a slight wall flanked at irregular distances by round towers. It had nine strong gates and a dry ditch round the walls. The people, around 12,000 families, were chiefly occupied in weaving fine cloth and other cotton manufactures. They also cut and polished Kapadvanj stones.[4] In 1804 the British took possession of Nadiad. In 1825 it was one of the largest towns in Gujarat, with 15,000 inhabitants.[5] In 1833 it carried on a considerable trade with Malwa and the interior, importing grain, drugs, gum and dye stuffs while exporting cotton, coarse cloth, calicoes, tobacco and coarse sugar.[6]

In 1847 it was a most thriving little town.[7] Its nine entrances are: Dabhan Bhagol, Pij Bhagol, Dumral Bhagol, Kolivada Bhagol, Chaklashi Bhagol, Salun Bhagol, Marida Bhagol, Bilodara Bhagol and Ahmedabad Bhagol.

The town has five divisions or Patis: Kakarkhad Pati, Kilidar and Halad Pati, Lakhavad Pati, Chaklasi Pati and Hirji Ratanji Pati.[8] Besides the main divisions there are wards known by the names of particular castes or tribes. Of these the chief are: Nagarwada, the Nagar Brahmin's ward, Lakhavad and Kakarkhad (inhabited by rich patidar peasants), Santh Pipli by Vanias, Bhavsarvad by calico printers, Mohoti Vorvad and Nani Vorvad by Bohoras, Desai Vago by Desais or superior landed proprietors, Mohota Por and Nana Por by Kanbi cultivators, Navagam by Khendaval Brahmins, Gazipura and Sakarko by Mussulmans, Mohota Bhatwada and Nana Bhatwada by Bhats or Rajput genealogists, Malharpura by Rawalias, and Vagrivad by Vagris.

The chief temples are the Santram Temple with large grounds where at every full moon a fair is held; the temples of Narayandev, Gosaiji or Vallabhacharya, Swaminarayan, Bhairav, Kalkamata and Jain Derasar. Besides the Government Revenue and Police Offices, there is a Subordinate Judge's Court, a Post Office, Haridas Desai Hospital and Desai Veterinary Dispensary. In 1877 including the Government High School, donated by Viharidas Desai, there were eight Vernacular Schools with average attendance of 1,039 pupils.

In 1872 over half of the population were from high castes of Patidars, Brahmins and Vaniyas. About one-fifth of the population were artisans and another fifth were labourers and agricultural workers. The largest single group, making up a quarter of the population, were the Patidars (Desais and Patels) and Kanbis. Most of the agricultural land surrounding the town was owned by Patidars and farmed by their Kanbi tenants. The leading Patidars were from the Desai Family and they lived in spacious mansions in the South-Eastern portion of the town, an area known as 'Desai Vago'. The remaining Patidars were divided into five lineages, each living in its own part of the town. The 1860s settlement report noted that some of the richest men of Kheda District were Patidars of Nadiad. Most rented their land out on long tenures. Two of the Patidar lineage were rather poorer than the rest; for the most part members of these lineages cultivated their own land. The Kanbi tenants were poorer and lived in a distinct section of the town called Por.[9]

The secret of the Patels' business acumen and financial responsibility lies in their being village accountants for over four centuries, when they managed and accounted for the entire land revenue collection of their respective villages. This inbred ability now brings them forward in any profession or trade that they pursue.

Nadiad municipality was first established by the British administration in 1866, and its President, who was nominated by the Collector, was Viharidas Desai, grandfather of Dadubhai Desai. Viharidas was succeeded by two sons, Bechardas and Purushottamdas as nominated presidents, followed by their nephew Girdhardas, who was nominated and later on elected, until 1918 when he was defeated by Gokuldas Talati, a Vania (52 years of continuous Presidentship by Desais of Nadiad Corporation).

In 1888, when the British established the Bombay Governor's Council, called the Bombay Legislative Council, Haridas was appointed the first member from Gujarat. After Haridas his younger brother and the father of Dadubhai Desai, Purushottamdas, became its member until 1912. Then Vithalbhai Patel won the position in an open election. He was succeeded, in 1920, by Dadubhai (the author's father) who was re-elected continuously until his retirement in 1930.

By 1911 Nadiad had a population of 27,000.

2

SIX HUNDRED YEARS OF THE NADIAD DESAIS

The present few thousand Nadiad Desais, together with their Patel relatives, are spread throughout the world. The latter are through marriages of Desai daughters to Patels of five villages: Karamsad, Bhadran, Dharmaj, Sojitra, Vaso and others outside the Six Gol. These are all descendants of one couple, Jetsi Patel and his wife (daughter of Ram Alhad).

Jetsi Patel belonged to the Khsatriya Dynasty which reigned over the Punjab in the time of Alexander the Great. His family subsequently migrated to Mathura, Jaipur, Ujjain (where one of its members was appointed Dewan), Adalaj, Somnath Patan, Singsur, Anhilawara Patan, Mehmadabad, Singrav.[1] Jetsi Patel had a son called Aalabhai, nicknamed Ram Allad. Allad's daughter, Ramba, was married to Rajabhai of Simraw. They had a son, Dohyabhai, who migrated to Nadiad in 1429 and founded the Desai Dynasty of Nadiad. The Dynasty progressed from Dohyabhai to his son Dahyabhai, to his son Kalubhai and to his son Khetabhai.

Rajabhai came to Nadiad in the year 1429 from the village of Singrav near Mehmedabad. At that time Mahmed Shah Begda was Sultan of Gujarat. Dohyabhai must have established his authority reasonably well in Nadiad as his grandson, Kalubhai the son of Dahyabhai, created the small lake in the eastern border of Nadiad which even now after more than six hundred years is still called after his son: Kheta Talav (talav means a small lake).

This lake has been used by Nadiad residents for bathing, swimming and for washing clothes, as well as providing water for the cattle. For drinking water an ornate stepwell was constructed. This is still used by some people, though this is no longer necessary as the whole city of Nadiad has running water supplied by the municipal water company. It draws its supplies from deep wells dug in the bed of the River Shedi, which flows to the North of the city. Shedi is a tributary of the River Sabarmati which flows into the Bay of Cambay (Khambhat). Shedi flows into River Vatrak at Kheda and from there Vatrak flows into Sabarmati near Kunjrav.

From Khetabhai up to his great-grandson Narandas, we do not have any history of the family except the knowledge of the lineage: Khetabhai's son Ramdas, his son Mahidas, his son Narandas.

In 1636 Narandas was summoned to the Court in Agra by Emperor Shah Jahan (the builder of the grand edifice, the Taj Mahal, in memory of his beautiful wife Mumtaz Mahal). There he received the title and position of Desai along with a rich sirpao (a head-dress of honour) and a palkhi. At the time the position Desai gave him the power from Agra to collect government taxes, mostly in the form of land revenue, on behalf of the Emperor and render the same to his treasury at Ahmedabad where the provincial governor of the Province of Gujarat was stationed.[2] At the beginning of the reign of Shah Jahan when Allami Sa'Dullah was appointed Wazir-i-azam (chief minister), he arranged paraganahs into groups and called them 'chaklas'.

In each 'chakla' he appointed an Amin/Desai. The 'chakla' was administered under Ijara or contract system, by a contractor here named Desai. He not only compounded for the revenue but also acted as governor for the establishment of law and order as well as the well-being of the subjects. Later in Gujarat 'chakla' was also used for the wards of a city or town in which they were divided. In all these 'chaklas' several footmen were posted to patrol the streets.[3]

This was the time when in 1638 Mandelslo and in 1680 Inigree Baldeos both speak of (Cambay) Khambhata as being twice the size of Surat. The British were barely holding on to their foothold in Gujarat and for that matter in India (for the first time) as they also gained permission in 1618 from the Muqarrab Khan of Surat (the Moghul officer controlling the Gujarat ports) and also from the Emperor to start a factory in Surat.

On 17 August 1608 William Hawkins landed in Surat on his ship 'Hector' after visiting Diu on the Saurashtra coast. In February 1609 he left Surat to reach the Moghul Court at Agra by land after ten weeks. There he delivered a letter from King James I addressed to Emperor Akbar, though Akbar was dead by then and had been succeeded by Jehangir who ruled from 1605 to 1627. In his turn Jehangir was succeeded by Shah Jahan ruling from 1627 to 1658. In 1658 Aurangzeb was crowned Emperor. Hawkins stayed three years in India, mostly as courtier to the Emperor. He even married the daughter of an Armenian Christian courtier in Agra. In 1615 the East India Company sent Sir Thomas Roe to the court of Jehangir in Agra. In the audience chamber of the Agra Fort when he reached the highseated king, he demanded a chair to sit, but was told: 'No one sits in this chamber.' The only concession allowed to the tired Roe was that he was allowed to lean against one of the supporting pillars of the audience chamber. Roe stayed at the court for three years.

In 1686, during the reign of Aurangzeb, Desaigiri was reaffirmed.[4] In 1663 Aurangzeb had revisited Gujarat and met most of the revenue officers and reaffirmed Desaigiri of Savadas but reduced the remuneration from 10 to 2½ per cent of the collected revenue. In 1807 the Gujarat Revenue Commissioner, K.L. Prendergrast, was appointed to inquire into the claims of the Desais and Majmoodars to Desaiship and emoluments resulting from it. Paragraph 32 of his report reads:

> We have however obtained through another channel an original official document comprising summary of the proceedings of Emperor Aurangzeb the first allumgeer about the year 1663. This document also specifies the duties and responsibilities of the Desais and was issued under the seal of the Subedar Mahomed Khan.[5]

After Akbar's reign (1556–1605) the revenue rates for different crops and also different lands were fixed by taking an average of the previous ten years' produce. The actual area under cultivation was supposed to be measured every year by the revenue officers in the presence of the Mukhi or Patwari and the owner of the land himself and forwarded to Nadiad where, based on the report, the actual amount of State demand was prepared and forwarded for onward collection of money or produce. In the case of natural or unexpected calamity, such as flooding, drought, family illness or death, fire or vandalism, the matter was thoroughly investigated, vouched and the HQ granted due remission of revenue. Akbar also defined the gaz, the tanab and the beega used in measurement of land and merchandise and thus set up a unified standard to replace different and varied values of gaz. He also replaced hemp rope by bamboo stick with iron ring for use as the measuring tanab.

A partial Family Tree, on page x, shows the links between Jetsi Patel and the Desais and Patels that appear in this book. A more comprehensive Family Tree is contained in a pocket at the end of the book.

3

GENERAL ADMINISTRATION OF NADIAD PARAGANAH (PERGUNNAH)

The lands of Kaira, except Thasra and Kapadvanj, were included in the settled and directly managed portions of the Anhilvada Domain of different Rajput dynasties from AD 746 to 1290. At the end of the fourteenth century they came under the rule of the Musalman Kingdom of Ahmedabad. In 1573 the Moghuls of Agra took control. In 1590 Todarmal, under the direction of the Emperor Akbar, undertook the survey of the whole district of Kaira except Kapadvanj. He reorganised the revenue system on what is known as the 'Ten Year Settlement'. This was in reality a system based upon the average yield of the previous ten years. The average produce of each crop per beega was worked out and one third of this average was the State demand.[1] The actual area under tillage was measured every season by the representative of Desai in the presence of the village Patel (Mukhi) and the cultivator and forwarded to the headquarters at Nadiad. There, on the basis of these returns, the schedule of the State demand for the year was prepared and the collection carried out. It was the Mukhi's duty to inform Desai of any unexpected calamity experienced by the farmer. This was thoroughly investigated and acted upon. Any remission of revenue was to be reported by Desai to the Governor's office at Ahmedabad.

This was the practice under the Moghuls. However, under Marathas from 1753 to the British arrival in 1803, the 'Ijara' system was employed. Under this system it was a kind of contract; it meant the farming-out of the revenue of a whole paraganah. Generally, the ijardar was required to pay a fixed amount as stipulated in the putta (lease). The ijardar had to give a qabuliyat (acceptance) and affirm his duty to pay it. He had to protect the interests of the state as well as that of the Ryots (farm labourers). The settlement was made for an amount that was a little less than the expected income from the area farmed out to the ijardar, thus leaving a margin of profit for him. Nadiad Desais were shrewd and by their personal efforts and vigilance increased the collection in the Nadiad Pergunnah beyond the official calculation and that too without oppressing the cultivators. The village Patel also received a bigger share from Desais. Thus, the revenue administration skills created a great clan of prosperous Patels which had connections and roots in all the villages of Nadiad Pergunnah. As time went by, the Patels became a vast integrated family. This is what made the Kaira District unique and especially fitted to carry out a consolidated and resolute mass movement. Kaira district became the power base of Gandhiji, for he knew that he could draw strength for his mass movements only from these 182 interconnected villages of Patels of Kaira district and Bardoli Taluka. Both places were abodes of Patidars.

The revenue administration was arranged thus: as sub-divisional officers, Desais guarded village interests, operated the channels of justice, saw that the cultivators were not oppressed, looked after village improvements and, where necessary, made advances for sowing, also managed the maintenance of the village wells and medical services.[2] On behalf of the Government he superintended the village headmen (Patels), supplied all local details likely to help him in fixing the revenue, settled boundary and other village disputes, as well as help in preparing the village accounts. The Amin/Patel, the Desais' assistants, prepared the different village accounts and settlements. Even though in these offices the son generally succeeded the father, the practice was tolerated rather than admitted as a right. These sub-divisional officers formed a well-to-do class. Besides their village fees, Dasturis, most of them had, chiefly by taking land in mortgage, acquired considerable estates. Locally Patels governed the village, managed its affairs and settled its disputes. In return for their services, the revenue farmer (Desai) gave a yearly allowance amounting in some cases to as much as Rs.6,000. The villagers also made them presents of grain from their crop. In Colonel Walker's opinion the above Maratha system had the merit of being simple and well calculated to ensure smooth collection of the revenue.

After the signing of the Treaty of Bassain with the Marathas in 1803 (Arthur Wellesley winning the Battle of Assaye in 1803), Colonel Walker made an engagement with Prabhudas Shankerdas Desai on 7 August 1804, under which the current revenue collection arrangement of Desais with the Peshwas was allowed to remain undisturbed and the Nadiad Pergunnah was again rented to them for payment of Rs.232,401 per year.[3] At that time the Neriad Pergunnah was made up of 39 villages. This arrangement remained in force until 1815 when the Aumany Management was forcibly introduced incorporating Tullatees in the management structure. The revenue letter from Bombay to London, 17 April 1816, reads as follows:

> In consequence of the seditious conduct of the Patels of Neriad, aided and countenanced by the Dessayes, Captain Robertson very properly superseded their agency, which they conceived indispensable to the security of the revenue, and determined to introduce the Aumany Management throughout the greater portion of that district... We anticipate the attainment of the fullest information of the actual resources of the Neriad Pergunnah under the operation of Captain Robertson's instructions to Lieutenant Barnwall, that they will be finally productive both of benefit to the Honourable Company and of much ease to the Collector's Department, as much as it will be the means of correcting abuses, of enabling us to dispense with an agency which at a future period might give us greater trouble than at present, and to substitute in its place a management which will finally lead to the establishment of Colonel Monroe's Ryotwary System, the seeds of which being already planted in a considerable portion of the Kaira Jurisdiction, it requires only some effort like the present to bring them to maturity and perfection.
>
> One great object of the Patels in resisting the Tullatee Regulations is to screen the illegal alienations and appropriations of the government lands... I would recommend the village expenses to your particular attention. These expenses have always been a considerable source of emolument to the managing Patels, the deprivation of which is another natural result of their proceedings. Under a careful control of the village expenses, I calculate that much ultimate advantage will occur

to the public. On this score you will receive much opposition from the Patels; but having so seditiously declined continuing their responsibility for collecting their revenue, they themselves must be aware that they have no plea of right to interfere in this branch of village management.[4]

On the same principle, they will have no right to any portion of the established enams, which it has always been usual to grant to the responsible Patels of each village. In the district of Neriad these enams amount to upwards of Rs.5,000. Policy may however dictate the necessity of rewarding where they may willingly afford the services of any Patel who may be proved never to have joined the combination or who may have the merit of first disentangling himself from its illegal resolves.[5] Considering also the degree of ill-will and the revengeful disposition of a cabal of disappointed natives, I shall deem it my duty to request that a military party should be allotted for your personal protection.[6]

Letter from Captain Archibald Robertson, first assistant collector of Kaira, to Lieutenant Robert Barnwall, assistant collector; dated 1 September 1815.

4

NADIAD SUB-DIVISION

This is situated in the centre of the Kaira District, bounded on the north by Kapadvanj and on the east by the Thasra and Anand sub-divisions, to the south is Petlad a former Gaikwar possession, to the southwest the Matar and to the west the Mehmadabad sub-divisions. Total area is 223 square miles. Its level surface with very few undulations, its well-grown groves of fruit and timber trees, its hedge-bound and highly tilled fields and its large strongly built villages, show Nadiad to be one of the richest parts of Gujarat. The climate is healthy; but in the south and southwest, where sea breezes blow from the Gulf of Cambay, the heat during the months of March, April and May is excessive.

The River Shedhi entering from the east passes through the sub-division on its way to join the Sabarmati. Near the centre of its course it is joined from the north by the 'Mohar' and the united stream passes westward winding between steep banks to join the Vatrak. Except in the usual dry season, when the water stands in pools, the streams of the Shedhi and Mohar flow throughout the year. Still the supply is scanty. The water of the Shedhi and the Mohar, carrying in solution some injurious salt, is unfit for irrigation. The want of clay in the soil makes storage in reservoirs difficult and the supply from wells, though plentiful and near the surface, is brackish.

Except some rice lands of medium-black besar, the whole sub-division is a light gorat soil, very rich and most carefully worked. Apart from ordinary grains and pulses, Nadiad produces all the better kinds of crops both early and late. The chief rainy season (Kharif) crops include rice, tobacco, Indian millet, pulses and several of the coarser grains. The cold weather (Rabi) crops are wheat and late tobacco, hot weather (Hari) late millet, pulse and gram. In the most fertile areas ginger, sunflower, tobacco, turmeric and sugar cane are grown.

The botanical names of these crops are: Bajri, Penicillaria Spicata, Dangar, Oryza Sativa, Bawta, Panicum Frumentaceum, Juvar, Sorghum Vulgare, Kodra, Paspalum Scrobiculatum, 'Ghaun', Triticum Aestivum, 'Jav', Hordeum Hexastichon, 'Makai' Zea Mays, 'kang', Panicum Italicum, 'Rajgara', Amarantus Paniculatus, 'Tuver' Cajanus Indicus, 'Math', Phaseolus Aconitifolius, 'Guvar' Cyamopsis Psoralioides, 'Chola' Vigna Catiang, 'Chana', Cicer arietinum, 'Mag' Phaseolus Radiatus, 'Adad' Phaseolus Mungo, 'Val', Dolichos Lablab, 'Tal' Sesamum Indicum, 'Serdi' saccharum Officinarum, 'Kasumba' Carthamus Tinctorius, 'Tambaku', Nicotiana Tabacum, Kapas Gossypium Herbaceum and Hemp, San, Crotalaria Juncea.

The people were grouped as follows: Brahmans; Patidars; Vanias; Shravaks; Luvanas; Kanbis; Rajputs; Kachhias; Malis; Bhavsars, calico printers; Sonis, gold and silversmiths; Kansaras, brass and coppersmiths; Luhars, blacksmiths; Suthars, carpenters; Kadias, bricklayers; Salats, masons; Ghanchis, oil pressers; Khatris, silk and cotton weavers; Barots, bards; Charans, genealogists; Ghandhraps, songsters; Darjis, tailors; Kumbhars, potters; Hajams, barbers; Dhobhis, washermen; Bharvads and Rabaris, herdsmen and shepherds; Machhis, fishermen; Golas, rice pounders; Bhadbhujas, grain parchers; Vagris, fowlers and hunters; Mochis, shoemakers; Chamadias, tanners; Bajanias, acrobats; Kalals, liquor sellers; Dhed and Bhangis, sweepers. This was the variety of professions on the arrival of the British at Nadiad in 1803.[1]

5

HISTORY OF KAIRA DISTRICT

From 746 to 1290 Rajputs reigned over the Kaira District which was directly managed as part of Anhilwad Kingdom. At the end of the fourteenth century, about 1370, it passed to the Mohamedan Kingdom of Ahmedabad and in 1635 was transferred to the Moghuls, during the reign of Emperor Shah Jehan.

Shivaji, born in April 1627, son of Shahji Bhonsle held a Jagir under the Bijapur Kingdom. In 1659 Shivaji killed the Bijapur's general, Afzal Khan. In 1666 he visited Aurangzeb in Delhi. On being dissatisfied with his treatment by Aurangzeb, he was arrested and imprisoned. He escaped in a fruit basket, raised an army and fought the Moghuls till he died in 1680.[1]

In 1720 the Marathas appeared. From that time to the fall of Ahmedabad in 1752, it was the scene of perpetual struggle between the Marathas and Mohamedan Viceroys for Gujarat which included the only real trading port (Khambhat) in upper western India, including Nadiad Broach and Surat Paragunnahs.

After the Marathas' victory in 1753, the district was shared between the Peshwas and Gaikwar, the Peshwas having suzerainty and Gaikwar the administration. In 1775, after the Battle of Arras (see Chapter 6), Vaghjeebhai effected reconciliation between Peshwas and Gaikwar. For this he received an inman (feudal grant), the village of Bilodara and a Palkhi.[2] This was enjoyed by the family until 1816 when during the Nadiad Rebellion of Patels the Desais of Nadiad were named as its ringleaders.

In the year 1742 Vaghjeebhai had built the Kalkadevi Temple and the small lake adjoining the temple and bestowed the surrounding land as a setting for the temple and also a covered resting place for pilgrims.

In 1780 Shankardas built what was then the tallest building in Nadiad, a six-storey mansion with carved wooden doors and windows. It is still standing and is called 'Shankardas Desai's Haveli'. It was so solidly built that even now it is being used as a family residence by some of his descendants. Shankardas was assassinated in front of his house by some conspirators in 1783. His son Prabhudas carried on Desaigiri until 7 August 1804, when he signed an agreement with the British. The sequence of events was as follows:[3]

1 The treaty dated 8 March 1802, signed 6 June 1802 between Jonathan Duncan and Raojee Apajee Dewan of Anund Rao Gaikwar, relating to Rs.125,000 of Neryad Pergunnah awarded to Mulhar Rao.[4]
2 On 18 February 1803 agreement with Anund Rao Gaikwar supplementary to the above treaty of March and June of 1802; disposal of Rs.125,000, being the part income of Neryad, as Mulhar Rao fled. So money now goes to the Honourable Company.[5]
3 A definitive treaty between the East India Company and Anund Rao Gaikwar, 10 September 1806.

In 1791 Peshwa made a ten year revenue collection agreement with Bhugwant Rao Gaikwar for management of Ahmedabad District. There is no mention of Neryad Pergunnah, perhaps because it was already a part of Baroda's Sovereign Region of 'Gaikwar'. In India the East India Company's servants were badly paid.[6] In Mr Fryer's time (1674) a writer received ten pounds, a factor two pounds, a merchant chief of factory 40 pounds and even the President at Surat only 300 pounds a year. These agents therefore also traded in India on their own account and reckoned to make money apart from the Company. In time they got into their hands the whole coastal trade and as the eighteenth century proceeded such men made great fortunes in private trade and returned to England immensely rich. These servants of the East India Company who made a fortune and returned to England to live in splendour were known as 'Nabobs'. By the year 1760 the whole standard of life in a gentleman's house had risen. London as well as large county towns were full of them and there they built three-storey properties of 'Upstairs Downstairs' fame, with servants' quarters and a kitchen in the basement.[7]

In the same year that the Arras campaign was going on, the first steps had been taken by American colonists to be independent of Britain's yoke. On 4 July 1776 America declared her independence – a day which has been celebrated ever since by all loyal Americans.

6

THE BATTLE OF ARRAS

The late 18th century was a turbulent time. The first Mysore War was fought in 1767, followed by the Second Mysore war in 1780 and the Third from 1790 to 1792. There were three Maratha wars, two Sikh wars and a host of lesser campaigns. All these hint at piecemeal policies and uncoordinated direction. Many short wars attract less attention than a few long ones. Moreover, they were usually fought and won before London's negative response could reach India. Viewing them now they would seem so jumbled together chronologically as to throw all but the most dogged historian off the scent.

The conquest of Bengal by the East India Company fuelled the ambition of its Madras establishment in Mysore. Then Mysore's conquest opened the way for intervention in the Maratha territories. Bombay in the early 1770s was growing in importance as far as commerce was concerned, although it remained far less politically significant than Calcutta and Madras. The Bombay Governors felt it important to possess the adjoining enclaves of Salset Island and Bassein Port. These had been Portuguese but were now in the possession of the Marathas. With unrest amongst the Marathas, Britain saw a growing opportunity to seize them and other territory. Thus started the first Anglo-Maratha War, in 1775. This was mainly fought in the Kaira District and was decided by the Battle of Arras. In Poona, the seat of the Marathas, a rupture had come about between the Peshwa, Ragunath Rao, and the Regent, Gangabai, who was supported by Sakharam Bapu and Nana Fadanvis. The Sindhia of Indore and Holkar of Nagpur also deserted Ragunath Rao. So he fled to the north of Poona with an army of about 40,000, hotly pursued by a Maratha Confederate Army of similar size. He reached Baroda on 3 January 1775 where he found Govind Rao and Khande Rao, the Jagirdar of Nadiad, besieging Fatesing, the Gaikwar of Baroda, in the city. Being hotly pursued by the Confederate Army, Ragunath Rao Ragobah could not afford to wait, bypassing Baroda and crossing the River Mahi in February 1775 encamped on the Plains of Arras, in the Kaira district. On 17 February, the Confederate Army, commanded by Hurra Punt Turkia, crossed the river at the Pass of Fazalpoor about 30 miles from Cambay. They crossed without any opposition from the enemy and commenced their attack on Ragobah's army. The engagement began at noon and lasted till after sunset.

The outcome of the battle was long in doubt, but victory was at last declared in favour of the Confederate Army which was occasioned by the disaffection of 12,000 Arabs, who at the critical moment refused to fight on account of the large arrears due to them – although they were also suspected of having been bribed to the treachery by the opposite party. These Arabs were posted with Ragobah in the centre, but he could not prevail upon them to draw their swords in his defence. There Hurra Punt Turkia made his grand attack; and Ragobah, after the Arabs stood neutral, found himself left with only 4,000 men – a force quite insufficient to withstand the superior number brought against them. Ragobah, perceiving that to gain possession of his person seemed to be the principle object of the enemy, resolved to leave the field; he retired to a village at some distance, upon which his right and his left wing gave way and the enemy remained the masters of the field. Ragobah immediately retreated towards Cambay with Himmat Rao, his adopted son, and several of his women. He carried with him his most valuable jewels, a few elephants and camels, and about 700 horsemen accompanied him in his flight. Ragobah reached Cambay at three o'clock next day. The Nabob of Cambay refused to admit him within the walls of the city. He left all his jewels in the charge of the Company's Resident at Cambay, Mr Malet. From there he left for Bhavnagar, where he abandoned his army and elephants and camels and departed by boat to Surat with his family. There, on 4 March, he was received by the Nawab and the British. Meanwhile from the battlefront of Arras, Ragobah's Generals, Sadasev Ramchandar, Succaram Horra, Apagee Madeu, Manackjee Phankria together with his allies Govind Rao, Gaikwar and Cunda Row Gaikwar of Nadiad, collected their scattered forces and retired to Copperwange (Kapadvanj), a strong post, 50 cos or 75 English miles from Cambay, where they now waited for Ragobah's orders. In this battle Ragobah had only two or three hundred men killed or wounded, but he lost all his guns together with a great number of elephants, camels and horses.

At Surat Ragobah was conducted by the Nabob to his palace of Mahomeda Bag and treated with great courtesy. The English provided a battalion of English Guards for him. On 5 March, Captain Field arrived from Cambay with the jewels and papers which Ragobah had left under Mr Malet's care; to the amount of 43 lakhs of rupees; six lakhs and 25,000 lakhs in jewels, the rest in bonds, grants and other government securities. The jewels were immediately sent into the Company's treasury in the Castle, as a deposit for the expenses of this expedition in his favour. Ragobah had signed a farman in which he promised the English the sum of thirty lakhs of rupees, to be paid on his arrival at Poona, and being established there as Peshwa. This donation being meant in lieu of all plunder, prize money or any demand whatever of the kind. This method of recompensing the English for their services in war has always been accepted by the Princes of India. Though this treaty was not signed till 6 March, the Bombay Government way back in February had sent a small contingent to Surat, under the command of Colonel Keating. As James Forbes writes: 'Bombay 16 February 1775, received an order from the Honourable the President and Council appointing me to officiate as Chaplain to the troops under the command of Lieutenant Colonel Keating now under orders to proceed to the assistance of Ragobah'.[1] The official report of James Forbes to the East India Company is used freely in the pages that follow.

The Indiaman, Calcutta, carried Colonel Keating and most of the English officers. The rest of the officers and the sepoys on board The Bonella Gallival, and several large boats forwarding under convoy of the Calcutta Indiaman. On 13 March the fleet left Surat in the direction of Cambay and first reached Domus (Dummas) on 15 March. They anchored a few miles south of Broach river to pick up Major Hassard and his detachment from Broach. A little after sunset on 17 March, Calcutta and its flotilla anchored in Cambay Road close to a steep bank which was flooded at the highest tide, about a mile and a half from the City of Cambay. At 8 o'clock on 18 March, all the troops landed and marched to

Narrangseer, a plain about half a mile north of the city, where the camp was formed. As Forbes writes:

'In the evening, struck camp at Narrangseer and the English forces marched to Ginnich, a village six miles from Cambay in a northerly direction. Captain Hartley with his division of sepoys remained at Narrangseer to take care of the stores we were obliged to leave there for want of cart and camels to remove them. The Army under the command of Colonel Keating, now it has been reinforced by the different detachments from Surat and Broach, consists of eighty artillery, three hundred and fifty European infantry, eight hundred sepoys and one hundred and sixty lascars, besides commissioned and non-commissioned officers; amounting in all to one thousand five hundred men. A further detachment of a hundred and fifty Europeans is expected to join us from Madras and six hundred sepoys from Bombay. Our train of artillery consists of the following pieces of ordnance:

2 iron eighteen pounders
4 brass twelve pounders
4 brass six pounders
2 eight inch howitzers
2 five and a half inch howitzers.

The officers of the present service are:

Lieutenant Colonel Thomas Keating, Commander-in-Chief

<u>Artillery</u>	<u>Infantry & Sepoys</u>	<u>Infantry & Sepoys</u>
MAJORS:	CAPTAINS:	ENSIGNS:
Gaspar Dagonas	Charles Michael Frith	William Hudson
Captains:	James Hartley	Philip England
John Westfhall	James Stewart	Simon Gottilick
John Nugent	Robert Scott	John Cliff
Lieutenants:	Lieutenants:	Edward Danoon
John Samuel Torriano	William Cuthbert	Charles Brown
Thomas Dighton	Robert Morris	John Brown
John Hallamby	Abraham Henney	George Dunn
John Bellaso	Alexander Canjano	Thomas Williams
John Wilkinson	Jacharich Cook	William Boyd
George St La Thomas	Thomas Dawson	Roger Brownrigg
Abraham Maximillian	William Hayes	John Riddell

Richardson	Thomas Kelly	<u>Cadets & Volunteers</u>
<u>Infantry & Sepoys</u>	Charles Yonger	Charles Stewart
Major:	Thomas Cheek	Henry Baker
Robert Hapard	Alexander Davis	Thomas Marshall
Captain:	William Proper	George Claney
John Hopkins	Thomas Anderson	. . . Bartlett
		Tudenic Dagons

<u>Staff – Double Appointments, etc</u>

Mr John . . .	Commissary
Mr James Forbes	Chaplain
Mr George Levibond	Judge Advocate
Mr Thomas Holmes	Paymaster & Secretary
Capt. James Stewart	Brigade Major
Capt. James Hartley	Quartermaster General
Lt. I.S. Jerriand	Captain of Prisoners
Lt. John Bellaso	Aide-de-camp
Mr Samuel Richardson	Surgeon Major
Mr Peter . . .	Surgeon
Mr John Blakeman	Surgeon
Mr Thomas Cumming	Surgeon.

While Col. Keating's army remained encamped near Narangseer, on 31 March they received intelligence reports that the enemy, the Confederate Army, had encamped near Kaira, about 30 miles away.

None of Ragobah's troops had yet joined him. They were supposed to be around Kapadvanj. Ragobah's forces now with him in Cambay were only about 2,000, most of whom had enlisted since his arrival in Cambay with the British Army. The majority of these men were untrained and undisciplined. On 1 April a fleet arrived from Surat with a detachment of 150 European infantry, 130 of them from Madras. This completed the force of 500 European infantry. Arriving with the Madras detachment were Captains Myers and Serle, Lieut. Stuky, Ensigns Green, Godfrei, Haliburton, Stafford and Tuning with Surgeon Mr Peter . . . Forbes describes it thus: 'That evening (3 April) Col. Keating introduced the gentlemen of the Army to Ragobah. We sat down by him on a carpet and he entered into a conversation about the Battle of Buxar, with which he seemed much pleased. After half an hour he presented us with betal nut and rose water and we took our leave.'

On 4 April Mr Bartlett (a volunteer) with a small party of cavalry arrived back from his reconnoitring mission to inform Col. Keating that he could not locate Ragobah's forces but saw the enemy encamped near Cairah (Kaira). Forbes:

Narrangseer, 12 April 1775 This morning Capt. Farrar arrived from Bombay with three hundred and ninety sepoys which, with two hundred that landed here on the 5th under Lt. Vocock and an Ensign, complete the detachment of sepoys expected from Bombay. Ensign Richardson and Capt. Farrar arrived with this battalion. The English line is formed into three divisions. The first under the command of Major Dagonas, the second Captain Hopkins and the third Capt. Farrar.

In the evening of 15 April 1775, struck the camp at Narrangseer. The English forces marched to Ginnich, a village six miles from Cambay in a northerly direction. Captain Hartley, with his division of sepoys remained at Narrangseer to take care of the stores we were obliged to leave there for want of cart and camels to remove them.

On the morning of 17 April 1775, at Ginnich, a thousand horse and as many foot, a body of Ragobah's forces under the command of Ledloy Bhoy and Sham Raw, joined us. I believe the fighting men may altogether amount to a third of that number.

Darah, 19 April 1775 Received intelligence that Ragobah's main army had arrived within a few miles of Ginnich. On which Ragobah and the Colonel with two companies of grenadiers, two divisions of sepoys and four six pounders, immediately marched to meet them at the village of Darah; where the junction, so much wished for and so long expected, was at last happily accomplished. This army is reckoned thirty-five thousand horse and foot exclusive of bazarmen, women and other followers of the camp. But in reality they do not amount to more than ten or twelve thousand fighting men. They are commanded by Sadasein Ramchander, Saccaram Hurra, Appajee Mahadev and Nanakjee Phankra; four of Ragobah's principal generals, who were with him at his defeat, who have since been collecting his scattered forces and waiting a favourable opportunity of joining their master. They very narrowly escaped the enemy encamped on the banks of the river Sabarmaty near Cairah, who marched to cut off their communication with us, but being three miles to the south they avoided them. The march this army has now performed is very great, no less than sixty cos or ninety English miles in two days and a half without a halt. They brought with them all their elephants, camels, bazar and baggages – several of their people, with a number of horses and camels perished in crossing the Sabarmaty and being unable to stem the tides thro' weakness and fatigue. In the evening the remainder of the English troops left Ginnich and encamped at Darah, three miles and a half due west, so that we were no further than Cambay.

Darah 21 April 1775 This afternoon we received the agreeable news that Govind Rao, at the head of a considerable force, was advanced to join us within a few miles of Darah – on which Ragobah and the Colonel marched with a strong detachment to meet them at the village of Tomsa, four miles west of Darah. Govind Rao's army is reckoned ten or twelve thousand, mostly good horse, but I am inclined to think the number greatly overrated. The forced march of Govind Rao has been more expeditious than that of Ragobah's army, tho' both of them are very great, considering the heat of the climate at this season.

By Indian calculations, Ragobah's army, including Govind Rao's and his other allies, is reckoned from forty to sixty thousand – but I do not think there are more than fifteen thousand at most that deserve the name of soldiers – threefourth of that number are horses. On 23 April, at sunrise, the whole of Ragobah's army headed by the smaller English army marched from Darah to Versara with a view to chastise the Maratha army.

Forbes continues: I exaggerate not when I say, there are a hundred thousand people who compose what is called Ragobah's army – but of this army I cannot allow more than fifteen thousand to be called good troops – others that please to style themselves fighting men, may be as many more, the rest are women, children and shopkeepers in the bazar of all trades and professions, of which there are several thousand that pay a considerable tax for the privilege of vending their commodities – exclusive of these, I am informed there are, no less than twelve thousand men who receive no pay from Ragobah, but gain their livelihood by plundering the villages and marauding for the rest of the camp – it may then be easily conceived, what a figure this army with their elephants, camels, horses and cattle of all kinds, must make, on a plain unbounded, with scarcely a tree to obstruct the view.

At two o'clock the army halted at a village called Versara, abounding with tanks and wells where the Colonel decided to encamp for a few days until the commissary, with the remainder of the stores and baggage arrived from Cambay.

Forbes writes: I will not attempt to describe the heat of the day and the burning winds that blow on us in this march – nothing but standing before Nebuchadnezzar's furnace seven times heated can give an idea of this fierce glow that impregnated the whole atmosphere – these hot winds together with what is called coup-de-soleil very often strike the European instantaneously dead on a march in this country – some of our men fell down to all appearance expired but by timely assistance recovered, the number of the cattle in the Maratha army perished through the excessive heat. The Colonel pitched his tent under a Banyan tree.

Versara, Darah and every village passed by the army had been burnt down by the Confederate army. No inhabitants were to be found. Versara is nine miles from Darah.

Our numerous army with elephants, camels and horses and cattle in one night exhausted all the tanks and wells at Versara, for which reason we were obliged to decamp earlier than intended and marched this morning, 24 April 1775, to the River Sabrematty. On our approaching the Sabrematty a detached party of the Ministerial army (enemy) who had been posted on the south side of the river immediately crossed and would not wait our arrival – the whole combined force was at a little distance on the opposite banks, all in motion and we supposed retreating. The principal officers in Ragobah's army were averse to crossing the river, when they saw the enemy so near them, and desired Colonel Keating to defer it until the next day – but he determined to pass over immediately and without a halt we descended the banks; and forded the river, in the place not more than two feet deep, tho' the opposite banks were steep, yet without loss of time, we ascended them and met with no opposition.

Here had the enemy ever meant to attack was the place; this was their favourable opportunity; but they neglected it for reasons I cannot discover – for they had long been encamped on the banks of the river and were as vigorous and as refreshed as possible – our army had marched in the heat for five hours and arrived at the river about noon when the sun acts with the greatest power and were greatly fatigued by the long march of this kind – the enemy would therefore most certainly have occasioned us no small trouble had they disputed our passage across the river. But so far from it that on the approach of our army, they retired with precipitation and we got up all our guns, ammunition and stores without the smallest loss. Our line was immediately formed on the banks and we were ready to give them a warm reception. Our worthy allies finding all quiet crossed the river and joined us. I am firmly of the opinion, that whenever we come to an engagement, on English courage alone must we depend for victory – for I place but a very poor reliance on that of our friends in Ragobah's army.

The enemy kept hovering near us the remainder of the day; we could plainly distinguish them from the trees at our encampment, but it would have answered no end to pursue them; they would have fled much faster than our fatigued troops could have followed them – and by being in possession of the banks of the river we have secured a grand advantage in constant supply of water, for our numerous army, and now only wait for the commissary with the treasure and stores from Cambay. The water is clean and very sweet – it abounds with carp and good fish of various kinds. What a blessing we have in so fine a river, where our harassed troops and cattle have abundance to drink, and so fine an element to bathe and recreate in the heat of the day. We crossed the river Sabrematty near the village of Anglah, seven miles from Versara in a northerly direction – on crossing this river, we left the territory of the Nabob of Cambay and entered that part of the Guzerat Province belonging to the Gaikwar Family.

27 April 1775 This morning Mr Torlesse arrived from Cambay with our stores, provisions and treasures. In the evening we marched a mile further along the river, to a stronger post.

Hossamlee 28 April 1775 At sunrise we marched from our ground near Anglah, along the banks of Sabrematty towards the village of Hossamlee; as we approached it, we perceived the enemy on the opposite banks of the river, coming down towards us – after performing a few manoeuvres they drew up in order of battle, and advanced – Colonel Keating immediately gave the necessary direction for an attack – a cannonading ensued on both sides – the enemy had twelve or fourteen guns; a few twelve, but most of them six pounders. We silenced their guns in about an hour and being there advanced close to the riverside, we obliged their left and centre to retreat – their right wing still stood the ground and part crossed the river; on which we marched in front of them and drove them off; a little after twelve the whole force retreated.

The number of the Confederate Army in this engagement was said to be from sixty to eighty thousand. Their artillery was well served, and at first kept up a very brisk fire – but their guns being too much elevated, their shots fell over our line into the village of Hossamlee. The loss of the enemy in this action from the different accounts is two principal officers killed, four hundred of different ranks killed and wounded, one elephant killed and three dangerously wounded, besides a number of horses and camels. Our detachment had only three Europeans and five Sepoys wounded, none killed. As to Ragobah's army, they were mere spectators, no part of them ever engaged.

The river dividing the two armies plus our men being much fatigued by a long march is the reason ascribed for not pursuing our advantage further, particularly in not taking their guns, which I look upon to be the severest blow they can sustain and what would strike them with the greatest terror. I hope therefore it will be our first grand object.

We then marched on about a mile further and at two o'clock encamped on a plain near the village of Hossamlee, which the enemy had left but a short time before, as the fires of their camp were not yet extinguished. From our encampment near Anglah to this place as measured by the parambulator is eight and a half English miles. The course ENE through a pleasant country until we reached this burnt plain where the Ministerial Army had encamped. They had either burnt or cut down all the trees in the adjacent fields and the country all around wears a most desolate appearance. A very large stock of grain and provender which they could not carry off, they set fire to. The hot ashes added to the natural warmth of the winds with the black dust and the stench of the carcasses form a combination that renders our camp extremely disagreeable. We are now four cos from Dolcah, a large town abounding with grain and refreshments of which our army stands in great need. The Confederates, we are informed, retired five cos before they halted and then encamped near the town of Kairah.

Hossamlee 30 April 1775 At nine o'clock at night we struck our camp at Hossamlee and marched with the intention of beating up the enemy's quarters at day break, being informed they are encamped only five or six cos from Hossamlee.

Chonwar 1 May 1775 At daybreak we found ourselves very far from accomplishing the scheme intended last night. It had proved to be exceedingly dark and we had the greatest difficulty in getting the guns and heavy stores over the river Sabrematty, which we crossed close to our encampment. Add to this the astonishing ignorance of our guides who marched us the whole night round every point of the compass, and at daybreak in a direct line we had not got two miles from the last ground. We then marched along the banks of the river, through a rich delightful country until eight o'clock; when an advance party of the enemy numbering eight or ten thousand, appeared on the opposite bank, coming towards us; but on firing a few shots among them, they retreated towards Cairah – and we encamped at Chonwar, nearly six miles from Hossamlee. The tents were pitched in a very pleasant situation, among a grove of mango trees, on the banks of a branch of the River Sabrematty, which here takes the name of Watruc.

Mantrah 2 May 1775 After sunrise we left Chonwar and marched four miles ENE until we came near the village of Mantrah on the opposite banks of the Watruc, which river we crossed there without much trouble; though we discerned the enemy very near and before we crossed, a skirmish ensued with our advanced and their rear guard of horse in which both met with a small loss. After halting while our baggage crossed the river for about an hour; we renewed our march towards Cairah; when suddenly the main body of the Confederate Army appeared on our right flank and rode on a full gallop as if resolved to charge; on which our line halted and wheeled up to receive them, our fire soon checked their progress and turned their attention to the rear of Ragobah's army, which they attacked with great vigour, in that part where he was posted on an elephant – but here they found themselves as mistaken, as two field pieces with fifty Europeans and as many sepoys had been ordered to the rear to prevent a consequence of the kind, which we had reason to expect; from knowing that Ragobah's person was the grand object of the enemy.

About this time a large body attempted an attack on our left, but not liking the reception they met with, they thought it most prudent to retire – our line advanced upon the enemy, as far as possible; but the ground between the two armies was so broken and full of holloways, that we could not without much difficulty get our guns further on and made it impossible to pursue the flying cavalry – in the ground however their horses could not act against us with success and our shot, both case and round, fell heavy among them in a quarter where they could not easily remove them.

The enemy's fire in this action was not near so smart, nor their artillery so well served, as at Hossamlee; but their horse made several resolute attacks – Ragobah's troops stood their charges and in general behaved tolerably well; several were killed and wounded, among the latter Sacaram Jurra, one of his ministers. He was cut in the head and neck by a sabre, but not very dangerously. In the English detachment not a man was hurt. From the report brought into headquarters we have certain intelligence that this cannonading cost the enemy no less than twelve hundred men killed and wounded; but I cannot help thinking most intelligence given there is meant to please and deceive; and that if they have lost a third of that number our artillery have done sufficient execution.

After the action we encamped on the field of battle, close to the river, in a very hot sandy plain, and no shade – but being on the banks of the Watruc, the advantage of the water is the primary consideration.

Mantrah 3 May 1775 This morning we left our ground intending to march against Cairah – but before our van had proceeded half a mile, the enemy seemed resolved to have another trial of our skills, and rode up very near us; we halted both armies, remained some time inactive, at last the Confederates wheeled off, and we immediately encamped on the spot for reasons I cannot pretend to assign.

Mantrah 4 May 1775 This day we remained encamped on the plains near Mantrah – I am quite ignorant of our manoeuvres, at present, nor can I guess why our progress is thus retarded – I cannot however help remarking the very disadvantageous terms on which we are now contending with the Confederate Army.

They have long been in this province, have collected all the grain and almost every other necessity of life, and destroyed the provender for our cattle; so that the difficulty of the numerous army is very great, and the expense of every article enormous – as to pursuing the enemy, it is in vain – the unwieldy elephant may as soon overtake the nimble deer. They generally send all their baggage, bazar and women several cos from them, to the banks of a river or a village abounding with water – being also the masters of the country and having the best intelligence of all our motions, they act accordingly.

As to attacking our encampment, I am well persuaded, that is never their intention; their conduct evinces them to be much wiser, after sending off their baggage, they choose an advantageous situation and there they wait us coming up to them. I do not say their experience in the art of war enables them always to make the best use of these advantages; as they have most certainly neglected them in several instances; but it gives them a superiority in choice of ground, by which means we engage them on unequal terms, they scour the country before us and leave us but ravaged plains. It's true when we come to action, we have the advantage and I doubt not let situation be the worst, that we shall always remain victorious.

Ragobah, we are informed is desirous of reducing Ahmedabad and Cairah – whether such are his wishes or not I cannot say – but it should be considered that was not the purpose of our expedition, not the intention of the Governor and Council in Bombay in sending so large a detachment from that garrison. The sole object was to conduct Ragobah to Poonah in the most expeditious manner and secure him firmly in government. The season is now far advanced and we are in greatest distress for money, the grand spring of war and are almost destitute of provisions and yet loitering in this ruined country that can afford us no assistance.

We have convinced the enemy in these two engagements of our superiority, why should we any longer pursue them? It would be much greater wisdom to direct our march to the Southward, on the road to Poonah. We may then cross the rivers Myhi and Nerbedah before the rains set in; and Canton during that season in some of the English settlements or adjacent towns, from whence we may easily have a communication, when we return towards Poonah, we command the country. The Confederates must then follow us with all their bazar and heavy baggage; which will make their motions much slower than at present.

Coomlah 5 May 1775 This morning after sunrise we left Mantrah camp and marched NE until we came opposite the walls of Cairah about a mile distant. Cairah is a large town belonging to Fatee Sing, next in sequence to Brodera. It is fortified with round towers mounting forty-seven guns. The building I could not easily distinguish, the town being full of trees loftier than houses. It is pleasantly and strongly situated between the rivers Watruc and Sherrie. No enemy appearing and encamped at a small distance near the village of Coomlah after a march of only two miles. The reason of our making so little progress or not at once attacking Camrah, is a mystery unknown to more than one in the English Army.

We pitched our tents in a pleasant spot on the banks of the river Sherrie, at this place not more than fifty yards broad. The banks very steep and the stream deep, abounding with fish of various kinds. This water was the softest and smoothest I ever saw. When we bathed in it, it felt like oil on the skin. The soil on the banks of the river is very different from that on the Sabrematty and Watruc being stiff and clayee. All around us the country is full of wild fruit trees bearing berries of different kinds, some of the most beautiful trees and pleasant flowers – among others is a large tree producing a fruit exactly resembling the fig but rather smaller and of inferior taste; the best I eat being comparable to an indifferent fig in England and has the leaves of the tree quite contrary, these being long and narrow, those are broad and larger. These wild fruits were welcome in a hot march, when we could get nothing better as the enemy had cleared the mangoes and tamarind trees of their productions.

It was this day given out in general orders, that Ragobah had signed a Pharman in which he promised the English forces, now on his service under Colonel Keating, the sum of thirty lakhs of rupees, to be paid on his arrival at Poonah and being established there as Peshwa – and this donation is meant in lieu of all plunder, prize-money or any demand whatsoever of that kind. This method of recompensing the English for their services in war, has always been adopted by the Princes on the other side of India.

Hyderabad 6 May 1775 At seven this morning we left Coomrah and marched three miles almost due east, this a fine enclosed country, until we came near the village of Hyderabad; when we were suddenly interrupted by the whole body of Confederate Army, who had posted themselves in an advantageous situation between a rising ground on the opposite banks of the River Serrie – so bad was our intelligence, that this very instant we supposed them many cos distant. They immediately began smart manoeuvering, which they kept up with spirit more than an hour. They had twelve pieces of cannon, but did not make use of the advantage their situation accorded them, by bringing their guns to the top of the hill, otherwise they must have done considerable mischief in our army; but keeping them behind the eminence, they were obliged to elevate them so much that their shot did but little execution. Our shots and shells at last silenced their guns which would, I suppose, have fallen into our hands had not the river parted the two armies in a place it was utterly impossible to visualize – after we had silenced their guns they retracted. We received intelligence that in this action they had a very considerable loss – among the killed was one of their principal officers – in the English detachment we had only one sepoy killed and one wounded, not an officer or European soldier hurt. Ragobah's loss was more considerable, upwards of thirty killed and wounded; as the greatest part of the enemy seemed directed in that quarter, where he got enthroned on his elephant and made himself conspicuous.

This engagement from first to last continued near two hours when we encamped in the field near Hyderabad – the sudden appearance of the enemy and then advantageous situation they had chose for this attack, occasioned this scene not unwittingly to be called 'The Hyderabad Trap'.

Dabaun 7 May 1775 Early morning Ragobah and his ministers held a council of war in which it was decided to drop conquering Cairah, Ahmedabad and other cities and march straight south, taking the town of Nariad in the route. About seven we left Hyderabad directing our march for Nadiad – on approaching the village of Dabaun the greatest part of the Ministerial Army suddenly appeared within three hundred yards of us, in a very woody part of the country, which prevented us seeing them before – observing them coming up to the charge at full speed, we immediately halted, formed the lines and got the guns unlimbered and as they then thought proper to draw up very near us, we fired a few rounds of cases shot and threw some shells into the very thickest of them, which occasioned the greatest disorder. They first wheeled to the right, then to the left and attempted to attack us on our left flank, but were so warmly received with round and shells and musketry, that they retreated in the greatest confusion, without firing a shot or doing the smallest mischief in our army – their loss this day must have been considerable; we did not expend much ammunition; and they were so near and so thick that every shot did great execution.

We then continued our march without further molestation to the village of Dabaun, where we found a large tank and fine shady trees, and encamped there the remainder of the day. Our march this day has been nearly SE, the distance from Hyderabad to Dabaun rather more than six miles, through one of the most delightful countries for a campaign I ever saw. The tufted groves, large tanks, beautiful enclosures and plenty of every kind of game, rendered it a most pleasing march. The enemy had not yet encamped in this part of the country therefore these natural beauties were unimpaired, but finding us marching this way, they had burnt down all the villages, stacks of hay and corn, which were found yet smoking as we passed them. To see so noble, so fertile a province laid waste and destroyed and bled by the severities of war, almost makes a heart of feeling to bleed.

Nariad 8 May 1775 A little after sunrise we left Dabaun and marching through a charming country, almost a continuous grove of mango trees, we reached the City of Neriad (Nadiad) about nine o'clock. It is two miles and a half from Dabaun, the road E by S. On our approaching Neriad the Subahdar (Desai) sent the keys of the gates to Ragobah in token of submission and to prevent the hostilities intended. Guards from the English Army were immediately posted at different gates to prevent anyone going in or out until everything was settled – we learnt the enemy left the place yesterday, on hearing we intended marching against it, and are now retired to a large tank nine to ten miles distant – we encamped near the walls of Neriad on an advantageous ground and pleasant situations, with plenty of wells and shady areas all around us.

Here a short resumé of the past will not go amiss. Cunda Row Gaikwar, the uncle of Govind Rao, was expected here to join forces with Ragobah. Instead he went over with all his forces to the Ministerial Army. Vaghjeebhai Desai also joined the Ministerial party as adviser of Cunda Row Gaikwar. Fateh Sing Gaikwar, who had signed a friendship treaty with Mr Lovibond of the East India Company and who had made friendly overtures to Colonel Keating to the extent that he had an ambassador in Colonel Keating's camp, had also joined the Ministerial Army and was on the move with them. So Neriad was naturally the enemy country. Ragobah, who was short of cash to pay wages to his soldiers, levied a tax of Rs.61,000 on thc inhabitants of Nadiad. They refused to pay at first, but being threatened with the worst consequences, most of the castes at last thought proper to comply. Each caste was taxed according to its wealth and numbers. The Brahmins and Bhauts claim a privilege from time immemorial of being exempted from impositions of any kind, the Bhauts are a set of people, chiefly employed in repeating verses in the Hindu scriptures. They also make verses themselves and pretend themselves as poets. These verses are generally in praise of some great men or battles. These Bhauts also stand security for debts of the villagers to the government. No security is looked upon so sacred and so certain. Upon failure of the bond or obligation between the parties, they certainly would destroy either themselves or one of the tribe and spill the blood before the face of that person who broke the engagement or refused the payment. This is looked upon as the most unfortunate circumstance and Hindus are taught to believe that the blood of the Bhaut thus spilt will most assuredly be demanded at their hands from Heaven. So that one seldom hears of an instance of a debt not being paid when a Bhaut stands security. Many of this tribe hold and cultivate lands, but pay no kind of taxes. An attempt to levy tax on them would result in suicide, which would create further upheaval of the entire Bhaut community.

Forbes writes: The Town of Neriad has been no less than twice taxed and plundered within these few months by Futtee Sing and Cunda Row, the tax now levied by Ragobah reduces the inhabitants to the most cruel distress indeed. The most shocking scenes at present, in every quarter of the town, of ruined families delivering up their last money which is insufficient to answer their quota of the tax. Their houses are instantly stripped of every movable and every accessory of life; and the poor creatures left to the severity of the poverty and want. Then under the pretext of their having buried valuables which perhaps they never possessed, tortures are inflicted and with no sparing hands. Sorry I am that an English Army has even the appearance of being concerned in such measures. If the master has offended let him suffer, not his innocent subjects. At least let not the British sword be drawn on behalf of such Asiatic cruelties and compulsions.

The City of Neriad is the capital of Cunda Row Gaikwar, where he usually resides. This town is nearly three miles in circumference, fortified in the Eastern manner with a wall flanked by round towers, This wall at present is mostly mud, but some parts lately have been built of brick and Chonam, very strong and from appearances this whole town will soon be surrounded by a wall of this kind. Neriad has nine gates, most of them very strong and neatly finished, seemingly just built – there is a small ditch around the greater part of the town not many yards over, between ten to fifteen feet deep. At the present day Neriad contains twelve thousand houses, several manufactures are carried on here, particularly fine Bafta and the colour stones from copperwange mentioned at Cambay, are cut and polished here. Contrary to most other large towns I have seen in India, Neriad appears in a flourishing condition, while the others are on the decline – its revenues are about three lakhs rupees I assume.

Adjoining Neriad are several groves of sandalwood of an inferior kind to that produced in the Bednur (Bangalore) country; but still might be turned to some account; its smell, though not so powerful, exactly resembled the true sandalwood, nor was it a bad colour.

Futta-Poor 14 May 1775 Having collected as much of the tribute as was possible and the advanced season not suffering us to lose any longer time, we left Neriad at eight o'clock this morning; and marching through a pleasant cultivated country, halted at eleven at the village of Futta-Poor, three miles from Neriad ENE. We found the village burnt down by the enemy who during our encampment at Neriad always kept within eight or ten miles from us – here were plenty of mango trees and wells and a tank not quite exhausted. About a mile from Neriad we passed the ruins of a mosque or some grand tomb; of a lighter and more elegant appearance than usual in Eastern architecture.

Boriavee 15 May 1775 At sunrise we left Futta-Poor and marched through a woody, but most delightful country. Could one lose the idea of its being the seat of war, it would appear a perfect paradise. By the large groves of mangoes and other fruit trees not being robbed of their produce, I suppose the Ministerial Army has not yet taken this road. A hard shower of rain in the night had laid the dust and refreshed the verdure.

A morning overcast and cool breezes from the south rendered the first part of our march very pleasant – but no sooner the clouds dispersed and Phoebus shone forth with intense heat, than the enemy thought proper to bear down upon us and interrupt our march. However a few rounds and shells dispersed a large body that appeared in front of our line near the village of Chiccalasee, which being neither burnt nor plundered we got plenty of forage a sure sign the enemy did not so soon expect us in this route. We found the large tank dried up, and the few wells insufficient to furnish us with water.

We therefore pursued our march about noon, and notwithstanding the violent heat, the enemy again attacked us on all quarters but could affect nothing. It was near sunset before we arrived at the village of Boriavee, built on an eminence, surrounded with a mud wall, as are most of the villages in this province, merely to prevent the coolies stealing the cattle in the night, for they are incapable of any other defences. The houses here were good and had hitherto escaped plunder, but Ragobah's troops soon dismantled them of everything they wanted – at Boriavee is a tank and several good wells.

Our course this day was on a medium SSE, we marched only about nine miles, though it took us up to twelve hours to perform it. The frequent halts for our baggages, taking care of Ragobah's Army and being harassed by the enemy were the principle reasons that retarded our march. Ensign Boyer who had been before a little indisposed died this day in a cart through excessive heat and fatigue, and I believe chiefly for want of Palanqueen or Dooley which is so highly necessary for the sick and wounded but not one has yet been provided.

Annant-Mogree 16 May 1775 At sunrise we marched from Boriavee through a country delightful as the eye could wish – resembling a nobleman's park and gardens richly cultivated – every hedge was set off with rows of leafy mangoes and other fruit trees which formed very beautiful vistas, though unadorned with buildings to terminate the view nor otherwise decked with any work of art. Every acre of this rich country in time of peace is cultivated and enclosed with multibush hedges – no part lies wasted – the soil though light is most excellent producing wheat, cush-cush, badgeree, cotton and tobacco, but seems unfit for rice, nor have I observed any batty grounds throughout the provinces. Here everything about the land a proper abode for all the rural pleasure attendant on peace and plenty. What pity then so noble a country should be the seat of war!

At ten o'clock we encamped at the village of Annant-Mogree, four miles and a half from Boriavee, our march south by east. This village is built on an eminence like Boriavee, is walled round, has a good tank and plenty of wells.

I imagine we stole a march on the enemy; since Ragobah mounted his elephant at sunrise – though it is his usual custom to pray an hour or two after the sun is above the horizon – and I suppose the enemy thought we should not leave our ground before eight or nine o'clock as has been customary – but for once they found themselves mistaken and cut off from water; which they expected at this village; for we had not well encamped before they came up in front of our lines parading with their elephants and tried by all means in their power to molest us – however they did not choose to venture an action; but after we had fired a few shots they rode off to seek for water elsewhere.

Nappar 17 May 1775 This morning we left Annant-Mogree and marched through a country like that described yesterday. Frequent halts for our baggage prevented our reaching the town of Nappar until twelve o'clock, though only five miles and a quarter from the last ground, south by east. Here we remained this day, one of the most stormy I ever saw. It blew a perfect hurricane, with a horrid cloud of dust that covered us and made our encampment very disagreeable. (The storm which we thought so disagreeable on land, was at sea attended with the most dreadful consequences. Of the merchant ships lying at anchor in Surat Road, nine were foundered and driven on shore, besides a number of small vessels and boats full of cotton. The damage sustained by the merchants in the City of Surat is estimated as upwards of thirty lakhs of rupees.)

Bettasee 18 May 1775 Soon after sunrise, we marched from Nappar towards the River Myhi; when we were a mile and a half from Nappar and had entered the Plains of Arras, we perceived a body of the enemy on the rear and to the left of our line.

It is here necessary to remark our detachment in the march is obliged to be divided for the protection of the Maratha Army, at Ragobah's particular desire, so that from it there have hitherto been formed two guards, one in the rear of the whole army, the other on the flank opposite to our main body. Each guard consisting of one hundred Europeans and sepoys with two field pieces. Orders have been given this day that, if the enemy attacked the flanking party, the rear guard were to move to their assistance and the division in the line, under the command of Captain Myers, to take up their ground; and if the rear guard alone should be attacked, Captain Myers was to reinforce them.

There was a small wood between the enemy and us when they commenced their attack from six guns on the rear, on which Captain Myers agreeable to orders moved to their assistance. When near enough our guns and howitzers fired on their canons until they were silenced and the horse displaced. Captain Myers' division was then reinforced by the Second Company of Bombay Grenadiers and he was ordered to march on and take the enemy's guns. His division advanced accordingly, but without any artillery, and when at a distance from the line, the enemy charged them from their left with a very large body, but they were repulsed from the division by the musketry and some round and case from the guns in the line. They charged a second time and were again beaten off. Just at this time a large body of the enemy with two war elephants got into a line immediately to the rear of the division, but declared they were Ragobah's own troops which was confirmed by Hurra Pont, an officer of horse in Ragobah's army, well known to the English and not mistrusted. This traitor was heard by many of our people, and also some of Ragobah's Scindian Horse, calling out to the enemy to advance on this division saying that was their time when the English were without their guns. This circumstance added to the endeavours of the horse and the elephants to break in on the rear of the division, soon convinced the English of the treachery. They immediately faced about and gave a general fire, which totally routed them. They were now repulsed both in front and rear with a very considerable loss, ours hitherto was trifling, except Captain Myers and Captain Serle who were both killed.

Thus had we met with success and obliged the enemy to fly before us, when a most extraordinary event happened. The Second Company of Bombay Grenadiers, who had been sent to the assistance of Captain Myers' division, suddenly faced to the right about and to the astonishment of the whole army made a running retreat from the ground. The Madras Infantry and Sepoys immediately followed their example. Though they retired in the greatest haste, it was somewhat regular until they came to the multibush hedges enclosing the fields in the scene of action. These hedges are not easily penetrated and the avenues were few and very small. Here then commenced their destruction. Here they broke their ranks and every man endeavoured to push through where he could without observing the least order. Though repeatedly called on by the officers to form, but all in vain. The officers did all that man can do to rally their fleeing party, but meeting with no obedience from their infatuated men, they fell a sacrifice. For the enemy now observing the surprising change in their favour, instantly faced about with renewed courage. From being the pursued they became pursuers and returning resolutely to the charge, sword in hand, cut and hacked our fleeing troops in a shocking manner. The officer alone could not long have remained by them, all fled to the guns as fast as possible.

The enemy having now advanced, near our line, in a large collected body, the cases shot and shells did great execution among them. The field was soon covered with dead, and what occasioned a much greater loss than they would otherwise have sustained, is the great attention they always pay to carrying off their dead and wounded. Never, if they possibly can avoid it, do they leave a body in the field. They will venture to the very mouth of the cannon sooner than not save the remains of a friend and pay him the last mournful office at the funeral pile. This day though they must have had several hundred killed in the action, and above remained on the field.

Notwithstanding the shameful behaviour of the Grenadiers, we drove them off with our artillery, and totally repulsed them. The loss of the English detachment in this action was very severe indeed, it was chiefly sustained in the retreat. Out of fifteen officers in Captain Myers's division, six were killed and five wounded. Captains Myers and Serle, Lieutenants Morris, Henney, Proper and Anderson were killed. Captain Faith, Lieutenants Dawson, Young, Davison and Ensign Toriw wounded, Mr Young mortally; besides eighty eight Europeans and one hundred and sixtytwo sepoys killed and wounded.

Thus ended this engagement which continued near three hours. We remained, it's true, victorious in the field of battle, but to use the saying of a famous general, two more such victories would equal defeat. It has cost us very dear indeed. The English officers behaved nobly and sold their lives very dear, but overpowered by numbers they bravely fell in the bed of honour. Mr Davison himself killed five, thereafter he was wounded; when he had lost his horse and sword he snatched up the musket of a dying sepoy but (so finely tempered were the enemy's swords) that before he could make use of it, a horseman cut it through the barrel and ramrod at one stroke; he seized another but it was instantly severed in the same manner and one of his fingers cut off with it. He then caught up a bayonet alone, with which he amply winged himself.

The loss the enemy sustained was very great, three elephants dead and a number of very fine horses. They lost several principle officers and at least a thousand men killed or wounded. Though the accounts brought to Ragobah and the Colonel made them more than double that number. Indeed the circumstances I mentioned of their exposing themselves to our heaviest fire to carry off their dead friends, must account for numbers falling that might have otherwise escaped. The generous attention much resembles the ancient custom of the Greeks and the Trojans. It is a circumstance that occurs in every battle in the Iliad, nothing was a greater disgrace than the arms or remains of a fallen hero to be in the possession of the enemy. I daily observe in these Asiatic armies, many customs that strongly reminded of the like scenes so beautifully described by the Grecian Bards.

As to the Ragobah's army, for their dastardly behaviour this day, I can compare them to nothing but a caravan of merchants with their women, children and baggage, travelling through an enemy's country and hiring us to protect them. For us to the name of soldiers, they are undeserving of so humble a title, a few exceptions only. When no danger is apprehended, no people are so ready at throwing the lance, more expert at flourishing a scimitar, parading their horses and showing their martial feats before the English troops. But the instant the enemy appears, their powerful and pretended courage leaves them. Then they flee like timid women behind our guns. Some of Ragobah's generals are brave men, but a general without troops is of little consequence. A few Arabs and Scindians deserve a better character, they have courage and want only conduct and proper discipline to make them good soldiers.

Nor do I, in the preceding description, mean to include the Confederate Army. Their whole conduct has been entirely opposite. They have only been defeated by superior military conduct and a better train of artillery. It is true that fifteen thousand of their horse are reckoned the best and most famous in India. Generally called the Deccan Horse. But I believe them superior to Ragobah's, they are like men of spirit while his are like cowards.

It seems the Ministerialists, notwithstanding the several repulses they have lately met with from us, were so highly elated with the signal victory they formerly gained over Ragobah on the plains of Arras that they determined to risk another engagement on those hitherto fortunate plains. The officers encouraged their men with hopes of a second conquest, notwithstanding the assistance of the English, which according to the superstitious notions all the Asiatics entertain, had the desired effect. However this day has convinced them of their mistakes. They have met with a defeat instead of a victory.

After remaining in the field to bury our dead and take care of the wounded, we marched toward the banks of the Myhi. As it was impossible, notwithstanding the fatigue of our men, to encamp on the spot for lack of water for which we were in the greatest distress the whole of this day's march, at sunset we arrived at the Village of Bettassee. There, finding a tank and wells, we encamped. This place is only six miles and a half from Nappar, the course ENE. The country we marched through this day ought to be as pleasant and delightful as any of the preceding, but my spirits were so much depressed on recollecting the fate of so many fine fellows, whom in the morning I had been conversing with in the greatest cheerfulness and familiarity; that I should have been incapable of tasting even the beauties of Milton's Eden. The battle was fought on the Plains of Arras in sight of the Pawgur Hill, a high mountain several miles distant to the eastward. The first rising ground I have seen in Guzerat Province.

Bettassee 19 May 1775 We remained in camp at Bettassee, taking care of the sick and wounded. We now have four hundred patients in the hospital.

Fazal-Poor 20 May 1775 A little after sunrise we left Bettassee and marched to the Mahi, intending to cross it at the Pass of Fazal-Poor. We travelled over a disagreeable heath, covered with a thorn three or four feet high, which rendered our march tedious and fatiguing. As we approached the banks of the river, we found the ground full of deep hollow ways. Some of them pits of a hundred feet deep with very steep precipices. The banks were bare of trees, but covered with prickly underwood. The Pass is a deep defile, where only one cart can proceed at a time and the road not very good. The bed of the river where we crossed it, is about four hundred yards broad, but the channel not more than fifty or sixty feet at this time of the year. The water is very clear and fresh-running over a bed of fine sand and shells. We crossed it close to the spot where Ragobah was defeated on the Plains of Arras. We encamped on the opposite side, in the place the Ministerial Army marched from the day of the defeat.

It was sunset before we could get across all our guns, stores, etc, and very hard work it was. Yet notwithstanding the steep banks and the heavy sand in the bed, we crossed them all without any accident. It was lucky the enemy gave us no molestation for had they posted themselves on the south bank they might have been very troublesome.

We encamped at night near a small fort in ruins, on the banks of the Myhi. It is square with a round tower at each corner to flank the bastions; but the builders have not chosen the most advantageous position they ought to have done. It has been dismantled on purpose as its present ruinous state is not the effect of time. We marched this morning two miles and a half north east until we crossed the river, the banks of which abound with a beautiful flowering thorn with a fragrant smell.

Coellie 21 May 1775 At nine o'clock we struck our encampment at Fazal-Poor and marched southward towards Baroche. There the Colonel proposes halting one or two days for the supply of money and stores and to send in our sick and wounded. The long fatiguing marches we now daily undertake, rendering their situation very unhappy; nor is it possibe to provide them with proper refreshment. The first two miles we marched.

Coellie 22 May 1775
Padrah 23 May 1775
Maun-Poor 24 May 1775
Mahter 25 May 1775
Soorban 26 to 28 May 1775
Baroche 4 & 5 June 1775
Dubhoy 19 June 1775

Early this morning we renewed our march to Dubhoy, where we arrived about noon through one of the worst roads imaginable. It was impossible to drag our heavy cannon through the stiff clay and the violence of the weather would not permit the men to remain out many hours on this service on an open plain. As to bullocks, they are not of the least service on these emergencies. I found the elephant the most useful beast in getting through this day's march, though in common the heaviness of his feet made an impression in the ground three feet deep.

Dubhoy 21 June 1775 This day Ragobah with his army moved from the encampment at Burrud to the banks of a small river called Ore, where he proposes remaining until we take the field at the commencement of the fair season. We have now got all our guns and most of our stores under shelter in Dubhoy. The officers and men are comfortably lodged and we only wait for a few supplies from Baroda, to make us pass the rains tolerably pleasant.

Dubhoy 30 June 1775 I shall now briefly mention the particulars that have come to my knowledge, respecting the Ministerial Army, since their retreat on 10 June. They remained in the villages around Dubhoy for two days waiting our motions, but hearing that we prepared wintering in this city, they then marched precipitately towards the Malwah country. They were greatly disaffected and chagrined at their late loss and not being able to join their bazar and baggage with the part of the army that had crossed the Nerbeda. We are informed Harri Pant Turkau with the remainder propose passing the river at a ford, about a hundred and fifty miles higher up. From thence marching at once into the Deccan with the intention of intercepting our progress to Poona, on the opening of the season.

A large body of the enemy were attempting to cross the River Nerbeda when the monsoon set in and numerous perished. Rumour says two thousand. It is certain that for several days a great number of bodies, of both men and cattle of all kinds, were seen floating with the stream when the rain came down.

Letter from Surat likewise mention that many of the Confederate Army men were drowned in the River Tappee near Surat in attempting to cross it. As elephant, camel, horse and human bodies in great quantities had been carried down with the floods. The coolies and Gracias plundered this party in their way to the Tappee and got a large booty.

Surat Nabob Hyder Ally has declared himself in Ragobah's favour and promised to assist him with both men and money. Nizam Ally, who has hitherto been a great supporter of the Ministerial, now relaxes. His Diwan, who had an uncommon influence on him and persuaded him to oppose Ragobah, has been lately cut off and it is thought Nizam Ally will now be glad to be on terms with Ragobah. Mhadojee Bouncelle, one of the most powerful chieftains among the Maratha, now has promised to espouse his cause on the commencement of the next campaign.

The Confederate Army has separated and most of the Generals returned to their own country. Nor is it supposed they will again unite. Tookajcc Holkar, the second in command, has promised to join Ragobah. Cunda Row Gaikwar is gone to Neriad, leaving behind his Vakils advisors. Futtee Singh Rav Gaikwar, like the crafty politician he has ever been esteemed, finding the Confederacy greatly broke and their cause almost reversed, now once more made overtures for peace. He is fearful of his Capital Brodera, a mere eighteen miles from Dubhoy, whither he has lately returned; and which his brother Govind Rao is in the hopes, we shall now put him in possession of, which will certainly be the case before we leave the Guzerat country. If Futtee Singh does not accede to such terms as Ragobah may insist on, which from his late contra-ordering conduct both to him and the English, he cannot expect to be very favourable. He has lately sent emissaries, which include Vaghjeebhoy Dessoy, to settle matters on amicable terms.

Dubhoy 1 July 1775 Ragobah lately moved his camp from the Ore to the north bank of Dahder River, six cos from here. The Colonel went out there this afternoon to reside a few days, it being only nine miles from Brodera from where he expects Futtee Singh to meet him to settle matters with Ragobah and the English Company on specific terms.

Bellapoor Camp 5 July 1775 This morning, by the Colonel's desire, I went out to Ragobah camp near the village of Bellapoor on the banks of the Dohder. In the afternoon Futtee Singh sent to request the Colonel would meet him at the village of Challenpoor on the north bank of the river. Which was halfway between Brodera and the camp. I accordingly accompanied the Colonel thither, but Futtee Singh not arriving by the time it was dark; I took a few horsemen and went on towards Brodera to conduct him to Challenpoor. It began to rain exceedingly hard soon after my setting out, which made the road so very bad that I did not reach Brodera until ten o'clock. I found Futtee Singh encamped without the walls but afraid of proceeding on account of Govind Rao's forces likewise encamped near Brodera. I assured him there was no danger and that Govind Rao would not dare to prevent his journey while under the English protection. But being very wet and tired I declined accompanying him. He then recommended me to the care of his brother Manekjee and himself with a party of horse proceeded on to Colonel Keating's. Manekjee conducted me to a large tent, provided me with a good bed, supper and cordials. After showing me every politeness in his power, left me to repose.

Brodera 6 July 1775 This morning my host renewed his hospitality in providing me with everything he thought would be agreeable. After breakfast I walked out to view the City of Brodera, but did not go within the walls. It appeared very extensive, the fortification in good repair, the gateways large and strong.

The Durbar made the best appearance, at the distance I was from it, of any I have met within India. The City altogether much exceeded Surat, Cambay or the other Eastern cities I have seen;

in its flourishing condition and good repair, it is situated in a large cultivated plain. The Moguls formerly possessed it and the large tombs and elegant ruins of their mausoleums still remain among the groves and gardens without the walls.

At eleven o'clock a letter came from Futtee Singh acquainting his brother that he was arrived at Ragobah's camp and desired that he would join him with his army and that I might accompany him. The Nobut was immediately beat and in half an hour we marched for the camp, where we arrived at one o'clock. About one thousand five hundred horse and foot came with us, which with those that last night escorted Futtee Singh, made up his troops; at camp about two thousand. He pitched his tent half a mile from the Maratha Army of Ragobah.

On Futtee Singh's arrival at camp with Colonel Keating, Ragobah came out to meet him at some distance from his tent, and received him with the greatest politeness. They then went in, where after a short ceremonious visit Futtee Singh retired to his own tent.

Bellapoor Camp 8 July 1775 In the morning I accompanied Colonel Keating in his public visit to Futtee Singh. His reception was very polite, all his ministers and great officers attending. We stayed about half an hour and then retired.

Dubhoy 15 July 1775 This morning I returned to Dubhoy, leaving Futtee Singh and the Colonel at Ragobah's camp. Matters not being yet finally settled to the satisfaction of all parties.

I think it is needless to particularise every journey I take in this country. I have already in many places observed that the greatest part of Guzerat Province is like an extensive garden or a beautiful park. If it appeared delightful in the dusty months of April and May, it is now since the commencement of the rains adorned with double charms. Everything appears in vernal bloom. Nothing can exceed the richness of the hedges about the houses and the fields, covered with vines and creepers of those varied greens that Thomson so elegantly described:

'United light and shade! Where the sight dwells, with growing strength, an even new delight.'

These visions are embellished with blossoms of a thousand mingled hue, that charm the eye and diffuse a most fragrant odour. The country is thereabouts watered by a number of small rivulets, which I suppose are the branches of Nerbeda or brooks that disembogue into the parent stream. I am informed that it will produce three crops a year from the material luxuriance of the soil and the fertility those rivers occasion. I think the Emperor Aurengzeb might have emphatically styled this province, as well as Bengal, 'The Paradise of Nations'. But indeed, since his flourishing reign, the face of things is entirely altered. Peace must for some years extend here before it can resume its former wealth and splendour. For now the lands remain uncultivated; the cities ransacked and destroyed, the smaller towns and villages burnt to the ground; all manufactures at an end; and no vestiges remain of that wealth, industry and population for which Guzerat was once famous.

20 July 1775 In consequence of a note received last night from the Colonel acquainting me that at last Futtee Singh had concluded everything to his satisfaction and left the camp for Brodera yesterday evening; and desiring me to go up to the camp to draw out the treaty and deliver to him at Brodera. I set out early this morning on an elephant, but the roads were so very bad that I did not reach the Dahder until two o'clock in the afternoon, though only nine miles from Dubhoy, it has rained incessantly since the 15th, so that the road was almost a continual sheet of water and when I reached the south bank of the Dahder at the Pass of Bellapoor where the water is seldom more than a ford deep, I found it rose to upwards of forty, running at astonishing velocity; owing to the freshets having come down from the mountains and neighbouring tanks and hollow ways being all overflowed, their streams have found a passage to this river; which in its rapidity sweeps down large trees and timber from adjacent plains. Several of Ragobah's Army lost their lives in attempting to stop these trees for firewood. For though the Indians in general are most expert swimmers, yet the stream was too rapid for their strength and carried many off from all assistance. Homer in the Iliad has a few lines on this subject.

Finding it in vain even for the elephant to cross and no boat or raft belonging to camp, I was in a most disagreeable situation. I could converse with those on the opposite banks and envy them their warm encampment, but had no place of shelter for myself. No tent or hut to screen me from the inclemency of the weather, which as the night approached seemed to indicate would be very bad; and so it turned out; for after sunset the clouds thickened apace and a most towering gloom instantly succeeded. Presently followed a deluge of rain; which continued with very little interruption the whole night. A night passed by me in the most cold and uncomfortable situation that can be imagined, in the open field, in dismal darkness and dreary solitude.

21 July 1775 No sooner did the morning dawn, then I looked at the river and finding the waters had risen in the night from the heavy rain, and seeing the utter impossibility of crossing to the Colonel for some time, I returned to Dubhoy and reached it in about six hours.

Bellapoor Camp 26 July 1775 This morning I went to camp by the Colonel's desire. I found the river somewhat abated but not fordable; however they had now got a sort of raft, on which I ventured over.

The following adventure happened in Ragobah's camp since my return to Dubhoy. A young man named Efsvant Row of some note in the army and a great favourite of Himmurat Row, Ragobah's adopted son was widely suspected of an amour with the most beautiful of Ragobah's women and his greatest favourite. Notwithstanding the Harram of women's apartment is generally well guarded among the Asiatics, yet as the lady herself felt a mutual flame, her lover found means to surmount all obstacles and bribing one of the female slaves of the Harram, to his interest, he gained access to her tent and indulged in all the soft delights of mutual love. Ragobah was however informed of it; he summoned Efsvant Row into his presence; who finding no evasion could befriend him, at last confessed to the crime. That night about nine o'clock, he was conducted by torchlight to the extremity of the camp, with his hands tied behind him and an executioner attending here, he was beheaded and his head laid on one side of a common road, his body on the other as a public spectacle; there they remained all the next day; at sunset his friends had the liberty to carry off his remains and perform the funeral ceremonies. The unfortunate brunette, now taken from her companions at the same still hour, sewn up in a sack and thrown alive into the river, to quench her flame and be an example to the rest of the sisterhood. The confidant escaped with only the loss of her nose; a common punishment in this part of the world. So much for all Maharatha intrigue, a warning to the cautious. How we behave to these damsels of the Peshwa in future; who are not very shy of the Europeans, but fond of displaying their skill in horsemanship before us; though generally well looked after by an old rogue of an eunuch.

Dubhoy 28 July 1775 I found Ragobah encampment very unhealthy from such number of people and their cattle having been in the same shed for this month past is the quantity of dirt and filth of all kind that now surrounds the camp is almost incredible; breeding vermin of all kinds, with such fetid smells and noxious vapours that in a morning we can scarcely see three yards before us; exclusive of the Dahder having overflowed its banks among the tombs, so that some hundred were obliged to be moved further off. These several disagreeable circumstances combined under it a most unwholesome situation. I was seized with a fever after the first night sleeping here and as the river was this day passable for an elephant, I crossed and returned to Dubhoy; judging there was very little hope of a recovery in such a pestilential air.

Dubhoy 29 July 1775 This evening the Colonel retired to town, seized with a very violent fever, which has also attacked Ragobah, Appajee, Mahadev and other principal persons in his army. Exclusive of those poor wretches, who are now enduring a second winter campaign in his service. Ragobah yesterday moved his camp for the benefit of a purer air and more cleanly soil.

Dubhoy 31 July 1775 It is here necessary to take a short review of political proceedings in Ragobah's camp this last month. We have seen Govind Rao Gaikwar, Futtee Singh Row Gaikwar, these two rival brothers long contending for their Father Damaji's possessions in the Guzerat Province. I shall here therefore only relate a few facts well known to all this part of the Eastern world. But without drawing an inference that must appear dubious to every impartial observer.

Futtee Singh, a few months older than Govind Rao, but born of Damaji's second wife, has since his father's death been in possession of Brodera and the dependent districts. On the commencement of the civil war in the Maharatha's Empire, he joined the Confederacy against Ragobah. From his thorough knowledge of the Guzerat Province (which for some months past has been the seat of war), he has not only had it in his power to assist the Ministerial cause with its best troops, but has also chosen for them the most advantageous situations to commence their attacks on our army; which has ever been the case, and owing to him alone. When first the English joined Ragobah at Cambay, he sent his Vakeels (presumably headed by Vaghjeebhoy) to enter into negotiations with the Company and Ragobah. A Treaty was accordingly concluded to his satisfaction; and Mr Lovibond sent with it to his camp to get it ratified. Here he first displayed himself. He pretended his dread of Hurra Pant Turkia discovering that he was treating with his enemies and requested Mr Lovibond to destroy the treaty as he would be searched; which he accordingly complied with. But I firmly believe that Futtee Singh had no thoughts then of concluding a treaty; but the true intent of his ambassador's errand was to spy the weakness of our camp and he was a man of as much cunning as his master, and I doubt not made all the observations he was directed to do. Instead of joining Ragobah as he promised the first favourable opportunity he has to the very conclusion of the campaign acted as his most inveterate enemy. And in the engagement of the 18th May led the van of the Confederate Army. But as I have lately observed, thinking the Minister's cause reversed, from the losses and disgrace they have lately met with and that Ragobah daily advances nearer an establishment in his government, like a true Maharatha, he immediately alters his conduct. He sees an English army within a few miles of his capital, well knows their powers and dreads the loss of his possessions, which he is certain is inevitable unless he speedily conciliates matters with Ragobah. Once more he sends an ambassador to the camp, and soon after arrives himself; submits to the terms imposed on him; returns to his house; enjoys himself in domestic peace and calm tranquillity and fleeces his subjects to pay his ransom.

Let us now take a short retrospect of Govind Rao. Since his father's death he has claimed his paternal inheritance; was besieging his capital with a large army and had been some months before the walls, when Ragobah in distress came into that part of Guzerat Province. There under promises of the most sacred nature (as we are told) to put him in possession of the Gaikwar lands in prosperous days, he engaged him to give up his own cause and join him with all his forces. At that time Govind Rao was thought a most valuable ally; and he has ever since been a faithful follower of Ragobah's fortunes; I do not pretend to say what promises were made to allure him to join us at Cambay, after Ragobah's defeat on the plains of Arras; but I am well informed they were great and most probably they were. Ragobah in such distress would most surely make him greater overtures than formerly, when he well knew that if the junction between him and his allies was not effected by a very near day, the English forces were immediately to return.

Ragobah had then a Kingdom at stake. The whole Guzerat Province with lakhs upon lakhs added to it, was but a trifle when weighed in the scale of empire. Govind Rao at the joined entreaty of Ragobah and the English representative came to us. He left his wife and children in a distant country without a home they could call their own; but protected under the hospitable roof of a friendly Rajah. To all these tender connections has he bid adieu and continued to this hour a faithful adherent to Ragobah.

On 18 August 1775 a treaty was finally concluded between Ragobah and Futtee Singh and guaranteed by the representative of the East India Company. Here Vaghjeebhai Desai played an important part in bringing about the compromise between Futtee Singh Gaikwar and Peshwa Ragobah, which culminated in the signing of this treaty. As a reward for his shrewd vakilat he received in Inam the village of Bilodara, north of Nadiad, in perpetuity.[2] Vaghjeebhai's family enjoyed the income from it until 1816 when the British took over the administration as well as its income from the hands of Ajubhai (the great-grandson of Vaghjeebhai) who had revolted against the British, when they enacted Talati regulations, which curtailed the power and remuneration of the Desais and Patels.

The terms of the treaty also rewarded the British (East India Company), also for effecting the reconciliation between the Gaikwar and Peshwa.[3] The Honourable Company got the remaining share of the Broach Pergunnah, being one tenth which belonged to the Gaikwar; also the Pergunnah of Coonal on the north banks of the River Nerbedah and those of Chickly and Veriow near Surat, yielding nearly Rs.277,000 per year. Ragobah granted to Futtee Singh under the seal of his brother Siajee all that part of Guzerat Country he now possesses, on the usual conditions the Gaikwar family hold it; viz Futtee Singh is to pay the Ragobah as Peshwa, the sum of eight lakhs of rupees per annum; to furnish Poonah with three thousand men at his sole expense, to be disposed of at the Peshwa's pleasure; and in time of necessity five thousand; the Peshwa paying the charge of the additional two thousand; that he is in the course of sixty days to pay the sum of six lakhs of rupees to the Circar of Poonah, the Peshwa ministers, great officers and servants of the Durbar, etc, etc.

That the Jagir of three lakhs of rupees per annum, formerly paid to Govind Rao from the Gaikwar possessions in the Guzerat Province, from that day cease for ever.

Ragobah, as a reward to Govind Rao for his long and faithful services and to make him ample amounts for the loss of his paternal inheritance amounting to many lakhs of rupees per annum; has promised to settle on him in some future prosperous day a fort in the Deccan and a Jagir of ten lakhs of rupees.

Thus Futtee Singh retained his hold over Brodera and Guzerat country, while Govind Rao lost almost everything.'

So ended, on the Plains of Arras, the First Anglo-Maratha War. However immediately after, Captain Stuart offered to march at once to Fazal-Poor with his battalion of sepoys and drive the enemy from the fort, but the Commanding Officer thought the risk too great for the proposed object. In the Second Anglo-Maratha War, Major General Arthur Wellesley triumphed over Scindhia's armies at Assaye in what the future Duke of Wellington always regarded as a stiffer contest than his victory over Napoleon at Waterloo.[4]

The ambition of Bombay to snatch the Maratha territories started the first Anglo-Maratha War in the Kaira district, resulting in the Battle of Arras. This war, important as it was, is often largely ignored by historians as though it was a non-event, perhaps because on this occasion the British Army fought as a mercenary force, charging for their services and also receiving large chunks of territory. The other two Maratha wars were fought by the British at their own expense. However, one must recognise that Arras was the first ever battle that the British forces fought against the Marathas. The Arras War taught the British an object lesson in the so-called 'mobile' war tactics of the Marathas. They rapidly moved thousands of horses as well as foot soldiers and guns, elephants and supply carts over the whole district of about 2,500 square miles. They attacked the pursuing enemy at their chosen time and place and this was perhaps a novel experience for Colonel Keating and his officers. Lessons were learnt for the future tackling of the formidable Maratha armies. The second Anglo-Maratha war was fought at Assaye in 1803. The third war took place at Poona in 1818 with Peshwa and Nagpoor with Bhonsle. It delivered the sovereignty of the whole of India, except for Assam, Sindh and Punjab, to the East India Company. The Pax Britannica started from this point.

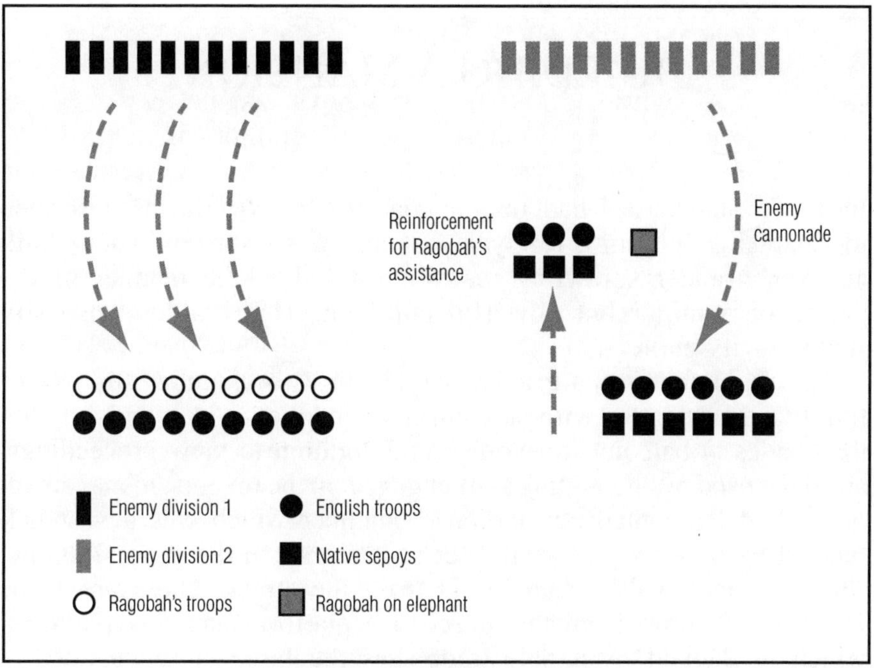

The Battle of Arras Troop Movements

7

BUILDING A MANSION

In 1750, Shankerdas had built a mansion in Nadiad, as described in Chapter 5. Within a few years Shankerdas's son Prabhudas built an even grander sprawling mansion, styled in the manner of the palace of a minor but powerful chieftain. This building also still stands in its entirety.

The main features are a kachery, a private chamber for use of family and friends, with a central chandelier and a balcony on three sides; a balcony for women and children to view proceedings; an adalat used by accounting staff engaged on the revenue management of Nadiad Paraganah; an audience chamber which was a vast hall flanked by a balcony all round for spectators and the general public. The entrance to this chamber is from the street. There are some 15 steps to climb from the street to a platform and this platform, which is flanked by a balustrade, has the large entrance door to the whole chamber. In the centre of the chamber is a very large chandelier with lamps using candles. Here is where the presiding Desai (Prabhudas) used to hold court to hear the complaints, grievances and disputes of all the people of Nadiad Paraganah.

There was also a jundarkhana room, next to the kachery, with strong doors and locks for storing the family jewels and ceremonial equipment including jewelled headgear and swords and daggers with diamond, ruby and emerald stones studded on their handles. There is an outer courtyard and as we go through we pass several access rooms and come to another large square courtyard with open verandahs all round and rooms above it. This was private and used as the family residence. This courtyard leads to further family rooms on the ground floor and after passing them you enter another open space with the kitchen area coming at the end of it. Here a well for clean water is situated. The water of this well is used by the household. Adjoining the well is a small worship place with idols of Deities. Every day a Brahmin priest would come and pray to the gods and would light incense and ghee lights.

The building also had a first, second and third storey with rooms on all the floors. On the second floor there was a library with some 20 cupboards full of books of various types. From the library rooms steps go up to the viewing tower, while the library itself is surrounded by open terraces some 20 feet long and wide. In fact this was the power base of the Desais. The largest, and for that matter the most magnificent and inspiring building in the whole of Nadiad Paraganah.

8

A DEFENSIVE ALLIANCE

Prabhudas was in power, as Kamavasidar of Neryad Pergunnah, when the Gaikwar surrendered the Nadiad (Naryad) Paragunah to the East India Company under the agreement dated 6 June 1802, which was consolidated in a definitive treaty on 21 April 1805.[1]

A definitive treaty of general defensive alliance between the Honourable East India Company on the one part and the Maharajah Anund Rao Gaikwar Sena Khas Kheyl, Sumsher Bahadoor and his children, heirs and his successors on the other, settled by Major Alexander Walker, Resident at Baroda, having full powers from the Government of Bombay, which is in like manner authorised by His Excellency the Most Noble Richard Marquis Wellesley, Knight of the Most Illustrious Order of St Patrick, one of his Britannic Majesty's Most Honourable Privy Councillors, Governor General in Council appointed by the Honourable the Court of Directors to direct and control all their affairs in the East Indies – 1805.[2]

Under this treaty the subsidiary force was increased: territories yielding Rs.1,170,000 were assigned for the payment of the Gaikwar's debts to the British, which amounted to Rs.41,387,325. The Gaikwar bound himself to submit his pecuniary disputes with the Peshwa to the arbitration of the British Government; and generally his relations with the British Government were defined. (In the first mentioned sum of Rs.1,170,000, was included the fund assigned and districts ceded, the Pergunnah of Neryad at Rs.175,000.)

From 7 August 1804 to 14 May 1805 Neryad was under the charge of Colonel Walker at Baroda. After that a collector was appointed for Kaira. At the time Neryad Pergunnah was calculated as yielding a revenue of Rs.175,000 to Anund Rao Gaikwar. This was the amount entered into the details of the above treaty. This amount was now ceded to the English East India Company by Anund Rao Gaikwar. The Neryad Pergunnah had 39 villages.

The first Englishman to meet Prabhudas was Robert Drummond, an officer of the East India Company, who did not seem to like him and described him as: 'The absolute arbitrator of all public measures in this Pergunnah in whom I had not yet beheld to possess the smallest particles of feeling except for his own person and private purposes…'[3]

However, the first Collector of the district, appointed on 14 May 1808 by the East India Company, Henry Diggle preferred to continue the tenure of Desaigiri describing him as: 'The most respectable Dessoy in this part of our possessions in Gujarat'.[4] This engagement was agreed by the East India Company with Purdoobass Sunkerdass (Prabhudas Shankerdas) on 7 August 1804.[5] From this date up to 14 May 1805 the whole district of Kaira including Neryad Paraganah was administered under Colonel Walker, the Resident at Baroda. During that time a European assistant and native officers (in case of Nadiad Purdoobass Sunkerdass) administered the area according to local usage, police, justice and revenue of the country. In 1805 a Collector was appointed with jurisdiction over the ceded districts, both those to the north of the Mahi River and those to the east of the Gulf of Cambay. The powers of the Desais over policing and dispensing justice were passed on to the Collector. Then the British, having felt the pulse of the district, began discreetly to assume sovereignty over it.

9

LAND REVENUE

The revenue letter from Bombay to the London Court of Directors of the East India Company reads as follows:

> Though ceded at Rs.175,000, yet your honourable court will observe that an engagement was made with the Dessayes so early as the year 1805 to pay a rental of Rs.232,401; on which occasion engagements were also entered into for the cultivation of the waste land in the Pergunnah, the success of which it is concluded has led to the great difference under the head lands cultivated.[1]

In 1806 Samaldas Desaibhai, the nephew of Prabhudas Desai, rose against him through a grievance against allocation of 'Desaigirry money'. He raised a body of horse and started plundering in the region of Nariad Pergunnah. The British considered him a 'Baharvatiya' and when chased he sought refuge in adjoining Gaikwar territory. Later he made his way to London by ship and returned from there in 1833 with the Board of Directors of the East India Company authorising him Rs.1500 per annum as part of his Desaigirry Huk.[2] In spite of this family defection the revenue collection powers of Prabhudas were not modified or reduced by the British who really wanted to establish themselves in a strange and alien country with long-established traditions and work ethics. However, they gradually began to suspect the sincerity of the Desais. A Mr Holford, a subordinate (with magisterial powers) to the Collector Dingle, wrote to Governor Duncan at Bombay (22 December 1806): 'There is hardly a single member of the whole Desai family in whom I would place much confidence'.[3] In 1805

Major Walker stationed the King's Brigade of 17 and 22 Dragoons at Nadiad, replacing the horse power of Prabhudas. In those days you needed the presence of troops and a show of strength to be able to collect the land revenue of the Paraganah. This was the first dent in the power of Prabhudas's family which they had enjoyed up to 1805; largely by maintaining 250 horse and 750 foot soldiers for revenue collection duties. Though the powers of Desais were diminished, the British still relied on them to deliver the revenue collected from the villages of the Pergunnah through the Patels (Mukhis) agency. The fact was that the revenue system being so complicated – torn between the Ruler's interests and the well-being and livelihoods of the ruled – it took several years for the British to understand fully its various unwritten rules and laws.

10

THE DESAI REVOLT

When the British decided that their position was strong enough to bear the strain, they enacted Regulations II and III of 1814 of the Bombay Government to introduce the 'Ryotwari (or Amani) system of revenue management', meaning thereby the appointment of Tullatees ostensibly to assist Patels and Mahudha Amins to supersede the office of Desai. Ajubhai organised a cabal of Prominent Patels and Mahudha Amins of the Pergunnah. They met secretly at his palatial building in Nadiad and decided to strike – the Patels of every village refused to co-operate in the collection of revenue. The Collector could now see a crisis engulfing his only recently established administration. Meanwhile, an insider Patel, Purbhudas Soonderdass, informed Collector Rowles of the full details of the Desai/Patel conspiracy and their future plan of action.[1] On the strength of this evidence, Barnwall and Robertson went to Ironside, the magistrate, to issue summons against Ajubhai and other Patels, who were immediately arrested and charged with crimes against the administration.

Subsequently, Ironside the Magistrate wrote to Warden the Chief Secretary to the Bombay Government on 15 September 1815 to the effect that by the prompt arrest and imprisonment of the perpetrators of the crime of conspiracy, their plans had happily been frustrated.[2] This conspiracy in its infancy might, if matured, have been productive of considerable difficulty and danger, as the number of perpetrators was growing and spreading rapidly.[3] The Government appointed a special and formidable court composed of the judges of Kaira and Broach and a third judge that of the Court of Circuit and Appeal. This court found Ajubhai Purbhudas and two accomplices guilty of the 'heinous offence' of trying to render Regulation II of the 1814 Act null and void and nonfunctional. The court, after a short session, convicted and sentenced Ajubhai Purbhudas Desai to five years imprisonment and a fine of 10,000 rupees. If the fine was not paid, an additional three years jail would follow. On that day, 25 September 1815, he was debarred for life from holding any office under the Government.[4] He was taken to Kaira where he was kept under house arrest. His wife was allowed to join him in a very comfortable Government-protected residence in the town of Kaira. It is here that his son, Bhau Saheb Rao Bahadur Viharidas Desai, was born in the year 1819.

Purbhudas was also prosecuted but not arrested or convicted, but the most powerful person of the Paraganah was stripped of his power and glory. The Patels also forfeited their power to collect the land revenue. Rowles the Collector had had this idea long before in 1810 when he wrote to Warden on 17 June 1810 suggesting that the Government collect the revenue without the help of village Patels. But it was his assistant, Captain Robertson, who insisted on continuing the Maratha-instituted system of revenue collection. After all, Rowles, though called a Collector, had no hand in collecting the revenue and thus was a non-functional collector. So for now, in 1814, the Patels were deprived of their power to collect the land revenue and also of their right to a share in the village inams or land grants which was always enjoyed by the responsible Patel of each village.[5]

Robertson also instructed Barnwall to check on the culpability of each Patel in the recent crime and to exclude all the guilty ones.[6] The Patels who were proved never to have joined the conspiracy 'were allowed to receive their share in the village inam'. In another letter Robertson ordered Barnwall to debar all Patels from their right to interfere in the management of village expenses. This village expense item was a source of income in kind to the Patels.[7]

The increase of land revenue was the main purpose of Amani management. To this purpose Robertson ordered Barnwall to swiftly establish whether all the revenue-free lands were legally so and also to calculate and draw up an accurate account of the resources of the District to enable the Government 'to rate it at its proper amount of revenue'.[8] To this purpose Barnwall began to survey the entire district, registering a name and a number for each field, measuring its extent and identifying its proprietor and cultivator.

Barnwall then, on 1 August 1816, made ‘an individual and separate assessment with each cultivator, to ascertain the true amount of his enjoyment and the rent he was equitably bound to contribute’.[8] Barnwall also registered the deeds of all alienated lands. When no deed was present he recognised the prescriptive rights, namely rights or titles established by a long unchallenged tenure. As a precaution he fined everyone who could not produce written evidence of their rights.[9] He also checked out village entertainment expenditure which seemed unnecessary and was calculated more for the private advantage of the Patels than of the village. To that end he instituted an annual audit of village expenses. In his letter of 1 August 1816 Barnwall reported that as a result the village expenses decreased by Rs.17,635 per year.[10] As these expenses were defrayed from the Government’s share of the revenues, this sum in effect amounted to an increase in the public (i.e. Government) revenue. Thus the status of Patels was reduced by depriving them of most of their powers which they had enjoyed before. Barnwall wrote to Rowles the Collector:

‘The temporary suspension of the Patel’s agency in the commencement of these proceedings, by weakening their power lessened their influence and gave an opportunity for the people to act with more freedom and independence. This tended to facilitate the earlier acquisition of information very essential to our successful progress; it also supplied the means of inculcating into the minds of the Patels, by the evidence of practical example, the degree of public confidence we possess and showed them how different the same communities will always act under a British and Mahratta rule.’[11]

In Barnwall’s estimation, the Patels had discovered the true limits of their power. With such confidence in his success in his struggle for power with Patels, Barnwall conceded to all those Patels who disavowed their past seditious conduct and agreed to co-operate with thc newly appointed Talatis, their right to resume their normal duties. This to him was an act of grace and favour on his part.

In 1816 the British got an increase of three lakhs of rupees in land revenue.[12] From 19 February 1819 the Court of Directors sent a letter to Napean the Bombay Governor reprimanding him for being too hasty in implementing the Bombay Regulations II and III of 1814 in the part of Gujarat that was ceded in 1817.[13] ‘It was quite impossible that you could have collected such accurate and ample information respecting the state of the districts as would in any case have warranted you in proceeding to frame for them a code of permanent legislation.' It cautioned Bombay in another letter: 'Above all things ... avoid sudden or considerable alterations, either in the amount or the channel of the collections'.[14]

As mentioned previously, Ajubhai's son Viharidas was born in 1819 in jail. This son was destined to play an important part in the civil life of Nadiad. For his public services, including the presidentship of the Nadiad Municipality, he was invited in 1877 to Queen Victoria's Silver Jubilee celebrations held in Delhi; there he was awarded the title of Rao Bahadur. In 1857 at the time of India's first war of independence (the Indian mutiny) he gave shelter to Nanasaheb and Tatyatopi. Subsequently, he named his younger son 'Nanasaheb' and his eldest nephew 'Tatyatopi' in memory of these celebrities. The minutes of Government 21 October 1815 show that Prabhodas was prohibited from holding any government office. Thus ended for a time the Desai supremacy and political influence. At the same time (23 April 1818) Dwarkadas, the younger brother of Prabhudas, was rewarded by the Collector for taking the government's side by being given, on 22 April 1818, 3,000 beegas of meadow land north of Nadiad on the banks of the River Sheree and permission to establish a new village on that land, which he called 'Dwarkapura', which the family enjoyed alone when all the other Desais of Nadiad lost their emolument powers and position at the seat of supreme power.[15]

When Ajubhai came out of prison he made a proposal to the Kaira Collector, Mr Archibald Robertson, to establish three villages in the district of Aleenah. Each new establishment to have attached to it lands to the extent of 5,000 beegas. Villages to be established were to be within the boundaries of Lasoondra, Ruvallya and Chetersumba (see Appendix 1).[16]

11

DESAIS REGAIN POWER

The other lesson the British derived from the upheaval of the first few years of their reign was that only the presence of what they called 'the European Agency' could provide accurate information on the condition of the district. Even Indian officers appointed by them were not to be relied upon. They were at variance with their official duties, and no salary or emolument, however high, would be adequate protection for the Government's interests. Barnwall gave Rowles his opinion that even honest Indian officers would not part with information unless their future employment depended upon their ability to convince the local British official of their usefulness.[1] Consequently, they parted with their knowledge of local conditions 'in quantities proportionate to the supposed stability of their appointments'.[2] Thinking that he had really succeeded in this land innovation of Nariad Paraganah, Rowles gave instructions to Barnwall to carry out the same reforms, namely appointments of tullatees and curtailment of the revenue powers of Desais and Patels in the remaining parts of their possessions in Gujarat. Bombay Government in their letter to the Court of Directors in London made a specific point that the actions taken were not an innovation. They were only reforms of the existing system of revenue collection.[3] However, they both fully realised that they had enhanced the British sovereignty *vis-à-vis* the revenue since the Patel power was curbed and their income and village prestige truncated. The East India Company was savouring a big mouthful of the sovereignty they accidentally acquired in the Nadiad District.[4]

By 1818 the Bombay Government began to change their tune as a result of their perception that keeping Desais out of public domain was not conducive to increased loyalty of the population.

The Desais' reign over the Nadiad population had been over a long period and their benevolent attitudes to the general population had made them natural leaders of their own people. Ajubhai Prabhudas Desai was released. The Gazette announced clemency and Desais were again allowed to resume their normal duties.[5] Later on, in 1827, a further proclamation was issued giving permission to Ajubhai and other senior members of the other branch of the Desai family to apply for Government employment.[6] Thus the leaders of the Nadiad conspiracy and perpetrators of seditious crimes against the State regarding the Tullatee regulations came out of it unscathed and retained their positions. Ajubhai even got permission to establish Ajupura and two villages on 1 November 1819. His uncle Dwarkdas also was given permission for the establishment of a village with 3,000 beegas of meadow land near Nadiad.

To conclude this account of the above period of upheaval in the Kaira district, the formerly unimportant office of Tullatee had by virtue of Regulation II of 1814 become a very responsible position and a threat to the Patels.[7] Governor Elphinstone also agreed: 'the greatest change without the least appearance was wrought by the appointment of new Tullatees'.[8] Though under pressure from the Court of Directors the Governor Napean halted further change in administration, although he did not reverse the decisions made between 1812 and 1819. Revenue surveys, Ryotwari system of revenue management and commissions for the recovery of alienated lands became the chief components of the embryonic revenue management of the Bombay Province in the nineteenth century. The British were planning to change the society and by their own admission they succeeded. The Patels lost power to Tullatees, while the Desais and Mujmudars lost power to local British officers and their favourites.

In 1821 Governor Elphinstone visited Kaira and came to the following conclusions: 'The facts that present themselves on a hasty view are that the grassias are weakened and depressed, that Dessees and all the hereditary officers including the Patels are stripped of power and influence and given security of persons and property in exchange; that the bankers are deprived of one large branch of their profits by the change in our system of revenue and of another by the decline of commerce occasioned by the downfall of so many native states and the equal diffusion of property that the Rhasti, once so important in Goozerat and now almost too insignificant to mention, and that the Ryots have gained much wealth, comfort and security among all the sufferers'.[9]

In Karl Marx's work, 'The Future of British Rule in India', he states: 'Britain has to fulfil a double mission in India; one destructive the other regenerative – the annihilation of old Asiatic society and the laying of the material foundation of Western society in Asia'.[10]

In later life Ajubhai Desai was appointed by the British and the people to arbitrate on the dispute concerning the Kharicut Canal. He gave his decision in favour of the Kalambandai villages and the British accepted it. In 1856 he constructed the steps to the well adjoining the Kheta Talav to make it a vav. Among other constructions he excavated and constructed Dhanji Kuva which even now provides potable water for people who may not have waterpipe connection from the municipal water supply. He also constructed temples of Shiva at Manjipura and Dumral. He died shortly after that.

In 1866 Nadiad Municipality was for the first time established by the Government to give people some semblance of local self-government. The President of the municipality was not elected but nominated by the Kheda Collector. The first President to be appointed was Viharidas Desai, the grandfather of Dabudhai Desai. Successive presidents to be appointed were Viharidas's sons Becherdas and Purushottamdas. They were followed by their nephew Girdhardas. In 1898 the British were not happy with the running of the municipality by the Desais, as they perceived nepotism, since the Desais were seen granting favours to their friends and associates. As a result the Desais were deprived of some of their powers as magistrates.[11] However, even after that the Collector continued to nominate Desais as presidents. The house tax rule of 1897, promulgated under the Desai presidentship, favoured the rich as the maximum tax on a building was fixed at Rs.10 irrespective of size and all were taxed the same amount. Thus a single room tenement paid the same as Desai's haveli of several rooms.[12]

12

A NEW COLLECTOR

In November 1913 the district collector Chuckerbutty was transferred from Kaira and a new Collector, Jyotsnanath Ghosal, arrived, who was to remain as Collector in Kaira right up until April 1918. He was a pragmatic administrator, always looking to improve the prosperity of the district.

By the time Ghosal came into office, Dadubhai Desai had completed many years in the mal at Ajupura where he stayed for a long period trying to experiment with growing various crops on about 500 bighas of the land the family had possessed for the last hundred years, when Ajupura was established by Ajubhai in the year 1818–19.[1] He concluded that cotton would be the most suitable crop for the soil, which was dry and received minimal rain. He sent the results of his experiments to the Royal Horticultural Society in London, who in return made him a Fellow of the Society. After Chuckerbutty had left Ghosal began a series of discussions with Dadubhai on the subject of the cultivation of the waste lands which were lying fallow. Ghosal was quick to see the benefits of cultivating the waste lands so that a good income would accrue to both the government and the cultivator. Dadubhai gave Ghosal the benefit of all the advice which could be perfectly fitted into the administration's machinery. The result was the Collector of Kaira Ghosal's famous letter No. R–1215 dated 23 February 1914 to the Revenue Department, Bombay (reproduced in its entirety in Appendix 5).[2] The letter was so well thought out both administratively and legally that the Under-Secretary to Government, C.W.A. Turner, sanctioned it on 7 May 1914.[3] This was one of the shortest times for the Government to consider giving away lands, about 82,051 acres of it (this amounted to one tenth of cultivatable land of the whole District of Kaira).[4] Dadubhai's long stay at Ajupura, a place surrounded by a bewildering wilderness, would have been daunting to any human being. The land, stretching mile upon mile in every direction, was full of dull yellowish grass called Dabhya in Gujarati, sparsely relieved with Babul trees having very few and lean leaves and the branches covered with prickly spikes. This was no tropical rain forest, it was semi-desert, uninviting wilderness.

Dadubhai visualised in this land miles of cotton plants, giving employment to hundreds of peasants of Gujarat. He also encountered dacoits, stationing themselves in the bushes, in between their raids on the villages of Thasra – Kapadvanj Talukas. Luckily these dacoits did not touch Dadubhai and his entourage. On the contrary they respected him and he used to advise them to mend their ways and become honest. The grasslands also harboured Rozes (the Gujarati name for an animal the size of a large horned deer) and rodents which frequently migrated to other cultivated surrounding areas and destroyed the crops of poor peasants. This land was annually auctioned by the Government to grass cutters at nominal rental. If the land was cultivated it could increase the prosperity and also Government's income. From these two Talukas, taking up this land was a gamble for agriculturists. However, a large number of people applied for and got the allocation of land. Dadubhai had full confidence in the venture and he took up about 8,700 acres adjoining his own lands at Ajupura and Chandasar. He established two further villages bringing in farmer workers from Bardoli Taluka of Surat District.[5] He called them Dajipura and Mugatpura, named after his family Saint Mugatram Maharaj and his Father Dajiram Maharaj. Village establishing and opening ceremonies were performed under the auspices of Mugatram Maharaj.

This was a straightforward depiction of 'enlightened self-interest' on the part of the British Administration.

13

DADUBHAI VILLAGES

Dadubhai invited all his cousins and all the Nadiad Desai families to consider taking up the land that the Government was giving free, although naturally with stringent performance criteria. Some of them visited the area and rejected it either as too far from Nadiad (about 20 miles) or too expensive a gamble to establish in such barren uninviting terrain. Later they all were to regret their decision. Dadubhai had to borrow a large sum from Banias and Bankers of Nadiad and Dakor and Thasra to finance the project, which in modern days is comparable to establishing a medium-sized industrial plant in the wilderness. Recruiting and enticing the farmers from 150 miles away in Surat District was also a problem. The villages you establish have to conform not only to Government regulations but also religious and social constraints. Each village had to have at least one family of Brahmin priests who could interpret Hindu scriptures in Sanskrit and perform religious ceremonies for birth, engagement, marriage and death, apart from other religious functions on Hindu holidays. Then came the appointment of village shopkeepers, mainly selling daily food and clothing requirements. Then came the ironmongers (village smithy) who could repair the blades of ploughs or shoes of animals and supply household iron tacks, etc. The village shoemaker, called chamadia, would take the hide of animals, cure it and make shoes and other items from it. The village vaidya (Ayurvedis practitioner) was needed. The village tailor was also invited if one could entice him away from his usual place. All the above had to be provided with land for houses as well as their minimum subsistence. The village well had to be dug first, so that potable water was available for humans and the animals. Also as the village grew in prosperity and population, certain adjoining land had to be reserved for future use. The new villages of Mugatpura and Dajipura turned out to be model villages of the Taluka.

Each farmer who settled in the new villages was given land in the village to build his own house with a big enough backyard to keep his livestock and equipment. Cultivators were allotted between 20 and 70 beeghas of land according to their family size and number of workers. Some who had grownup sons, who could help them, got more land. Dadubhai also imported 'John Deere' soil-breaking machines and tractors from America, the first such machinery in the Kaira District. The Collector Ghosal made a special visit to Ajupura to see for himself the fruits of his task. All the farmers received the land already broken up by the machinery. The land which had remained uncultivated had become hard as stone. There was not enough rain as the average total rainfall in the monsoon was never more than ten inches. So hardened plants, like dabhia and babul, were able to sustain life by sending their roots deeper than other plants. Their deep roots made them difficult to eradicate. Hence the need for deep-digging John Deere machines. Dadubhai had already retained the lease of about 800 acres, which the family possessed in the grass-cutting days, plus 500 acres in Ajupura and 8,700 acres of newly acquired uncultivated land. All together this amounted to about 10,000 acres.[1] Furious activity followed to bring these lands into cultivation before the June rains in 1914. The first crop of cotton came into hand by 1915. The First World War was already on. The price of cotton hit a record high and Dadubhai's prosperity knew no bounds. In the year 1915 his income was more than Rs.65,000 (equal to £5,000), in today's terms about £400,000 per year tax free! As the land was broken, more and more cultivators also became prosperous. Within the five years, from 1915–1920, the northern part of Kheda District was transformed from a low-income area, barely subsisting from small agricultural income, into a rich area with unheard-of prosperity for all the cultivators. Dadubhai's popularity increased in the Kaira District to such an extent that he could now afford to move into wider provincial politics like his father and uncles who were all well known politicians and administrators. His uncle Haridas Desai had been the Dewan of Junagadh (the premier State of Kathiawad) from 1883 onwards. His father was President of Nadiad municipality and a member of the Bombay Governor's Legislative Council. Dadubhai marked his time to consolidate his public position first in the district before going provincial. In 1917 he became Vice-President of Kaira District Local Board, which managed local taxes and primary and secondary schools in the whole Kaira District. He was 36 years old then. To this position he was nominated in 1917, by the Collector who himself was the President of the District Local Board.[2]

In 1916 Baraiya Satyagraha at Mal tract was the feature. The events were as follows. In the famine of 1899–1900 caused mainly by failure of rain, many Baraiyas had given up their land and migrated elsewhere. Now this very same land was allotted by the Government to rich landlords. The landlords needed Baraiyas to work on their lands. The Baraiyas were unwilling to work as labourers on the very same land they previously owned. The landlord offered them higher wages to get them to work. However, the other Baraiyas, who owned lands, also had to pay higher wages to their labourers.[3] So, in September 1916 the leading Baraiyas held a meeting and decided that all Baraiyas should withdraw their labour from non-Baraiyas owned lands. Caste penalties were threatened on whoever broke ranks. This non-cooperation, by withdrawing their labour, spread to some 240 villages in Northern Kaira District. The landlords and the Collector tried hard to break the strike. Outside labourers were brought and the Government pledged their support to the landlords. Collector Ghosal asked Dadubhai to negotiate and settle the dispute with the strikers. Dadubhai tried but the strike continued though on a lower scale. One month later it fizzled out owing to dissensions among the Baraiyas themselves. The poorer ones started to feel the pangs of hunger and poverty and began creeping back to work. This movement made the landlords realise, for the first time, that the Baraiya community was a force to be reckoned with on all future occasions. Neglecting their genuine needs was not an option.

14

TAX COLLECTION AT NADIAD

Under the presidency of the Nadiad Desais, tax collection in the Nadiad Municipality was lax, the rich being often allowed to get away with paying only a part of the tax due, while traders could avoid the town octroi tax by taking their goods from the train at the stop before Nadiad and then bringing them by road into the town. The municipal finances were in perilous state as the greed and apathy of municipal officers could be said to promote it. In 1913 the exasperated Collector wrote: 'The congested state of the town, the number of hollows surrounding it which during and after the monsoon are converted into stagnant pools, the absence of any drainage system and the use of Khalkoovas (cesspits) for the disposal of night soil are jointly responsible for its appalling insanitary condition, its frequent epidemics and very high death rate'.[1] The Collector thought that, to solve the problem of Nadiad municipality mismanagement, he should appoint a Mamlatdar-grade government officer as chief officer of the municipality. He would then work with the municipal council and its president, as a counterbalancing force to stop corruption. Girdhardas Desai, who was the President, protested against the unnecessarily expensive appointment.[2] In spite of that a Sunni Bohra of Broach, Valibax Adam Patel, was appointed as the first chief officer. His appointment was soon put to the test when a council resolution passed by a huge majority supported by the Desais and Gokuldas Tullatee demanded that Valibax be dismissed on the ground that he was too highly paid and that a lower-grade officer would suffice.[3]

The Collector ignored the resolution. In the 1918 election for the presidency of the Nadiad municipality, Gokuldas Tullatee opposed the incumbent Girdhardas Desai and won by the narrow majority of one vote, thanks to the defection of a Patel voter. So, after nearly a quarter of a century of service to the Nadiad municipality Girdhardas Desai's, and for that matter Nadiad Desai's, power was broken by the Nadiad Arya Samajist nationalists who included Fulchand Bapuji Shah, Chandulal Desai and Batuk Mehta, with Gokuldas Tullatee as their leader. By then the Arya Samajist had by charity collection built a Hindu orphanage, 'Hindu Anath Ashram'. Gandhiji visited the Ashram in 1916 and expressed his support. Later he made it his stopping station in Nadiad when he acted as recruiting agent for the British in their war against Germany. In 1918 Gandhiji had made Nadiad Hindu Anath Ashram the headquarters for the failed Kheda land revenue Satyagraha, this being the only venue large enough for such work.[4]

15

MORLEY-MINTO REFORMS

Under the Morley-Minto reforms of 1909, a new elected legislative council was formed for Bombay. The members were to be elected from Northern Division local boards and Northern Division municipalities. Prior to that, members for the Bombay Legislative Council were appointed by the Government. The last incumbent before the elections was Purushottamdas Desai (the Father of Dadubhai). For the new electorate of 1911 new Desai contestants were Girdhardas Desai and Gopaldas Desai. For the first time there was a threat from outside. Gopaldas Desai was opposed by Gokuldas Talati, a Vanya lawyer from Umreth; while Girdhardas Desai was opposed by Vithalbhai Patel who was virtually a Desai as his mother was a Nadiad Desai distantly related to both the contesting Desais. He had spent a major part of his childhood in Nadiad and had his matriculation from Nadiad Government High School. Both the Nadiad Desais were defeated in the election. Vithalbhai won with 72 per cent of the votes in his favour in the local boards seat, while Gokuldas won the municipality seat. So for a while the Nadiad Desais lost some of their power in the municipality. That was in 1911. Up to that time Purushottamdas Desai had attended regularly the Legislative Council at Bombay, of which he was a member. In fact Purushottamdas was the first person holding any office under the British to broach the subject of land revenue charges. By asking at the meeting of the Bombay Legislative Council on 25 June 1910: 'Does it appear advisable to Government to institute inquiries with regard to judiciousness of the assessment rates, especially in the Thasra Taluka where lands have continued to be relinquished in spite of the concession continued since 1902'.[1] From this it will be observed that Purushottamdas Desai had stirred up the hornet's nest which in later years served as focal point for Vithalbhai, Vallabhbhai and Gandhiji to attack the British. From this point onwards for twenty years the focus of the freedom fight of India remained in Gujarat. By then Dadubhai had turned 32 and was the joint author of his Father's enquiry about the justice of the land revenue collection in Kaira. At the time he was content to look after the family interests. Until 1920, when he entered the Bombay Legislative Council as an elected member representing the Kaira District, Purushottamdas Desai also took an active part in the Bombay Legislative Council to protect the interests of Gujarat and especially the Kaira District landowners and subjects in general: for example he gave his opinion on Bhagdari and Narvadars tenures of land.[2] All this was possible because Viharidas took special care to see that all his sons learnt the English language, its grammar and prose. In 1911 Vithalbhai J. Patel arrived on the political scene of the Kaira District and also that of Gujarat and even of all India. Soon he was to tower over everyone. First he was elected to Taluka and District Local Boards in 1911 and from there to membership of the Bombay Legislative Council – one Desai taking the place of the other. An account of his life appears later in Part 3, Chapter 25.

PART 2

STRUGGLE AND INDEPENDENCE

16

BARDOLI SATYAGRAHA

BRITISH PARLIAMENT 1919

Bardoli is a small town in Gujarat and Satyagraha is a strategy of nonviolent, nonco-operation with the government administration. The maps at the end of this Chapter and at the end of Appendix 5, Document 17, show most of the locations mentioned in the following pages.

In 1919 the British Parliament set up a Joint Select Committee on the Government of India Bill. The recommendations of this Committee were to have far-reaching consequences. In pursuance of Resolution No. 18 of the Indian National Congress at Delhi in December 1918, it was decided to send a delegation to England. The All India Congress Committee which met on 21–22 April 1919 agreed that the delegation should be composed of Vithalbhai (joint Secretary of the Congress), Dewan Madhav Rao and N.C. Kelkar and should be asked to sail at once to England. Following the Delhi sessions of the Congress in December 1918, the Rowlatt Act had already been imposed upon the country. The three members sailed on 29 April 1919, Lokmanya Tilak and Horniman joined them later. It was the work of the delegation to seek interviews with the members of the Joint Select Committee and make representation to the Committee for self-determination in India.[1]

Giving an account of his work with the Congress deputation in England, Vithalbhai has placed the following on record: 'Most of the members of the deputation left for India early in November 1919, to be in time for the Amritsar Congress. They directed me to stay on till the Bill was through and I did so. My principal duty was to see that the Congress view was represented before the

Joint Committee, which had not till then completed its labours, and before the House of Commons when the Bill was discussed there. The only member of the Committee who sympathised with Congress demands was Mr Spoor, with whom I kept in constant touch noting the deliberations of the Committee. I passed hours and hours with him and explained to his satisfaction the justice of our demands. He then consented to move before the Joint Committee all the amendments which I had prepared on the lines of the Delhi Congress resolutions. He also expressed his willingness to move similar amendments in the House on the Bill as revised by the Joint Committee and asked me to interview prominent members of his Party and explain our case to them. This I did and I am glad to say successfully. I then prepared draft amendments and sent a copy to every prominent member of the Labour Party. I requested Mr Spoor and three other members to convene a meeting of their party to consider these amendments. At that stage Mrs Besant was exerting herself to induce the Labour members to support the Bill as revised and not to give notice of my amendments. I am glad to say that, in spite of Mrs Besant's adverse intervention, the Executive of the Labour Party met and decided to move our amendments in the House. I tried some members of the other party but the only member whom I could convince was Mr MacAllum Scott. He gave notice of our amendments after I had four interviews with him. I then interviewed every member who had given notice of our amendments and gave them instructions and supplied them with supporting material. I was asked by some of them to prepare notes on amendments. Thereupon such notes were prepared on all our amendments and a copy supplied to every member who had given notice. The Bill was discussed in the House of Commons for three days and the Congress case was fully represented. I had been fortunate enough to get a seat under the gallery from where I could not only hear the debate properly, but also give instructions on points raised in the debate. As an instance of these instructions, I should like to mention one. During the debate on Mr MacAllum Scott's amendment for transfer of all subjects, other than law, justice and police in the Presidency of Bombay, Commander Kenworthy asked Mr Montagu, who was replying, whether the Government of Bombay itself had not recommended the transfer of land revenue and irrigation? This question was asked on my instructions. Although not a single amendment was adopted by the House, the discussion had in my opinion served a very 'useful purpose'.'[2] Thus Vithalbhai's efforts opened up a second front of our struggle in England. Until Vithalbhai adopted these methods, they had been either unknown or not practised. It was taken to be almost axiomatic, that we should never mix ourselves up in English politics, and also that propaganda in England was absolutely futile. In the final India Bill a provision was inserted which recommended that the Land Revenue Regulations be brought under legislative control. This was solely due to Vithalbhai's efforts. He provided the intelligentsia of the Labour Party with a new platform to fight the Conservatives and he laid the foundation of the Indian alliance with the Labour Party which certainly has been an important factor in the independence which was later secured. Annexing the Labour Party to the Indian cause was Vithalbhai's great service to India. These same tactics were disallowed by Gandhiji at the Second Round Table Conference and that was the reason for issuing The Bose-Patel Manifesto of 9 May 1933[3] and the most exasperating letter of Vithalbhai dated 11 May 1933, to Dadubhai from Vienna.[4] What Vithalbhai understood of the working of the modern capitalist system, Gandhiji failed, or was unwilling, to understand and exploit to India's advantage. Independence came, but rather late when the Hindu-Muslim split had already infected Indian politics. Who knows, maybe the Hindu-Muslim amity, which was the hallmark of Akbar's empire would have pervaded now, but for the untimely withdrawal of Vithalbhai by the almighty god?

SEEDS OF SATYAGRAHA

The seeds of Bardoli Satyagraha were thus sown in 1919 by the British Parliament's Joint Select Committee on the Government of India Bill, which recommended that the Land Revenue Regulations be brought under stricter legislative control.

The last revenue settlement of the Bardoli Taluka had taken place in 1896 and a fresh revision, according to the existing practice in the Bombay Presidency, became due in 1926. The work was entrusted to Sjt M.S. Jayakar, a member of the provincial civil service, who had certainly no previous experience of similar work to his credit. He started his work sometime in 1924 and finally submitted his report to the Government on 11 November 1925. Let us summarise this report which recommended an increase of 25 per cent over the existing rates, but also raised 23 villages from a lower group to a higher group, with the result that the increase in the total assessment of the Taluka amounted to something over 30 per cent. The old assessment which was Rs.514,762 was raised to Rs.672,273. The summary of his reasons for the increase in his own words are as follows:

‘1) Communications have considerably improved, including the opening of the broad gauge line of the Tapti Valley Railway.
2) Population has increased by about 3,800.
3) The increase in the number of milch cattle and carts.
4) The increase in wealth as judged by the new and well-built Pucca houses springing up all over.
5) Improved condition of the Kaliparaj, spread of education and prohibition among the Kaliparaj.
6) Abnormal rise in the prices of food grains and of cotton.
7) Agricultural wages have doubled.
8) The prices of land have risen and assessment represents a steadily decreasing proportion of the rent.’

The consideration however that weighed with him most was that the price of the total products of the Taluka ‘represent a clear increase of Rs.1,508,077 over the price of the products during the previous settlement’. This report was not published as such reports are never published, not even in the Government Gazette. What usually happens is that one copy is kept at the Taluka Kacheri. You have to go to Kacheri to see the report. No one gets a copy of the report. How can a peasant travel, in some cases 20 miles, from his village to see a report which is in English, a language that he probably never learnt. The Government also considered a separate report by the Settlement Commissioner Anderson who suggested an entirely new grouping of 32 villages and enhancing the rates of some of these villages by 50 to 60 per cent. In making their choice between the two reports – Jayakar’s and Anderson’s – the Government found a way of escape by recommending a 22 per cent increase in the land revenue. There was something sharp however about the circumstances in which the revised assessment was applied to Bardoli. Government resolution No. 2973 of 5 May 1903 lays down that the year of introduction of a new settlement must be the first year of the new settlement and not the last year of the current settlement; and Section 104 of the Land Revenue Code expressly provides, that in the year of introduction of a new settlement: 'The difference between the old and the new settlement of all lands on which the latter may be in excess of the former shall be remitted and the revised assessment shall be levied only from the next following year'. With the Government Resolution 2973 and Section 104 read together, the new settlement rates in Bardoli could be introduced only in the revenue year 1927–28 and levied in the year 1928–29, that is in February 1929.

To get around Section 104, the new settlement was introduced on 19 July 1927 (July being the last month of the revenue year 1926–27), in contravention of the above cited Government Resolution, so as to enable the Government to levy the new rates in 1927–28.

In 1923 Dadubhai Desai, Bhimbhai Naik and H.B. Shivdasani had set up an organisation called Khedut Mandal at Bardoli.[5] Its objective was to adopt constitutional methods to ameliorate the condition of the peasants. The social position of members of this group and their constitutionalist stance enabled them to have some influence on the Government officials at different levels. Their views carried weight with the Government, even if the latter would not very often see eye to eye with them.[6] There was also another group called the Ashram Group which represented the views of Mahatma Gandhi. They operated from the Ashram established by Gandhi in 1922, when he wanted to start Satyagraha from Bardoli (the satyagraha which was aborted before it was started). This group was headed by two brothers, Kunverji and Kalyanji Mehtas (who were Patidars although called Mehta).

When, on 11 November 1925, Jayakar's proposal to increase the land revenue by about 25 per cent became known, both groups jointly opposed it. Under the leadership of Dadubhai Desai it was proposed to make a final presentation to the Government before starting any agitation. Pamphlets containing the following instructions were issued and distributed in all the villages of Bardoli Taluka:

'Within two months of this announcement, peasants should acquaint us about their views on the problem of land revenue rise. Rao Saheb Dadubhai Desai is to visit the Taluka 18, 19 and 20 February 1926 in this connection. Those who want to convey their views to him, should see him. Their cases will be presented by the Members of the Legislative Council (by Dadubhai and other

M.L.Cs.) but do not be under the impression that you will get justice through the Legislative Council. The Government generally does not pay heed to any appeal and keeps room for public agitation. If you do not get justice before the time of paying the first instalment of land revenue, we will launch Satyagraha shown by Gandhiji as a last measure.[7] This requires unity, firm decision, and a sense of sacrifice on the part of the peasants.'

The first phase of the movement was dominated by the Khedut Mandal, as they were supported by most of the peasants. The Ashram group of the Congress, which had a reduced hold on the peasants, were only too happy to accept a secondary role.[8] On the advice of the members of the Legislative Council the peasants began sending petitions to the Collector of Surat, J.W. Hartshorne. The moderate leaders finally collected all the petitions and handed them over to the Commissioner, W.W. Smart. None of these petitions was ever acknowledged.

In 1924 the Bombay Legislative Council, in which Dadubhai Desai represented the constituency of Kaira District and was also the leader of the opposition for Gujarat, had passed a motion for a committee to be set up to consider the recommendations of the Joint Select Committee of the British Parliament. This motion also demanded that until the Committee Report came forward, the Bombay Government should not make further revenue settlements – the Government opposed this. However a Committee of eight officials and 14 non-officials was established on 28 June 1924.[9] Although the non-officials were in the majority, those like Dadubhai who wanted radical reform found themselves in a minority. Dadubhai made several speeches to the Committee arguing strongly against any revision of the scale of Land Revenue. It may be noted that the grandfather of Benazir Bhutto, Khan Bahadur Shah Nawaz Khan Bhutto, who represented Sind constituency, was also a member with government leanings.

Dadubhai Desai was one of the most vocal members of the Committee where he made several speeches against further enhancement of land revenue.[10] The Report of the Committee came to hand in March 1927. Its recommendations were:

1 Revision settlements should be limited to 25 per cent of the present levy;
2 A Committee of the Legislative Council should be formed

with the direction to review all revision settlements and demand alteration where necessary.

If the Government wished to overrule these, it would need a resolution of the Legislature. In effect, the Government, having a clear majority in the Bombay Legislative Council, had manoeuvred to retain the same powers as before over revenue settlements. Dadubhai clearly saw the game and refused to sign the report.[11] He inserted a long minute of dissent in which he demanded that the peasants be recognised as owners of their land, rather than as tenants of the Government, that there should be permanent settlements, that those farmers with an annual income under Rs.5,000 be exempted from revenue and that a landowner should have the right to go to a court of law to get his assessment revised in the same manner as the income tax paper. Dadubhai also protested that, in spite of the Legislative Council's motion of 1924 that revision settlements should cease, the settlements had continued unabated.[12] Thus, the Bombay Government was not yet prepared to concede any control over land revenue policy to the members of the Legislative Council. After the Bombay Government rejected the proposals of the Bombay Legislative Council Land Revenue Committee in May 1927, the downtrodden peasantry of Gujarat was ready to start a revolt against their harsh treatment by the Government who professed to look after their well-being.

The budget session of the Bombay Legislative Council commenced in February 1927. Throughout the session the issue of Bardoli figured prominently. Dadubhai, Bhimbhai, Shivdasani and others made several speeches pointing out that there was no justification for any increase in the land revenue.

Their Council Representatives, viz Dadubhai and others, had waited patiently till early 1927 for the Revenue Member of the Bombay Government to act. Later Dadubhai and Bhimbhai Naik submitted a long memorandum dealing not only with the Report but also detailing the real economic conditions and the hardships of the people. In spite of all this the Government finally announced the revised settlement as *de facto*. After this, having exhausted all the avenues of redress by constitutional means and waiting to see a change of heart by the Government, the peasants led by Dadubhai in a Conference held, on 6 September 1927, at the famous Jain Temple (which had been the centre of the 1921 proposed civil disobedience movement) and attended by thousands of them, announced and unanimously passed a resolution to withhold payment of the 22 per cent enhanced payment.[13] Thus was started the BARDOLI SATYAGRAHA led by Dadubhai Desai of Nadiad and his Khedut Mandal.[14] The meeting was also attended by the Ashram group leaders Kunverji, Khushalbhai, Keshubhai and others.

On 19 December 1927, Ashram leaders Kunverji, Keshavji and Mohanlal Pandya saw Vallabhbhai at Ahmedabad.[15] Vallabhbhai said he was busy and at the time when the moderate leaders Dadubhai and Bhambhai were still active, it would be inexpedient to launch a direct action which would divide the leadership. He was also not sure about the degree of support which the local Ashram workers enjoyed from the peasants.

The local leaders with encouragement and advice from the M.L.Cs., especially Dadubhai, Bhimbhai and Shivdasani stepped up their activities among the peasants. They wrote letters to the leading peasants, landlords, Patels and Talatis of the Taluka and explained the pressing need for a campaign. The leaders also started a programme of touring the Taluka to canvas support for the campaign.

Immediately after the conference at Bardoli, Dadubhai went back to Nadiad and Ahmedabad and saw Gandhiji and Vallabhbhai separately. Having briefed Vallabhbhai with full details of the situation in Bardoli, he asked him if he would take over the leadership. Vallabhbhai was reluctant to discontinue his still unfinished work as the President of Ahmedabad Municipality and go to Bardoli. Dadubhai then went to Bardoli and asked the two local leaders, Kalyanji and Kunvarji (brothers) to go and see Vallabhbhai alone. Vallabhbhai said he could not interfere with the work of Dadubhai and Bhimbhai who were perfectly capable leaders. So now Dadubhai again asked Gandhiji to persuade Vallabhbhai. He also sent Kalyanji and Kunvarji to Gandhiji. After a long talk, Gandhi saw Vallabhbhai and asked him to go to Bardoli and check for himself about the suitability of a struggle of no revenue payment. Gandhi also stipulated that the peasants should not pay the enhanced 22 per cent as well as the present revenue charge. Thus no money should be paid to the Government if the campaign was to succeed. So now Vallabhbhai accompanied by Dadubhai went to Bardoli, on 4 February 1928, and reluctantly accepted the Presidentship of the Conference from Dadubhai who resigned.[16] Vallabhbhai was the obvious leader for the campaign and was finally persuaded by Dadubhai with the assurance that he could conduct the campaign in his own indomitable way without any interference. Dadubhai also promised the full support of the M.L.Cs. as a channel of communication with the Government at every stage of the movement and to keep the channel of negotiations with the Government open. Vallabhbhai was ceremoniously installed at the conference on 4 February 1928.

This Satyagraha was destined to be the first so-called 'Gandhian' agitation of any magnitude capable of ruffling the feathers of the British Raj. This most notable and successful campaign was joined by Vallabhbhai Patel who became its leader after persuasion by Dadubhai and it catapulted him into an all-India leadership of unassailable power. So far none of the leaders of the Indian National Congress had ever conceived of let alone led and won such a mass awakening and effective struggle. From now on he was given the pseudonym of 'Sardar' (meaning a commanding leader) of the peasants.

Vallabhbhai, along with Dadubhai, immediately called a Conference of all the workers of the 79 villages of Bardoli Taluka. Amongst them were men of every community, Kanbis, Anavlas, Kaliparaj and Parsis, who were paying between Rs.300 and Rs.500 as land revenue.[17] At this Conference there was a wide range of opinions. Men of five or six villages said that they would rather pay the existing rate and decline to pay the 22 per cent enhancement. The rest were determined to refuse any payment whatsoever to the Government. Representatives of two villages discussed the situation frankly with Vallabhbhai.[18] 'Are you speaking for the whole of your village?', they were asked. 'I am', said one of them with stubborn determination. 'But if all the rest fall back what will you do?', he was asked. 'I will stand alone', he replied. Then came another who was asked the same question. He said: 'My village will stand together so long as the Talukas stands together, not afterwards'. A third man said: 'We are all determined Hindus and Musalmans, but I must say that 25 per cent of the Musalmans are rather shaky'. Then came another who said: 'Sir, if four true people can be found to stand firm come what may, I am sure of success'. 'What do you mean by four?', he was asked. 'By four I mean four of the top men', he replied. Next he was asked: 'Do you consider yourself one of them?' His reply was: 'No Sir, I am the fifth and I will follow the four'. 'Are there four people who are prepared to stake their all in resisting the enhancement?', asked Vallabhbhai. Immediately four stood up to express their determination. In the meanwhile the representatives of the five villages had been conferring with the rest and now announced their decision to go with the Taluka. It was after this that Sjt Vallabhbhai Patel addressed the conference. After criticising the Government's revenue policy, he gave as his opinion that the farmers' cause was just and that they were fully justified in resisting the payment of revenue. He asked them to search their hearts and ask themselves if they could carry on a non-violent and honest struggle for any length of time against a Government which might mobilise all the forces at its disposal.[19] The question ultimately affected not one Taluka but many Talukas and many districts, that is to say the whole of India. He warned them against coming to a hasty decision and gave them seven days to think it over, so that he might in the meantime communicate with Government and see if he could persuade them to reconsider the matter and announce an impartial enquiry.

There were three M.L.C.s, Sjt Dadubhai Desai, Bhimbhai Naik and Dr Dixit, present there on the dais, who emphasised the point that they had exhausted every constitutional means at their disposal and, as they had failed, they had gladly entrusted their case to one who could take them along the path of non-violent resistance and suffering.[20]

SATYAGRAHA STARTS

This was on 4 February 1928 and the Bardoli Satyagraha started in earnest. Vallabhbhai then went back to Ahmedabad and, on 6 February, wrote a letter to His Excellency the Governor of Bombay stating the case of the Bardoli peasants and suggested to him: 'To afford a fair opportunity to the people to place their case before an impartial tribunal clothed with adequate authority'. He also added that unless this was done, 'with all his anxiety to avoid a serious conflict with Government, he would have no alternative but to advise the people to refuse to pay the assessment and peacefully and quietly suffer the consequences of such refusal'. At the end he added: 'Should Your Excellency think it necessary that we should meet in this matter, I would gladly wait on you'. He also mentioned in the letter the settlement officer's recommendation of regrouping a number of villages and placing them in a higher group, where a serious irregularity had occurred.

The Government saw the correctness of the argument on regrouping and, without admitting it, at the end of the month they announced at the next meeting of the Bombay Legislative Council in March that the grouping of 22 villages had been reduced. However, the Governor's reply to the main argument of Vallabhbhai's letter came in the form of a note by his Private Secretary that the letter 'had been sent to the Revenue Department for official consideration and disposal'. Thus the Governor deliberately refused to deal with Vallabhbhai directly. The Governor had met and known Vallabhbhai and his work at the time of his visit to Kaira District for flood relief. A golden opportunity for a peaceful settlement was lost.[21]

Vallabhbhai waited until 11 February for the Government's reply. Having received no reply by 12 February as arranged, the representatives of all 139 villages assembled in a conference with Vallabhbhai, Dadubhai, Bhimbhai Naik and Dr Dixit on the dais. The villagers had taken, and brought with them, thousands of signatures to a tentative pledge for non-payment of assessment. Vallabhbhai glanced at these papers and, after asking them a few relevant questions, delivered his oration. He told them that he had written to the Government, but their reply had been to pass on his letter to the Revenue Department for consideration and disposal. This was not acceptable. Then he said:[22] 'I have nothing more to say. Do what you do with eyes open, with God as witness and fully counting the cost. It is possible that the Government might pick up the leading men among you first to set an example. Government might first confiscate the lands of those who move the resolution today. If you are sure that these things will leave you unshaken take up and fight the good fight.'

The following resolution was moved then seconded and supported by men from different villages and drawn from various communities in the Taluka – Kanbis, Anavlas, Vanias, Parsis and Musalmans:

> This Conference of the people of Bardoli Taluka resolves that revision settlement in Bardoli is arbitrary, unjust and oppressive and advises all the occupants to refuse payment of the revised settlement until the Government is prepared to accept the amount of the old settlement in full satisfaction of their dues

> or until the Government appoints an impartial tribunal to settle the whole question of revision by investigation and inquiry on the spot.[23]

The first speaker made a very brief speech. Two of those who followed made brief observations and the rest simply supported the resolution. There were no more speeches, but after recitation of sacred text from the Koran and of a Hindu hymn and repetition of Ramanama – the whole Conference participating – the resolution was passed in solemn silence.[24]

The final date, 15 February 1928, for the payment of the first instalment of the land revenue had passed, the period for forfeiture notices had expired. The four members of the Legislative Council, Sjt Dadubhai, Bhimbhai Naik, Shivdasani and Dr Dixit, attended many mass meetings on the outskirts of various villages and were impressed with the strength and solidarity of the people.[25] Meanwhile, Sjt Vallabhbhai was taking stock of the situation and he took a conciliatory step about which he was in correspondence with the Government for some time. The 'Inam' lands were not subject to any enhancement, so he thought that there should be no objection to them paying their land revenue. So he issued instructions to owners of 'Inam' lands to pay up their revenue. The total assessment of these lands was only Rs.8,756–12–0 out of a total revenue demand in excess of 6 lakhs of rupees. This step was taken to show the correctness of his attitude, but it made no difference to the Government. In early April Vallabhbhai came to Bardoli with Dadubhai and other M.L.C.s and he was so impressed with the solidarity and determination of the people of Bardoli that his confidence in the ultimate success was shown in his speech to the mass meeting there. His mastery of rhetoric came into full play.[26] His speech went on: 'These M.L.C.s are all our men but their methods of work and fight are different. They fight the Government on the Government's ground. It is a game of chance arranged by Government in which they play whenever they like with loaded dice. Our M.L.C.s call it a constitutional fight. Well that constitutional fight is not for me ... Mine is a game arranged by myself, and I am quite at home in it. These friends, the M.L.C.s, also agree with me that there is no hope for us otherwise ... Agriculturalists today are like the road – metal crushed flat under a steamroller, which let us call the 'Anderson Patent Steamroller' (alluding to Mr

Anderson the settlement Commissioner who conjured up the enhanced revenue under his theory of rental value of land) we are fighting to see that in Bardoli at any rate we will not consent to be crushed under that steamroller ... The fight is not for the purpose of saving a lakh and a few thousand Rupees. If I could be convinced that there was a case for enhancement, I should not have hesitated to advise the people to pay up ... When, before the launch of the Bardoli campaign, I wrote to the Government that the condition of agriculturalists was everywhere getting worse and that they should not try to bring one or two Talukas that may be comparatively better on a level with the rest, they said to me that I was an 'Outsider'!'[27]

By 14 April 1928, the no-tax campaign was proceeding vigorously. Nobody had paid the revenue which was due. Attachment and forfeiture notices found their place in wastepaper baskets. The Government now envisaged resorting to more drastic measures. The Commissioner of the Division cut short his seaside holiday and came to Surat on orders from above. Similarily, the Collector was obliged to decamp from the hills in the neighbouring State and return to Bardoli for the first time since the start of the campaign. So far he had been looking at the campaign through the eyes of his Deputy Collector. What he saw at Bardoli depressed him – all the shops closed, the shopkeepers having resolved not to open the shops during the day in order to avoid attachment processes. They took away the licences and the brass badges of the nonco-operating taxi drivers. The Collector marched to Sarbhon at a late hour in the evening. He saw all the doors closed on him. Then he went to another village and met with the same disappointment. Next day he called a meeting of all Talatis, asked them to prepare a map of suitable lands which on confiscation could be given away to intending purchasers and left for Surat, evidently boiling with rage. A campaign of attaching buffaloes had already begun. Three special officers were now appointed with special powers to employ summary methods of house-entry and attachment. The Hindu Mamlatdar was transferred to a distant district and a Muslim Mamlatdar appointed in his place, so that he might be better able to bring pressure on Muslim agriculturalists and divide them from the Hindus. Undaunted by these measures, the people were strengthening their organisation more and more. During this first stage of the campaign Vallabhbhai was still coming to Bardoli from

Ahmedabad for three days in the week, as the rest of the week needed his presence in Ahmedabad as President of the Municipality. Dadubhai, however, and other Surat members of the Council, spent all their time going round the villages making speeches and hearing about events and giving advice to the people and supporting their enthusiasm. The response of the people was so great that no one could envisage the collapse of the movement. However, to keep spirits up, more rabble-rousing speeches that Vallabhbhai alone was capable of were thought advisable. Consequently Dadubhai again requested Vallabhbhai to leave Ahmedabad resign his Presidentship of Ahmedabad Municipality and make a fulltime home and speech making platform in Bardoli Ashram. Vallabhbhai, realising this was a sure winner, resigned from Ahmedabad in May and started devoting all his time to the movement. No one was more pleased with this than Dadubhai who was anxious for the success of the movement he had originally started.[28]

On 18 April 1928, while the peasant campaign was in full swing under the leadership of Vallabhbhai, Dadubhai wrote to the Governor, Sir Leslie Wilson, on behalf of eight M.L.Cs. from Gujarat exposing the discrepancies in the settlement report amd requesting him to appoint an independent inquiry committee.[29] Dadubhai also threatened that if the inquiry committee were not appointed the eight M.L.Cs. from Gujarat would resign from their membership of the Bombay Legislative Council and would seek re-election to prove that the whole of Gujarat was behind the demand for an inquiry. J.C. Ker, private secretary to the Governor, replied: 'Your resignation is one that must of course rest with yourselves. It would prove that you are opposed to any increase in the land revenue in Bardoli Taluka and perhaps in any other part of Gujarat and if you were re-elected it would prove that electors of Gujarat were equally opposed to any increase and were desirous of avoiding any further taxation themselves... If each section of the community were consulted separately, no taxes would be levied at all by any Government Municipality or Local Board'.[30]

The Government published the whole correspondance in the *Times of India* (23 April) to prove the parochial character of the Gujarat members. Further the *Times of India*, which was always pro-Government, writing in its editorial on the same day condemned the Gujarat M.L.Cs.:

'Gujarat does not intend to bear its share of the general taxation of the country and that its people expect all their share of the benefits of a peaceful administration, without contributing towards the increased cost of governing the Province. What do their sections of the Presidency think of such a selfish policy?'[31]

The Government considered the M.L.Cs. were only bluffing about their resignation from the Council. A secret confidential report of the Home Ministry of the Government of India stated: 'None of these gentlemen desires to resign, and for the moment they are keeping quiet. In the event of the incident finding its way into the newspapers, Government will probably publish the correspondence and the effect must be to cause a split between the M.L.Cs. and Patel (Vallabhbhai) and his party. If this should happen the collection of revenue should be facilitated ... The movement does not appear to have the support of the more moderate section of the politicians'.[32]

Dadubhai replied coolly to Ker's letter. Stating his position he wrote: '... it was not the intention of Gujarat members to object to any equitable and just taxation, but to request His Excellency to order a fresh inquiry into the recent revision settlement of Bardoli and Chorasi Talukas, with a view to set right grave mistakes both in data and in the decision arrived at on that data ...'.

On the same day (23 April 1928) Governor Wilson wrote to Lord Irwin that he was not afraid of the threat of resignation of eight Gujarat members and that the Government's position was very sound.[33] On 18 May, as the Government turned down their demand, the eight M.L.Cs. tendered their resignations and the Government accepted them on 20 May 1928. The Government had not expected the M.L.Cs. to take such a drastic step. This happened more than three months after the movement started and yet the resistance of the peasants had not declined in any way.

On 18 May 1928 the Congress Working Committee met in Bombay. Vallabhbhai went there and pressed for, and passed, a resolution congratulating the peasants of Bardoli for their valiant struggle, appreciating the work done by Vallabhbhai and other Congress field workers and congratulated the Gujarat M.L.Cs. on their efforts and for their resignations.

Meanwhile Lord Irwin wrote to Wilson: 'To use Vithalbhai as a vehicle to transmit ideas to his brother Vallabhbhai',[34] Wilson in reply refused.[35] On 17 May 1928 Vithalbhai wrote directly to Wilson, stating that the demands of the Bardoli peasants for an independent inquiry was just and legitimate. The measures adopted by the Government of Bombay were far beyond what a civilised government could lawfully do.[36] In reply, Wilson defended his Government's measures as well as his officials. He also accused Vithalbhai of playing into the hands of the agitators while occupying a responsible position in the Central Government. He demanded his resignation.[37] Wilson also wrote to Irwin dismissing Vithalbhai's arguments and casting doubt on the accuracy of his sources of information.[38]

Vithalbhai, as a true Desai, persisted with Lord Irwin till Irwin sent the following telegram to Wilson:[39] 'Patel, who is the President of the Assembly, had an interview with me today. He expressed very strongly the hope that a settlement would emerge. He was emphatic that there was no political *arrière pensée* in the trouble of any kind on the side of his friends, and that no one wanted trouble, but that they were solely actuated by the conviction that a bona fide miscalculation had been made. He went on to say that passive resistance would be abandoned and settlement could probably be arrived at if, pending result of an independent inquiry, Government could agree to collect the original revenue assessment.' The substance of the argument of Vithalbhai clearly shows that he was in close contact with Vallabhbhai and Dadubhai. In fact, when he started the Bardoli campaign in September 1927, Dadubhai at the conference exhorted the peasants not to pay the enhanced 22 per cent, but to pay the original assessment, and the conference had passed a resolution to that effect. It was the Bombay Government who by their actions had turned a simple complaint and grievances into a political storm.

To the Bombay Government (Wilson) the prestige and authority of the administration was the issue. The very next day he sent a reply telegram to Irwin:[40] 'Patel has misled you in saying that there was no political *arrière pensée*. This is a deliberate attempt to coerce Government by using the weapon of civil disobedience and the movement is headed by his brother. They thought government would give way and now they find that they are mistaken. They are spreading stories such as Patel tells you. I am confident of your support in our action which has unanimous agreement of all my colleagues, European and Indian, to uphold the authority of Government'.[41]

Wilson followed up that telegram with full details in his letter of 1 June 1928.[42] Then in a letter on the next day, 2 June, he stressed that he had reduced the enhancement from 30 per cent (as proposed by Jaykar) to 20 per cent to pacify the opposition, but the agitators had not accepted it. That was proof positive that the agitation was politically motivated. After due consideration of Wilson's arguments and the facts relayed by him, Irwin wrote to Wilson on 25 June:[43] 'Your grounds for suspecting politics in Bardoli look pretty strong. I assure you full support in the matter and I hope that your difficulties may gradually diminish'. This reduction of the enhancement placated Vithalbhai and nullified his intervention – but was still worried about the consequences in the event that his correspondence with Patel was published.[44]

Now another intruder had to be placated. Kanayalal M.Munshi, an M.L.C., jumped in to try to secure a settlement. He went to see Gandhi and Vallabhbhai, ascertained their position and wrote a letter to Wilson on 27 May, stating that as an impartial observer he was convinced that the demands of the Bardoli peasants were neither excessive nor unreasonable. He criticised the Government's policy of repression. In reply, Wilson stated that no government worth the name could concede to private individuals the right to usurp the functions of the Government.[45] Later Munshi resigned as an M.L.C.

Next came Sir Purshottamdas Thakerdas, a member of the Central Legislative Assembly and a cousin of Sir Chunilal Mehta, the finance member of the Bombay's Governor's Executive Council. On 2 June 1928 he wrote to Sir Chunilal:[46] 'I am convinced that Government have put themselves in the wrong by refusing the request of Dadubhai Desai and other M.L.Cs for an inquiry by an officer of Government … I feel strongly that the Government now wish to show their power. No Indian can encourage them in this tendency of theirs. I fully realise that Government have lost their head and ruined the Bardoli farmers. At this stage in the name of prestige, I cannot by any means sympathise with Government's most thoughtless insistence on their own point of view'.

Then Sir Purshottamdas, along with H.P. Mody and Lalji Naranji, all three representing the Bombay Indian Merchants' Chamber, met Wilson on 22 June. At the meeting, Wilson was adamant that the old revenue plus the enhanced one must be paid by no one else except the occupants of the land. Unless this was done, the Government would not move in the direction of the requested inquiry.[47]

The frustrated Chamber leaders asked their representative in the Legislative Council to resign in protest. Accordingly, Lalji Naranji resigned from the Council on 3 July 1928.[48] On learning of this latest resignation, in addition to those of the Gujarat members led by Dadubhai, Lord Irwin sent the following message to Lord Birkenhead in London: 'Moderate opinion is ranged very strongly against Government and this opinion represents genuine conviction and is not merely swimming with the tide. There is a genuine belief that settlement has not been a fair one to the cultivators and requires to be re-examined'.[49]

By the end of May 1928, Bardoli was the talk of all India. It had withstood the fire beyond all expectations. It had belied all the gloomy forebodings of doubters and cynics. The much abused Vania in Bardoli had amazed all his traducers. The immolation of one Parsee was enough to attract the attention of the entire Parsee community and the machinations of the Musalman Mamlatdar had failed to touch the two brave Musalman Khatedars of Bardoli who were a real tower of strength to the movement. The heroism of simple unsophisticated women of Bardoli was an inspiration to all women outside Bardoli. As one went from Ahmedabad to Bardoli one could not fail to notice the remarkable public awakening about the Bardoli Satyagraha.

Now the Government brought Pathans from outside to tyrannise over and oppress the gentle and more sophisticated population of Bardoli. The Pathan-Raj soon took over the Taluka. They even tortured the buffaloes belonging to the peasants. They forcibly entered their houses and broke the kitchen utensils, water pots and beat the children and men.[50]

When the Government began to attach the property, cattle and agricultural produce, the people locked their houses and went out in the open, where they stayed for days and days together, braving all sorts of extremes of weather. They also exercised one of the most potent non-violent weapons of all. Social boycott of all government employees who were still working and who by reason of that boycott could not even procure the bare necessities of daily life. Thus, the Government too was under pressure to make a settlement. Government authorities from the Commissioner, Collector and Mamlatdar to the lowest peon in the district court, for once felt uncertain and realising that they might not be able for long to withstand the strain of this acute social boycott that was being practised against them by the solid phalanx of these determined villagers of Bardoli Taluka. Congress leaders, viz Vallabhbhai and Gandhiji, were also aware of the frailties of human nature and that they could not trust the villagers to hold out indefinitely. They too wanted a compromise, though all the while proclaiming loudly that they would not pay this additional tax and would fight to the finish until victory was won. So there was an undercurrent of willingness to settle, from the Government as well as from the Congress.

In the meantime the Government's hope, that with the advent of the monsoon in June the movement would be abandoned by the peasants, was proved wrong.[51] In the last such (smaller) revenue campaign in Kheda in 1918, the peasants had given up the campaign the moment the rains appeared.

Anticipating that the monsoon would disrupt the campaign, Wilson had made elaborate arrangements to crush the movement by increasing the number of police in Bardoli and threatening to take the sternest measures against the land revenue defaulters.[52] Commissioner Mr Smart was quoted by Wilson in his letter of 2 July 1928 to Irwin,[53] as saying: 'The main as well as the subsidiary headquarters of the campaign were crowded and busy. The pressure upon the people not to pay their land revenue remained effective as heretofore'. Even the pro-government *Times of India* admitted that the administration in Bardoli was completely paralysed.[54]

In the months of May and June and early July, Vallabhbhai had already propagated the news to various leaders and organisations of the Bardoli campaign, together with its purposes and repercussions on the entire fabric of British administration in India. So Bardoli now gained wide support in the country. As a result leaders like Motilal Nehru, Sir Ted Bahadur Sapru and Hridaynath Kunzru issued statements supporting the Bardoli peasants. Calcutta newspapers *The Statesman* and *Pioneer* also began to support the Bardoli rebellion in their editorials and, last but not the least, the British Parliament was beginning to be disturbed by some MPs who questioned the wisdom of the Government of India in the matter of Bardoli. One MP asked what measures were being taken by the Bombay Government to redress the grievances of the peasants of Bardoli? Also how far the agricultural activity in Bardoli suffered due to Government actions? The Under-Secretary of State for India, Earl Winterton, stated that he could not give a reply to these questions until he received information from India, for which he was waiting.[55] Furthermore by the end of June, as per Wilson's letter to Irwin on 26 June, he stated that two members of his Executive Council, Sir Chunilal Mehta and Harilal Desai, the former acting as Finance Minister and the latter as Education Minister, who had been supporters up till then, were now doubting the wisdom of his policy.[56] Wilson now found it very difficult to keep his Cabinet firmly with him.

On 19 July 1928 Wilson, who was under a terrible strain, wrote to Irwin after visiting Surat: 'I have arrived here this morning (to Poona) and have little to add to my telegram. It was perfectly hopeless with Patel, who started straightaway on the subject of the assessment. I thought later that I had got the Member of the Legislative Council for Bardoli to agree to pay this himself, which I could have accepted; but then after seeing Patel, who told him he would be a traitor if he did so, he said he could not do it ... As there was no agreement possible on the assessment question after two and a half hours of discussion, we separated from his deputation ... I received a cable from Birkenhead, early this morning, after I had been to Surat; but I thought you might like to see it together with a copy of my reply.'[57]

Birkenhead's telegram of 19 July 1928 stated: 'I understand from Viceroy and from press that you are going to Surat and will meet a delegation of which Patel might be a member. I trust you will make it plain that you are there to announce decision of Government and not to negotiate, and you will bear in mind, it is not our policy to save Patel's face. But on the contrary to discredit him and his supporters by all possible means and even at the cost of some prolongation of the struggle. I entirely approve your personal attitude...'[58]

Wilson explained to Birkenhead the same day as follows: 'Your private and personal telegram No. 1992 received on my way back from Surat. I laid conditions, as agreed with Viceroy, before deputation headed by Patel yesterday, and said they were final. He was unwilling to accept, trying for some way to save his face, but I naturally refused to go any further. Hope you will not credit everything reported in the press, some very misleading statements are being made. Government quite firm. Am addressing Legislative Assembly Council on Monday and feel sure you will agree with what I propose to say. Shall proceed as agreed with Viceroy. Position can easily be misunderstood at home, as powers of Government to deal with passive civil disobedience are very limited unless we proceed under CRIMINAL LAW AMENDMENT ACT as suggested in the Viceroy's telegram, which we shall do unless complete surrender to our conditions. I hardly expect full agreement by my Executive Council to this, but can carry with majority. Very grateful for your support in most difficult circumstances'.[59]

In Wilson's report of 19 July 1928 to Birkenhead, paragraph 5 states the Goverment's mistakes:

'*First* The Revenue Commissioner, who is apt to let his tongue and his pen run away with him – made certain remarks about the Settlement Commissioner's settlement of Bardoli which have caused a great deal of trouble.

Second The Collector of Surat, who is in charge of Bardoli, did not take immediate action which he should have done. When I returned to Mahabaleshwar at the beginning of April, I found that he was not at his headquarters, and I personally telegraphed him and the Commissioner of the Northern Division to proceed to Surat at once and give me an immediate report. By that time however the crops were all in and a great opportunity of realising the assessment on the crops was lost.

I now find that under paragraph 7 of the Criminal Law Amendment Act I am advised that Patel's organisation can be declared an unlawful assembly. Until I went to Simla, I did not know of this. Although I had asked my legal advisers, on more than one occasion, to tell me whether there was any law under which it was possible to bring Patel or his followers to trial for inciting others to break the law, otherwise than by the special ordinance and I was advised that there was not, and that under the Land Revenue Code as it stood, non-payment (and therefore incitement to non-payment) of revenue was not an offence.'[60]

Thus the Government, in their ignorance, had allowed the Bardoli Satyagraha to grow into a monster. If they had imprisoned Patel and others from the very start, the Bardoli campaign would never have begun. This was luck for Vallabhbhai Patel which allowed him to conduct the campaign for many months, unmolested by the imperial forces. At this point in the history of Congress, all the avenues of successful mass movement had been closed, as we shall see in the second such movement the salt Satyagraha where all the relevant leaders were put away in jail before they could do any damage. In the changed circumstances, only the constitutionalists,

Vithalbhai and Dadubhai, realised the ruinous consequences of the imprisonment of campaign leaders. In Dharasana they contrived to run the show without being arrested. Thus the Viceroy and the Governor were guided into their worst defeat.

Wilson, after describing his speech of 24 July in the Council, wrote that if his conditions were not accepted within 14 days, sterner measures will be taken. To this effect he mentioned the steps he proposed to take:

1. A Home Department resolution putting in effect the Criminal Law Amendment Act.
2. To instruct Inspector-General of prisons to be ready to provide the necessary accommodation.
3. The question of drafting into the Taluka an adequate number of police.
4. To see General W.C.L. Hanekar, the head of Southern Command, with a view to having troops standing by at Ahmedabad or sending a company or two to Surat to be on the spot.[61]

Next he saw Hanekar and decided that military personnel should be moved to Divisional Headquarters in Sarbhon, Valod and Kadod in the hour of need. Also they needed to install wireless connections to facilitate communication in case the telegraph wires were cut by the agitators. Troops were to be deployed to Surat immediately and to wait there for further orders.[62]

The Governor in his speech had threatened dire consequences, if the Council members representing the Surat District failed to fulfil his conditions, which were of course that either the full assessment shall be paid forthwith or the difference between the old and the new assessment be paid into the treasury on behalf of the peasants. Mahadev Desai wrote: 'In Bardoli as I have said before, all was peaceful, the Sardar's arrest was regarded everywhere as a foregone conclusion, and rather than succeed him after he was taken away, Gandhiji thought it better to anticipate the Government and to go to Bardoli ready to do what the Sardar wanted him to do. Accordingly he moved to Bardoli on 2 August.'[63]

SETTLEMENT AGREED

While the parameters were set on the 13 July meeting of Wilson with Lord Irwin – the Surat members, led by Dadubhai, were searching for ways to settle the dispute in the one week remaining before the opening session of the Bombay Legislative Council. Sir Chunilal had conveyed to them that an inquiry will be instituted if the full revenue was paid.

Dadubhai hurried to Bombay to Ramchandra Bhatt's Mansion. This being where he always stayed as a guest of the Bhatt family during his visits to Bombay for sessions of the Legislative Council. There, while having breakfast with Mr Bhatt, they discussed the Bardoli issue. The cultivators had no objection to paying the old assessment. It was the revised element they objected to pay. If the Government accepted to appoint an inquiry commission with full powers, they would pay. However, the Government wanted payment first, the inquiry commission would only come after the payment of all dues. There would be an inquiry, provided they pay the full revenue, which includes the revision element, first. Crystallizing the problem, Dadubhai knew that the cultivators were ready to pay the old settlement revenue. It was now the question of paying the revision amount in advance, which of course he knew from his detailed study that it will be returned after the finding of the Committee of Inquiry. Dadubhai could raise the money for the revision settlement, but who would pay it? After all, it was the responsibilty of the peasants and no outsider could step in to pay. Ramchandra Bhatt said: 'My family comes from Mota, which as you know is in Bardoli Taluka, and if I pay it on behalf of other cultivators, it should be acceptable to the Government. You do not need to raise the money, I can guarantee the entire amount myself.' Dadubhai replied: 'Are you sure you are willing to risk this amount of money?'. Bhatt responded: 'You can go ahead and put forward my name to the Government. I am paying this on behalf of cultivators of my own Taluka and I am proud of it.'

It was Dadubhai who had evolved this formula and had first acquainted the Surat members of the Council and secured their approval. After all they were supposed to act as a united front of the villagers to the Bombay Government. Sir Chunilal Mehta was then informed of the proposal. He alone, as the senior member of the Governor's Council, had to accept it on the floor of the House.

The final question was with Vallabhbhai, who was leading the Satyagraha campaign. Sir Chunilal agreed to have a talk with Vallabhbhai and get his consent to call off the civil disobedience movement and recommend to the villagers to pay their original revenue assessment.

In spite of Vallabhbhai's obduracy, Mahatmaji made his way to Bardoli and set himself up in the Ashram there on 2 August, with the intention of staying put until the victory was achieved and he could share the glory jointly with Vallabhbhai. Mahadev Desai writes in his diary: 'Whilst Gandhiji had thus settled down in Bardoli, Sjt Vallabhbhai received a telegram from Rao Saheb Dadubhai Desai who invited him to Poona on behalf of the Gujarat members.'[64] Dadubhai required Vallabhbhai to agree with the terms of the settlement which he had hammered out for its signing by the Surat members of the Bombay Council![65] Without wasting a moment Vallabhbhai took the train and reached Poona on the next day, 3 August. The Government had realised that though they had addressed the ultimatum to the Surat members, it had ultimately to treat with Sjt Vallabhbhai. The Council members, led by Sjt Dadubhai, who were negotiating with the Government for a settlement, refused to give any undertaking or to commit Sjt Vallabhbhai in any way. It was only Vallabhbhai who would speak for himself while informal discussions were going on at Sir Chunilal's place. After two days of lengthy talks all the terms of the agreement were accepted by both parties. It was felt that Government were no less eager for a settlement than were the Council members, but everyone seemed to be at a loss to discover a formula that would preserve Government prestige. A neutral draft was framed by the Council members (really by Dadubhai) but that was not acceptable to Sir Chunilal. Then in the evening, Sir Chunilal came with the draft of a letter to be addressed by the Surat members to the Revenue member of the Bombay Government. This read: 'We are glad to be able to say that we are in a position to inform Government that the conditions laid down by his Excellency the Governor in his opening speech to the Council dated 23 July will be fulfilled'. (In his speech to the Bombay Legislative Council on 23 July, Sir Leslie Wilson had specified that, unless the agriculturalists paid their land revenue in full, no inquiry into the amount of assessment would be established.)

On seeing this draft, Vallabhbhai wondered: 'What can be the meaning of the M.L.Cs signing the letter saying that the conditions will be fulfilled, when they have to fulfil the conditions before any inquiry is granted? And if anyone can fulfil the conditions it is we, and we say that it is impossible for us to pay even the old assessment until after the inquiry is announced'. Then Vallabhbhai was told that this was a compromise on the part of the Government to save their face. It is an agreement between Surat members and the Government. It did not involve the Congress. This agreement is shown to Vallabhbhai as a matter of courtesy, so that he can make up his mind as to whether the conditions which he seeks are fulfilled, and so that he can call off the Satyagraha. Then Vallabhbhai said: 'Well then if they sign it I should have no objection.' So, the moment Vallabhbhai said that, if the Surat members had no objection to signing the document, he would have none, the settlement was agreed. All that Vallabhbhai wanted was a full independent, judicial inquiry and a restoration of the status quo. The Government were perfectly agreeable, provided here too they could keep their prestige intact.

Ramchandra Bhatt's proposal to pay the enhanced assessment was accepted by the Government. Thus the condition which the Government had laid down for instituting an inquiry was fulfilled. Shri Vallabhbhai had now to call off the Satyagraha and advise the cultivators to pay up the old assessments. Though in fact Vallabhbhai's victory was a pyrrhic one, it was hailed as an unprecedented success. The Government's prestige remained intact. The Government had saved their honour and Vallabhbhai had saved his movement from annihilation.

Dadubhai later admitted that this had been their only way to avoid defeat. The peasants were on the brink of giving up. They would have had to suffer a further period of privation and the Government's severe treatment which, though verging on illegitimacy, was really hurting. Vallabhbhai privately thanked Dadubhai for saving the movement and escaping a disaster. Gandhiji also tacitly approved, although it scarcely fitted into his moral code. The official historians of the Congress – Pattabhai Sitaramayya and Pande – conveniently omitted these details of the terms of the compromise from their story of Bardoli. Of course, the Government also realised that it was not in their interest to do anything that would provoke another Bardoli elsewhere in India. Lord Irwin's letter bears testimony of that perception: 'I hope we may be able to take such steps in consultation with other provincial governors, as may avoid a recurrence of this potentially very dangerous situation.' Thus, the Government agreed to set up the committee of enquiry to review the Bardoli settlement after Ramchandra Bhatt paid the enhanced settlement of 22% on behalf of the peasants of Bardoli. Both sides declared this capitulation a victory. If the money of the enhanced settlement had not been paid by Ramchandra Bhatt, no matter how hard Vallabhbhai strained to keep the campaign going, the Government were not going to give in. With failure staring him in the face, Vallabhbhai had to accept the settlement under the Government's terms.

The enquiry, in the exact words suggested by Vallabhbhai, was to be announced immediately after the Surat members had addressed that diplomatic letter, and the restorative measures would be taken on the members writing a formal letter to the Revenue member to reinstate the Talatis, to restore the lands and to release the Satyagraha prisoners. The compensation clause cancelling all the penalties and compensating the liquor seller in the village of Valod was not included in the letter, as these things would be done by executive orders. For Vallabhbhai nothing more was necessary. He was there to win the substance and not the shadow.

The seven Surat members who signed the settlement document virtually guaranteeing the deposition of the total value of the enhanced revenue settlement included the cousin of Dadubhai, J.B. Desai, whose constituency included the Surat region.[66] The settlement document was as follows:

'APPENDIX II

The Settlement Documents

The letters exchanged between the Surat M.L.Cs and the Government recording the terms of settlement.

1.

The following letter was addressed by the members of the Legislative Council representing Bardoli Taluka and Surat District to the Hon'ble the Revenue Member:

'POONA, 6TH AUGUST 1928,

To

The Hon'ble The Revenue Member,

Sir,

With reference to your letter dated August 3rd 1928, we

are glad to be able to say that we are in a position to inform Government that the conditions laid down by His Excellency the Governor in his opening speech to the Council dated 23rd of July will be fulfilled.

Yours sincerely,

Sd. A.M.K. DEHLAVI
Sd. BHASAHEB (Thakore of Kerwada)
Sd. DAUDKHAN SALEBHAI TYEBJEE
Sd. J.B. DESAI
Sd. B.R. NAIK
Sd. H.B. SHIVDASANI
Sd. M.K. DIXIT

2.

Announcement of the Enquiry

Government thereafter announced the following enquiry:

The enquiry will be entrusted to a Revenue Officer and a Judicial Officer, the decision of the Judicial Officer to prevail in all matters of difference between the two, with the following terms of reference:

To enquire into and report upon the complaint of the people of Bardoli and Valod.

(a) That the enhancement of revenue recently made is not warranted in terms of the Land Revenue Code;

(b) That the reports accessible to the public do not contain sufficient data warranting the enhancement and that some of the data given are wrong;

and to find that, if the people's complaint is held to be justified what enhancement or reduction, if any, there should be upon the old assessment.

As the enquiry is to be full, open and independent, the people will be free to lead as well as test evidence before it with the help of their representatives including legal advisers.

3.

The following further letters were exchanged between the members of the Legislative Council representing the Bardoli Taluka and the Surat district and the Hon'ble the Revenue Member:

Poona, AUGUST 7, 1928.

To

The Hon'ble the Revenue Member.

Sir,

Now that the principal point about the Bardoli question is settled satisfactorily we hope and trust that Government will

(a) Release all Satyagrahi prisoners.

(b) Restore all lands forfeited.

(c) Reinstate all Talatis and Patels who resigned their offices.

Yours sincerely,

Sd. A.M.K. DEHLAVI
Sd. DAUDKHAN SALEBHAI TYEBJEE
Sd. BHASAHEB (Thakore of Kerwada)
Sd. BHIMBHAI R. NAIK
Sd. H.B. SHIVDASANI
Sd. J.B. DESAI
Sd. M.K. DIXIT'

4.

The following letter dated 7 August 1928 was addressed by the Hon'ble the Revenue Member to the above members of the Legislative Council: 'Gentleman,

With reference to your letter dated the 7th instant, Government, in exercise of their prerogative, will release all Satyagrahi prisoners and will be pleased to issue orders granting your second request.

The Talatis and Patels will be pardoned if they apply in the proper form.

Yours sincerely,

Sd. J.L. RIEU

N.B. The price paid for the lands which were sold by Government and were transferred to R.B. Naik as stated in para 86 of the Report was about Rs.11,000 or double the assessment in respect thereof. The excess of assessment thus received was also remitted by Government to the individual cultivators with the result that the land was restored to them without their being out of pocket to any extent.'

As soon as the news of the settlement had spread round the country, Sardar Vallabhbhai was overwhelmed with telegrams and letters of congratulations. The entire press of India showered praise on him for his astuteness and ability to conduct such a vast campaign in the 137 villages of Bardoli Taluka. His proficiency at managing a campaign on such a huge scale was universally acclaimed. Gandhiji was now freed from the shackles of Sardar and made a few speeches and wrote in the columns of Young India his congratulations to the Governor of Bombay, to the people of Bardoli and to Sjt Vallabhbhai. Of the latter he said: 'Without his firmness as well as gentleness, the settlement would have been impossible'. He added: 'The Satyagrahis have achieved practically all that they had asked for. The Terms of Reference to the Committee of Enquiry are all that could be desired. True, there is no inquiry into the allegations about the coercive measures adopted by the Government to enforce payment. But it was generous on the part of Sjt Vallabhbhai to waive the condition, seeing that the lands forfeited, including lands sold, are to be restored. Talatis are to be re-instated and other minor matters are to be attended to'.

The following excerpts from Mahadev Desai's account clearly reveal how Vallabhbhai jealously guarded his pitch once he knew he could succeed and present himself as the sole architect of this success, to the exclusion of even Gandhiji:[67] 'The Sardar, though he had issued an appeal for public funds, was firm in his resolve, to retain the local and circumscribed character of the Bardoli issue. Sjt C. Rajagopaalachari and Sjt Gangadhar Deshpande, who were in Ahmedabad about the time, were anxious to visit Bardoli to see things for themselves. Gandhiji advised them not to go, and Sjt Vallabhbhai appreciated the advice. On hearing the news of the death of Maganlal Gandhi, Gandhiji's best comrade, Sjt Vallabhbhai was anxious to go to Ahmedabad. Gandhiji wrote to him not to do so and said: "It is a heavy loss, but it should not disturb your programme. You cannot stir out from Bardoli at the present moment. Do not hesitate to write to me for any help you may need. Please understand that I am at your beck and call, ready to start whenever you want me." Much as the Sardar would have loved to have Gandhiji in Bardoli, he refrained as he knew that Gandhiji's presence there would be a signal to all India to rush to Bardoli.'[68]

The Sardar, who was in Bombay for a day, had an occasion to meet the members of the Working Committee of the Congress, many of whom would have run up to Bardoli if he had wished. Pandit Motilalji, who greeted him warmly, humorously asked Lala Girdharlal how long he would be prepared to insure Vallabhbhai's freedom? Everyone appeared to be sure that in a few days the Sardar would have been a guest in one of His Majesty's prisons, that Gandhiji would have to take his place and that Bardoli would become an all-India issue. But Sjt Vallabhbhai did not even, out of courtesy, invite the various leaders to go to Bardoli. Their visit would if possible advertise Bardoli a little more, but it would soon give an opportunity to the opposite side to misrepresent the case as political.[69]

Pandit Motilal Nehru congratulated Gandhiji and Vallabhbhai on their 'Splendid Triumph'. Sjt C. Rajgopalachari wrote: 'Vallabhbhai's part in Indian history has been great'. Pandit Madan Mohan Malaviyaji congratulating Sardar Vallabhbhai said: 'The first signal triumph of Satyagraha was Champaran. The second and equally great triumph has been in Bardoli.' Sjt Subhas Bose wired: 'All India rejoices with you on a glorious victory. All honour to Satyagrahis and their leader.' Later, in his book 'The Indian Struggle', he wrote: 'The Bardoli campaign was the precursor of the larger fight that Bombay was to wage in 1930', (the Dharasana Salt Satyagraha).

Out of this campaign, Vallabhbhai Patel emerged with a great reputation. Prior to this he was of course known as one of the sincerest and staunchest lieutenants of the Mahatma, but the Bardoli victory brought him into the front rank of India's leaders. In appreciation of his heroic service, the Mahatma gave him the title of 'Sardar' (meaning leader of the peasants) by which he is now generally known.[70]

The newspaper the *Lahore Tribune* stated on 16 August 1928:

'If 30 to 35 crores of people from the Himalayas to Rameshwar and from Karachi to Burma rise to a man as Satyagrahis, the arms of the British Government would prove a matter for mere jest. This is what Bardoli has brought home to the people of India.'

While Gandhi had failed in his attempt to start a satyagraha in 1921 at Bardoli, Vallabhbhai had succeeded. Victory in the Bardoli struggle gave the Congress leaders an infallible tool against the British Raj. From now on in every political action, the Congress leaders vigorously championed the cause of the peasants to further their own political power. Pandit Jawaharlal Nehru belatedly acknowledged in his autobiography, written 5 years later: 'The Bardoli Satyagraha under the leadership of Sardar Vallabhbhai Patel was gallantly carried through to the admiration of the rest of India. The Bardoli peasantry met with a considerable measure of success. The real success of their campaign however lay in the effect it produced amongst the peasantry all over India. Bardoli became a sign and a symbol of hope and strength and victory to the Indian peasant'.[71]

A centenary history of the Indian National Congress, written by B.N. Pande, published by the All-India Congress Committee and released by Shri Rajiv Gandhi on 28 December 1985, dismisses the whole Bardoli campaign in a small, unsubstantiated and false account in which it does not even mention its real political influence.[72] This is amazing when one considers that this history of Congress is written in five volumes and each volume has more than 600 pages. Such was the bias of subsequent Nehru descendants against any accomplishment by Gujarat and its residents. The only Gujarati who gets full praise in this history is Gandhi, whose alliance with Nehru has been beneficial to them throughout by linking the surname 'Gandhi' to all their subsequent progeny, whether male or female.

However the importance of Bardoli's struggle was not unnoticed by the Viceroy Lord Irwin, who writes to the King Emperor on 18 July 1928: 'Your Majesty, I do not doubt you will have noticed with concern the reports of the situation in Bardoli in the Bombay Presidency. The position there has been and is very difficult and has been causing a great deal of anxiety both to Sir Leslie Wilson and myself. The area of land round Bardoli was due for re-assessment of Land Revenue, which was accordingly made. Against the assessment, which passed through all the usual procedures, the cultivators have protested and have refused to pay the revenue due. Bardoli, as Your Majesty may remember, has a certain unfortunate historical association, in that it was the first place where Mr Gandhi sought to inaugurate his Civil Disobedience Campaign, six or seven years ago. It is not easy to be wholly certain how far the movement of refusal to pay the revenue was originally political. I have no doubt in my own mind that the cultivators have a certain case, due to some mistakes made by the officers of Government, but they have undoubtedly gone the wrong way to remedy it and have created a situation in which it is obviously extremely difficult for Government to do anything to meet them.

Sir Leslie Wilson came up to see me for a day on Sunday, and has gone to the Bardoli District today. We discussed together the limit to which, he could rightly go in seeking a settlement with those who could speak for the cultivators, and I hope his visit there may bring peace. If not I am afraid we are in for a difficult time which may bring quite serious trouble.'[73]

Lord Birkenhead, the Secretary of State for India, had this to say on 12 July 1928 in the following letter to the Indian Viceroy. 'Bardoli was discussed at Cabinet yesterday. The Cabinet, like myself, was much perturbed by the situation, as it is described to us. It seems to me that it might develop in a variety of ways. At present only a small part of the PRAIRIE has caught fire, but there are other, and very inflammable, PRAIRIES in the vicinity... Primary consideration, in my judgement, is to break the movement before it has gone any further and to show the whole of India unmistakably that no such attempt can succeed'.[74]

Later, on 22 August 1928, after the settlement at Bardoli Lord Birkenhead wrote to the King: 'You will, I think, Sir have been relieved to see that Sir Leslie Wilson has secured a settlement of the Bardoli trouble on the conditions which he felt it necessary to lay down. Although, as was to be expected, his political enemies have done their best to distort the facts of the settlement, to their own advantage, the fact remains that the terms he delivered in his speech to his Council have been met. I hope we may be able to take such steps, in consultation with other Provincial Governors, as may avoid a recurrence of this potentially very dangerous situation'.[75]

In the House of Commons, reviewing the Bardoli campaign, Lord Winterton said that Sjt Vallabhbhai had achieved 'a measure of success' but 'law was being enforced against tenants who refused payment'.

AFTERMATH OF THE SETTLEMENT

The Bardoli victory, won after a very short and swift campaign, only redressed a local grievance, but the triumph was unique in that it compelled not only the nation's but the whole Empire's attention, and the justice and moderation of the people's demands won practically all the nation's sympathy. The Governor of the province, who for a time seemed only to listen to dictation from Whitehall, did all that he personally could to bring about peace. That is why Gandhiji and Vallabhbhai emphasised in their speeches, throughout the week after the settlement, the duty of congratulating the Governor as much as that of congratulating those who had won the campaign. Of course we now know, following the release of the Halifax letters after the 40 years closed period, that Lord Irwin was equally involved in the settlement in as much as he allowed the agreement to go through.

Lord Irwin, later after the Bardoli settlement, wrote two letters to the Governors. The first went to all six Governors, dated 6 September 1928 and the second to five Governors (the Bombay Governor received a separate letter) dated 29 October 1928.[76]

The first letter states: 'I have been thinking a good deal over recent events at Bardoli, and I should like to put you privately in possession of the way my reflections have been moving. I can feel no doubt that the Bardoli episode and its settlement are likely to have permanent reactions in other parts of India. The terms offered by the Bombay Government and finally accepted by those organising the movement of non-payment had the full approval of the Government of India, and I think in the circumstances they were inevitable. But we should, I suspect, delude ourselves if we thought that the settlement was likely to leave the situation unchanged.' Addressed to the Governors of Madras, Bombay, United Provinces of Agra and Oudh, Punjab, Central Provinces and Assam.

The second letter states: 'It appears that when organised opposition in Bardoli first began to show itself, the local officers were not sufficiently alive to the situation, and the movement was allowed to grow without adequate steps being taken to counter it, and without Government even receiving full information of what was going on. A movement like this must obviously be dealt with at the very beginning; if it is allowed to develop, it soon becomes formidable... The Criminal Law Amendment Act enables a local government to declare an organisation to be unlawful if it has for its object interference with the administration of the law and it would seem that as soon as a definite campaign of non-payment of taxes or revenue is launched, it would be feasible to declare the organisation unlawful.' Addressed to the Governors of Madras, United Provinces of Agra and Oudh, Punjab, Central Provinces and Assam.

One could ask – has Pandit Nehru or any other Congress leader done anything to force the Viceroy to write such letters to all Provincial Governors asking them to remain alert about repetition of Bardoli anywhere else in India? If anything, the British Government was truly alarmed as a result of Bardoli Satyagraha. Later, when Viscount Peel replaced Lord Birkenhead as Secretary of State for India, Lord Irwin wrote to him:

> 'I had long been coming to feel that it is this question of land revenue that our flanks are most dangerously exposed. We must be prepared to consider means of strengthening them.'[77]

Thus Bardoli put Vallabhbhai on the political map of India. He was the first man in the entire leadership of India, to have fought and conducted the largest mass movement against the Raj and succeeded in it. He could now sit alongside the Mahatma, who had been a successful campaigner in South Africa, and ahead of any other leader. This situation was perhaps rather unwelcome to the Mahatma, though he knew the unbending self-discipline of his loyal follower who would never challenge his leadership. Dadubhai was extremely happy to have helped Vallabhbhai to attain this position as he himself had never any ambition to go on the All-India stage. In all his political dealing, Dadubhai took the lead only if the circumstances and his comrades forced him to take that position. He always preferred peace and quiet in place of the limelight of leadership. Vallabhbhai understood his debt to Dadubhai and until his own death he always kept in close contact with him and wherever possible sought his advice.[78]

We have noted earlier that Gandhiji also entered the Bardoli campaign, in spite of Vallabhbhai's wishes, under the pretext that he had to step into the shoes of Vallabhbhai should he be arrested by the British. Gandhiji knew that Dadubhai was working towards a solution and that he was about to succeed. So better now than never the Mahatma accepted a secondary position. At this point in the history of India, Vallabhbhai was the leader of All-India importance. Gandhiji marked time and sure enough his time came after his Salt Satyagraha when again with the help of Dadubhai and Vithalbhai he was able to maintain the position of unchallenged supreme leadership of India, leaving Vallabhbhai again in second position behind him.

While the Bardoli campaign was in progress Dr M.A. Ansari was the Congress President (from 26 December 1927 to 29 December 1928) and for the next year (starting 29 December 1928) it was the turn of Pandit Motilal Nehru to be the President of Congress. At this Calcutta Congress, on 29 December 1928, the main focus was on the boycotting of the SIMON COMMISSION, which was touring the country. Among the usual resolutions was one offering congratulations to Vallabhbhai Patel on the success of the Bardoli struggle.[79] The praise of Vallabhbhai and Bardoli was not very extensive or ecstatic, since the victory had been so sudden and also the Bardoli struggle had been brought under the wing of Congress only in the later stages. Congress was also not well organised enough to understand immediately its wider implications and importance. The significance of the Bardoli movement went far beyond its immediate objective and its impact was felt at the All-India level. It helped the Congress to broaden its popular support because the success of the Bardoli struggle was largely due to its being linked with the freedom movement. The new battle cry of the peasantry in various parts of the country was: 'Bardolise our Agitation'. There is no doubt that the success of Bardoli strengthened the hold of the Congress on the Indian peasantry.

The next session of the Congress was to be at Lahore in 1929, where Vallabhbhai in view of his Bardoli success was the logical choice as President. In the provincial voting for the election of the Congress President, ten provinces voted for Gandhi, five for Vallabhbhai J. Patel and three for Jawaharlal Nehru.[80] Gandhi was declared duly elected, but he resigned. All eyes now turned upon Gandhi as the man who would rescue the Congress once more and lead it on the path to victory through some sort of movement. What next? Nothing but civil disobedience would be the logical consequence of such a course. Gandhiji had now to select between his loyal soldier Vallabhbhai and the wayward, socialist left-winger, Jawaharlal Nehru. The general feeling in Congress circles was that the honour of being the Congress President should go to Sardar Vallabhbhai Patel, but the Mahatma decided to back the candidature of Pandit Jawaharlal Nehru.[81] Motilal's persuasion also played a big part in it, since he was very anxious to bring back this revolting son into line.

Lord Irwin's assessment later on in his letter to the King on 5 February 1931 (two months after Nehru came into prominence as the Congress President) stated: 'Jawaharlal Nehru is frankly communist and subversive. He has been influenced by Russia, regards the States as tiresome anachronisms and thinks that revolution would be an admirable way of getting rid of them and of introducing the new order to which he looks'.[82]

To all intents and purposes the Mahatma eschewed any competitor in his power base of Kaira, while Gujarati Vallabhbhai, though a disciplined disciple, had achieved a victory that still eluded the Mahatma. After all, prior to Bardoli, the Mahatma had barely recovered from his depressed state of mind. By selecting Jawaharlal, against the democratic vote of five states against three, Mahatma had tried to put Vallabhbhai in his place (though not for long as in the next Congress of 1931 he had to accept Vallabhbhai as President). Vallabhbhai, in his presidential oration, acknowledged the tribute paid in his election as President, not to him a mere peasant, but to Gujarat, which had played such a large share in the fight for freedom.[83]

Subhas Bose wrote: 'The Mahatma took a clever step in supporting the canditure of Pandit Jawaharlal Nehru and his election as President opened a new chapter in his public career. Since then Pandit J.L. Nehru has been a consistent and unfailing supporter of the Mahatma'.[84]

Dadubhai said: 'It was the result of repeated requests of Motilal'. He said he had heard one such conversation at the time of the 1929 AICC.

Pandit Jawaharlal Nehru himself was surprised at the support he received from the Mahatma for his election as the President of the Indian National Congress of 1929. He wrote in his autobiography: 'At the AICC meeting, at the last moment he pressed my name forward. The AICC was taken aback ... I have seldom felt quite so annoyed as I did at the election. It was not that I was not sensible of the honour, for it was a great honour, and I would have rejoiced, if I had been elected in the ordinary way. But I did not come to it by the main entrance or even a side entrance; I appeared suddenly by a trap-door and bewildered the audience into acceptance. They put a brave face on it, and like a necessary pill swallowed me. My pride was hurt and almost I felt like handing back the honour. Fortunately I restrained myself from making an exhibition of myself, and stole away with a heavy heart. Probably the person who was happiest about this decision was my father'.[85]

So J. Nehru, at the age of 39, entered the frontmost ranks of the Congress organisation without really working for it.

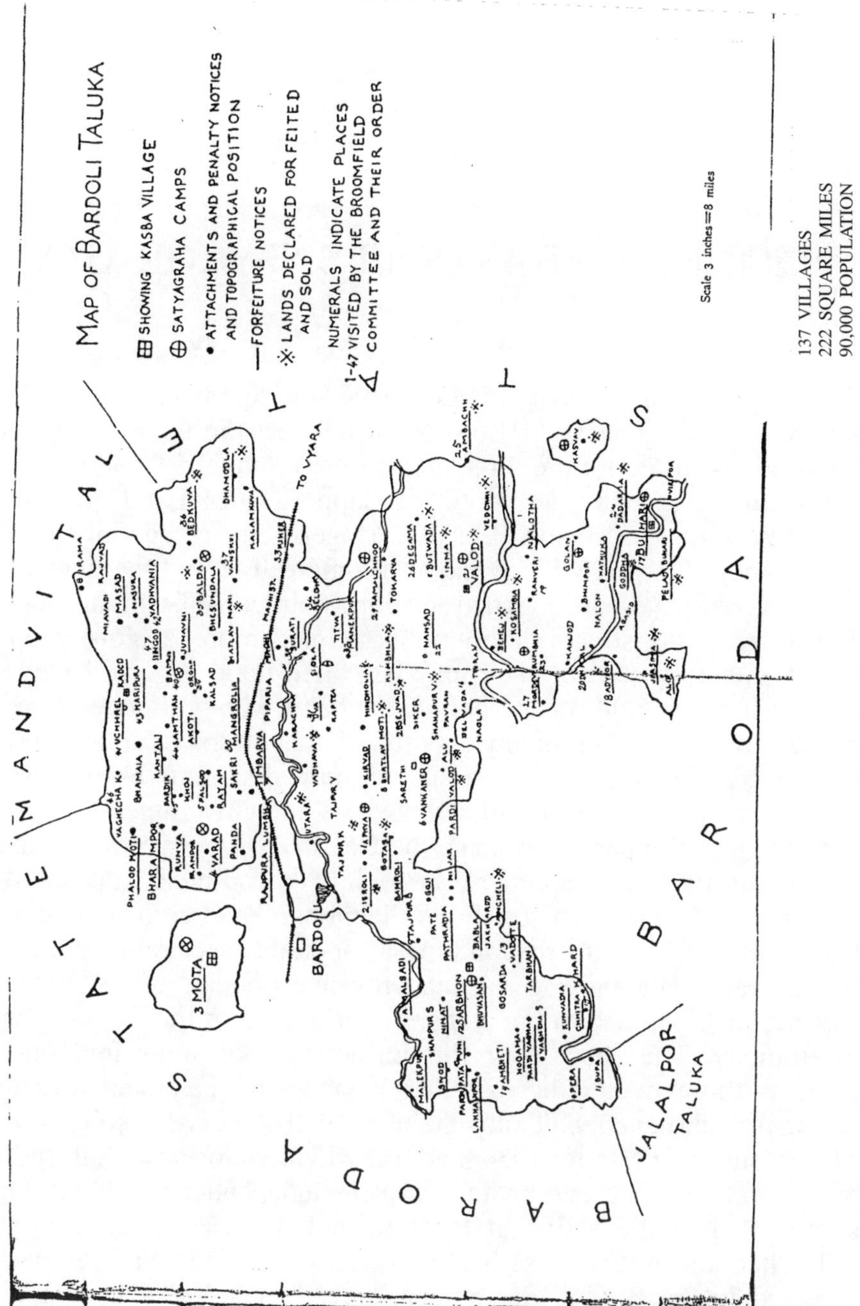
MAP OF BARDOLI TALUKA
⊞ SHOWING KASBA VILLAGE
⊕ SATYAGRAHA CAMPS
• ATTACHMENTS AND PENALTY NOTICES AND TOPOGRAPHICAL POSITION
—FORFEITURE NOTICES
※ LANDS DECLARED FORFEITED AND SOLD
NUMERALS INDICATE PLACES 1-47 VISITED BY THE BROOMFIELD COMMITTEE AND THEIR ORDER
MANDVI STATE
BARODA STATE
BARODA
JALALPOR TALUKA
TO VYARA
BARDOLI
3 MOTA
VALOD
Scale 3 inches = 8 miles
137 VILLAGES
222 SQUARE MILES
90,000 POPULATION

17

SEQUEL TO BARDOLI SATYAGRAHA

'The Governor of Bombay, Sir Leslie Wilson, lost twelve pounds in weight with sheer worry'.[1] Lord Irwin felt that the issue had grave implications for the future. In a letter to the Provincial Governors, in the form of advice, he wrote: 'I suppose that Land Revenue Administration has always been the danger point of administration and I fancy that this will be more and more true as time goes on. Land revenue payers are bound to develop a political self-consciousness and as they do so are likely to scrutinise more zealously any enhancement of revenue they may be called upon to pay. There is here an obvious field for the political agitator who will certainly not be slow to avail himself of any opportunity that offers for organization of a mass movement on an issue of immediate interest to large numbers of persons, which may embarrass the Government'.[2]

Bardoli thus appeared to make the Gandhian Revenue Satyagraha into a formidable weapon, by attacking the colonial state at its very heart. It also transformed Vallabhbhai Patel into a national leader.[3] Bardoli was the first and most important successful challenge so far made. Not only to the land revenue policies of the British Government, but also to the authority and power of the Government in Bombay. The success of the Bardoli peasants inspired other peasants throughout India to rcfuse payment of their land revenue during the subsequent Salt Satyagraha of 1930, the Civil Disobedience Movement of 1930 to 1934 and the final victorious Quit India Movement of 1942 ending in complete independence.[4] It is very surprising that the action at Bardoli, and its effects, received so little attention by Congress historians. A total of 137 villages were involved in the Bardoli Satyagraha, spread over 222 square miles and with a population of 90,000.[5]

In August the Government had capitulated and set up the Maxwell-Broomfield Committee of Inquiry to review the Bardoli settlement. In September the Bombay Government abandoned their land revenue code amendment bill. The Maxwell-Broomfield report came in May 1929. It showed that the settlement in Bardoli had been made in a slipshod manner and that unauthorised methods had been used. This called into question every single revenue revision settlement made in the Bombay Presidency during the 1920s. On 16 July 1929 the Bombay Government announced that all the settlements which had not been finalised were to be abandoned, thus vindicating the stand Dadubhai had taken throughout the past ten years. There were to be no new settlements for Kheda district until after the constitutional reforms which were being discussed by the Simon Commission. This meant that R.G. Gordon's proposed revision settlement was to be abandoned and the old rates of the 1890s were to be maintained. This capitulation was the real victory of Bardoli. By 1929 Peasant Satyagraha was seen as a most potent force; as a form of protest it was considered to hold the key to swaraj. It was against this background of wild enthusiasm that civil disobedience was to be launched in the Kheda district after January 1930. This was Vallabhbhai's own project.[6] In the letter of 16 January 1930 he mentions that intention. But Gandhiji, being a realist too, questioned the wisdom of starting another non-revenue campaign hot on the heels of Bardoli Satyagraha. He had written in *Young India* on 5 September 1929: 'Vallabhbhai needs a Bardoli to make good his leadership. How many Bardolis are there ready in the country today?'. Dadubhai agreed with Gandhiji's view of the uniqueness of Bardoli. He also did not think that Bardoli could be recreated in Kheda or for that matter in any part of India. He told the writer, in the later years of his retirement, that after the hard won Bardoli success he was torn between various ideas of confronting the British.

He had already done so for the ten previous good years in the Bombay Legislative Council, to constitutionally confronting the British Raj and showing them by arguments how unjust and undemocratic they had been to the Indian nation in many directions. He had also seen the sacrifices and privations that the peasants had had to undergo in a non-revenue payment Satyagraha. Surely there must be a better way of involving the whole population, including of course the peasants, in a minimum physical sacrifice which would leave untouched the financial structure of the village communities including peasants, women and all other adults. In the Bombay Legislative Council in the past ten years he had, as leader of the opposition to the Government, argued about salt workers and salt taxes. He also knew very well that salt tax was one of the sacred cows of the British Government, to such an extent that even the slightest change that a provincial government might want to effect in the working of the collection of the salt tax and the work and condition of salt-pan workers had not only to be sanctioned by the Viceroy but also had to be communicated to the Secretary of State for India in London for his confirmation. The salt tax was one of the major sources of revenue of the Government of India, and in critical times helped to balance the Central Government budget.[7] Lord Lytton had experienced the salt issue during his Viceroyalty.[8] He felt it is quite wrong that salt should be taxed at all in a country like India where it was a necessity of life. However, as the tax brought in a considerable revenue, he did hope to be able to reduce it. In Rajputana, where there were salt lakes and salt mines, the salt was cheaper and smuggling was going on continuously. To prevent smuggling the Government had put up a prickly hedge extending about 1,500 miles across India. There were 12,000 inspectors and tax collectors posted along this hedge. He negotiated a deal with the Maharajas of Jaipur and Bharatpur to take over their mines and salt works in return for the British giving them a money consideration.

By saving on the inspectors and tax collectors at the customs barrier hedge, Lytton was able to reduce the tax on salt and standardise it throughout British India within two years. This he achieved in spite of his advisers who had told him it was impossible and that if he 'touched a stone of the Temple of the Fiscal Solomons of the past' he would be 'buried alive under the ruins'. Such was the importance of salt tax to the Colonial Office in London. Dadubhai had argued about the terms of employees of salt pans. Refer to his intervention in the Bombay Legislative Council where he was the leader of opposition to the Government.[9]

In 1923, as Dadubhai Desai, who was an elected member of the Bombay Governor's Council constituted under the new Government of India Act of 1919, was seeking re-election, Lord Reading the Viceroy on 25 March 1923 certified the doubling of the tax on salt from Rs.1.4 to Rs.2.8 to balance the Central Government's budget, as mentioned earlier. Salt duty had always formed a large portion of Government revenue (in the fiscal year 1929/30 the total revenue from salt tax was Rs.67,646,354, a sizeable amount at the time). On 23 March Lord Reading sent to all the Provincial Governments a confidential telegram asking their advice on the unprecedented increase in salt duty. Sykes, the Bombay Governor, in his telegram of reply dated 25 March, cautioned the Viceroy and alluded to the advantage the politicians would gain in this matter in the forthcoming elections under the new Montague Chelmsford reforms (see below) which would come into force in October.[10]

Sure enough this did not escape the watchful eyes of Dadubhai. In his electioneering speeches at Dakor, Nadiad, Anand and other villages, from April till 31 October (the polling date), he continued telling the people he would fight in the Bombay Council to prevent any increase in the forthcoming revision settlement in Kaira. He also mentioned forcefully that the Government has doubled the duty on salt to Rs.2.8 and, as this was done by the Viceroy in Delhi he could do nothing in the Bombay Council, but he would protest about it to the Governor in Council and ask him to approach the Central Government to reduce rather than increase this duty which was already hurting the population and especially the very poor. In the election, Dadubhai Desai retained his seat by a majority of 1,067 votes.[11]

Under the Montague Chelmsford reforms of 1919, the new Legislative Council franchise gave the vote to those paying Rs.22 land revenue. Previously, under the Marley Minto reforms, this had been Rs.45 per annum. The new reform resulted in the number of voters in the Kheda District doubling from about 10,000 to 20,000! So it was that the British began introducing democracy in stages and this was considered the beginning of full adult enfranchisement for enslaved India.

In 1867 the British Parliament passed the 'Representation of the People' Act, which for the first time enfranchised the adult male householders in the country who occupied houses with a rateable value of at least £12 per year. This resulted in over a million men receiving the vote. Then, in 1872 the 'Ballot Act' was passed, which introduced the ballot with secret voting.[12] In 1870 the 'Education Act' had been passed, whereby ratepayers would elect school boards. Their task was to open schools where religious organisations had not done so. This was followed in 1876 by an Act to make elementary education compulsory for all children.[13] Prior to that, the Municipal Reform Act of 1835 had created Municipal Borough Councils. Thus, by 1876 Britain was well on the way to being a fully-fledged democracy. A similar process was being carried out in India, bit by bit. Each step was about 40 years behind a similar reform in Great Britain. In the year 1832 of the 16 million souls in Britain there were only 160,000 electors – a mere 1 per cent franchise.

Dadubhai, having firmly convinced himself of the efficacy of a no-salt tax campaign simply because a salt tax was so important to the Government, he had to devise a way of doing it. The salt tax became liable as soon as the salt was produced in government-owned works. The salt was then distributed to dealers against the payment of the full price which already included the tax. So no-tax payment is out of the question. How about raiding the salt pans? But that would be theft and a criminal act. How about making salt by boiling salt water? Would the Government bother about an individual manufacturing salt like that? Between 29 August and 29 November he made several visits to Gandhiji at Sabarmati and introduced and discussed the salt issue with him. Dadubhai took copious notes and Bombay Legislative Council Hansards on salt regulations (in which he himself had taken an active part) as well as historical and monetary papers about salt tax, which he had accumulated while being a member of the Bombay Legislative Council for the previous ten years. During this time the 'salt issue', though of serious consideration between Dadubhai and Gandhiji, was not discussed by Gandhiji with any other national leader. He knew that unless he produced a detailed programme, nobody would ever understand salt. For none of the leaders was supposed to understand the importance of salt to the Government. Even when Tagore met Gandhiji on 18 January 1930 only a few days before he started the salt satyagraha, when asked about his future campaign if any after Bardoli, Gandhi replied that he was still waiting for the inner soul to tell him what to do (concealing that he was in the final stages of his plan for salt satyagraha).

In the meantime, on 21 November 1930, Vithalbhai had arrived at Nadiad and decided to stay at the country house of Dadubhai for the period of the recess of the Central Legislative Assembly in Delhi (of which he was President). Dadubhai broached the subject of salt satyagraha and Vithalbhai rejected it outright. On questioning him about any other alternative he had no reply except the legal-constitutional path. They both thought deeply about how to get even the Dominion status which looked as remote as the nearest star. By this time Vithalbhai had already been diagnosed as having tuberculosis. The cause must have been, as we now know, his heavy smoking. He needed fresh air and prolonged undisturbed rest, which he got at the Nadiad country house. This was surrounded by an orchard full of flowering shrubs and trees such as sandalwood, mango, amla, nefoc, custard apple, borsali and orange groves. He knew he had only a short time to complete his work of gaining independence. Ultimately, after long discussions and hesitation, he agreed to give as much help as he could to Gandhiji if he were to start a salt campaign of some sort. It was also decided that he would persuade the Viceroy to delay Gandhi's arrest as long as possible. If absolutely necessary, he would sacrifice his brother Vallabhbhai's freedom rather than Gandhiji's. This would not be difficult as Vallabhbhai was planning to start a land revenue campaign in the Kaira District. He never bothered about any campaign which Gandhiji had devised. Gandhiji in the meantime was slowly and steadily gathering together the mechanisation and requirements of the salt campaign. To arrange the logistics of the salt campaign was not as easy as it looks. They both considered various options. Merely making salt was a crime. Of course, looting the salt from salt pans or salt works looked like dacoity. Violence was always ruled out by Gandhiji's principles of non-violent struggles. Where to make salt? Would boiling sea water provoke the Government into taking notice of such an act or would they dismiss it as a prank? The months of July to October 1929 occupied the thoughts of Gandhiji and, to a lesser extent, of Dadubhai who frequented Sabarmati Ashram from his Nadiad home and power-base. In early December Vithalbhai went back to Delhi to preside over the winter session of the Central Legislative Assembly. Gandhiji was still planning and thinking and in 14–16 February 1930 the Congress Working Committee met at Ahmedabad. Not a word was spoken about a salt satyagraha which Gandhi kept between himself and Dadubhai. Gandhiji only told them that he was thinking of civil disobedience and needed Congress approval. They passed the following resolution:

> In the opinion of the Working Committee, disobedience should be initiated and controlled by those who believe in non-violence for the purpose of achieving Purna Swaraj as an article of faith and welcomes the proposal of Mahatma Gandhi and authorises him and those working with him who believe in non-violence as an article of faith to start civil disobedience. The Working Committee further hopes that in the event of a mass movement taking place, all those who are rendering voluntary co-operation to the Government, such as lawyers and those who are receiving so-called benefits from it, such as students, will withdraw their co-operation or renounce benefits as the case may be, and throw themselves into the final struggle for freedom.[14]

At this meeting Pandit Motilal Nehru and Jawaharlal (who was now the Congress President) were also present. This resolution did not mention salt satyagraha since none of the members were privy to the thoughts of the Mahatma. After Vithalbhai went back to Delhi in December, Dadubhai, who normally communicated with him frequently, ceased to do so. This was because he feared a letter about his talk with Gandhi might go astray in the post, which would give the whole game away. Vithalbhai was only the third person to know of the salt satyagraha, of which he did not approve. So on 6 March he wrote to Dadubhai: 'You have been purposely silent for a long time; the cause of this I do not understand. I think Gandhi has made a great mistake of selecting salt for satyagraha. I now need your advice as to what step I should take?'.[15] From this it could be seen that only Dadubhai knew the salt secret and did not send any news of it to his most trusted friend Vithalbhai.

The secret of the salt was let out of the bag for the first time on 2 March 1930 when Gandhiji sent an 11 point, politely worded, ultimatum to Lord Irwin through a young British Quaker, Reginald Reynolds, who was going to Delhi after a short visit to the Sabarmati Ashram. Unless the Viceroy accepted his eleven points and honour them, he would disobey the salt laws on 11 March 1930. Lord Irwin regretted that he was unable to comply with Gandhiji's request. On 12 March Gandhiji again wrote to Lord Irwin: 'On bended knees I asked for bread and received stone instead. I repudiate this law and regard it as my sacred duty to break the mournful mandatory of compulsory peace that is choking the heart of the nation for want of free vent'.[16] The choice of salt as the central issue of the Satyagraha movement at first appeared eccentric even to Gandhiji's close associates. Motilal Nehru wrote to Dr Ansari that: 'The thing was incredibly small.' To Motilal salt had become like the charkha and fasting, another of Gandhi's hobby horses. Jawaharlal Nehru was bewildered; to connect ordinary salt with the national independence movement seemed incredible to him, since he just did not understand the importance of salt to the British Raj.[17]

Pattabi Sitaramaya writes in the History of Congress:

> Every age and every clime has its miracles and India was to produce its own. It was to witness this miracle of the twentieth century in their own motherland that thousands of people gathered round the banner of Gandhi at the Sabarmati Ashram on 6 March 1930, and accompanied him as far as their legs could carry their bodies or their enthusiasm could sustain their energies. Among those who accompanied Gandhi and his pilgrim fighters were newspaper correspondents from various parts of India and from abroad. Photographers, cinemamen and of course the vast concourse of village people from round about, with batches of leading men from different provinces. Gandhi had all along said that: 'Gujarat will bear the brunt of the fight for Indian emancipation and if Gujarat did it, and was allowed to do it, the rest of India need not pass through the agonies and anguish inevitable in the struggle.'[18]

Here is a description by a correspondent who was with the party: 'Early on the morning of 12 March, Gandhi left the Ashram on a campaign of civil disobedience with his 75 volunteers picked and chosen for Dandi, a sea-side village 200 miles distant for the manufacture of salt.'

In the words of S.A. Brelvi of the *Bombay Chronicle*: 'The scenes that preceded, accompanied and followed this great national event, were so enthusiastic, magnificent and soul-stirring, that indeed they beggar description. Never was the wave of patriotism so powerful in the hearts of mankind as it was on this great occasion, which is bound to go down in the chapters of history of India's national freedom as a great beginning to a great movement.'[19]

18

SALT SATYAGRAHA

P.C. Ray said: 'Mahatma Gandhi's historic march was like the exodus of the Israelites under Moses. Until the seer seized the promised land he won't turn his back.' In the prayer meeting of 11 March 1930, which had a record attendance, Gandhiji said: 'Our case is strong, our means the purest and God is with us. There is no defeat for Satyagrahis till they give up truth. I pray for the battle which begins tomorrow.'

Next day (12 March) Mahatma started his historic march. At first the Viceroy, Lord Irwin, thought that the salt march would end and the movement fizzle out in a fiasco. Next day he wrote to the Secretary of State for India, Wedgwood Benn: 'Most of my thought at the moment is concentrated on Gandhiji'.[1]

Sir Frederick Sykes, Governor of Bombay, was in favour of the instant arrest of Gandhiji, but Lord Irwin stopped him. Vithalbhai played his part. Lord Irwin later wrote: 'The will-power of the man must have been enormous to get him through his march'. He wrote a few days later: 'I was always told that his blood pressure is dangerous and his heart none too good, and I was also told a few days ago that his horoscope predicts that he will die this year, and that is the explanation of this dangerous throw. It would be a very happy solution'. Lord Irwin was really misled by this advice. He later realised it, but that was of no avail.

Meanwhile, in the Kheda District things were moving fast on an entirely different plane. Vallabhbhai had complete faith in his ability to carry his own no-revenue campaign to a successful conclusion like that of Bardoli. Throughout the last months of 1929, and early in January 1930, Dadubhai also kept Vallabhbhai well informed about his discussions with Gandhiji on plans for the salt Satyagraha. Vallabhbhai, however, also did not favour the idea in the same way as his brother, Vithalbhai. Dadubhai also tried in every possible way to help him in this project. Being an elected member of the Bombay Governor's Legislative Council he had more access to the various government organisations and their executives. From Taluka Mamlatdar to the Governor, he could talk freely and could ascertain their views in general. This he passed on to Vallabhbhai, by letters and by personal meetings, as and when it was necessary or expedient. This can be clearly seen from the two letters (printed in Appendix 4) of 16 and 20 January 1930, both of which were in response to Dadubhai's letters (the only ones saved from destruction or government raids).[2] Thus, he acted more in a friendly advisory capacity to help Gandhiji for his Salt Satyagraha and to Vallabhbhai for his independently started no-revenue payment campaign restricted to Kheda districts – Matar, Mehmedabad, Borsad and Nadiad Talukas. His campaign was to be launched at Ras on 7 March with a fiery speech to a meeting of the people of Borsad Taluka. But as he rose to make his speech Vallabhbhai was arrested by the District Collector, Master, and summarily sentenced to three months imprisonment. Under the powers he had as District Magistrate, Master was entitled to impose a maximum sentence of three months only. The Bombay Government had in the meantime cabled to Master, ordering him not to arrest Vallabhbhai.[3] When they discovered what had happened, they were annoyed but, in the interests of collective responsibility, they and the Government of India had to defend the arrest as Government policy. Vallabhbhai's arrest sent a wave of indignation through Kheda District. Merchants closed their shops, meetings were held throughout the district and a rousing speech, which Vallabhbhai had made a fortnight before, was printed up and circulated around the villages.[4]

The Patidars of Ras, insulted by the arrest in their village, resolved to refuse their land revenue. The Gandhian leader, Ashabhai Patel, went to Borsad to inform the Taluka leaders of their decision. The Congress leaders tried to dissuade him, arguing that Congress had not sanctioned land revenue refusal and only Gandhiji could give permission for such a campaign. Ashabhai therefore waited for Gandhi to come through Borsad Taluka on the salt march, and in the meantime visited several other villages of the Taluka to persuade them to join Ras. During the next ten days he received assurances from the Patidars of 14 villages that they would refuse their revenue. Vallabhbhai's arrest thus triggered off the no-revenue campaign in Borsad Taluka. This comprised the villages of Ras, Sunav, Pagaj, Porda, Piplav, Isnav, Amod, Bochasan, Davapura, Rupiapura, Dhundakuva, Vadala, Golel and Danteli.

Then suddenly on 21 March Dabudhai received a communication from the jail at Ahmedabad that Vallabhbhai wished to see him and that the date of 24 March was fixed for the purpose. As it was so important, Mahatma's secretary also wrote a postcard to him reminding him of the meeting (letter of 21 March 1930 reproduced in Appendix 4).[5] Vallabhbhai knew that in his absence Dadubhai will take over his work, but he was also anxious about how the campaign which he had started on 7 March 1930 was coming along and whether various other local leaders were also doing their bit. Above all else he had to discuss the negotiation points in case the Government wanted to negotiate, of course this was to be restricted to revenue Satyagraha only. He also wished to merge his campaign with that of Gandhiji for better results. The other local leaders of Kheda, Darbar Gopaldas, Goraldas Talat and Phulchand Bapuji, were for the moment only engaged in the work of the Salt Satyagraha. On 6 April 1930, the day Gandhiji was also to break the salt law, Salt Satyagraha took these leaders to Badalpur where they broke the salt law and were arrested. These were Darbar Gopaldas, Phulchand Bapuji and Gokuldas Talati. By mid-April the salt campaign was going on well in spite of arrests. Master then decided he had to resort to brute force. He relaxed control over the police so they were allowed to use their lathis at the slightest provocation. Individual Salt Satyagrahis who were offering Satyagrahi sabras (salt) were brutally beaten up. The officialdom had gone crazy and run riot. In Nadiad people, especially women and children, were scared to come out of their houses. In Nadiad the writer himself has known that D.A. Laher, the Police Superintendent, entered Satyagrahis' houses and beat them up. This was a common occurrence in the whole district. Gandhiji, who was now in Dharasana, wrote in Navjivan on 4 May 1930: 'In Gujarat at present the Kheda District seems to have become the centre of our struggle. Nowhere else in Gujarat do we find the same repression as in that district. There they arrest or release whom they like, beat up or abuse all and sundry.'

Desai Vago at Nadiad, the place where all the Desais resided, gave the Police Superintendent, Laher, the main excuse for repression and atrocities. Desais were at the forefront and remained so in spite of their suffering. Their spirit was indomitable. The Government felt they were rapidly losing control in Kheda and for that matter to a certain extent the whole of Gujarat. Congress volunteers going from village to village persuaded Government officers to resign and join the movement. One by one hundreds of Mukhis, Talatis, Matadars and Ravaniyas resigned. The position on 20 June was as follows:[6]

TALUKA	Villages in which there were resignations	Total of Narva & Ryotwari Villages	Percentage of first to second column	Number of resignations Mukhis	Matadars	Ravaniyas
Borsad	64	73	88	83	260	135
Anand	54	67	81	51	228	84
Mehmedabad	47	59	80	43	149	60
Matar	56	78	72	51	163	47
Thasra	37	59	63	33	65	38
Nadiad	59	97	61	61	247	98
Kapadvanj	23	77	30	9	48	15
	340	510	67	331	1160	477

Meanwhile Gandhiji's march had begun on 12 March 1930 from Sabarmati. The attention of the world was focused on his itinerary through the villages of Gujarat. Every detail of the march was covered by the newspapers. Even midday and evening bulletins were printed to satisfy the insatiable demand for news.[7] The march was gruelling and several of the party had to give up through exhaustion. Huge crowds flocked from miles around to see the march. As they came the onlookers stirred up clouds of dense, choking dust through which Gandhiji and his followers had to pass. Everywhere there was a carnival atmosphere, with cymbals clashing, drums beating and bugles blowing, the long folk-trumpets of Gujarat, blasting out a raucous chorus as Gandhi entered each village. Local politicians could be seen at different stages of the march. As it took place during the dry months of blue skies and scorching sunshine, the major part of it had to be completed each day during the cool hours, immediately after sunrise. After the early morning march, food was taken in the village reached and a meeting was held. During the heat of the day they rested. They then walked for about an hour to the next town or village, where they spent the night. Whenever possible, Gandhi chose to stay in Dharmashalas attached to temples. People flocked to these Dharmashalas for Gandhi's darshan. Another meeting was held in the evening when Gandhi made a speech.[8]

During the march Gandhi laid great emphasis on the resignation of officers. Congress workers scoured the villages of the three districts collecting the government officers' promises of resignation. Gandhi told the people to boycott officials who refused to resign, but not in a spirit of bitterness or with undue social pressure. By the time he left Kheda (19 March) 60 resignations had been handed in. He also asked Congress volunteers to come forward. He asked all students over the age of 15 and all teachers to leave their schools and take up Congress work.[9]

On 15 March Gandhi reached Nadiad, his beloved Nadiad, the population of which had never let him down – the centrepiece of his political career. Here in Nadiad, in days gone by, he first used the expression 'Himalayan Miscalculation' about prematurely launching, in 1918, his first civil disobedience movement on the soil of India. With the people not yet ready to qualify as true Satyagrahis, in his own words: 'I had called on the people of Nadiad and the whole Kheda District to launch upon civil disobedience before they qualified themselves for it and this mistake seemed to me to be of Himalayan magnitude'.[10] But now, however, the people of Nadiad were well trained to offer true Gandhian Satyagraha, which was in the end going to be a torch-bearer for the wider All-India movement to defeat the British imperialism. Nadiad was Gandhi's starting point as well as the operational base for his first political act on the soil of India: the recruitment services he rendered to the British war effort. As he entered Nadiad at the Ahmedabad gate of the town, the leaders of Kheda, led by Dadubhai then President of Kheda District Congress Committee, and Darabar Gopaldas, Raojibhat Patel, Phulchand Bapuj Shah and Gokaldas Talaki, welcomed him with flowers, garlands and respects. He was taken straight to Santaram Temple where Janakidas Maharaj welcomed him. He spent the afternoon closeted with the leaders. In the evening, after a welcoming speech by Dadubhai, Gandhiji addressed a crowd of 50,000 from the balcony of the impeccably white Santram Temple. It was a sea of white caps which proved beyond doubt the following he had was real. One of those on the march wrote: 'Seated on a chair on the balcony, the uncrowned King of India, whose regalia consists of a simple spotless white dhoti and an equally simple white khaddar piece of cloth wrapped about the waist.[11] This uncrowned King of India looked upon his adoring and expectant fellow-countrymen and exhorted them to follow him unto death. In the course of his public life of over 35 years, the Mahatma had addressed many a monstrous meeting, but none has ever filled him, or his army, with greater delight than this one at Nadiad. The sight thrilled me – its impression will abide with me for ever.'

The writer was then 10 years old and distinctly remembers the image of Gandhiji delivering his speech from the snow-white balcony of the Santram Temple. It was a magnificent, soul-stirring sight.

On 19 March, Gandhi arrived at Ras in Borsad Taluka. There Ashabhai Patel requested him to allow no-revenue campaign along with his salt non-cooperation movement.[12] After listening carefully to his request, Gandhi agreed to accept their initiative. In Navjivan on 29 April 1930, Gandhi wrote: 'The Government is unlikely to tolerate any campaign of non-payment of land revenue assessment. Nor is it at present a part of our programme. Let him who has the courage not to pay his land revenue assessment, as was done by the Pancha Patel of Karari, but whoever does it must realise the risks he is running. His household, his cattle, his land and everything in fact will be sold by the Government in order to collect its dues. The position in Kaira will be very different from what it was in Bardoli. The struggle in Bardoli was of a totally different character. It was limited in its scope. There it was a question of establishing a right. Here we are talking of removing a government. The difference between the two is as far removed as the earth is from the sun. For this reason before Ras proceeds to implement its resolution, its people should develop strength of character and a spirit of sacrifice, while the other villages which wish to follow in the footsteps of Ras should, without any excitement or anger, make an objective assessment of their strength.'

Gandhi had hoped, by concentrating on the salt laws, to emphasise the grievances of the poor peasants, but this the Patidars would not allow and once again he found himself leading them in their favourite form of protest – revenue refusal. Gandhi left Kheda District on the evening of 19 March, after the Ras meeting, crossing the Mahi River in a boat to Broach District. As he had marched through Kheda during the previous week, the movement had swelled in strength and fervour. People from all castes, classes and creeds had turned out to welcome him. Even groups previously hostile to Congress had garlanded and showered him with rose petals. By 19 March the authority of the British in Kheda District lay in shreds.[13]

The onward march of Gandhiji lasted 24 days. After walking 241 miles, Gandhiji reached Dandi on the morning of 5 April 1930 (the eve of the anniversary of the Amritsar Massacre). He had lost a bit of weight and looked thin and frail, but he was in the jovial mood of a victorious general. The first phase of the campaign was now complete and the second one was to begin. When Gandhi was asked what he wanted to achieve by this campaign, his answer was: 'I want the world sympathy in this battle of right against might'.

The night of 5 April was spent in prayers by the Satyagrahis. The next morning Gandhiji walked to the sea and took a ceremonial dip in the water as an act of purification. At 8.30 a.m. Gandhiji emerged and solemnly bent down with 'Om Shree Ram' and picked up a small lump of salt. The Satyagrahi followers then picked up salt too. Immediately after breaking the salt law, Gandhi issued the following press statement: 'Now that the technical or ceremonial breach of the salt law has been committed, it is open to anyone who would take the risk of prosecution under the salt law, to manufacture salt wherever he wishes and wherever it is convenient. My advice is that workers should everywhere manufacture salt, make use of it and instruct the villagers likewise. At the same time, telling the villagers that they run the risk of being prosecuted. In other words the villagers should be fully instructed as to incidence of the salt tax and the manner of breaking the laws and regulations connected with it, so as to have the salt tax repealed.

It should be made absolutely clear to the villagers that the breach is open and in no way stealthy. This salt, being manufactured by nature in creeks and pits near the sea-shore, let them use it for themselves and their cattle and sell it to those who will buy it, it being well understood that all such people are committing a breach of the salt law and running the same risk of a prosecution, or even without a prosecution are to be subject by a so-called salt officer to harassment.

This war against the salt tax should be continued during the National Week that is until the 13th April. Those who are not engaged in this sacred work should themselves do vigorous propaganda for the boycott of foreign cloth and the use of Khaddar. They should also endeavour to manufacture as much Khaddar as possible. As to this and the prohibition of liquor, I am preparing a message for the women of India, who I am becoming more and more convinced can make a larger contribution than men towards the attainment of independence. I feel that they will be worthier interpreters of non-violence than men. Not because they are weak, as men in their arrogance believe them to be, but because they have greater courage of the right type and immeasurably greater spirit of self-sacrifice'.[14]

As mentioned earlier, on that same day, 6 April, Darbar Gopaldas, Phulchand Bapuji and Gokaldas Talati led a group of volunteers to the seashore at Badalpur and as they picked up salt they were all arrested and taken away under the orders of Collector Master. Since these leaders were arrested, people took over and hundreds of Satyagrahis broke the salt law and the police started beating them at random. This beating did not attract any attention in the national or international press because they were all focusing their attention on what Gandhi was doing on the seashore at Dharasana.

On that day in the morning at Dandi, where Gandhi broke the salt law for the first time, police were not there and no arrests were made. Satyagrahis of the Mahatma were seen walking and wandering along the seashore at Dandi free and without any molestation by the police, a real anti-climax. They had invited a storm and in return there was not even a ripple. However, elsewhere in India a storm really did break out. People of every walk of life started making their own salt by boiling sea water or gathering salt from the seashore. Even Jawaharlal at Allahabad, who like other Congressmen knew nothing about salt, read up about it and started making it. 'We ultimately succeeded in producing some unwholesome stuff which we waved about in triumph and often auctioned for fancy prices. It was really immaterial whether the stuff was good or bad, the main thing was to commit a breach of the obnoxious salt law and we were successful in this, even though the quality of the salt was poor'. So wrote Jawaharlal in his autobiography.[15] Perhaps he had realised, late in the day, that Gandhiji had some idea which seemed to work.[16] During the following week people also started picketing liquor shops and burning foreign cloth all in the line of protest against the British Raj. People seemed determined to violate the laws as peacefully as possible. The police everywhere seemed to be quiet. Again, on 8 April, Gandhiji broke the salt law at the nearby village of Aat, near Dandi. This time he expected to be arrested and even delivered a parting message, in which he said: 'Let not my companions or the people at large be perturbed over my arrest, for it is not I but God who is guiding this movement. At present India's self-respect in fact her all, is symbolised as it were in a handful of salt in the Satyagrahis' hand. Let the fist holding it therefore be broken but let there be no voluntary surrender of the salt.'

While Gandhi was at Dandi, events took place elsewhere in India which generated equal interest and important consequences. In Peshawar, Abdul Gaffar Khan was arrested on 23 April and as a result of his arrest an angry crowd set fire to a military vehicle and demonstrators plundered and set fire to the police station there. In response to that, the Government three days later sent two platoons of the second Battalion of the 18th Royal Garhwali Rifles. These Hindu Garhwalis, when ordered to fire on a crowd of Muslims, refused the order. So from 25 April to 4 May the City of Peshawar was in the hands of Abdul Gaffar Khan and his red shirts. The British sent a Gurkha Regiment with air support and re-took Peshawar. After their refusal to shoot, the Garhwalis were at once disarmed, placed before a court-martial and sentenced to long terms of imprisonment. When these facts became known, the Working Committee of the Congress appointed a committee under Vithalbhai Patel (who had already resigned the Presidency of the Central Assembly).[17]

Despite needing to inquire into and report on the facts, this

Committee was not allowed to go to the Frontier Province and collect evidence there. Nonetheless, they collected facts and prepared a report. As soon as the report of the Committee was published, it was banned by the Government.[18] As a result of the Garhwalis' refusal to fire, the Viceroy Irwin realised that for the first time he could not rely on the military for full, unqualified support. In a confidential memorandum to King George V, he spoke of his fear that the next uprising might have even more dreadful consequences. 'Above all', he wrote: 'This was obviously the sort of thing on which the less press comment there is the better'.[19] Consequently he tried to muzzle the press. The Bengal Ordinance was renewed on 23 April and the Viceroy promulgated on 27 April another Ordinance reviving the powers of the Press Act of 1910, with certain amendments. As a result, Gandhi's '*Young India*' had to be issued in cyclostyle. Gandhi, in a press statement, declared: 'Revival in the form of an ordinance of the Press Act, that was supposed to be dead, was only to be expected, and in its new form the Act contains additional provisions, making the whole piece deadlier than before. Whether we realise it or not, for some days past we have been living in a veiled form of Martial Law... I hope however the time for tame submission to dictation from the British Rulers is gone for ever. I hope that people will not be frightened by this ordinance. Press-men, if they are worthy representatives of public opinion will not be frightened by the ordinance ... I would therefore urge the press-men and publishers to refuse to furnish security, and if they are called upon to do so, either to cease publication or to challenge the authorities to confiscate whatever they like...'.

Gandhi subsequently asked the manager of the Navjinan press to allow it to be forfeited rather than deposit security, if security was demanded by the Government under the press ordinance. Navjinan was seized and printing stopped. Many journalists in the country paid the securities demanded of them and thus forfeited their freedom to print the true picture of the ongoing struggle.

Kaira District became the theatre of war in Gujarat and Gandhi in an article in cyclostyled Navjivan wrote: 'People have preserved peace but there are anger and malice and therefore violence in their intensive social boycott. They censure and harass Government officers in small matters. They will not succeed in this manner. We should expose the evils of the office of Mamlatdars and Fozdars. There should be sweetness and respect in our intense boycott ...

People of Kaira District should take a warning and enforce boycott within limits. I have indicated for instance boycott of village officers should be with regard to their office only. Their orders should not be obeyed, but their food supplies should not be stopped. They should not be ejected from their houses. If we are not capable of doing this, we should give up the boycott'.[20]

After finishing his report on Garhwali rebellion, Vithalbhai Patel came to Nadiad having visited Calcutta and Bombay. That was early May. Dadubhai informed him of the ongoing civil disobedience in Kheda District and news of Dharasana salt campaign, which seemed to be slowing down a bit. Then Gandhiji, being unable to make any impression on the authorities, tried a fresh letter to Lord Irwin in which he expressed his intention to raid the Dharasana Salt Works and take possession of it. The letter ran: 'Dear Friend, God willing, it is my intention to set out for Dharasana and reach there with my companions and demand possession of the salt works. The public have been told that Dharasana is private property. This is mere camouflage. It is as effectively under Government control as the Viceroy's house. Not a pinch of salt can be removed without the previous sanction of the authorities. It is possible for you to prevent this raid, as it has been playfully and mischievously called, in three ways:

1. By removing the salt tax;
2. By arresting me and my party unless the country can, as I hope it will, replace everyone taken away;
3. By sheer goondaism, unless every head broken is replaced as I hope it will. You may condemn civil disobedience as much as you like. Will you prefer violent revolt to civil disobedience? If you say, as you have said, that the civil disobedience must end in violence, history will pronounce the verdict that the British Government, not heeding because not understanding non-violence, goaded human nature to violence, which it could understand and deal with. But in spite of the goading, I shall hope that God will give the people of India wisdom and strength to withstand every temptation and revocation to violence. If therefore you cannot see your way to remove the salt tax and remove the prohibition on private salt-making, I must reluctantly

commence the march, adumbrated in the opening paragraph of my letter.

I am your sincere friend, M K Gandhi.'[21]

Gandhiji, after writing this letter on 24 April, was arranging to break the law by a big raid on the Dharasana salt works, taking with him hundreds of volunteers, all of whom were to virtually loot the salt from there. This spectacular show of strength and courage on the part of volunteers, was meant to be the international showpiece of Gandhian ideology. But this was not to be. The Viceroy had by now woken up from his sleep and had realised that he should prevent Gandhi from going on further in inciting the public and making capital internationally.

On 24 April 1930, Lord Irwin wrote to the King: 'The general situation in India naturally gives cause for some anxiety, but not serious alarm. The active state of the civil disobedience movement began when Gandhi reached the seashore and by personal example gave the signal for the breach of the salt law. This example has been followed in varying degrees in other provinces, but as a threat to the monopoly of the Government, this part of his programme may be pronounced a failure. The extremists could hardly have expected any other result, for their main object was to prepare the country for widespread defiance of the law. We have up to now met this by the arrest of popular leaders in different parts of India, though we have not as yet arrested Gandhi. The opinion, both of Local Governments and of our own police advisers here, was pretty unanimous that if we could we should avoid his arrest. At all events in the early stages Indian opinion distinguishes very sharply between Gandhi whom they regard rather in the light of a venerable impracticable saint and the more avowedly political and subversive leaders... If we could get through the whole movement without arresting him, that would be worth considering, but if we cannot expect to do this – as I doubt if we can – then it seems to me that we shall gain nothing, and perhaps lose much, by delay. We are accordingly consulting local governments again on this general question of strategy'.[22]

In the same letter, Lord Irwin wrote: 'Mr Vithalbhai Patel, President of the Assembly, has intimated to me that he intends to resign at once. His attitude is quite illogical inasmuch as he has frequently assured me that he thinks that the whole movement is mistaken. But I suppose one must make some allowance for the feelings of anyone who sees all his old comrades in jail. I predict it may not be very long before he is there too'.

On 5 May Lord Irwin struck and arrested Gandhi before he could lead the raid on the salt works. At 12.45 a.m. about 30 policemen, some of whom carried rifles, entered the camp at Karadi under the command of two British officers and one Indian Fozdar, as well as the District Magistrate. Gandhi was awakened. One police officer said: 'Please wake up'. Gandhi sat up and said: 'Have you come to arrest me?'. 'Yes', said the District Magistrate: 'Your name is Mohandas Karamchand Gandhi?'. Gandhi asked if he could brush his teeth and wash his face, but the superintendent of police indicated that there was very little time and he could only brush his teeth. The commotion woke up everyone in the camp and all rushed to the reed hut. While brushing his teeth, Gandhi asked: 'Am I being arrested under Section 124-A of the Indian Penal Code?' The whole edifice which Gandhi had created was in danger of collapsing.

'No not under Section 124', the District Magistrate said, 'I have a written order'. 'Would you mind reading it to me?', said Gandhi. The Magistrate began to read the warrant: 'Whereas the Governor in Council views with alarm the activities of Mohandas Karamchand Gandhi, he directs that the said Mohandas Karamchand Gandhi should be placed under restraint under Regulation XXV of 1827, and suffer imprisonment during the pleasure of the Government and that he be immediately removed to the Yerawada Jail'. This Regulation XXV was enacted in Bombay by the East India Company for the purpose of punishing defecting Indian Princes.

Then Gandhi and the followers in the camp sang this short prayer:

'Raghupati Raghav Raja Ram
Patitapavan Sita Ram
Sita Ram, Sita Ram
Bhaj Pyare Tu Sitaram'

Afterwards, each Satyagrahi bowed down before Mahatma and touched his feet as a sign of their continued devotion and affection. Then Gandhi was placed on a truck and whisked away to a place a few miles from Karadi Camp, where the Gujarat Mail was prearranged to stop. A special coach was reserved for the party. The train stopped at Borivli at 6.40 a.m. From there Gandhi was transferred to an automobile, arriving at Yerawada Jail at 10.30 a.m. There at Yerawada Jail he was detained without a trial for an indeterminate term at the jail as an enemy of the State.

As soon as the news of the arrest was out, the whole country had hartals and strikes. For a few days the country was very near to anarchy. However, this could not last long since most of the Congress leaders, as well as Gandhi, were in jail. Vallabhbhai was in jail even before the start of the Salt Satyagraha.

On 14 April Pandit Nehru was jailed. Without criticising him, it is difficult to understand why he was so determined to break the salt law at Allahabad and prematurely to court prison there, rather than take Gandhi's place at Karadi Camp and direct the salt campaign from there? After all, the whole country and the entire army of foreign correspondents were concentrating on this nerve centre of salt Satyagraha. When he had started his march, Gandhi had expressed his wish that, once he was arrested, Jawaharlal, as the Congress President, should take his place and continue to direct the salt campaign. Now, with the sudden forced withdrawal of Mahatma from the base station of the struggle, the leading workers were in disarray. After all, Gandhi had been providing the leadership and directing an hour-to-hour programme. As the hours ticked by the movement at Dharasana was about to hit the buffers. There were other leaders at the camp, but they needed direction, encouragement and help. None of them had an effective power base in any district of Gujarat from where they could inspire more volunteers. Shri Iman Saheb and Manilal Gandhi, who were great friends of Dadubhai, sent an urgent message to him and Vithalbhai (who also was back in Nadiad then) to come to Dharasana and save the campaign.[23] At this time Dadubhai, being the President of Kaira District Congress, was running the civil disobedience movement in the district and also enlisting volunteers for Mahatma's campaign at Dharasana. They were following the movement at Dharasana with keen eyes on the requirements of men and materials.

Their volunteer recruiting plan for the Dharasana campaign, which was already in full swing, led to another week of frenzied activity throughout the Kheda District. Dadubhai also wrote to leading figures in Bardoli to hasten the volunteer programme. Dadubhai even took with him his eldest son Balwantrai and his two nephews Harshadbhai and Hirubhai to volunteer and take part in the projected, massive raid on the Dharasana salt works. Vithalbhai, having 16 years experience in the legislatures, and Dadubhai having over 10 years experience at Bombay Legislative Council, knew exactly where to strike a blow against the British Establishment. They knew they were the only organisers left who could deliver. They took their volunteers from Kheda and Ahmedabad with them and merged them with the volunteers of other parts of Surat District (especially Bardoli). A 'War Council' was formed to carry out a fight that Gandhi would approve, non-violent civil disobedience carried out without malice. Their mode of operation was entirely different from the other leaders who were already in prison. Those leaders had dared the British to imprison them and the British obliged, knowing full well that they were less dangerous inside the prisons than outside and that the movement would die once they were out of it and in jail. The two constitutionalists did not want to go to jail to pass their days in anxious laziness. They knew that remaining outside they could damage the Raj more than by being inside. They knew that when the authorities realised the damage they are inflicting on them they would surely arrest them. They were not afraid of the jail. The rise or fall of the entire Salt Satyagraha had passed into their hands. They began to plan a series of massive volunteer raids on the Dharasana Salt Works – one after another as circumstances permitted, and if the Government were foolish enough to permit it. The British had little reason to arrest them on salt charges, as they were determined to direct the movement without themselves breaking the salt law, and the Raj was concentrating on the salt law only. They simply acted as generals on the battlefield.

The 'War Council' was as follows:[24]

1) Vithalbhai J. Patel – until recently the first elected President of the Viceroy's Central Legislative Assembly at New Delhi and member of the Congress Working Committee;
2) Dadubhai P. Desai – President of Kheda District Congress Committee, elected member of the Bombay Governor's Legislative Council successively for the last four terms; (These two were leaders directing overall policy and addressing meetings to whip up enthusiasm);

3) Sarojihi Naidu – member of the Congress Working Committee;
4) Pyarelal – Mahatma's secretary;
5) Imam Saheb – a seasoned Moslem leader of great reputation, a co-worker with Gandhi in SA and Dadubhai at Kheda District;
6) Narhari Parikh – a local leader at Ahmedabad and that of Gujarat Provincial Congress Committee;
7) Manilal M. Gandhi – son of Mahatma and himself a great Satyagrahi, see a letter written by him to the writer (in Appendix 4);
8) Ambalal Sarabhai – a well-known industrialist who helped sustain the Sabarmati Ashram and a trusted follower of Gandhiji.

Gandhi had hoped that the civil disobedience movement would spread like a prairie fire across India, but instead it had the appearance of thousands of bonfires glowing brilliantly and then dying out. He believed that he had found a weapon which would destroy British morale, and that Swaraj would be the inevitable result of a mass disobedience carried to its logical conclusion, but he lacked a powerful organisation and a carefully worked-out programme. What was needed was a series of symbolic acts, perhaps four or five such acts, to create an atmosphere of mounting tension, with each new act being progressively more demanding and more challenging. But there was only the solemn lifting of a thimbleful of salt from the ground.[25]

On 21 May 1930, following the instructions of the 'War Council', a number of groups of Satyagrahis from Gujarat had run down to Dharasana to embrace death. The Satyagrahis who were without lathis, sticks or any other weapons, commenced the non-violent battle against the British Government which was armed with rifles and machine guns, canons and lances and other weapons. On the 20th in every train batches of volunteers from Surat, Ahmedabad, Kaira and other districts came one after another. Before the 20th about a thousand Satyagrahi had arrived in Satyagrahi camps at Dharasana, Bilimora, Punwri and other places. It was only the day before that 1000 other volunteers had arrived to join the battle. So that in the Satyagrahi camp, there arrived an army of about 2,000 to 2,500 Satyagrahis ready to raid the salt pans. Simultaneously, it was Maniben Patel, the only daughter of Sardar Vallabhbhai Patel, who was to be in charge of so-called Red Cross volunteers composed of doctors, nurses and others to treat, bandage and nurse wounded Satyagrahis.

They were ready to march towards the salt pan under the leadership of their respective leaders: Shriyut Sarojini Naidu, Shriyut Imam Saheb, Shriyut Narhari Parikh, Shriyut Manilal Gandhi and Shriyut Pyarelal; each had his or her own party to march with against the opposing forces of the Government, which consisted of the Commissioner of Gujarat, Garret, Braham the Collector of the Surat District, Robinson the Superintendent of Police, Antia Deputy Superintendent of Police, Mr Alam Shah the Divisional Inspector of Police, Sabwala the Sub-inspector and a sizeable posse of constables carrying lathis with iron tops, all standing ready to protect the salt pans at any cost.

At about 6.15 a.m. the army of Satyagrahis, chanting Vande Mataram and Mahatmaji Ki Jay, marched towards the salt pan. The officers gave orders to the sepoys to beat the Satyagrahis. They started hitting randomly but with good aim at the bodies of the Satyagrahis. The advance guard fell but a few behind them reached the pan and tried to cut the barbed wire of the fence with cutters. This was about 20 minutes after the start of the march. One volunteer cutting the fence was attacked by a policeman who forced him to the ground and still the volunteer was trying to reach the fence to cut it. A second policeman rushed to beat him, while a third one hit his hand with a lathi. On seeing this brutality, Shri Manilal Gandhi, the second son of the Mahatma, rushed to his aid. As Manilal was trying to help, Antia, the deputy Superintendent of Police, came forward and shouted: 'Mr Gandhi, I arrest you'. Simultaneously, one policeman, thinking Manilal was a volunteer, dealt him four or five blows with an 'edipolo' stick. Soon Manilal Gandhi along with Shri Imam Saheb were taken into police custody within the salt pan. In such a short time the police had created havoc and the scene was gruesome. The ground was covered with the bodies of Satyagrahis groaning with pain from the beatings and wounds created by the iron-ring lathis. The Red Cross volunteers carried the wounded on stretchers to the field hospital where doctors and nurses were waiting. Within quarter of an hour the police broke the heads of 60 or 70 volunteers. As Chimanlal Modi of Nutan Gujarat wrote: 'Today in the presence of Savita Narayan (i.e. the sun) the Satyagrahi have fulfilled the desire of Mahatma Gandhi by dyeing the salt pan with their blood'.

Alam Shah, the Inspector of Police, kept shouting to the police: 'Maro Saleko', to make them beat more and more volunteers. Even Mr Garret the Commissioner, Mr Braham the Collector and Mr Robinson the Superintendent of Police, all of them British, also joined in the beating of a few Satyagrahis. The handle of the 'edipolo' stick of another officer was broken while beating the Satyagrahis. The police even kicked the volunteers who had fallen on the ground. Shri Narhari Parikh received lathi blows on legs, head and shoulders, but this calm warrior did not shirk his duty. He did not resist nor raise his hand – non-violent to the limit, even with 20 to 25 lathi blows. At this point the Excise Officer intervened and reprimanded the sepoy. Shri Narhari Parikh got back safely to the camp and had his wounds treated. He was not arrested then. While this was going on, the Field Commander, brave Sarojini Devi had arrived and took her stand in the midst of her people. On seeing her, Antia, the Deputy Superintendent of Police, ran to arrest her and Shrimati Sarojini Devi went away with him saying: 'I am going'. The salt pans resounded with shouts of: 'Vande Mataram' and 'Mahatma Gandhi Ki Jai'. Sarojini, after exhorting her warriors to become martyrs by demonstrating non-violent heroism, went away with Mr Antia smiling. With the Commander under arrest, the longing for martyrdom welled up in the hearts of the Satyagrahis. Those who had retreated began to rush forward. The sepoys tried to stop the charge by holding their lathis across in a line. The marchers had reached the salt pans and some sat down there in front of the police cordon of crossed lathis. The Police brutality was now increasing, blow after blow raining on the heads and shoulders of sitting Satyagrahis. Two or four sepoys began lifting them up by their legs and arms and dragging them along like cattle. After releasing them at a distance and pulling them to their feet they continued beating them. Even the Red Cross volunteers were beaten up. As the news of the many wounded reached Bulsar and Billimora, doctors arrived from these places to help. Women of the villages came with water pots and gave water to the wounded. The men who had come to witness the fight gave all the help they could. Every ten minutes ten or twelve Satyagrahis were joining the wounded. All the doctors and nurses along with Shrimati Maniben Patel and other sisters had tirelessly and heroically nursed the wounded. By now the authorities had arrested four leaders who had led the volunteers to the battlefront. These were: Shrimati Sarojini Devi, Shri Imam Saheb, Shri Manilal Gandhi and Pyarelal. The volunteers, though leaderless, now carried on the task they were assigned to. While the fight was going on Shri Vithalbhai Patel and Shri Dadubhai Desai arrived at the Satyagrahi camp and after visiting and comforting the wounded went straight to the officers, especially Mr Garret whom they knew personally very well, and asked for permission to see Shrimati Sarojini Devi.[26] This was refused with: It is regretfully not possible to allow you to see her.

After talking with Narhari Parikh and Maniben Patel they went back to Dungari camp, exhorting the volunteers to carry on the campaign. At 10.15 a.m. as the Satyagrahis who had been carrying out a sit-down strike in the salt pan itself were being lifted out of the pan, one officer shouted: 'All of you are arrested'. The volunteers stood up to be arrested. As soon as they got up they were ordered to leave the salt pan. When the volunteers refused to leave the salt pan and remained immovable, they were again assaulted with lathis in a resumed show of sepoy strength. As a result of this sudden unexpected attack the sepoys caused them to retreat. After some time the Satyagrahis again made their way to the salt pan. This time the sepoys surrounded them in the compound of latrines erected for the 224 Satyagrahis who had been arrested some days before. There they wounded half a dozen volunteers in a short time. Volunteers would retreat and after some minutes regroup and come forward to the pan and again the police would drive them back. This cruel game was played continuously for five hours from six o'clock in the morning. At this time, eleven o'clock, Shri Vithalbhai Patel and Dadubhai Desai, the two organisers of the current campaign, returned to the Dharasana battlefield and camp. They talked to and examined the condition of the wounded. After conferring with Shri Narhari Parikh, they went back to Dungri Camp, which served as the headquarters of the campaign. Narhari Parikh, who was the only field commander still free, tried his best to continue the fight by sending a few Satyagrahis to the pan. The police would then give them lathi blows. About 1,500 volunteers were left to do this job. Up until six o'clock in the evening this cat-and-mouse game went on resulting in about 750 volunteers being beaten by the police, of whom 320 were badly wounded and were bandaged and treated by the staff of Maniben Patel. One or two of them were dying and about 50 were in a serious condition. Towards the end the police also turned their forces on to about 2,000 spectators who ran helter skelter into the field and the police cordon. The police chased them up to the nearby village of Untadi. The Satyagrahis received the order to retreat to the camp at about six o'clock. During the entire struggle at the salt pan, all the Satyagrahis remained strictly non-violent though beaten mercilessly again and again. Shri Vithalbhai and Shri Dadubhai came to the camp twice, saw and assessed the situation in consultation with Shri Narhari Parikh and Maniben. They sent an SOS to Bombay to get more medical supplies and returned to Dungra at eight o'clock in the evening. The volunteers were summoned into the compound opposite the camp to hear Shri Ambalal and Dadubhai. Shri Ambalal exhorted the volunteers to maintain the courage they had shown. The spirit of non-violent fight should be sustained.[27] Shri Dadubhai then spoke of Mahatmaji as a divine spirit who should be followed. The oppression perpetrated by the police and officials should be endured with a cheerful face. The aim of this fight is to bring about a change of heart of the Government by enduring the oppression of Government with love. Those who have perfect confidence in this doctrine, should receive the lathi blows with non-violence as they had done today. Some volunteers wished to go back to their villages and they were allowed to go to Billimora or Bulsar where they could catch their respective trains.

After due deliberation with Shri Ambalal, Shri Narhari Parikh and Shrimati Maniben it was decided, to allow time for the wounded to recuperate and to find and recruit further batches of volunteers, and to postpone the next big raid on the Dharasana Salt Pan until 25 May (four days after the first raid). However, the Government fully realising they met with defeat in the first raid brought considerable reinforcements in the field. In the evening of 21 May a company of nearly 200 Maratha soldiers commanded by European sergeants alighted at the railway station of Dungri. A special train carrying troops from Ahmedabad had arrived at Billimora. In the morning, at six o'clock, a special train full of soldiers was waiting at the nearby Surat station. To all intents and purposes it looked as if the Government had realised the gravity and importance of the events of 21 May. It seemed that the whole might of the British Raj was to be employed in the next showdown. Shri Vithalbhai and Shri Dadubhai were fully prepared to meet this force. However, other events were to intervene before the start of another salt-pan raid.

On Thursday 22 May Antia, the Deputy Superintendent of Police, arrived with his force at the Dharasana camp/hospital and ordered Shri Jivanlal Diwan, who had just arrived from Ahmedabad with a group of volunteers and who was helping with the treatment of the wounded in there, to vacate the camp/hospital and take away the wounded. Simultaneously, the sepoys started beating the volunteers, breaking the earthen pots of water, hitting anyone and everyone and destroying the medical equipment and cots and furniture. The unreasonable order of Antia was to vacate the camp in three impossible minutes. After wanton destruction, some Satyagrahis who could walk, walked away in silence, but the rest remained. The police then went away leaving behind the destruction they had wrought. Narhari Parikh was now left with 30 volunteers. The camp was thoroughly destroyed. On 23 May a large group of volunteers arrived with Shri Jivanlal Diwan and more volunteers were due shortly. The Government closed the railway crossing on the road to Dharasana from Bulsar for all traffic including pedestrians. No train was to stop at Dungri station. So all the routes to Dharasana were closed. In addition, Braham, the District Magistrate, read out Section 144 of the criminal penal code which prohibited the meeting of five or more persons within the limits of the villages of Dharasana, Chharwada and Umarsadi.[28] Thus the Government made sure no more raids were possible.

Shri Vithalbhai and Shri Dadubhai, with great reluctance and disgust, suspended the salt campaign for the time being. Meanwhile, as the struggle was going on on 21 May, Webb Miller, who had been detrained by the authorities at Bulsar, which is the next station to Dungri, took a goods train and reached Dungri. From there he walked six miles to Dharasana battlefield. He wrote as follows in his dispatch to United Press: ‘In eighteen years of reporting in twentytwo countries, during which I have witnessed innumerable civil disturbances, riots, street fights and rebellions, I have never witnessed such harrowing scenes as at Dharasana. Sometimes the scenes were so painful that I had to turn away momentarily. One surprising feature was the discipline of the volunteers. It seemed they were thoroughly imbued with Gandhi’s non-violence creed’.[29]

Louis Fischer wrote: ‘Gandhiji made England powerless and

India invincible'.[30] Webb Miller also confirmed the size of the volunteer army as 2,500 and described what happened. He found them in thatched sheds after prayer. Sarojini Naidu led the half mile march of the Satyagrahis to the salt depot at Dharasana. Among the Satyagrahis were Imam Saheb, Pyarelal and Manilal Gandhi, who moved forward at the head of the marchers shouting 'Inquilab Zindabad'. The salt pans were protected by barbed wire and ditches and were guarded by 400 policemen and half a dozen British officers. The Satyagrahis refused to obey when police ordered them to retreat. The large force of police then methodically and mechanically rained lathi blows on the heads of the Satyagrahis. Miller tells us that not one of the marchers raised an arm to fend off the blows and that there were no signs of wavering or fear. Three hundred and twenty Satyagrahis were arrested and two of them died. The Dharasana raid, in Miller's mind, clearly demonstrated the spirit of fearlessness, self-sacrifice and self-discipline which Gandhiji had instilled in the minds of the Satyagrahis. The British were extremely sensitive about American public opinion on India, especially when the reports of Webb Miller on the Dharasana Salt Satyagraha received widespread publicity in the USA. A large number of Americans, including William Kirk of Pemona College, Herbert A. Miller, Professor of Sociology at Ohio State University, Sherwood Eddy Secretary of the Asian branch of the YMCA, Kirby Page the editor of World Tomorrow, went to India and met Gandhiji in prison and all wrote about the power he had over his people. A force the British Government ought to recognise and respect. In the wake of Salt Satyagraha a few books were written and published, for example William James Durant's 'The Case for India', C.F. Andrew's 'Mahatma Gandhi's Ideas Including Selections from His Writings', Rev. J.T. Sunderland's 'India in Bondage'. These books laid the blame for India's ills upon the British imperial policies of exploitation. All senior politicians in Britain had by now realised that the damage done to British prestige in the USA was immense. Finally on 17 July 1930, Senator John Blaine raised in the Senate the question of Indian independence. The Springfield *Daily Republican* compared Gandhi's Salt Satyagraha with 'Boston's short way with tea'. The *Baltimore Sun* proclaimed that the civil disobedience movement would influence the whole course of history.

The *New York World* remarked that it was unfortunate that the most civilised Empire of the West had failed to reach an understanding with such a noble leader as Gandhi. The American liberals were deeply moved when they read about the police atrocities committed during the Dharasana salt campaign.

Judith Brown in her book wrote that the Salt Satyagraha probably marked the peak of Gandhiji's political influence over his countrymen and the British Raj.[31] Thus the Salt Satyagraha confirmed Gandhiji as the supreme and unchallenged leader of the Indian Independence Movement. From now onwards it was difficult for anyone to challenge his control of All India leadership.

Dadubhai's interest in the success of the Salt Satyagraha was twofold. First it was his idea, adopted by Gandhiji after laborious persuasion and meetings at Sabarmati and, second, if the Salt Satyagraha was accepted by the whole nation, then Gandhiji will be enthroned as the unchallenged supreme leader of the whole country, towering above all leaders together. Such was his devotion to Gandhiji.

Of all the fires raging across India in the name of Salt Satyagraha, the Dharasana fire was not only the most brilliant and spectacular but also the most politically effective and was taken notice of by the international community which for the first time noted down in every detail the oppression carried out by one of the most powerful countries in the world which had so far enjoyed the unquestioned trust of other lands. From now on every move by Britain would be watched and assessed by civilised peoples elsewhere and especially America. This was the unexpected and unsolicited reward that Vithalbhai and Dadubhai procured for the imprisoned Mahatma. This was the most successful Satyagraha of Gandhi's entire life. All other Congress leaders having contributed very little towards its success, Gandhi's position now became unassailable. The British Government did not lose sight of what had happened at Dharasana, though Lord Irwin was upbeat when he wrote to the King: 'Your Majesty can hardly fail to have read with amusement the accounts of the several battles for the salt depot at Dharasana. The police for a long time tried to refrain from action. After a time this became impossible and they eventually had to resort to sterner measures. A good many people suffered minor injuries in consequence, but I believe those who suffered injuries were as nothing compared with those who wished to sustain an honourable contusion or bruise or who, to make the whole setting more dramatic, lay on the ground as if laid out for dead without any injury at all.

But of course, Your Majesty will appreciate the whole business was propaganda and, as such, served its purpose admirably well.'[32]

Robert Payne writes: 'The Viceroy was highly amused, but there were many who were considerably less amused'.[33] Webb Miller's report of the incident was circulated by United Press around the world and, since it was patently honest and factual, it served as a warning that the British in India would be watched more closely in future. Like Amritsar, Dharasana would acquire the status of a legend and the shadow of Dharasana would remain over the British Raj to the very end.

That afternoon, as the wounded arrived in the hospital of the nearby town of Bulsar, Madeleine Slade caught up with the Satyagrahis and watched them as they were being carried in on blood-soaked blankets, still bleeding. She toured the hospital wards and saw the men lying in agony in their beds with swollen testicles and broken heads, gashed faces and lacerated limbs. Later that day she wrote: 'What has become of English honour and English justice? No amount of argument can excuse what they have been doing at Dharasana. India has now realised the true nature of the British Raj and with this realisation the Raj is doomed'.[34]

With Gandhi in prison, his spirit was, as always, inspiring India. The news of the Dharasana atrocities reached all over India and civil disorder was the order of the day everywhere. The British owned shops and textile mills closed due to Hartals. British-made cloth and goods were everywhere heaped up and set alight in bonfires. The liquor shops were closed and women joined the men in picketing all the bazaars and factories and Government offices. Salt Satyagraha had paralysed the country to the point of suffocation. At the same time the land revenue campaign of Vallabhbhai and Dadubhai was winning on all points in the Kheda District (as described in the next chapter). The Government's policy was in total disarray. Something had to be done to stop this agitation, but what? Only a truce called by Gandhi would save the situation. To this end the Viceroy immediately agreed to talks with Gandhi and released eleven of the leaders from detention. The Viceroy was at his wit's end. He allowed intermediaries – Slocombe, Sir Tej Bahadur and M.R. Jayakar – to interview Gandhi and all other important imprisoned Congress leaders to discuss a settlement of the dispute. Lord Irwin soon realised that Gandhi was the real leader and that he should himself hold talks with him. To preface his approach to Gandhi, Lord Irwin made a speech on 17 January 1931 in the Central Legislative Assembly: 'However mistaken any man may think him to be, however deplorable may appear the result of the policy associated with his name, no one can fail to recognise the spiritual force which compels Mr Gandhi to count no sacrifice too great in the cause, as he believes, of the India he loves.'[35]

Within ten days of his speech to the Assembly of true realisation, Lord Irwin set free from jail Mahatma and 19 other leaders of the Congress. This included Vithalbhai J. Patel and Dadubhai P. Desai along with Jawaharlal Nehru, Raj Gopalachari, Sarojini Naidu and others. Motilal Nehru had already been released by reason of his ill health and shortly afterwards he died. The release was unconditional and Congress as an organisation was reinstated as a legal entity by withdrawing the Government ordinance on 14 February. Gandhiji wrote a letter to Lord Irwin to seek an interview for talks with him face to face. On the 16th Gandhi received a reply from Lord Irwin granting him the desired interview. The working committee had formally passed a resolution investing him with the powers of a plenipotentiary to negotiate a settlement in the name of Congress. Now Post-Dharasana Gandhi's authority among the Congress was supreme. In the working committee it was suggested that Gandhi should go alone to negotiate with the Viceroy, no one seemed to oppose this. Vallabhbhai was also accepted as the best organiser of civil disobedience movements in the whole of India – thanks to his victory over the British in Bardoli Satyagraha – thanks also to Dadubhai who always remained unassuming and who shunned power.

Within one year a Nadiad Desai was instrumental in establishing two great leaders as all powerful All-India leaders. From now on until their deaths the control of the entire Congress organisation lay in their hands. The reader has to understand that, until the 21 May raid on Dharasana by 2,000 volunteers organised by Vithalbhai and Dadubhai, the Salt Satyagraha was very low key everywhere and the British Government was not concerned and though there was some disruption, business went on as usual. Lord Irwin wrote to the King, on 24 April 1930: 'As a threat to the monopoly of the Government, this part of his (Gandhi's) programme may be pronounced a failure'.[36] The Government had known that by withdrawing the Congress leaders from the field by arresting them, the people of India and especially those of Gujarat were leaderless and without guidance. They had not counted on Vithalbhai and Dadubhai who had deep insight into the weakness of the Government. Through their parliamentary experience, they knew how and where to hit the Government. Congress leaders mostly opposed constitutionalism because it was not the place for everybody to fight and win the elections to the Councils and Assembly. If you are a constitutionalist, however, you have to deal with people as well as with the Government in the debating chamber where you have to confront the best brains of the Government in person and demonstrate a disciplined and sophisticated approach.

Gandhi had received a favourable reply to his letter to Lord Irwin of 14 February 1931 and they met in Delhi on 17 February for four hours. On the second day the Viceroy was understanding but did not accept any of Gandhi's proposals. There was a long delay until the 27th when the talks were resumed after Lord Irwin received some instructions from Whitehall. In the discussion on 3 March, a formidable difficulty arose in the form of restitution of lands and property in Kheda District and Bardoli Taluka.[37] In the whole civil disobedience movement, until now, no other province or district of India had really suffered seizure of land, except Gujarat, which only involved Kheda District and the Bardoli Taluka. Gandhi insisted that the Viceroy should instruct the Bombay Governor to restore all the land and property. Gandhi was asked to see the Provincial Government, because he (Irwin) had passed a letter to the Government of Bombay, when the Bardoli no-tax campaign was at its height, stating that he would not ask for the restitution of properties to the peasants under any circumstances. He would naturally be most unwilling to go against his own previously stated policy. Gandhi wanted the Viceroy to do it. At last the Viceroy agreed to give a letter to the Bombay Government to help the two gentlemen (the Finance Member and Revenue Member of the Bombay Government) in recovering the confiscated lands. Before this, on 18 February, only on the second day of talks, Gandhi raised the question of Borsad atrocities on women. He demanded an inquiry with the words: 'History offers no parallel to the atrocities committed on women in the Kaira District'.[38] Lord Irwin could not agree and Gandhi did not persist.

Eventually on 5 March 1931, the Gandhi-Irwin Pact with its 21 clauses was signed and released to the press.[39] The Pact included:

Clause (5) – Civil disobedience will effectively be discontinued; Clause (17) – Immovable property, of which possession had been taken under Ordinance IX of 1930, will be returned. Where immovable property has been sold by the Government to third parties, the transaction must be regarded as final, as far as the Government is concerned.

Vallabhbhai saw his nine years' work with the Patidars of Kaira come to nothing. The peasants were disappointed that the sold lands would not be returned. The reinstatement of the Mukhis who had resigned on the advice of Congress leaders during the struggle was in doubt. The Patidars had the impression of being cheated and that Gandhiji's desire for peace took precedence over their vital interests. For the peasants the pact had won nothing. Lord Irwin might have had 'a change of heart' but not local officials, like Garret and Collector Master, who despised Congress as much as ever for its sedition. These officers were not going to pursue a 'liberal policy' in restoring lands and Mukhiships. Vallabhbhai gave his verbal support to the pact and told the peasants to pay their land revenue, but after that made no further attempt to conform to the 'spirit of the pact'.[40] He encouraged the peasants to boycott those who had sheepishly paid their revenue during the civil disobedience, or who had bought Government-confiscated land or taken up resigned Mukhiships. People who associated with these blacklegs were to be fined by their caste Panchayais. Above all, Vallabhbhai insisted that the pact was merely a truce and that within months the struggle would be resumed.

19

LAND REVENUE AGITATION 1930

With the Bardoli victory in his pocket (in January 1930), Sardar began to examine the potential in his own district for starting a similar disobedience movement. Gandhiji had come to know of Sardar's intention in September, immediately after the successful conclusion of Bardoli agitation. He wrote in *Young India*, on 5 September 1929: 'But he needs a Bardoli to make good his leadership. How many Bardolis are there ready in the country today?'. To him the Bardoli situation was extraordinary and that people of Bardoli, unlike the people of Kheda, were exceptionally well prepared. If he tried an All-India campaign, it would in all likelihood result in violence and thus negate the effort. Dadubhai did not entirely dismiss Vallabhbhai's idea. His only worry was that the peasants would lose their land, which is unbearable for any human being. That was the reason why he advocated the Salt Satyagraha to Gandhiji. However isolated, Vallabhbhai needed Dadubhai's help and co-operation, which was readily given. A great deal of correspondence passed between the two of them on this subject. Unfortunately, almost the entire file of Vallabhbhai's letters has been destroyed by the white ants which plague Gujarat in the hot summer months. After my father, Dadubhai, passed away at Nadiad, I came from London and saw the wanton destruction of numerous files of Dadubhai's letters which had been attacked by the white ants. Miraculously, two letters in Vallabhbhai's own handwriting survived. They tell the story of the close friendship of these two leaders who were the shining light of the Kheda District. These letters are reproduced in Appendix 4.[1] Sardar always addressed Dadubhai as 'My Dear Brother' (Priya Bhai Dadubhai). The author has never seen any letters of Sardar to other persons where he has addressed them as 'Priya Bhai'. Such was the brotherly love between the two. Another colleague on similar terms was Vithalbhai Patel, the elder brother of Sardar. Of course, Gandhiji also had great love and affection for Dadubhai.

There is very little correspondence between them that has been saved. However, Nadiad being near Ahmedabad (Sabarmati Ashram) Dadubhai used to drive down in his car as and when Gandhiji needed to be consulted; but especially a once-a-week visit was always made to Sabarmati. When they met they either discussed the situation and progress in the work of Harijan uplift or other social services in Nadiad and the entire Kaira District, or the events in Bombay with the Governor's Legislative Council in which Dadubhai was leader of the opposition from Gujarat (from 1920 to 1930). Also they discussed any new legislation passed by the Council and what effect it would have on any of the future campaigns of Gandhiji. Dadubhai's frequent meetings with the Governor and members of his executive (ministers) were helpful in finding out the general attitude and direction of the Government. Gandhiji was very interested in what went on in Bombay (from Dadubhai) and in Delhi (from Vithalbhai Patel who was President of the Viceroy's Legislative Assembly, from 1925 to 1930). In those days, Gandhiji's politics were much influenced by Vallabhbhai, Dadubhai, Vithalbhai and Motilal Nehru, because these were the leaders representing their regions and also holding important public positions which gave them access to the high echelons of the British Government – Collectors, Commissioners, Governors and the Viceroy and also, lower down in the Government Hierarchy, all the officers – Mamlatdars, District Superintendants of Police and District Judges who treated them honestly and with respect. After all they were members of the Viceroy's Council and/or Governor's Council. In every major campaign that Gandhiji started, he had a prior discussion with one or more of these four leaders; after all they had also to take the field with Gandhiji. To take one example: it was the constant persuasion of Vithalbhai that resulted in Lord Irwin meeting Gandhiji,[2] from which followed the Gandhi-Irwin Pact of March 1931. This was the first pact negotiated and accepted by the Congress. Before that the Government of India did not recognise Congress as an All-India force which could deliver the majority of the people of India. They treated what the Congress said with a pinch of salt. Vithalbhai's letters are there for all to see in Appendix 4.

Jawaharlal Nehru was never in Gandhi's inner circle, nor was he ever consulted about any planned movement. He and Subhas Bose belonged to the youth wing that believed in a violent revolution, like the Russian one, to produce independence. Lord Irwin, even as late as 1931, portrayed Jawaharlal as a communist and a wayward soul.[3] It was only in 1929, when Gandhiji promoted him to be Congress President, that he joined the inner circle and won over the Mahatma in support of his own political ambitions.[4] Partly as a result, after 1930 Vithalbhai changed his opinion of the Mahatma.[5] From 1931 to the end, Vallabhbhai and Dadubhai remained in the Mahatma's camp but with reservations. They clearly saw the Mahatma leaning disproportionately towards Jawaharlal Nehru. From then onwards, Sardar nicknamed Jawaharlal 'Gandhi's Son'. The writer has heard this from Sardar's own lips. Pandit Nehru harvested rich rewards from this relationship – Presidency of Congress at the age of 39! Later, Prime Minister of Independent India. From 1929 to 1946 he remained in the front rank, always seen with the Mahatma, and from 1946 to 1964 he wielded supreme power as the first Prime Minister of India and regularly re-elected to this office until his death. More rewards were to follow from the surname 'Gandhi', which enriched the Nehru dynasty. After Pandit Jawaharlal Nehru, the surname of his descendants is 'Gandhi' instead of 'Nehru' (Indira Gandhi, Rajiv Gandhi, and now the behind-the-curtain prime minister Sonya Gandhi). When K.M. Munshi, the Agriculture Minister of the Government of India, wanted to plant some trees in the Gandhi Samadhi, Sardar told him not to touch the Gandhi Samadhi because that was the monopoly kingdom of Nehru the 'Son of the Mahatma'! (Personally heard by the writer when he visited him in 1950).

In 1929, in the Kheda District, the monsoon was weak. The last few days of showers, which were the most important, had not arrived. Consequently, there was crop failure in the parts of Kheda District lying along the Vatrak river, especially the Matar and Mehmdabad Talukas. Early in January, Vallabhbhai went to these spots at the request of the farmers. Similar requests were received by Dadubhai, who made a speech on the subject from the floor of the Bombay Council Chamber. He also made a representation to the Revenue Member of the Council of Bombay, who subsequently ordered the Collector of Kheda, Alfred Master, to send him the crops report. The Governor had personally taken an interest and had intervened. Vallabhbhai had asked Dadubhai to see the Governor with a view to getting his intervention. The Governor did intervene – Sardar's letter of 20 January 1930 testifies to that. The two letters of 16 and 20 January 1930 clearly show the closest co-operation both enjoyed in the Matar/Mehmdabad peasants' struggle. They clearly show that Vallabhbhai's work was complementary with Dadubhai's efforts and vice versa: full agreement with each other and no divergence as was the case with Jawaharlal Nehru. Nehru had to recognise Sardar's strength in the Congress organisation, but never trusted Sardar. In short, Nehru never considered Sardar in his camp – while Vallabhbhai, Vithalbhai and Dadubhai trusted each other implicitly.

A satyagraha camp was established at Mehmdabad and Congress workers Pandit Ravishankar Maharaj, Pandyaji Mohanlal and others began touring the Taluka advising the peasants to refuse payment of land revenue.[6] The Collector of Kheda, Alfred Master, ordered the Mamlatdar at Mehmdabad to suspend revenue collection in those of the villages of the Mehmdabad Taluka. Vallabhbhai was not satisfied with that. He wanted overall suspension in both Matar and Mehmdabad Talukas.[7] The Collector retreated a little more by ordering more generous suspensions of revenue. Still Vallabhbhai was not satisfied. Finally at the beginning of February, Collector Master announced that all the revenue in Matar and Mehmdabad Talukas would be suspended for the year.[8] So having staved off the Matar and Mehmdabad District agitation, the Bombay Government swiftly acted in accordance with the second letter (29 October 1928) of Irwin to the Governors and arrested Vallabhbhai on 6 March. This was just before he was to begin organising the campaign of non-payment of revenue on a wider scale in the Borsad Taluka. This was the campaign Vallabhbhai started on his own and that also without Gandhi's approval or blessing. It was always going to be a success; Gandhiji had no hand in it yet he received the credit, in the same way he had received the credit for the 21 May 1930 Dharasana raid organised by Vithalbhai and Dadubhai. Throughout the whole period, for nine months (from 4 May 1930 to 25 January 1931) Gandhi was in jail in Poona far away from the action. Jawaharlal was also in jail for nine months (from 14 April 1930 to 25 January 1931, except for seven days from 11 October to 19 October 1930). It is Vithalbhai, Vallabhbhai and Dadubhai who organised and conducted the campaign on all fronts

– salt satyagraha to land-revenue refusal satyagraha. Throughout this period of the first formidable struggle/movement, Dadubhai was the only one of the big leaders to remain for any length of time free to carry on the work. He was put away the last time on 13 October 1930, see Appendix 5. But the work he began, carried on until the Government buckled in January 1931. The lesser leaders and volunteers had the momentum to maintain the progress of the struggle.

Dadubhai had participated continuously in Bardoli (1928), salt (1930) and Kaira land-revenue refusal movement from May to October 1930 more than any of the other Congress leaders. The strain told on him and he decided to retire from active political work. From 1931 to 1936 he played a passive role. Only in 1936, after persuasion from Vallabhbhai, he contested the election for a seat in the Bombay Legislative Council, in which he was successful. He did not accept any ministerial portfolio even though Vallabhbhai requested him to do so. However, he remained a member of the Council until its term ended. From then on he remained an elder statesman in an advisory capacity until his death in 1958.

The efforts of none other than Vithalbhai, Vallabhbhai and Dadubhai first established the Indian National Congress in its role as the major institution of the people of India, in their fight against British Imperialism. From this beginning Congress went on from success to success until it wrested independence from the Raj.

Historians wrongly attributed Vallabhbhai's arrest to Collector Master, assuming that Master acted against the will of the Bombay Government. However, at that time they had no access to the thinking behind this action. Of course we are now in possession of the official thoughts in the form of two letters of Irwin to the Provincial Governors.[9] Also Lord Irwin himself wrote to His Majesty The King on 11 March 1930, just after Vallabhbhai's arrest in the following words: 'The Bombay Government arrested one of the Patel brothers two days ago, the brother of our Assembly President. So far as I can judge, this has been quite a good thing. He was Gandhi's righthand man in organisation and was supposed to be going to lead the movement when Gandhi himself had been withdrawn. The adjournment was moved in the Assembly yesterday to protest against his arrest, but I am glad to say was defeated by a very handsome majority, which is all to the good'.[10]

Lord Irwin was led to believe that Vallabhbhai was going to

join in the Salt Satyagraha and so should be arrested. This was Vithalbhai's plan arranged with Dadubhai when the former was in Nadiad.[11] Attention was drawn to Vallabhbhai whose extraordinary organising capacity was not unknown to the Government. The Government thought that by withdrawing Vallabhbhai, Gandhi would be crippled and would not be able to achieve his objective. In the same letter to the King, Irwin wrote: 'Meanwhile Mr Gandhi has announced his intention of starting off on his march tomorrow, and his march is calculated to take him five days. We have considered the whole situation very fully, and I am quite satisfied that, though it will have regrettable repercussions on our moderate friends, we cannot afford to let the would-be law-breaking forces gather momentum, and that therefore, if and when Gandhi reaches the point of breaking the law, we shall have to arrest him. The only exception to this necessity that I can possibly foresee would be that if his march had been such a fiasco and the whole thing were so ridiculous as merely to be exciting derision, one might be able to leave it alone. But I do not anticipate that this is at all likely to be the kind of setting in which the play will be acted'.[10] Thus it looks as if Irwin kept his options open and that he retained the initiative; Bombay Government to act on his orders.

In the meantime Dadubhai received a letter from the jailer of Sabarmati Prison and also a letter from Gandhiji's secretary, Shri Mahadev Desai, that Vallabhbhai Patel wanted to see him in the gaol on 24 March 1930 at 12 p.m.[12] Dadubhai went to Ahmedabad and met Vallabhbhai in the prison and acquainted him of the situation. By that time Gandhiji had already crossed the River Mahi in a boat to Broach District. Sardar was told of the tumultuous reception that greeted Gandhi in Nadiad on 15 March.[13] He also told him about the developments at Ras on 19 March, when Shivabhai and others requested Gandhiji to allow the 14 villages that had voted, to start non-payment of revenue satyagraha concurrent with the Salt Satyagraha. Gandhi was not in favour of it, but after full discussions he agreed and asked them to act non-violently.[14] Dadubhai told him that he himself was trying to keep the non-revenue campaign alive, but the Salt Satyagraha took priority. He told him that after Gandhiji had broken the salt law at Dandi, the situation would be clearer and perhaps the non-revenue campaign would again have precedence. Sardar wanted to know what his men were doing in the field. Of course, they were at that moment engaged in breaking the salt law, as it needed their urgent attention. Sardar was happy with the progress of the salt campaign, but he was hankering after the non-revenue satyagraha which he considered the key weapon against the Government. At the moment Dadubhai, who had also promised Gandhiji, was engaged in a recruiting campaign for volunteers to go to Dharasana and join Gandhiji in breaking the salt law.

Vallabhbhai remained in jail until 26 June 1930 and during his absence Dadubhai skillfully managed both campaigns. The Congress workers who really went from village to village encouraging Vanar Senas to keep Prabhat Ferries going; selling unlawful salt in small packets to the population, persuading Mukhis, Matadars and Rawanias to resign, worked with redoubled enthusiasm after Gandhiji was arrested on 4 May.

Before Vallabhbhai came back from the jail, Dadubhai had addressed several meetings and gave instructions and advice to the local leaders in the Kaira District. After all, Vallabhbhai had created a giant network of Congress workers in every town and village. These were the same people who kept Dadubhai in touch with local developments. Wherever it was necessary, Dadubhai went to the spot and gave all the advice and support that was possible. He also got in touch with local officials and explained to them their duty to the country. As an example, in Appendix 4, the Patrika of one such meeting and the letter covering such meeting will give an idea of Dadubhai's work in the absence of Vallabhbhai.[15] The letter is from Shvabhai Ashabhai, joint secretary of satyagraha Chhavni Borsad, of 30 April 1930 addressed to Dadubhai Desai informing him of a conference on 5 May of Mukhi, Matadars and Rawanias of various villages, who had resigned their Government posts. The conference's aim was to set up a Mukhi Matadar Mandal. Also ten villages had definitely decided to refuse payment of the current year's land revenue. They needed to give proper instructions to these peasants and thank them and encourage them in their efforts to aid the independence struggle. For this Dadubhai's presence was necessary. So a request was made by him and Lallubhai Patel for Dadubhai to come to the conference. This was a typical conference among a number of similar ones the leaders had to attend and to influence their outcome. Sardar was a great organiser and, before he was arrested, the whole structure of the campaign was in place and was functioning. Dadubhai had to run the machinery in an efficient way, and that is what he did till Vallabhbhai came back on 26 June 1930 after his release. Subsequently, Sardar took the reins and carried on the campaign until 1st August when he was arrested again.

On 20 May 1930 Dadubhai, as detailed in Chapter 18, went to Dharasana in company with Vithalbhai to manage the massive historic raid by over 2,000 volunteers. Having accomplished the work he returned to Nadiad.

After 25 May Dadubhai left Dharasana and, returning to Nadiad on 31 May, he organised a mass meeting of the peasants of Gujarat, as a challenge of war to the government by the Kaira District. That meeting passed several resolutions including one for non-payment of land revenue, Bardoli-style. Its effectiveness can be judged from the report of Bombay Government to the Central Government in New Delhi.

On 10 May 1930 Bardoli Taluka also voted to refuse payment of land revenue. On 31 May a Kheda District Peasant Conference was held at Nadiad and a resolution proposed by Dadubhai Desai (Chairman of the reception committee) calling for land revenue-refusal.[16] He said that the non-cooperation movement had been initiated by this very district and that the first sacrifice in the present war of independence had been made by this district. There was a greater veneration for Gandhiji in this district than for anyone else. This district could not tolerate in any way his internment by Government. It would not be regarded as improper if this district has taken any step for his release. The necessity for convening the conference had been felt to be especially urgent in order to express resentment at this policy of repression adopted by the Government. The duty of non-payment of revenue devolved upon all peasants.

After discussion by delegates from various Talukas of Kheda District, seven resolutions were passed. They included those regarding non-payment of land revenue, wearing pure (genuine) Khaddar, prohibition of liquor and one resolution urging the Government servants, who had not resigned, to do so now. A further vow was taken that until Mahatma Gandhi and Sardar Vallabhbhai were liberated, no land revenue would be paid at all.

In the absence of Sardar, Dadubhai kept up the momentum of the movement, making speeches and visiting village after village. As a result the Kaira District came to the forefront of the freedom struggle. The principal centres were Nadiad, Anand and Borsad

Talukas in Kaira, Jambusar in Broach and Bardoli in Surat. The non-revenue campaign was successful enough to annoy Governor Sykes. From Bardoli up to the Gandhi-Irwin Pact only Rs.20,000 out of a revenue quota of Rs.397,000 could be collected by the Government. In Kheda the non-revenue campaign involved 15,000 peasants. The Bombay Government's problems in dealing with the situation were further complicated by the weakness of the police in Kheda. Recruiting, as well as discipline, were not up to standard. In the face of police cruelty there were mass desertions to the villages. Villagers moved to the adjoining Baroda State. According to the official Government's fortnightly report, Kheda Patidars were seen camped on the Baroda border.[17]

By May 1930, most villages in Kheda had already paid their 1929/30 land revenue instalment. However, those numbering about 20 villages in Nadiad and Borsad Taluka had yet to pay their instalment. These were the villages on which the satyagrahi leaders concentrated. As a result these villages refused to pay. By late June the growing solidarity amongst all classes of Patidars was beginning to worry the Government of Bombay. On 17 June they wrote a long and confidential letter to the Home Department of the Government of India, stating that the campaign for the non-payment of land revenue has been strongly organised in the districts of Ahmedabad, Kaira, Broach and Surat. To collect the land revenue they proposed, and asked for, Government of India's consent to utilise the coercive powers which they possess under the provision of the Bombay Land Revenue Code, such as the attachment of moveable property and the arrest of defaulters. The matter which they wished specially to bring to the notice of the Government of India, was the policy which they propose to enforce in respect of the forfeiture and sale of all holdings of defaulters.[18] The Bombay Government asked for assurances from the centre that once the forfeited land had been sold to a third party, that land will not be returned in future. The same applied to those Mukhis who had resigned from the Government.

The Congress volunteers were assuring the peasants that the confiscated land would be returned to them as soon as a settlement was arrived at with the Government and Mukhis were also told that they will get their jobs back, as had happened after the Bardoli settlement. The Government of India, on 3 July 1930, replied in affirmation to the policy spelt out by the Bombay Government and assured them that whatever action they took as regards the forfeiture of land and the Mukhis who resigned, would be permanent and there would be no going back on that assurance in the future.[19] This concession by the Government of India was to limit its negotiating powers with the Congress at a future date.

As for the non-revenue campaign, it was in full swing in the Nadiad Taluka and the area south of the River Shedi, especially among the Patidars. Most of them removed their cattle and belongings to the Gaikwar Territory of Baroda.[20] The 1930 crop was going to be good as the monsoon had arrived and the timing of the rains was favourable. Payment date of full revenue was in December. The villagers expected to harvest and sell the produce before that date and transfer the proceeds to Baroda State, thus escaping the revenue collectors. To forestall this, the Collector Master brought forward the revenue collection date to 8 October. He also gave the police and revenue officers carte blanche to use any methods they liked on the Patels who failed to pay in time. In Borsad Taluka, the new Mamlatdar Mohanlal Shah (from OD), who had become notorious as a strict and strong-handed revenue collector during the 1928 Bardoli Satyagraha, perpetrating 'Zulum' by each time taking with him a lorry-load of policemen and letting them loose on the unsuspecting villagers and their families. Peasants were beaten, their gold ornaments snatched from their bodies and necks, their kitchen earthenwares smashed, anyone wearing a white cap (Gandhi cap) being specially selected for harsher treatment. They were tied up with rope and then thrashed with sticks.[21] These atrocities continued for several months. In November 1931, Verrier Elwin who toured the Borsad Taluka verified these reports of brutality by police in the *Bombay Chronicle* and found 'overwhelming and consistent evidence of severe beating and the grossest insult and abuse…', by Indian officials, connived at by their British superiors.[22] In the Kaira District south of the River Shedi about three-fifths of all Patidar-dominated villages participated in the non-revenue campaign.

In the civil disobedience movement kinship link through the gol played the most positive part. Patidars of the following five gols resolved to support the movement: Vallabhbhai, Dadubhai and the local leaders like Ashabhai Shivabhai, Lallubhai, Raojibhai and others attended meetings of these gols and exhorted them to follow the campaign by non-payment of the revenue:[23]

Borsad Taluka	–	Gol of 21 villages
	–	Gol of 16 villages
	–	Gol of 14 villages
Nadiad Taluka	–	Gol of 22 villages
Petlad Taluka	–	Gol of 16 villages.[24]

Another pressure to join the movement came from contacts based on hypergamous marriages. Patidars of superior villages who had taken wives from the Patidars of lesser villages were in a position to influence them to make them follow their path. Usually these Patidars of lesser villages were rich and influential in their own villages, and hence they were able to get their whole village Gol to join the movement.

As for the superior gols of six, five, nine and twenty-seven, the gol could not be used for supporting the movement. Vallabhbhai himself was angry with some of the Karamsad Patels who did not follow him. On one occasion he told Dadubhai that Karamsad had betrayed him and that he had greater faith in the loyalty of Nadiad Patidars. They never let him down. In these superior gols the Patidars were prosperous and consequently they followed their own ways. However, the majority contributed heavily towards the movement by offering funds as well as suffering – in fact they were also a source of strength for Vallabhbhai.

Some of the Nadiad Desais, especially Gopaldas, Girdhardas and Bhagwandas, opposed the agitation and paid land revenue on their lands. Being one of the principal leaders of the movement Dadubhai refused to pay the land revenue on his lands in Salun and Ajupura.[25] Strong support for the movement came from the villages in the area bordering the Baroda State territory; 71 per cent of Hijratis to Pij and surrounding Baroda territory; from Nadiad Taluka came from villages surrounding Narsanda. The lead of the Narsanda Patidars was valuable to the revenue campaign because villages around it naturally followed their leaders who were full of patriotic fervour. In the gol of five, Pij was a prominent member and its younger Patidars helped the Hijratis as much as they could. 'Kheda Jilla Patrika' was secretly printed in Pij and then distributed to the villages. In the British India of Chaklashi and Uttarsanda the movement was weak. Some Patidars refused to pay, but not all. In Uttarsanda the Congress leader Khushalbhai Patel came from an impoverished family and as such he could not influence richer peasant families. In Matar Taluka six villages dominated by Patidars took part in the campaign, but the villages Barayias and Rajputs took no part. Patidars of Alindra in Matar Taluka paid their revenue, so also those of Traj which was dominated by its landlord, Mukhi Chhotabhai who remained loyal to the Government. There was strong movement in Limbasi, Tranja and Devataj. These villages were near Sojitra which though in the Baroda Territory strongly supported the movement. Raojibhai Manibhai Patel came from Sojitra and he was a pillar of strength at the Nadiad headquarters of the Kheda Jilla Samiti. In Anand Taluka Boriavi stood out as the leading centre of the campaign. Some Patels from Anand and Karamsad took up the banner, but many of them remained loyal to the Government. Those Patidars who joined the movement and also became Hijratis went over to Bakrol which was in the Baroda State. The town of Umreth failed to provide a lead. It was dominated by Khandelval Brahmins who opposed the Gandhi creed. In Od the movement had collapsed but the adjoining village of Thamna gave solid support to the Congress.[26]

Soon after the Hijrat started, Master boasted that within two weeks the movement within Kheda District would be dead.[27] His confidence was based on the announcement earlier that the Congress organisation was declared unlawful in the Bombay Presidency. Sixty-seven Congress-linked organisations in Kheda were declared unlawful and 17 Congress buildings, including the headquarters of the District Congress Committee in Nadiad, were taken possession of by the police. Dadubhai's haveli was also raided and officers took away sacks of files and papers.[28] However, the Congress organisation moved to Baroda just before the seizure by the Government. For instance, Borsad Taluka Congress Committee was quickly moved to Bhadran, which was not only Baroda Territory but also the very town of Shivabhai Ashabhai Patel who was for a long time a stalwart of Congress there. One of his letters to Dadubhai is quoted earlier in this chapter. He kept away in person from Congress demonstrations which he had actually organised. He would move to Gaikwar Territory the moment police were searching for him. He regularly produced the Borsad Satyagraha Samachar Patrika and distributed it in British Territory. Sojitra (Baroda State) became the headquarters of Matar Taluka Congress Committee, Nadiad Taluka Congress Committee as well as the Kheda Jilla Congress Committee. Quarters were moved to Pij (Baroda), out of reach of British Authorities. Congress Chhavnis of Bodal and Anklav were taken to Joshikua (Baroda). Ras Congress establishment was removed to Jhardla (Baroda). All these were set up as camps in the Gaikwar Territory. The Congress workers used to visit these camps and tried to keep up the spirit of the Hijratis assuring them that their lands will be returned to them once the Congress got a settlement with the Government.

Collector Master also employed other tactics to encourage Baraiyas, Patanvadias and Muslims to buy cheaply the repossessed land of the Patels. Normally, being the traditional enemies of Patels, they were helpful to the Government.[29] It ran like this: 'A scheme is now on foot to sell Patidar lands to Dharalas, and if this materialises, the chief difficulty of land revenue collection will disappear. Once Dharalas buy Patidar lands, the rest of Patidars will pay up at once.'

The local officials and police also encouraged the lower castes to loot the properties of absent Patidars, plunder their crops and burn their houses, as mentioned earlier. The Mamlatdar of Borsad, Mohanlal Shah, was one of the chief instigators of these criminal activities. At the village of Asodar, Shah told an assembly of Dharala peasants:[30] 'Those who took away your land during the great famine of 1899–1900 now pose as servants of the people. I have now come to offer you back your land for five seers of corn. If you have ten rupees you can buy 200 bighas of land. I can give you ten bighas of land with standing crop for ten rupees. I can give you police protection so that you can harvest the crop safely. If your neighbour does not pay his revenue, you can pay it for him and get his land transferred to your name.'

In another village he said:[31] 'Those who want Mukhiship, Patidar lands with standing crops and Patidar houses, come to me. Those in debt to Patidar should not repay the money. Do not pay any rent either. If they come to ask for payment, refuse them and beat them if necessary. If anybody gets killed, I will support you. If somebody threatens you to get money from you, come to my office and declare that you are unable to pay. I was born to emancipate the Barayias and Patanvadyas.'

On 26 June Vallabhbhai was released from prison and immediately took over the reins of the movement from Dadubhai. But Sardar's presence was not to be for long for, as he went to Bombay to attend the ceremony of Lokmanya Tilak's anniversary, he was arrested and taken away. On 1 August he was sentenced to three months in jail. So once again Dadubhai was left to carry on the direction of the Kheda campaign alone. However, he too was withdrawn on 10 October and sentenced to five months' imprisonment on 13 October 1930.[32] Nonetheless the movement carried on with the same vigour through the work of local leaders and other Congress activists, as well as its own momentum.

On 24 October Mohanlal Shah violated the Baroda State Government area by entering it at Joshikuva and beating up some peasants who were in fact Baroda subjects. When he was told that he was in Baroda Territory, he remarked: 'Who is the Gaekwad? He is our slave!' The Baroda State authorities did not like that and they became very angry.[33] H.M. Brailsford, who visited Kheda in October, had witnessed the lathi charge ordered by Shah and had complained to the Divisional Commissioner Hugh Garrett, who promised to look into the matter.[34]

A delegation of Kheda Hijratis went to Bombay in November to acquaint the Indian Merchant Chambers and Diamond Merchants' Association as well as Mulji Jetha market with the atrocities perpetrated by the authorities. As a result they sent representatives to Borsad to see for themselves. When they saw the atrocities, they reported what they had seen to Bombay newspapers who published them. So now 'Borsad Atrocities' were known all over the country.[35] By November the policy of repression was seen as a failure. The Patidar peasant could not be intimidated. The Government's strategy and its prestige were in tatters.

In December the Bombay Government sent its revenue member, Frank Hudson, to see for himself and weigh up the deteriorating situation in the Kheda District. He soon realised that the policy of repression had failed miserably and that the Patidars were more resolute than ever. As a placatory measure he replaced Mohanlal Shah with the more lenient Solomon Benjamin who was the Mamlatdar in Mehmdabad. His orders were to confiscate the land and property of Hijratis rather than terrorising them. However, when the land came up for auction, the local people were scared of the wrath of the Patidars or did not have enough money to buy the offered land. Consequently only some land changed hands. By the end of February 1931, 1,742 acres of land were confiscated in the Kheda District. In Borsad Taluka 785 acres from ten villages were sold at an average price of eleven rupees an acre, this price being about one-tenth of the real value. By 15 March the Government had collected Rs.169,933 against the total due revenue of Rs.396,324.[36] This was not satisfactory, especially in view of peasant determination and resistance which showed no sign of abating. As Hardiman writes: 'In March 1931 Congress was in a position of great advantage. The British had failed to break the movement and had lost control in key areas of rural Gujarat. With the start of the slump in agricultural prices, civil disobedience was set to flare up on a scale which would have made 1930 seem insignificant. It was at this stage that Gandhi called off the movement.'[37]

Prior to that, the British had realised that they were on the losing side and in order to woo the Congress the following statement was issued by His Excellency the Governor-General on 25 January 1931: 'In order to provide opportunity for consideration of the statement made by the Prime Minister on 19 January, my Government, in consultation with local Governments, have thought it right that members of the Working Committee of the All India Congress Committee should enjoy full liberty of discussion between themselves and with those who acted as members of the Committee since 1 January 1930.

In accordance with this decision and with this object and in order that there may be no legal bar to any meeting they may wish to hold, the notification declaring the Committee to be an unlawful association under the Criminal Law Amendments Act, will be withdrawn by all local Governments and action will be taken for the release of Mr Gandhi and others who are now members of the Committee or who have acted as such since 1 January 1930.

My Government will impose no conditions on these releases, because we feel that the best hope of restoration of peaceful conditions lies in discussions being conducted by those concerned under terms of unconditional liberty. Our action has been taken in pursuance of a sincere desire to assist the creation of such peaceful conditions as would enable the Government to implement the undertaking given by the Prime Minister that if civil quiet were proclaimed and assured, the Government would not be backward in response.

I am content to trust those who will be affected by our decision to act in the same spirit as inspired it, and I am confident that they will recognise the importance of securing for those grave issues calm and dispassionate examination.'

The above announcement by the Viceroy shows clearly the defeat of the British. The mass movement was truly successful enough to merit the close attention and respect of the Government. This was after the Government's repeated efforts through Jayakar-Sapru negotiations to effect a compromise with the jailed leaders of Congress, including Gandhi. The last letter rejecting any compromise by the Congress leaders from Yerawada Central Prison was on 5 September 1930. After that the Round Table Conference met in London on 12 November 1930 with 86 delegates in all, 57 from British India and 16 from native states, the remaining 13 being from the British political parties. There was no Congress delegate as they had declined to join the Round Table Conference.

On 19 January 1931 the plenary session was held. The British Prime Minister's closing speech ended with: 'If in the meantime there is response to the Viceroy's appeal, from those engaged at present in civil disobedience, steps will be taken to enlist their services.' Within a week of the utterance of these words of the British Prime Minister, the Viceroy made the statement of 25 January 1931 (see above). On 31 January Gandhi wrote a letter to Lord Irwin drawing his attention to the police excesses in the country and particularly to the assault on the women at Borsad on 21 January 1931, and asked for an enquiry into the conduct of the police.

On that day, 21 January, there had been a demonstration by 1,300 women in Borsad. Most of these women were Patidars from Hijarat (camps in the Gaekwad territory). Police resorted to a lathi charge to break up the meeting. In the course of this action some women received severe beatings. Gangaben Vaidya, who was a member of Sabarmati Ashram, was the leader of the demonstration and she wrote to Gandhi in Allahabad about how she and others were beaten by the police.[38] As a result, on 31 January, Gandhi wrote in a letter to Irwin: 'History offers no parallel to the atrocities committed on the women in the Kaira District.'

Immediately after his release from jail on 26 January, Gandhi and Vallabhbhai had gone to the Allahabad hospital to see the ailing Motilal Nehru. Gandhi stayed in North India until after Motilal's death (7 February 1931). He had had talks with Vithalbhai in the hospital. Vithalbhai noted that Gandhi was all out for peace at any cost. He told Gandhi that negotiations and talk of peace in the midst of a raging battle would be its undoing, would deprive it of all momentum, would sidetrack the essentials and would kill all enthusiasm. If a compromise had to be resorted to, it would have been infinitely more beneficial for the Congress to have attended the First Round Table Conference. It would have at least spared the country of untold suffering through which she had to go.

Vallabhbhai returned to Gujarat on 4 February and stayed there until 18 February, touring the districts and meeting the peasants. Dadubhai was also released on the same day, 26 January, and going straight to Nadiad he toured the whole Kheda District and assessed the situation. He repossessed the sequestered headquarters of the Kheda District Congress at Nadiad, of which he was the President. He met Vallabhbhai at Ahmedabad on 5 February and acquainted him with the situation in Nadiad, Ras, Borsad and other parts. Later they both toured the areas and encouraged the population in what they were doing. The civil disobedience movement was going on well and at full speed, even in their absence. They asked the Hijratis to continue the struggle, since they did not know the real intention of the Government in releasing them while the struggle was going on. The Congress was still at war with the Government and was on a winning path. Vallabhbhai weighed up the situation *vis-à-vis* the peasants and their problems. He had discussions with Dadubhai about the requirements of the peasants if a negotiated settlement was to be produced by Gandhi in Delhi. It had been the peasants who gave substance to the movement and how could anybody flout their rights?

As Vithalbhai was sick in Bombay, he could not attend the Working Committee meeting at Delhi which appointed Gandhiji as the sole representative of Congress to negotiate with the Viceroy. Vallabhbhai also was in Kaira and reached Delhi on 18 February, by then Gandhi had already met Irwin for two days. Thus neither of the two Patels was present to stop Gandhi making any mistake at the start of the negotiations. Further in the negotiations, Vithalbhai also would not have allowed the Government to escape the scrutiny of the atrocities of the police and other officers.

As mentioned in the last Chapter, Gandhiji had sent a letter to the Viceroy asking for an interview to talk to him as man to man. An affirmative reply came on 16 February on which date Gandhi and the members of the Working Committee left for Delhi from Allahabad. Vallabhbhai was at the time in Kheda and could reach

Delhi only on 18 February, one day later than Gandhiji. Gandhiji saw the Viceroy on 17 February and talked with him for four hours. On the second day of his meeting with the Viceroy (18 February) he raised the question of the Borsad atrocities, but failed to make the return of confiscated land a priority.[39] Vallabhbhai came to Delhi just after this and he was furious about such an omission. He told the Mahatma if the land was not returned to the peasants, the pact would not be accepted in Gujarat.[40]

Gandhi found himself trapped in this quagmire, mainly on account his being away from Gujarat for the period he was in jail and not knowing at first hand the feelings of the people of Gujarat. When he saw the Viceroy on 17 February he had no time to go to Gujarat and feel the pulse of the peasants and Congress activists of Kheda and Bardoli. Perhaps, while confined at Yerawada, he did not realise that Kheda District and Bardoli Taluka had done more than any region of India; the weight of numbers and the persistance they displayed were not matched by the rest of India. To Vallabhbhai's mind the entire power displayed by the Congress lay in Gujarat and its peasantry.

The Congress Working Committee, in their wisdom, had nominated Gandhi alone to deal with and negotiate with the Viceroy. So he had gone alone to the Viceroy's mansion (the new mansion designed by Lutyens) and faced not only the Viceroy but an array of his advisers. Talks went on intermittently till 4 March. Every evening Gandhi came back to tell the Working Committee the essence of the talks. On the first day he pressed more about an investigation of police atrocities at Borsad rather than the restoration of confiscated land. Next day, in the evening, when Vallabhbhai joined the Congress Working Committee at Delhi, he asked Gandhiji why he had not made the issue of restoring the confiscated land of Gujarat cultivators as the basis for negotiations? Hardiman writes in his book:[41] 'Without Vallabhbhai's guidance, Gandhi misjudged the feelings of Gujarat peasants. He thought they were more upset by police atrocities, particularly the incident of 21 January'. Thus Gandhi made a Himalayan mistake in not making the return of confiscated land a priority. All along Vallabhbhai, Dadubhai and all the Congress activists had told and promised the peasants that confiscated land would be returned to them once a settlement was reached. So on 27 February Gandhi, belatedly but firmly, raised this question with Irwin.[42] In reply Gandhi was told that the Government of India could not go back on the promise given to the Bombay Government on 4 July 1930, that all land and property confiscated will remain confiscated and also the Mukhis and other office holders who resigned would not be reinstated.[43] All that Gandhi received from Irwin was a promise that confiscated land not yet sold would be returned and that the Government would pursue a liberal policy in regard to the reinstatement of the Mukhis.

On 5 March the Mahatma and Irwin put their signature to the so-called Gandhi-Irwin Pact.[44] The terms of the pact in brief were as follows: Gandhi and Congress agreed:

1 To suspend the civil disobedience movement;
2 To participate in the forthcoming second Round Table Conference in London;
3 To forget the demand for an investigation into the allegations of police atrocities in different parts of India.

The Viceroy, on behalf of the Government, agreed:

1 To release all political prisoners in connection with the non-violent movement;
2 To restore confiscated land and property to owners where it had not already been sold or auctioned by the Government;
3 To withdraw the emergency ordinances;
4 To permit people who live within a certain distance of the seashore to collect or manufacture salt free of duty;
5 To permit peaceful picketing of liquor, opium and foreign cloth shops. The last item designed not as a discrimination against British goods but as an encouragement to the Swadeshi movement (i.e. indigenous industries).[45]

This pact had really nothing of value for Congress. For a long time the Congress had always insisted on an assurance from the Government regarding the granting of dominion status. The 1930 fight was launched for attaining this. Who would suspend the movement without such an assurance belies belief. How could Gandhi, an astute politician, miss this point? In the entire negotiations there was no assurance from the Government about Dominion status.

Subhas writes in his book:

> On the demand for an enquiry into the police atrocities, the Mahatma had been informed that if he stuck to it till the breaking-point, the Government would yield. Nevertheless he voluntarily gave up the demand on an appeal from the Viceroy. With better bargaining, even in March 1931, one could have extracted more from the Government, because they were really anxious for a settlement. But men with fixed ideas are not well qualified for political bargaining. So far as Mahatma is concerned, he alternates between obstinacy and leniency, and moreover he is too susceptible to personal appeals. With such habits of mind it is difficult to get the better of one's opponent in political bargaining. The Delhi truce was a great help to the Government. It gave them time to inquire more deeply into the tactics of the Congress and thereafter to perfect their machinery for dealing with that body in future. In the case of the Congress, the pact had a soporific effect. The enthusiasm of the people began to evaporate and it was out of public enthusiasm that one got men and money for a non-violent mass movement. While the Government could resume their activities at any time, because they had no dearth of men or money; the Congress would have to wait till public enthusiasm could be worked up once again.[46]

If the pact had provided for an enquiry into atrocities by the police and other officers, it would have resulted in a proper investigation of such actions by officers in future. In the later movements spread over ten years, the police excesses continued without restraint. The 1942 Quit India movement experienced unbelievable atrocities. The writer of this book personally experienced such police brutality. The occasion was on 15 September when the writer was a student at Bombay University. He organised a peaceful protest meeting at 'Bhat Bazar' in Bombay. A crowd of about 2,000 had assembled and, as the writer was about to make his speech from the dais, police with sticks and military police with bare bayonets charged on the crowd. Many were beaten severely along with the writer who after a few hours woke up in the Worli temporary prison. He was seriously bruised and was bleeding from his right leg and from the right side of his head. He was kept in atrocious conditions in the prison until released after six months. Later, after India became free, he was awarded 'Sanman Patra' by the Bombay Government. All those who had been jailed were awarded this title. Vithalbhai was released on 25 January 1931, along with all others. But after his release, he went straight into hospital because he was seriously ill.

Another embarrassing situation had arisen when nominations for the Presidency of the ensuing session of the Congress were invited from the Provincial Congress Committees. Vithalbhai came to know that he was going to be proposed by most of the Committees. However, it was suddenly decreed from high command offices that due to abnormal and unsettling conditions during the year, the normal procedure would not be adopted. In its place the Working Committee would elect the next President. This Working Committee, under the inescapable influence of the Mahatma, nominated Vallabhbhai to be President. This was the unkindest cut of all, Vithalbhai certainly would not have put up his name against his brother. But the implied humiliation could not but rankle in his heart. After this, on 24 February 1931, Vithalbhai left for further treatment in Europe.[47]

To Vithalbhai's mind what the Government agreed to was simply this: that if the civil disobedience movement was withdrawn, Government would also withdraw the consequent repression. Concerning the question of the constitution, the Government did not give even an inch beyond what the first Round Table Conference had already arrived at. The salt laws were to remain almost as they were and picketing did not permit the distinction in respect of British goods. Most thinking people could not believe their eyes when they saw the terms of the pact in print. They asked: 'Was it for this that thousands of men and women invited the rigours of prison life? Was it for this that thousands of men and women underwent the privations and sufferings which had been inflicted on them by petty officers of the Government? Was it for this that the Dharasana volunteers bore the lathi charge and suffered serious injuries?' They complained, but to whom? Such was the hold of Gandhi on the masses of India, that no one dare tell him that he was wrong, except for the people of Gujarat who were in a minority. Motilal Nehru had passed away, Vithalbhai was out of India and there was no third man in the whole Congress who could take any liberty with Gandhiji. Jawaharlal could do it, but he was Gandhi's obedient son. The All-India Congress Committee met on 26 March. When Dadubhai asked Gandhiji why he succumbed to such easy terms for the Raj, his reply was: 'Dadubhai, this is the first step, future struggle will see us victorious. No one should worry about the present because truth will ultimately triumph'. When asked about the confiscated land that had been sold, his reply was that we should all work to persuade the purchasers to give back the land to the real owners. At the Congress session held on 29 March at Karachi, the resolution supporting the pact was passed. Gandhi was vindicated even though the pact gave nothing to the country nor to the suffering people of Gujarat. But the Gandhi-Irwin Pact had betrayed them. Sardar's nine years' work had come to nothing.

To sum up, Gandhi was in prison from 10 March 1922 to 5 February 1924. Thus he could not attend the Gaya Indian National Congress meeting in 1922, nor the Special Delhi Session September 1923, nor the annual session at Cocanada in 1923. He was also absent from doing any relief work in Gujarat after the flood damage of 1926. By the middle of 1927, the leadership of the Congress was on the whole found wanting. While Mahatma Gandhi was suffering from acute mental depression brought on by the failure of his satyagraha and was living in retirement from active politics right until the start of the Salt Satyagraha on 12 March 1930. Motilal Nehru had left for Europe on private business. In the circumstances the responsibility of leadership was vested in Srinivas Ayengar who was not really an all-India figure at that time.

When Dadubhai started the Bardoli Satyagraha on 6 September 1927, Gandhi was in Ahmedabad and did not visit Bardoli until 6 August 1928. By then the Bardoli settlement had been nearly finalised by Vallabhbhai with the help of Dadubhai.

During the entire period of 1922 to 1927 Vithalbhai, Vallabhbhai and Dadubhai were ceaselessly furthering the Nation's cause in various ways. Vithalbhai was President of the Central Legislative Assembly, Vallabhbhai was working constructively as President of Ahmedabad Municipal Corporation. He was involved in relief work also in training and organising the Congress volunteer force for future satyagraha. Dadubhai was busy as leader of the Gujarat opposition in the Bombay Governor's Legislative Council as well as helping Vallabhbhai in his work whenever required. It was these three stalwarts who maintained the struggle for freedom and kept the Congress in the public limelight.

The charts which follow show the Office Bearers of the Indian National Congress for the period discussed in Part 2 of this book. Also shown are the dates when the leaders were imprisoned.

INDIAN NATIONAL CONGRESS; OFFICE BEARERS

	VITHALBHAI	VALLABHBHAI	GANDHIJI
Bombay Sept 1918	Chairman of the Reception Committee		
Delhi 26/12/1918	Joint General Secretary		
Amritsar 26/12/1919	Joint General Secretary		
Calcutta Sept 1920 Special Congress	Joint General Secretary		
Ahmedabad 27/12/1921	Chairman of the Reception Committee		
Cocanada 28/12/1923			
Belgaum 26/12/1924			President
Gauhati 26/12/1926	Joint General Secretary		
Madras 26/12/1927	As President of		
Calcutta 29/12/1928	Legislative Assembly		
Lahore 25/12/1929	He resigned C.W.C. membership		
1930	No Congress meeting – illegal due to Salt Satyagraha		
Karachi March 1931		President	
Delhi April 1932	Held while under ban		
Calcutta March 1933			
Bombay 24/10/1934			

Vithalbhai's absence from holding any post in the Congress was due to his involvement in constitutional affairs – being a Member of the Central Legislative Assembly from 1923 till 1930 continuously, which period included the Presidency of Central Assembly from 22 August 1925 till May 1930. As its President, he had to resign from Congress.

INDIAN NATIONAL CONGRESS; LEADERS' PRISON TERMS

GANDHI	VALLABHBHAI	VITHALBHAI	DADUBHAI	NEHRU	MOTILAL
10/3/1922 arrested 5/2/1924 released		21/5/1930 arrested 27/5/1930 present at Rawalpindi committee meeting			
4/5/1930 arrested	7/3/1930 arrested	28/8/1930 arrested		14/4/1930 arrested (salt act)	30/6/1930 arrested
	26/6/1930 released				
	1/8/1930 arrested		13/10/1930 arrested		
25/1/1931 released 17/2/1931 met Irwin 4/3/1931 Gandhi-Irwin Pact	25/1/1931 released	25/1/1931 released to hospital 24/2/1931 left for Europe	25/1/1931 released	25/1/1931 released	20/1/1931 released 7/2/1931 died
4/1/1932 arrested	4/1/1932 arrested				
1933 released					
	14/1/1934 released			?/2/1934 arrested	
				4/9/1935 released	
	19/11/1940 arrested			22/10/1940 arrested	
	20/8/1941 released			4/12/1941 released	
9/8/1942 arrested	9/8/1942 arrested			9/8/1942 arrested	
6/5/1944 released					
	15/6/1945 released			15/6/1945 released	

Also the present Author was imprisoned from 15/9/1942 to 15/3/1943.

20

THE TRUTH DISTORTED?

The preceding chapters detail the main battles in the struggle of the Indian people against British rule. The grievances were everywhere but active resistance was centred on the region of Gujarat, the dynamic nerve centre of India. There the leadership was concentrated in the Patidar community, which produced the authoritative figures of: Purushottamdas Desai, Vallabhbhai Patel, Vithalbhai Patel and Dadubhai Desai. Their initial efforts were built upon by Gandhi and later by Nehru.

A study of existing histories will perhaps show a different emphasis to the above. Credit and publicity have been showered upon Gandhi and Nehru so as to overshadow the major and decisive contributions made by others in the struggle to achieve freedom.

What would seem to be an authoritative record of the period is the five volume 'A Centenary History of the Indian National Congress (1885–1985)', written by eleven contributers under the general editorship of B.N. Pande. This was published in 1985 jointly by the All India Congress Committee and Vikas Publishing House Private Limited of Bombay. Triumphantly released by the Prime Minister, Rajiv Gandhi, with a foreword in praise of Nehru's leadership. On page 466 of volume two of the above, the Bardoli Satyagraha is described as follows:

> When months of petitions, demonstrations and protests organised under the leadership of Vallabhbhai Patel and the overall guidance of Mahatma Gandhi failed to move the Government, a Satyagraha was launched declaring that the revenue demand would not be paid.

Then comes the following quotation:

> 'The Mahatma', highlights this grim yet fascinating mass struggle launched under the Congress banner.

These statements do not have any supporting references and are patently untrue. An accurate account, fully supported by historical documents, is as follows:

> The months of petitions, demonstrations and protests, organised under the leadership of Dadubhai Desai and without any guidance from Mahatma Gandhi, led to the Bardoli Satyagraha. This was launched by Dadubhai and his Khedut Mandal on 6 September 1927. Gandhiji had neither directed this nor did he have anything to do with its inception or beginning. From 6 September 1927 until 4 February 1928, only Dadubhai and Khedut Mandal kept the campaign going. Then Dadubhai went to Ahmedabad and acquainted Gandhi and Vallabhbhai with news of the movement. What was needed was a rabble-rousing speaker such as Vallabhbhai. After prolonged discussions, Vallabhbhai was persuaded to join and take over the movement. He accompanied Dadubhai back to Bardoli on 4 February 1928, i.e. a full five months after the start of the no revenue payment campaign. On their arrival, a conference was held of the peasants of Bardoli Taluka. It was there that Vallabhbhai reluctantly agreed to become President of the conference, taking over from Dadubhai who resigned in his favour.

Gandhiji had attempted, in 1921, to organise a non-cooperation movement in Bardoli, but this had been a complete failure. However, in 1927–1928 Dadubhai and Vallabhbhai had succeeded. Victory in the Bardoli struggle now gave the Congress leaders an infallible tool against the British administration. From this time on, in every political action, the Congress leaders vigorously championed the cause of the peasants to increase their own political power.

This aspect of the Bardoli struggle is supported by Shirin Mehta in her book 'The Peasantry and Nationalism'. She writes:

> In fact after the failure of the non-cooperation movement of 1921, the Bardoli struggle came as a god-sent opportunity to the Congress workers. The failure of the 1921 movement had demoralised a large number of workers and even the efficacy

> of the Gandhian techniques of political agitation had come to be questioned. The Bardoli struggle revived people's faith in Gandhi's leadership. Even the leftist leaders were impressed. It is not without significance that Subhash Chandra Bose went to meet Gandhi at his Sabarmati Ashram in May 1928, when the Bardoli Satyagraha was at its height and requested the Mahatma to come out of his retirement and lead the country. Bose thought, as he later wrote, that the political situation in the country was ripe for action and therefore did not appreciate Gandhi's hesitation because: 'Before his eyes the peasantry of Bardoli were demonstrating through a no-tax campaign that they were ready for struggle.'[1]

Further distortions of the truth surface in the account of the Salt Satyagraha given by Pande and his colleagues. This is particularly so in relation to the very important raid on the Dharsana salt-depot which took place on 21 May 1930. Their book contains only a very brief mention of this bloody battle and which seems to be based entirely on the description given by the American newspaper reporter, Webb Miller (who only watched as an outside onlooker with no knowledge of the internal organization of the raid). He implies that the raid was motivated by and led by Sarojini Naidu. Although the real leaders and organisers were Dadubhai and Vithalbhai, they are not mentioned even once. Furthermore, no mention is made in the book of the vital War Council which was overseeing the whole Satyagraha operation. The sketchy description given does not do justice to what was the most important event of the whole salt Satyagraha, which needs a full and honest account.

A fuller and more truthful narrative of the action at Bardoli and at Dharsana will be found in Chapters 16 and 18. While Pande and colleagues appear to have done little research into these important occurrences, the present Author has had access to a number of reliable sources. He has discussed the events personally with Dadubhai and with Manilal Gandhi (Gandhiji's second son and one of the group leaders of the march). One of Manilal's letters to the Author is reproduced in Appendix 4. Manilal confirmed that Vithalbhai and Dadubhai took over the direction of the Salt Satyagraha and controlled the entire proceedings of the salt raid on 21 May 1930. Further authentication of what the Author has written is contained in documents held at the British Library. This is the official account of what happened at Dharsana detailed by the Government of Bombay, dated 28 May 1930.[2]

Reading all five volumes of Pande's History of the Congress, one is made to believe that the interaction of members of the political elite, rather than the popular mass agitations, brought about independence. The reality is that the British largely ignored all the politicians' conference speeches and statements, taking no action based on them. However, they watched with rapt attention the mass movements like Bardoli and Dharasana, even getting scared by them. For the first time since the Freedom War of 1857 (Indian Mutiny) the British felt insecure and perceived that power was slipping away from their authority in this jewel of the British Crown.

Another so-called 'History' is 'Freedom at Midnight' by Larry Collins and Dominique Lapierre. It is often claimed that this work seeks to project the history of the times to which it relates and that its completion involved extensive and painstaking research. Lapierre is reported to have said: 'The book is an authentic tribute to history'. While the book is a dramatisation of the events leading up to freedom, it is replete with distortions and inaccuracies. Its treatment of the personalities involved does not appear to have been done with a true historical approach. The authors show a profound and surprising ignorance, or lack of appreciation, of the basic facts of the situation. Sardar, a most important and effective participant, is here treated in an almost casual manner. The brief references to Sardar are unreliable; for instance the book states that he left school to work in a textile mill – but this is something he never did! Amazingly, the authors are apparently unaware of the mass struggle of the Bardoli Satyagraha. This was an event of the greatest significance yet the word 'Bardoli' does not appear even once in 572 pages!

Another example of their research is this story (page 243): 'The Maharajah of Orissa was trapped in his palace by a mob, which refused to let him leave until he had signed.' However, as any Indian could have told them, Orissa did not have a Maharajah!

After Independence a new set of leaders were installed. Soon it was only the facts (proven and unproven) and evidence showing these leaders in a favourable light which were thought to be relevant. The vital work of many others was allowed to slip into obscurity.

Part 3

MAJOR CHARACTERS

21

HARIDAS DESAI

Haridas was born on 29 July 1840 at his mother's place in Vaso. For his primary education his grandfather, Ajubhai, engaged a teacher to teach him at home and for learning the English language he sent him to Ahmedabad. In those days the railways had not yet been constructed in the region. If you required to go to Ahmedabad you had to go by horse power or camel power, and you had to cross the Shedhi, Meshvo, Vatrak, Khari and Sabarmati rivers. The bridges for crossing these rivers were ramshackle, unreliable and sometimes non-existent owing to flooding in the rainy season. Since Haridas could not commute every day to Ahmedabad, his father rented a house in Hazira's Pole and set up a full comfortable household with a cook and a servant. There he used to entertain his student friends. Among them were Mansukhram Suryaram Tripathi, Manibhai Jasbhai, Ambala Sarabhai, Motibhai Lalbhai, all of whom became famous as holders of various positions in the Gujarat political and social world. Later in life they all continued to co-operate and to help each other. This was because the learning of English language was a distant vision for all but a very few Indians then. You needed money and inclination as well as perseverance to learn and master English grammar and prose. As mentioned in Chapter 1, Viharidas the Father of Haridas constructed in 1857 the first primary school in Nadiad at Mogulkot. Later, in 1872, a large building was constructed which was then named 'Government High School Nadiad'. So from 1872 onwards, the Nadiad children were not obliged to go to Ahmedabad for English education. The Government school at Nadiad is still functioning and is a premier institution in Nadiad. Nowadays in Nadiad, apart from some private schools, there is a D.P. Desai High School of the Maniba Dadubhai Desai Trust. The creator of this charity was a great-grandson of Viharidas Desai. He, Dharamsingh Desai, also donated a large Technical College for engineering studies leading up to University Degrees.

At Ahmedabad, Haridas studied up to 'First Law Class Book', the prevalent highest diploma of that time, so he was now equipped with knowledge of English as well as the English legal system that was prevalent in India. At the age of 24 he was appointed a member of the Local Fund Committee of Mehmdabad Taluka in Kaira District. Prior to that at the age of 21, when he had finished his education, his wife of a few months died. After a year, yielding to family pressure, he re-married. While acquainting himself with the social services structure of Nadiad Taluka, he came into personal contact with E.H. Percival the Collector of Kaira District, who appointed him the Municipal Commissioner of Nadiad in 1867. Prior to that he undertook a journey to South India and toured Madras and Trichinopally areas by foot and bullock cart, to study the tobacco industry of South India. Percival had a great confidence in the capacity of young Haridas and he was sent as an administrator of Bhavnagar State during the minority of the Maharajah; further, in 1870, he appointed Haridas as Nyayadhish (Chief Justice) of Bhavnagar. In 1872 the British appointed him as a member of the Finance Committee to give evidence before the British Parliament about the management of the finances of the Indian Empire. During his work as a judge in Bhavnagar, he showed a sense of integrity in delivering justice, the most important attribute necessary for occupants of high public positions. The newly appointed Political Agent of the whole of Kathiawar (now Saurashtra) James Braithwaite Peile singled out Haridas for these qualities. He quickly appointed him as Diwan of Vadhvan State during the minority of Thakor Saheb Dajiram. From that time onwards Haridas became successively Diwan of many states in Kathiawar. From Vadhvan he became Diwan of Vankaner State in 1881. Then in 1882 he was shifted to Diwangiri of Idar State. Ultimately in 1883 the Nawab of Junagadh selected him as his Diwan. Junagadh was then the largest State of Kathiawar. While in Idar State his greatest contribution to reform was his land revenue policy. Desais were born and bred on the eternal subject of land revenue, by reason of being large landowners and thereby unwilling payers of land revenue to the State. Haridas reduced the level of land revenue in the whole State of Idar. The result was that cultivation areas were increased. The cultivators of poor lands, which were left as fallow lands to avoid paying revenue, were now enticed to bring that land into cultivation. The result was that Idar State's annual income increased instead of falling because of reduced revenue demand. The Maharajah, who had initial misgivings about reducing the level of revenue, was delighted by this 'magic trick'. After serving only 14 months in Idar, when Haridas was transferred to the bigger appointment at Junagadh, the Maharajah of Idar wrote him a heartrending letter in which he expressed his eternal gratitude for improving his State's financial situation. The Ruler wanted to give him a village too, which Haridas declined. After all, he was going to a much higher position of power and emolument. The years Haridas spent at Junagadh were his glorious years of just and powerful administration. His first act was to restore peace and tranquillity to the state which had been the battlefield of the Makarani and Maiya rebels. With a firm hand and grave risk to his own personal safety, he faced the rebels with Junagadh army and police and quelled the rebellion. Nawab Bahadurkhanji now felt secure for the first time in his life and offered Haridas a gift of one lakh of rupees (a huge sum in 1884). Haridas had no need for the money, but to keep the Nawab happy he suggested a formula whereby he would accept the annual interest on that sum, this interest to be added to his wages. In return, his wage would be reduced by that amount. So his wage included the Ruler's gift but it actually remained the same. By this means he respected the gift but did not take it. However, the Ruler insisted that the interest from one lakh of rupees would remain to be paid not only to Haridas but to his descendants in perpetuity. This sum the family received annually from Junagadh till the Republic of India took control of Junagadh State. Taking up the case of his Cousin Prabhudas (Sadhuram), Dadubhai wrote to his friend Sardar Vallabhbhai, the Deputy Premier and Home Minister who was handling the accession of the States to the Indian Union Government.[1] This was done when the Union Government merged the whole region of Junagadh State. In the letter Sardar mentions that the matter of Sadhuram's endowment was solved and he was satisfied with the outcome.[2]

Throughout the second half of the nineteenth century there was a race for construction of regional railways networks all over India and Haridas played a great part in persuading the authorities to agree to the construction of a link line between Jetalsar and Junagadh.

Haridas was mindful of the troubles of the pilgrims going to the top of Girnar without steps. So he conceived the idea of floating a lottery to finance the building of steps to the top of Girnar Mount.

Whenever Haridas had to dispense justice he disregarded the vested interests and their influence. In one case the nephew of the Ruler Nawab Bahadurkhanji was prosecuted under the criminal procedure code and Haridas disregarded the Nawab's request and delivered the judgement against this offender. He faced the Nawab courageously and told him: 'Your rule, and its continuity, depends on your administration being impartial and just to your subjects. We must inspire loyalty in the population we rule'.

The Nawab had no answer and the sentence, which was the death penalty, was carried out.

In 1872, thirteen years before the Indian National Congress was founded, Haridas was appointed to the Committee which reported the state of the finances of the whole Indian Empire including Ceylon and Burma to the British Parliament in London.

In 1888, Haridas became the first man from Gujarat to serve in the Bombay Governor's Legislative Council. On his death, his younger brother served on the same Council until 1911, the year that the Morley-Minto reforms came into force. It was then that Vithalbhai took over the membership of the Council. To summarise: from 1888 to 1930 only the members of the Desai family occupied a seat on the Governor's Bombay Legislative Council, i.e. for 42 years. The sequence was as follows:

Haridas	1888–1895
Purushottamdas	1895–1911
Vithalbhai	1911–1920
Dadubhai	1920–1930.

By 1893 the British public was greatly disturbed by reports in the British press about the continuation of the notorious 'Opium Trade' carried out under the (British) authority of the Indian Government, to the detriment of the Chinese people. To quell that disquiet the Parliament in London appointed a commission styled as 'The Royal Opium Commission', to report on the working of the opium trade and suggest reforms if necessary. The Commission was constituted as follows:

Lord Brassey (Chairman)
J.A. Lyall
Lakshmesh War Singh (Maharajah of Darbhanga)
W. Roberts
R.G.C. Mowbray
A.U. Fanshawe
A. Peae
Haridas Viharidas Desai.

The Commission went through the entire history of the opium trade, including the monopoly exercised by the East India Company, starting from its administration by Warren Hastings to the present day. They also visited opium growing areas and the centres of export from India to China, and went through the financial implications of such trade for the Indian Government as well as for the British treasury. The final report was handed over to the Parliament in London on 16 April 1895, by the Commission members in person.

With the dual strain of the Dewanship of Junagadh and extensive touring with members of the Commission, Haridas developed heart problems. As a result he could not undertake the long journey to London in company with the other members of the Commission who personally presented the report to the full House of Commons in London. Denoting his absence he affixed his personal memorandum to the report. Exactly two months later on 17 June 1895 he died peacefully at Nadiad from a massive heart attack.

In his memorandum to the Commission report, he had courageously pointed out startling truths about the British administration of India. He wrote:[3] 'As regards the exportation of Indian opium to China. To abolish it would result in a great loss to Indian revenue. This loss the Indian people are unwilling and unable to make up by accepting the imposition of any additional tax. They have no voice to check or reduce the expenditure made in India, or in England to be born by India, which is admittedly poor and already over-taxed. Its resources are constantly drained off to foreign countries without adequate and substantial return from them. It may also be mentioned that India is a dependency of England, while China is not that of India. Under these circumstances it cannot be for a moment imagined that those British people, who have disinterestedly taken up this cause for the good of India and China, would ever expect India, helpless as it is, to extend its generosity, at a great loss, towards China, in the manner proposed before the Commission. Again viewing this point in another light, it is the Chinese Government that should take stringent measures, against the importation of Indian opium, if it believes that it is either injured or ruined by accepting the drug from India. This it can well do now, when it has been publicly announced before Parliament on behalf of the British Government that the Chinese Government are under no treaty obligation to accept Indian opium, if they choose to refuse it. But if the Chinese Government from past experience still entertain any fears as to the bona fide carrying out of the authoritative announcement made before the Parliament, I would suggest that an official communication be sent from the British Government to the Chinese Government, informing the latter that any action on their part towards the stoppage of the importation of Indian opium into China, would be unhampered by the treaty obligations entered into by them with the British Government. I am however afraid China would not be prepared to do so, so long as it allows an extensive growth of opium on its land, and also accepts importation of the drug from Turkey and Persia. Thus any attempt from outside, for the benefit of China, would if I have been able to see through the subject correctly, be ineffective unless China takes the initiative in adopting the strictest measures, first against the cultivation of opium on its own land, and then gradually against the importation of the drug from foreign countries.'

The history of the opium trade in short is this: 'The trade in opium was officially recognised by the Directors of the East India Company, at least as early as 1769. As Commissioners sent out to India in that year to supervise the management of the Company's affairs throughout India were instructed to encourage the export of silk, yarn and opium... The records indeed show that opium was provided on account of the Company for export to Bencoolen and Balambangan in Sumatra, before any attempt was made to interfere with or regulate the arrangements for its production.'[4]

'Opium is received from the contractors at the factory at Patna and sent down to the Presidency, with a part being reserved for trade of the settlement of Balambangah. The rest is sold at public auction; and the produce, after deducting the prime cost and charges, is set apart as a fund for payment of gratuities proposed to be allowed to members of the late Council, in lieu of their advantages of trade from which they interdicted themselves.'[5]

In the same year (1775) that the question was raised as to the management of opium business, the Patna Council of the Governor-General were directed by London to submit their opinion on 'what mode it will be most advisable to adopt for the future provision of the opium'.[6] In a letter dated 25 March 1775, the Patna Council recommended that a monopoly of the trade should be established in favour of the Company, and suggested that the Company should export the opium on their account to China. As an indication of the demand for opium and the extent of the trade then existing, it is noteworthy that the Council estimated that, if the French and Dutch were excluded from the trade and smuggling stopped, they would be able to provide at least 33,000 chests (each chest weighing approximately 133½lb) a year. The profit on this, if sold on the Company's account in China with a contract price in Bengal of Rs.230 or 240 a chest, would as they said be prodigious.

The Council, composed of Governor-General Hastings, Barwell, Francis Monson and Clavering, decided that the opium in its crude state should be brought by the contractor to a place fixed by the Patna Provincial Council and be there manufactured by him under the provision of a person or persons appointed for the purpose by the Board.[7]

Tenders were accordingly invited and contracts for one year were assigned to the lowest of 13 bidders.[8] This was to a Mr Griffith for the provision of 2,980 chests in Bihar at Rs.180 a chest and 2½ per cent commission on the sale at Calcutta, and to a Mr Wilton for the provision of 1,000 chests in Bengal at Rs.240 a chest without commission. Again, for one year 1776–77, Messrs Griffith and Wilton received an extension on the contract on the same terms. In 1777 a Mr Mackenzie received the whole contract for three years on the same terms as the former contractors, a measure which called forth a strong protest from the Court of Directors.[9] They wrote: 'We observe Mr Mackenzie's offer was to pay 10,000 sicca rupees per annum as a consideration for holding the opium contract on the terms of his predecessors and of being indulged with such additional advances of money as he might require. These proposals you accept without acquainting the former contractor or any other person with the terms therein contained. But after two years experience providing opium by contract, you should have ascertained, by advertising for other proposals, whether the price hitherto paid to the contractor had been reasonable or whether any other respectable person would engage to provide it on terms more advantageous to the Company; and as you acted otherwise, and so far as appears to us, concluded a contract of great importance without advertising for proposals, or making previous enquiries necessary to guide your judgement therein and to warrant the measure, we therefore disapprove your conduct on that occasion.'

Notwithstanding this disapproval, Mackenzie received in 1780 an extension of his contract for another year. Then again in 1781 Warren Hastings awarded Stephen Sullivan a contract for the supply of opium for four years on the terms upon which the contract had been held by Mackenzie. The contract was condemned by the Board of Directors in their letter of 12 July 1782 and formed the most important of the charges of 'glaringly extravagant and wantonly profuse' in the 4th article of Hastings' impeachment. At Hastings' trial by the Parliament in London, it was proved that Sullivan resold the contract at a large profit. However, Hastings had managed the whole affair so well that corruption on the part of Hastings was never established. The verdict was acquittal on the charge by 19 votes against 5.

The proceeds of 'Opium Trade' helped finance the purchase of tea from China for export to England. Now in 1784 the Commutation Act was passed which drastically reduced the customs duty in the UK for tea imported from China. This gave a fresh impetus to the tea trade, and to pay for additional quantities of tea the East India Company had to devise ways of financing it. Trade with China had its problems. Chinese trade was not open to foreigners thanks to an Imperial decree in force then. Also the Chinese economy was more or less self-sufficient. So there was hardly any merchandise that could be sold to generate enough funds to purchase tea from China. Trade with that country was thus conducted through a few authorised merchants at the port of Canton, which was the sole point of entry to China. The only way to buy tea was to exchange it for bullion. For this, opium provided the answer. In 1795 Sir John Macpherson succeeded Warren Hastings as Governor-General and this subject of providing the Company's super-cargoes in China with funds for the purchase of tea, was considered. In London the Court of Directors, as well as the newly appointed Board of Control, were seriously considering the same question. Sir John directed that opium for the year 1785 be offered for sale to an association of merchants residing in Calcutta, on the understanding that payment for it should be made at the Canton treasury of the East India Company in Spanish dollars (gold). Sir John Macpherson and his Council determined, subject to the approval of the Court of Directors, to apply in future the proceeds of the opium monopoly to the 'exclusive benefit of the China trade' (in tea).[10]

In short this is how the system worked, in Judith M. Brown's words in her book 'Modern India' (Oxford University Press 1994): 'As opium was a prohibited import into China, the Company sold the drug to English "private" traders who smuggled it into China with the Company's connivance, and then paid their illegal proceeds into the Company's treasury at Canton, where the money was used to buy tea for shipment to England. The trader-smugglers recouped themselves by drawing on the Company in Bengal or London.' (For more details of this procedure see Appendix 3.)

As a result of this devious manoeuvre a range of powerful British interests were satisfied. The British Government got its revenue from tea; and this amounted to one-tenth of total Government revenue in the early nineteenth century. The Company also gained a large revenue from opium monopoly – nearly one-seventh of its total revenue at that time. It also financed its tea business and contrived a method of transmitting money to London, for pensions and other 'home charges' generated by the Government of India, while the private traders found a way to send their profits home. Little wonder that a contemporary could enthuse in 1839 about the benefit to the British of the opium trade: 'From opium trade the Honourable Company have derived for years an immense revenue and through them the British Government and the Nation have also reaped an incalculable amount of political and financial advantage'.[11]

Simply opium traded for tea poured an abundant revenue into the British Exchequer and benefited the nation to an extent of 6 million pounds annually. In effect, this benefit should have been returned to India as foreign trade surplus, but in those days such surplus was absorbed by the rulers. India received the opium value in the form of local currency, but no benefit from the trade surplus. However, the local currency earned from opium trade was useful for the Indian administration of the Government of India. Thus, to Britain, opium provided a permanent additional help throughout the nineteenth century to finance the industrial revolution which had just begun. No doubt the memorandum to Royal Opium Commission, by Haridas Desai noted: 'The Indian people have no voice to check or reduce the expenditure made in India or in England to be borne by India, which is admittedly poor and already over-taxed, while its resources are constantly drained off to foreign countries without adequate and substantial return from them'.

This was heartfelt sentiment, based entirely on truth, expressed by the very man appointed by the British administration. Perhaps this is the first voice of protest, from a man whom the British trusted for his integrity and honesty, against the colonial exploitation of India. Immediately after the work of the Royal Opium Commission was finished, Lord Brassey recommended Haridas for a knighthood. Alas, Haridas died of a heart attack before he could be honoured.

Haridas's other triumph was an early and close association with, and support of, Swami Vivekananda who virtually considered him as his: 'I love you and respect you like a father'.[12] He befriended Swami Vivekananda very early in the latter's career as a torch-bearer of Hindu civilisation and helped him in his visit to USA when he was attending the Parliament of Religions in Chicago. Vivekananda wrote him various letters from Chicago and New York. In one of them he asked Haridas to send two or three pieces of rug from Agra or Lahore. The Americans liked those rugs and Vivekananda intended to present them to some of his hosts there in America.

In his letters he describes events in the Parliament and also gives his views in general on various matters relating to Hindu religion and the nature and conduct of Indians in general. In spite of being a very busy person, Vivekananda took time to visit Nadiad and meet the Desai family.

Vivekananda was still in the USA (New York) when Haridas passed away, but he wrote a letter from New York to Girdhardas (nephew of Haridas): 'Your Uncle was a great soul and his whole life was given to do good to his country, hoping you all will follow in his footsteps. He was a strong and noble friend and India lost a good deal in losing him. Remember me to your Uncle and friend, ever always, well wisher of your family'.[13]

The family has been able to save 14 of Vivekananda's many letters and they have been bequeathed to the Ramkrishna Centre in the United States. Three of these are reproduced in Appendix 4. Haridas died on 17 June 1895, leaving a wife, two sons and two daughters.

22

PURUSHOTTAMDAS DESAI

To celebrate the birth, in 1852, of his son Purushottamdas, Viharidas donated the land for the construction of Sat Swarup Temple (Haveli), at Santh Pipli in Nadiad. Purushottamdas studied at Nadiad in the Nadiad High School endowed by his father, and finished his secondary school certificate with a good command of English grammar and prose. In his youth he stayed mainly at Nadiad looking after his father's estate. At the age of 44 he was appointed Vice-President of the Nadiad Municipality of which he became President from 1898 to 1902. In 1904, under the Local Boards Constitution, he was elected to the Bombay Governor's Legislative Council, which seat he occupied till 1911 when the new Council, under the Morley-Minto Reforms, was elected in major provinces. During his membership of the Council, he took a keen interest in all the bills that related to revenue matters. He had strong views on Bhagdari and Narvadari tenures of land. In his submission of suggestions concerning these tenures, he proposed to regulate the powers of interference by the Collector and that the law should be amended to do that. In the end the Government decided not to pursue reforms of the Bhagdari and Narvadari tenures and left them as before.[1] Under his Presidency of the Nadiad Municipality, street lamps were installed and the roads metalled for the first time. For the communal services he performed, the Government awarded him the title of 'Sardar' (one step less than a knighthood). The peasant nationalists of Kheda District were seen as being among the most dedicated of Gandhi's supporters. On several occasions they refused to pay their land revenue to the British Government in support of the nationalist movement and a good deal of land and property was confiscated as a punishment.[2] On 3 November 1917 in a speech at Gujarat Political Conference, Gandhiji announced that the Nationalist movement in Gujarat was to be for the peasants. He believed that it was impossible to win Swaraj without widespread peasant backing for the Nationalist programme.[3] Again on 20 April 1918 in a speech to the peasants at Ajarpura, he said that Swaraj would not be worth winning unless the peasants learnt to demand their rights.[4] On 15 September 1931 at the Second Round Table Conference in London, Gandhiji claimed in his speech that the Indian National Congress was essentially a peasant organisation.[5]

The most important service that Purushottamdas rendered to the Indian Nation was in the area of revenue settlement. To his historic question, which he placed on the table of the Bombay Governor's Legislative Council on 25 June 1910, the Government's reply was: 'The matter will be examined!'. Having heard no further statement from the Government, he reiterated the same question on 22 November 1910. This time the Government machinery was set in motion and the sequence of events was as follows:

Of the token but the first real questionning of the judiciousness of some revenue settlements by Purushottamdas.

P.V. Desai's questions:

Question No. 1 – Asked on 25 June 1910:
'Government to institute inquiries with regard to judiciousness of assessment rates in Thasra Taluka?'
Government's reply: 'The matter will be examined.'

Question No. 2 – Asked on 22 November 1910:
Same question
Same reply.

Government Memorandum No. 2232: 4 March 1911:
Copy of question and reply (The matter will be examined) sent to Settlement Commissioner and Director of Land Records.

Government Memorandum No. 10657: 25 November 1913:
Asks Commissioner N.D. to expedite submission of report called for in Memorandum No. 2232 of 4 March 1911.

Letter from Commissioner N.D., No. 670: 25 February 1914:
Forwarded the Report No. 2441 of 4

December 1913 by B.R. Mehta – Superintendent Land Records and Registration N.D. – which was reviewed both by Collector of Kaira-Ghosal and the Settlement Commissioner, copies of whose remarks are forwarded.

Government Resolution No. 4697, 20 May 1914:

Concession regarding the Land Revenue assessment granted on 16th July 1909, to cease with effect from 1 August 1914.

The above sequence of events clearly shows that the Government, acting on behalf of the people they represented, were seriously concerned about anyone, and especially a council member, asking questions about land revenue and implying that the rates were unjust. It took the Government and the revenue officers (the Settlement Commissioner N.D., the Collector of Kaira and Commissioner of Northern Division) from 25 June 1910 to 20 May 1914 – nearly four years of procrastination – to work up a plausible defence. Such was the sensitivity of the British Raj to land revenue, which in reality formed the bulk of the Government of India's annual income! This appears to be the first attack anybody had made on the land revenue system. Nevertheless, this attack on land revenue assessment later became the main target of Gandhiji in 1918 and Vallabhbhai and Dadubhai in 1928. This is what gave life to and sustained the mass movement throughout almost the entire life of the Indian National Congress, which was to achieve independence from Britain in 1947. The Congress movement needed the help and co-operation of both peasant farmers and landowners, as well as the intelligentsia, for its widespread and sustainable mass actions. This whole episode of the Government's land revenue settlement policy is reproduced in its original form from the India Office records (see Appendix 2).[6]

In 1908 a retired schoolteacher and a follower of Mahatma Gandhi had founded an institution called Patidar Yuvak Mandal in his village of Vanz in Bardoli Taluka. He was Kunverji Mehta, a Lewa Patidar, and as such its membership was restricted to Lewa Patidars only. Later on it was open to the entire Patidar community. However, in 1908 one Motibhai Narsinhbhai Amin had also started Patidar Yuvak Mandal in Petlad. The aim of both of these institutions was to raise the educational level of Patidars of Surat and Kaira districts. Purushottamdas took great interest in the activities of both the Mandals and had supported them whenever possible.[7] In 1910, under his Presidency, he convened a conference of all Patidars of Gujarat and Kathiawar at Vanz in Bardoli Taluka under the auspices of the 'Patidar Yuvak Mandal'. The purpose was to solidify the community and set in motion various reforms to the system of dowry payment and child marriages as well as furthering the educational facilities of the region. They passed eleven resolutions aimed at reforming the social customs and developing agriculture. The Conference exhorted the Government to establish an agricultural college in the region, similar to Poona Agricultural College. It also asked the Government to give the cultivators their own elected representative to the Bombay Legislative Council. Of course Purushottamdas was an M.L.C who was elected under the District Local Boards Constitution.

Three years later, in 1913, the peasant community in the United Provinces of Agra and Ayodhya (now called Uttar Pradesh) invited Kunverji to preside over an All-India Peasant Kshatriya Conference to be held at Barabanki. Kunverji proposed the name of Jethalal Swaminarayan, a professor of mathematics at the Gujarat College Ahmedabad. Kunverji and Swaminarayan took Vallabhbhai (who was practising in Ahmedabad) to the Conference. The Barabanki Session seemed quite successful and the next session was convened in 1914 at Ahmedabad under the newly elected M.L.C Vithalbhai Patel as its presiding officer. Under the Patidar Yuvak Mandal, Kunverji founded a boarding-house called Patidar Ashram for the Patidar students at Surat. When Gandhi, coming from South Africa, landed at Bombay in 1915, Kunverji was also there to receive him. At the time he invited him to visit the Patidar Ashram. Subsequently, Gandhiji visited the Ashram on 2 January 1916 and said:

'I feel as if I were in the midst of my own family members… I have come to regard the Patidar Yuvak Mandal in high esteem ever since I was in Africa. I was told that I was sure to get full cooperation of the Patidar Mandal on my return to India. I was helped by many of my Patidar friends there. But I shall see how far and to what extent you are going to help me here?'[8]

So it can be seen from the above that Gandhi, immediately upon arrival from South Africa, made a first contact with the Indian Patidar community and annexed it for all his future programmes to increase his political clout with the British Government. Although his origins were in Rajkot (Kathiawar), he hardly tried to harness the people of Kathiawar for his political campaigns. From now on to the end of his life, this part of Gujarat stretching from Ahmedabad to Surat, provided him strong and faithful support. It would be true to call his political power base a most formidable and reliable one, Nadiad Desais in the form of Vithalbhai, Vallabhbhai and Dadubhai became his great pillars of strength throughout his political career. Without their unflinching political support in all the agitations in Gujarat, one wonders how far Gandhiji would have achieved what he did?

Purushottamdas Desai retired from political life in 1917, when his son Dadubhai took up the baton when he was appointed to the Vice-Presidency of the Kaira District Local Board. In 1929 he suffered from a heart attack and died in his sleep, content that his son, Dadubhai had achieved one of his great successes with the Bardoli Satyagraha.

The Author vividly remembers the evening rides to surrounding villages in company with him in his automobile (Willys Knight). An evening ride in a horse carriage (Victoria) or a car was a daily routine for him and he would take one or two of his grandchildren with him.

23

DADUBHAI

Dadubhai was born on 26 May 1878 and died on 1 March 1958, i.e. he lived for a few days less than 80 years. He was educated at Nadiad Government High School and also at Junagadh where his uncle Haridas Desai, whom he called 'Motabapa', was the Divan. Later he went on to Elphinstone College where he read history and politics and took a BA degree at Bombay University in 1903. Vithalbhai Patel and Vallabhbhai Patel were also educated up to Matric standard at the same Government High School in Nadiad. Thus the Nadiad Government High School had the distinction of producing the three foremost political opponents of the British in the form of nationalist leaders. He had barely passed his degree exam when his brother Ganpatidas, who was organising the establishment of a cotton spinning and weaving mill in Nadiad, called him to assist in his work.

The two brothers, with the additional third brother Thakordas, started the Nadiad Swadeshi Spinning Weaving and Manufacturing Company Limited, with Ganpatidas Krishnarao Company Limited as managing agents, on 7 September 1906 (see Appendix 5).[1] He was then 27 years old. Simultaneously in 1908 the three brothers also took up Government forest land, on 10 yearly leases, to cut the grass and sell it to the newly opened tram company in Bombay. The motive power of trams in those days was provided by horses. This grassland was situated not in Charatar but in the region to the north called Mal Tract. This area consisted of land that was abandoned by the peasants during the great famine of 1899–1900. As it had no natural source of water, even the trees that grew there were stunted and with few thin leaves, only grass could grow there naturally after the annual monsoon rains. The textile mill went into liquidation in 1909, mainly because his brother Ganpatidas, the managing agent, suffered from tuberculosis and died in 1909. As mentioned the grass cutting lease of the land at Ajupura and Chandasar gave a reasonable but not fabulous income to the family for three years from 1908 to 1910.

In 1911 the Government resumed ownership of the lands under the terms of the lease which were: (a) that for the first ten years i.e. from 1908–1909 to 1918–1919, full assessment and local fund cess should be paid every year and (b) that if during the period of the lease, Government should in any year need the grass for their own purposes, the land should be returned and no assessment or local fund cess levied upon it for that year.[2] Under the pretext of the great scarcity of fodder, the Collector, Chuckerbutty a Bengali Christian, activated Clause (b) of the lease and took possession of the lands in 1911 as well as the following year 1912. On a petition by Dadubhai Desai on 20 April 1913 and Memorandum No. 4796 from Commissioner Northern Division No. 2659 dated 5 July 1915, the Commissioner stated that it should now be pointed out to the Collector that the original intention of condition (b) of the lease was that the lessee should be deprived of the grass from leased lands only when the Government had some urgent need for grass, as for example during a famine, and that the resumption ordered in 1912 should be confined only to that year and should not be renewed except when urgent need arose. Thus Collector Chuckerbutty's tirade against the Nadiad Desais (see below) lost effectiveness. Apart from the above mentioned lease of lands at Ajupura and Chandasar, Dadubhai had also acquired further leases on lands in other adjoining villages via the annual auctions. The Collector accused the Desais of using their influence with Indian officials, ranging from the Deputy Collector to the village Headman of the area, to ensure that nobody would bid against them so that they managed to obtain the grass at nominal rates.[3] They allowed the other Patidars to take the remaining plots at very low rates. The Government later calculated that during the previous years, in which there were rigged auctions, they lost between Rs.50,000 and Rs.150,000 each year. Chuckerbutty was a very thorough and ambitious collector and thought he had a chance to advance his, as well as the Government's, cause by bringing the Desais to justice. He collected evidence both false or true against the Patidars whom he described as exercising 'Baronial Power' behind crime and corruption in the District. In September 1911 he arrested Vithaldas Patel who was a son-in-law of a Nadiad Desai, on a charge of rigging the grass auction.

Commenting on this episode, Hardiman writes: 'This was an unwise move. In his attempt to be more British than the British, Chuckerbutty had failed to understand that the survival of the Indian Empire depended on not alienating influential and loyal families like the Nadiad Desais'.[4] A few days later the Sessions Judge of Ahmedabad, B.C. Kennedy, ordered that Vithaldas be released on bail. Chuckerbutty was furious and wrote an angry letter to Kennedy pointing out that the whole case would be ruined as, once out of the jail, Vithaldas would destroy all the compromising evidence.[5] Chuckerbutty was censured for criticising his judicial superior and was forced to apologise to Kennedy. Although Vithaldas was subsequently found guilty, he was let off with only a warning. The ostensible reason was that, as the frauds had been going on for eight years and had involved officers of all grades, it would have been unfair to have convicted Vithaldas and not the officials.'

Chuckerbutty tried to institute an inquiry into the conduct of Deputy Collector Mr Manilal Ajitrai Thakore by calling upon him to answer charges of suspected misconduct in connection with grass frauds in the Kaira district. Whereupon the Private Secretary to his Excellency the Governor wrote to the Commissioner of the Northern Division, that the Government considered that as members of the Provincial Civil Service were appointed by them it was only the Government that should order a formal departmental inquiry under No. XIX of the rules for regulating admission to and promotion within the Bombay Provincial Civil Service. It was quite wrong of the Collector to institute an inquiry. Chuckerbutty also tried to indict the Mamlatdar of Thasra, Kathavat, and called upon him to submit an explanation of many points which appear to weigh very much against him. No further action was taken against Kathavat. In the end none of the officers was ever punished. Thus the Nadiad Desais came away scot-free with their power in the government enhanced.[6]

After Vithalbhai's death in 1932, Dadubhai, having lost a formidable comrade, decided to retire from active politics. However, he kept up his social and Harijan improvement work. He remained President of Harijan Sevak Sang. He also took an active part in the creation of Vithal Kanya Vidpalaya, named in the memory of his friend

Vithalbhai. However, when the Congress decided to contest the elections under the new Government of India Act of 1935, Vallabhbhai persuaded him to stand for the Bombay Council election. This was the place where he had played an active part since he was first elected in 1920. Having won the election Congress formed a Ministry in Bombay, as in eight other Provinces. Vallabhbhai offered him the Revenue portfolio, but Dadubhai rejected this saying: 'I do not want to take part in power'.

After the Council term he retired and did not fight any further elections. He left the Congress work to three of his sons. While two of them took part in the 'Quit India' movement in 1942 and were jailed, another son, Chittaranjan (the Author) was a member of Congress from August 1939 until independence. During participation in the 'Quit India' demonstrations he was beaten unconscious and in September 1942 he was sent to prison for six months. Later, after graduating as a doctor, he went to Malaya on a mercy mission called 'The Congress Medical Mission'. There he served as a missionary doctor for six months. Subsequently the Government bestowed on him the title 'Sanman Patra' (This was awarded to all those imprisoned for supporting the 1942 'Quit India' movement).

The second son, Madhubhai, after having served his prison term in 1942, took up active work for Congress until Indira Gandhi broke the Congress into two. Then he joined the 'Swatantra Party' and was elected to Gujarat State Assembly called Vidhan Sabha.

The third son, Dharmsinh, joined the Congress and was elected to the Indian Parliament in Delhi and served for two terms until his untimely death in 1980. Before his death he established an Engineering College at Nadiad from his own private charitable trust (Dharmsinh Desai Trust). The College now has university status.

After Dadubhai's term at the Bombay Legislative Council, he passed his last years in retirement in Nadiad; except for the 1942 'Quit India' movement in which he played his part in Nadiad and the Kaira district, as well as undertaking work with the peasants on their land revenue refusal. Of course he kept in constant touch with his lifelong co-worker and friend, Sardar Patel. In 1958 he passed away without any terminal illness or suffering.

24

SARDAR VALLABHBHAI PATEL

Vallabhbhai was born in Nadiad, his mother was Ladbai Desai, whose father Jijeebhai Vastabhai Desai descended from the original founder of the Nadiad Desai Dynasty. His childhood friend, Dadubhai, also shared the same ancestry.[1]

His Father hailed from Karamsad which, like Nadiad, belonged to the Chh Gam Ekda. His real education in English was to come from Nadiad Government High school. In those days none of the other Chh Gam villages had an English school. In the Nadiad High School, Vallabhbhai, his brother Vithalbhai and Dadubhai were all great friends. Their friendship continued throughout their whole lives including the political one. To all intents and purposes Vallabhbhai and Vithalbhai, though called Patel, were culturally really Nadiad Desais. In 1897 he passed the matriculation examination from the Government High School Nadiad. This High School was donated to the people of Nadiad by Viharidas Desai, the grandfather of Dadubhai Desai. After matriculating, for the next three years he studied the law books at home and passed the District Pleaders Examination in 1900. Vithalbhai had gone to Bombay to study law and passed the District Pleaders Examination in 1895 and had already started legal practice in Godhra, about 66 miles north-east of Nadiad. From there he moved to Borsad in 1898. Vallabhbhai did not accept Vithalbhai's invitation to come and join the Borsad practice but instead went to Godhra to try his luck there. In Godhra his practice thrived, but after some years Vallabhbhai moved to Borsad to join Vithalbhai in his criminal court practice. The practice prospered reasonably well and was enough to finance both the brothers' foreign education. They both became barristers in England and returned to India for further practice of law. In 1914 Vallabhbhai's father, Zaverbhai, died. Prior to that, in 1909, his wife Zaverba had died leaving a daughter four and a half years old and a son three years old. He travelled to London in 1910 and joined the Middle Temple, where in 1912, he qualified as a barrister. In 1913, returning to India, he started a criminal lawyer practice in Ahmedabad. Then in 1916 he attended the Lucknow session of the Indian National Congress, where he made the acquaintance of Gandhiji.

In 1917 he entered the Ahmedabad Municipality as an Elected Councillor. He also became the Secretary of Gujarat Sabha, of which Gandhi was the President.

In 1918, Gandhi started the Kheda Satyagraha but, for over half of the duration of the agitation, he was away at Champaran and Ahmedabad leaving Vallabhbhai in charge. When Gandhiji was there, Vallabhbhai always accompanied him on his tours of villages. Compared to later agitation at Bardoli, the satyagraha organisation was rudimentary. There were no trained Congress workers as there were to be in Bardoli. Also, the scope of agitation was vast as it involved seven Talukas viz: Matar, Anand, Borsad, Nadiad, Mehmedabad, Kapadvanj and Thasra. A total of 510 villages were involved, though only about 70 really responded to the call for non-payment of land revenue. The participants were not strict about non-violence. Gandhiji was becoming disenchanted with this sort of practice. In April he spent 20 days in the district but in May only ten. On 12 April he wrote to his son Devdas, that he did not get the same joy working in Nadiad as he got in Ahmedabad and that many were failing to understand his message of non-violent non-cooperation.[2] Not being at that time seasoned or experienced enough, Vallabhbhai could not succeed in spite of his fiery speeches. The agitation ended in early June. Gandhiji called it his 'Himalayan Blunder'. Gandhi writes in his autobiography: 'A Satyagrahi obeys the laws of society intelligently and of his own free will, because he considers it to be his sacred duty to do so. It is only when a person has thus obeyed the laws of society scrupulously that he is in a position to judge as to which particular rules are good and just and which unjust and iniquitous. Only then does the right accrue to him of civil disobedience of certain laws in well-defined circumstances. My error lay in my failure to observe the necessary limitation. I had called on the people to launch upon civil disobedience before they had thus qualified for it and this mistake seemed to me of Himalayan magnitude. As soon as I entered the Kheda

District, all the old recollections of the Kheda Satyagraha struggle came back to me and I wondered how I could have failed to perceive what was so obvious. I realised that before a people could be fit for offering civil disobedience, they should thoroughly understand its deeper implications. That being so, before restarting civil disobedience on a mass scale, it would be necessary to create a band of well-tried pure-hearted volunteers who thoroughly understood the strict conditions of Satyagraha. They could explain these to the people and by sleepless vigilance keep them on the right path'.[3]

Vallabhbhai being the co-worker of Gandhi for the first time in the Kheda Satyagraha learnt a lesson from this failure and began training volunteers on the above-mentioned Satyagraha principles, when he became President of Gujarat Provincial Congress Committee in 1921. From then onwards, for each district as well as Taluka Congress Committee he picked his own lieutenants, who were utterly faithful to him and in the normal run of events were not ambitious to be political leaders. To attack these men would amount to attacking Vallabhbhai. In the Kheda District especially, he created a strong band of such workers in each town and village. This was the volunteer army which he later took with him to Bardoli for the 1928 Satyagraha. These were his men who took his message from village to village. The villagers followed their example and gallantly suffered privations and all the repressive measures of the Government until their objective was achieved. Organising a fight in 137 villages extending to 222 square miles needs exceptional organising abilities. Neither Nehru nor any other Congressional leader had such capacity. Later on, Sardar controlled the All-India Congress organisation in the same way and Nehru was the main beneficiary of it. Again the same ability allowed Sardar Vallabhbhai to amalgamate all the Princely States into one united India.

That was a feat unparalleled in the history of mankind. The saga of Indian unity achieved by Sardar will be written in history in letters of gold. The miracle was performed in defiance of history, against tradition, in the face of many adverse circumstances and forces, and in the short span of just two years. The contemporary generation may not appreciate the difficulties and complexities of the situation and may regard it as an achievement easily obtained, but that was not so. Sardar was a colossus on the Indian political stage, who took time as well as problems in his stride, who got out of every hour 60 minutes of work and out of every minute 60 seconds of exertion, who never lost the initiative nor missed the tempo and who was conscious in himself of the little time left to him. Yet he applied himself heroically and energetically to the task, exuding confidence in himself and imparting faith to others, spreading goodwill and trust, and animating everyone with a sense of urgency and the call of patriotism. Thus the message of integration was translated into action from Kashmir to Kanya Kumari and from Kamrup in Assam to Kutch. It was a vision of unity seldom before converted into action.[4]

On 20 February 1947, Prime Minister Attlee made a declaration in the House of Commons, in the course of which he set a date not later than June 1948 for Britain to transfer power to responsible Indian hands. It was also announced that Viscount Mountbatten of Burma would replace Lord Wavell as Viceroy. Prior to this, the Cabinet Mission Plan of 16 May 1946, though expressed as a recommendation, was really an award, as the Mission was unable to bring about a general agreement between the Congress and the Muslim League. The Congress agreed to participate in the Constituent Assembly to be convened under the plan for the forming of a new constitution. The Muslim League at first accepted the plan, while reiterating that their aim of the attainment of a separate sovereign Pakistan remained their final objective. However, after an acrimonious controversy between Congress President Nehru and League President Jinnah over the interpretation of the plan, the Council of the Muslim League revoked its acceptance. At this time, if Sardar had been the Congress President in place of Jawaharlal Nehru, this split with the League would not have happened. Sardar was a mature and seasoned negotiator and statesman while Nehru was inexperienced and still learning and so apt to make mistakes. Even Maulana Abul Kalam Azad, who had no love for Sardar, writes in his autobiography: 'My second mistake was that, when I decided not to stand myself, I did not support Sardar Patel. We differed on many issues, but I am convinced that, if he had succeeded me as Congress President, he would have seen that the Cabinet Mission Plan was successfully implemented. He would never have committed the mistake of Jawaharlal which gave Mr Jinnah the opportunity of sabotaging the Plan. I can never forgive myself when I think that if I had not committed these mistakes, perhaps the history of the last ten years would have been different'.[5]

This mistake of Maulana was made on 26 April 1946. On 10 July 1946, triumphant Nehru held a press conference in Bombay and in response to questions from news correspondents he stated emphatically: 'The Congress has agreed only to participate in the Constituent Assembly and regarded itself free to change or modify the Cabinet Mission Plan as it thought best'.[6] Jawaharlal's statement came to Jinnah as a bombshell. Now that the Congress President had declared that the Congress could change the scheme, through its majority in the Constituent Assembly, this would mean that the minorities would be placed at the mercy of the majority. The Muslim League Council met on 27 July 1946 and passed a resolution rejecting the Cabinet Mission Plan and decided to resort to direct action for the achievement of sovereign Pakistan. On 8 August the Congress Working Committee met to remedy the situation. Jawaharlal was not willing to call such a meeting and the Committee was now in a dilemma. To repudiate the President's statement would weaken the organisation; on the other hand, to give up the Cabinet Mission Plan would ruin the country. Sardar's mind worked hard to balance the situation. Finally the Committee drafted a resolution which made no reference to Jawaharlal's controversial statement, but reaffirmed the Committee's decision of 7 July 1946 that the Congress had accepted the Cabinet Mission Plan in its entirety and that it will seek the largest measure of co-operation in drawing up a constitution for free India, allowing the greatest measure of freedom and protection for all just claims and interests. The Committee hoped that the Muslim League and all others concerned, in the wider interests of the Nation as well as their own, would join in this great task.

The hope was that if the Muslim League accepted this resolution, it could return to its earlier position where it had accepted the Cabinet Mission Plan. Jinnah did not, however, accept the position and knew that Jawaharlal's statement represented the real thinking of the Congress. He argued that, if Congress could change so many times while the British were still in the country and power had not come into its hands, what assurance did the minorities have that once the British left, Congress would not change its mind again and go back to the position taken up in Jawaharlal's statement.

On 12 August 1946 the Government of India issued the following statement: 'His Excellency the Viceroy, with the approval of His Majesty's Government, invited the President of the Congress to make proposals for the formation of an interim government and the President of the Congress has accepted the invitation. Pandit Jawaharlal Nehru will shortly visit New Delhi to discuss this proposal with His Excellency the Viceroy'.

Jinnah issued a statement the same day rejecting Jawaharlal's invitation to co-operate in the formation of an interim government. The cause was the same suspicion aroused by Nehru's press statement of 10 July 1946. The Muslim League Council decided to resort to direct action; Jinnah declared 16 August 1946 as the Direct Action Day. Mob violence plunged the great city of Calcutta into an orgy of bloodshed with murders rampant everywhere. Maulana writes: 'Sixteen August 1946 was a black day not only for Calcutta but for the whole of India. The turn that events had taken made it almost impossible to expect a peaceful solution by agreement between the Congress and the Muslim League. This was one of the greatest tragedies of Indian history and I have to say with the deepest regret that a large part of the responsibility for this development rests with Jawaharlal. His unfortunate statement that the Congress would be free to modify the Cabinet Mission Plan, reopened the whole question of political and communal settlement. Mr Jinnah took full advantage of that mistake and withdrew from the League's earlier acceptance of the Cabinet Mission Plan'.[7]

Sardar moved to Aurangzeb Road in October 1946, a month after taking office (before that he was in Birla house, New Delhi). In January 1947, Azad joined the Cabinet. The Constituent Assembly was conceived on 16 May 1946, formed in Autumn 1946 and met in December 1946.

Lord Wavell wrote in his diary: 'I saw Vallabhbhai Patel for the first time this morning. Not an attractive personality and uncompromising, but more of a man than most of the Indian politicians I have met... Patel at once began with allegations that the British were supporting Mr Jinnah and the Muslim League, that Jinnah had been allowed to wreck the Simla Conference, that his manners to Azad had been intolerable and so on...'

He said that he did not see how there was ever going to be a settlement between Hindus and Muslims while the British were in India, and that the British should clear out and leave Indians to settle matters themselves. I said he really could not expect us to leave India to chaos and civil war and that there must be some sort of settlement.

I did not introduce the issue of Pakistan, as the tone of his approach did not seem to favour it and merely said that it was my business to see that law and order was maintained until some new form of government was settled. He agreed with this'.[8]

From the end of March 1946 to the end of June, in Delhi, Simla, and again in Delhi, Congress had talks and discussions with the Cabinet Mission composed of Lord Pethwick-Lawrence, Secretary of State for India – Sir Stafford Cripps, President of the Board of Trade – A.V. Alexander, First Lord of the Admiralty. Lord Wavell the Viceroy was in effect the fourth member of the negotiating team. In the negotiations: Vallabhbhai and Jawaharlal were for a strong centre, though Nehru was willing to accept a weaker central government if that would retain the Muslim areas; Gandhi and Maulana thought that the strong provinces would blunt the edge of separation. Thus these two, and Nehru, wanted to disprove the two-nation doctrine.[9]

The Cabinet Mission had two tasks: first, to convert the Viceroy's Executive Council into a representative interim government and, second, to devise a long-term constitutional solution.

The Congress negotiators (representatives) were Maulana Azad who was still the President, Vallabhbhai for the first time as an official Congress negotiator, Jawaharlal Nehru who did much of the speaking and Abdul Gaffar Khan whose inclusion in the team signified the importance they gave to the North-West Frontier Province. The Mahatma's role was unofficial but not inconsequential. Jinnah represented the Muslim League. Wavell, in his diary, described Patel thus: 'Rather a Roman face, powerful, clever and uncompromising'.[10]

The main controversy was about the Central Government and its power. Wavell writes: 'Congress wishing the Union Centre to have powers of direct taxation and to be self-supporting, while Jinnah advocated that it should be given a lump sum and should have to go to the Groups if it wanted any more money… On the matter of Central Legislature, Jinnah stonewalled obstinately but we eventually got him to admit that parity of representatives from the two Groups would be the 'least objectionable' form… Finally it seemed to be generally agreed, at least Jinnah did not dissent, that a Central Judiciary would be necessary.

We finally got down to an announcement by Jinnah that he would accept the Union Centre if Congress would accept Groups. Nehru said something very near acceptance of Jinnah's proposition and Patel's cold face of angry disapproval was a study.

At one moment Jinnah seemed to claim the right of a Group to secede after five years; and Patel exclaimed triumphantly: 'There we have it now, what he has been after all the time'. The damage had been done in Patel's mind and he had been given an handle for his contention that the League are not really in earnest about entering a union and mean to get out as soon as possible'.[10]

After long drawn-out deliberations with the Congress and the League, who did not see eye to eye, the Cabinet Mission prepared an 'Award' on 16 May 1946. This became the final offer of the British Government.

Congress thanked the Mission for ruling out Pakistan and also the compulsory grouping; while the League held that Section 19 of the Plan constituted Pakistan's 'Foundation and Basis'. Sir Stafford Cripps claimed in the House of Commons that he kept the wording of the Plan's language 'purposely vague'. Getting both Congress and the League to 'accept' different and contradictory provisions was the purpose.[11]

On 6 June 1946 the Council of All-India Muslim League passed a resolution accepting the Cabinet Mission Plan, subject however to a number of reservations. The Cabinet Mission left India on 24 June 1946, after a stay in India of three months. On 25 June 1946 the Congress President, Maulana Azad, asserted that his party accepted the statement of 16 May, but with several reservations. The Congress Working Committee's resolution accepting the Cabinet Mission Plan was submitted for ratification to the All-India Congress Committee which met in Bombay on 6 July 1946. At this session Jawaharlal Nehru (nominated by the back door as Congress President on 26 April 1946) took over the Presidency.

On 10 July 1946, as mentioned earlier, Nehru made the great blunder at his press conference. Speaking to the press, Nehru admitted that, having agreed to participate in the Constituent Assembly, the Congress had agreed to the Cabinet Mission Plan 'but what we do there we are entirely and absolutely free to determine'. Referring to the two conditions laid down by the Mission, namely proper arrangements for minorities and a treaty between India and Great Britain, he stressed that he would have no treaty with the British Government if they sought to impose any conditions on India and, as for minorities, it was our domestic problem. 'We shall no doubt succeed in solving it. We accept no outsiders' interference in it, certainly not the British Government's interference, and therefore these two limiting factors to the sovereignty of the Constituent Assembly are not accepted by us'.

Nehru's viewpoint was at once taken up by Jinnah who characterised it as 'a complete repudiation of the basic form upon which the long-term scheme rests and all its fundamentals and terms and obligations and rights of parties accepting the scheme'. At the meeting of the Council of the All-India Muslim League in Bombay on 27 July 1946, Jinnah accused the Cabinet Mission of bad faith and of having 'played into the hands of the Congress'. He said the Congress did not appreciate the sacrifices the League had made. The League therefore had no alternative but to adhere once more to the national goal of Pakistan. A resolution to that effect was drafted by the Working Committee and placed before the Council. It was passed without dissent. The Working Committee of the League followed upon the Council resolution by calling upon Muslims throughout India to observe 16 August as 'Direct Action Day'.

Thus Nehru's childish mistake made Pakistan a certainty. The Congress President's words were all that mattered to the League and Mr Jinnah. If Sardar had been the President, he would never have made such a blunder. Subsequently, Sardar, and other leaders, tried to repair the damage but to no avail.

To rectify Nehru's mistake, the Congress Working Committee met on 8 August 1946, at which Maulana Azad pointed out that if we wanted to save the situation, we must make it clear that the statement of the Congress President at the Bombay press conference was his personal opinion and did not represent the policy of the Congress.[12] However, Nehru objected to this, saying it would be embarrassing to the organisation and also to him personally, if the Working Committee passed a resolution that the statement of the Congress President did not represent the policy of the Congress. Ultimately a resolution, which Sardar played a great hand in, was drafted which made no reference to Jawaharlal's statement but reaffirmed the decision of AICC in which it accepted the Cabinet Mission Plan in its entirety. Sardar Vallabhbhai was greatly perturbed by Nehru's blunder.

An exasperated Sardar wrote on 29 July 1946 in the following terms to D.P. Mishra (who was dropped by Nehru from his new

Working Committee): 'I have had numerous complaints about the formation of the new Working Committee by our President, and I fully appreciate the depth of feeling among comrades who have worked with us for so many years and who are upset at the revolutionary change in the personnel. I am therefore not surprised at the unrestrained manner in which you have expressed in your letter'.[13]

'Though the President (Nehru) has been elected for the fourth time, he often acts with childlike innocence, which puts all in great difficulties quite unexpectedly. You have good reason to be angry but we must not allow our anger to get the better of ourselves... He has done many things recently which have caused us great embarrassment. His action in Kashmir, his interference in the Sikh election to the Constituent Assembly, his press conference immediately after the AICC are all acts of emotional insanity and put tremendous strain on us to set matters right... His present action is also the result of a burning desire to take the younger elements with him and although in doing so he has committed a grave mistake, he will not hesitate to rectify it when he realises the grave injustice he has done to others and to the organisation. You may however rest assured that so long as one of us is inside the group that governs the policy of the Congress, the straight and steady march of the ship will not be interrupted.'[14]

Before Sardar wrote the above letter, he wrote to Jawaharlal on 19 July 1946 saying: 'The Punjab situation is in a hopeless muddle... The Sikhs are not in our discipline... I had a telephone call just now from Bhim Sen Sachar. He wants to resign his leadership'.[15]

On 27 July 1946 Sardar wrote to Bhim Sen Sachar:

> Last week I had a telephone call from you suggesting that you proposed to resign from the leadership. I could not understand what you meant and why you wanted to take my permission? You were appointed by Maulana Sahib as leader and you should have asked him to permit you to resign, if you wanted to do so. I have heard nothing from you except this telephone call ... I am sorry about the Punjab muddle, particularly the bungling in the Constituent Assembly elections by the Sikhs. We expected three seats from the Unionist group – at least two – but we got only one. The Sikhs did not contest at all in spite of my efforts, and I was surprised to

> hear that, in spite of my instructions, you had contacted Pandit Nehru and conveyed his message to the Sikhs, which resulted in this unfortunate situation. Its repercussions have been very serious.[16]

Thus Nehru's uncalled-for interference created the crisis for Congress in the Punjab Province, and that lasted even after Independence. Gopichand Bhargava was the Premier of Punjab at the time of partition and remained so till June 1949 when a large number of party members withdrew their support from him in favour of Bhim Sen Sachar. But Sachar did not survive for long as he was really unsuited to be a premier. The then Governor of East Punjab, C.M. Trivedi, wrote to Sardar on 11 June 1949 describing Sachar as hasty, impulsive, tactless, obstinate, vain and a difficult person to work with. This was the man of Nehru's choice who polluted the Punjab politics. If Nehru had given a free hand to Sardar, this situation would not have occurred. Sardar had asked for Government's Rule, for a spell until conditions stabilised. But Nehru and the Cabinet did not agree. As we shall see later, the Punjab situation remained the same in the reign of Prime Minister Indira Gandhi, who became the first victim of Sikh discontent paying with her life.

By the act of partition, India lost an area of 364,737 square miles and lost a population of 81.5 million to Pakistan. However, the integration of 554 princely states, which was organised by Sardar, brought in to the new Indian nation an area of over 500,000 square miles with a population of 86.5 million (not including Kashmir and Jammu).

In the words of Sardar: 'The great ideal of geographical, political and economical unification of India had for centuries remained a distant dream. After the advent of Indian independence, it still seemed as difficult to attain as ever. Nevertheless, it was indeed consummated through the policy of integration.'

The new Constitution came into force on 26 January 1950. By this time, Sardar had integrated geographically all the states and brought them into the same constitutional relations with the central government as the provinces. The administrative integration into the union was proceeding apace. The scheme of financial integration had already been worked out and would come into operation within a few months. It was settled that the armed forces of the princely states would be absorbed into the Indian army.

Over a period of years Sardar, because of his organisational ability and his reputation for discipline, realism and straightforwardness, came to be looked upon as the only person who could handle the Party machinery with judgement, competence, to general satisfaction and with emphasis on results. Congress Presidents usually consulted him on important matters and his advice was usually accepted. He was virtually in charge of the election machinery both in 1937 and in 1945–46. He was also the guiding genius of the parliamentary programme and the ministering angel of party funds.[17]

Sardar's role in the Congress organisation was a decisive one. He enjoyed both popular trust and confidence. The rank and file looked upon him with awe. He had a reputation for fair-mindedness and sound judgement. His knowledge of local politics was deep and his understanding of local situations quick and instructive. He was fearless and set great store by stability. At the same time he took a moral stand when the occasion demanded. As a leader he would influence local judgement through the faith and confidence he inspired, but he was capable of refraining from pressing his view to the point of going against democratic principles. His handling of the Madras affair involving Rajaji's leadership demonstrated this.[18]

Sardar organised the Bardoli Satyagraha Campaign almost like a military one. He anticipated all the possible moves by the Government and he devised the strategy to counter them. Mass imprisonment, attachment of land, cattle and household property and various kinds of harassment were all taken into account. He divided the Bardoli Taluka into thirteen Satyagraha camps (or Chhavanis as they were called); each under the control of one of his trusted lieutenants. Each camp encompassed the surrounding villages. Most of the camp leaders were outsiders, from other parts of Gujarat, mainly from Kheda District. The location of the camps was chosen on strategic, geopolitical and socio-ethnic grounds.

The Bardoli Taluka (British) was surrounded by the territories of Baroda State at many points and Sardar wanted the striking peasants to move their cattle and household goods to Baroda territory to prevent them falling into Government hands.

He divided the Taluka into four regions:

I Northern Region, consisting of:
- Mota, the village of Ramchandra Bhatt
- Varad, a stronghold of Patidars
- Bamni, also a stronghold of Patidars
- Balda, this camp was in the midst of the Kaliparaj population

II Central Region, consisting of:
- Afva
- Sialda
- Vankaner, again a stronghold of Patidars
- Bardoli

III Southeastern Region, consisting of:
- Siker
- Bajipura
- Valod, has concentration of Banias
- Buhari, situated in the midst of the Kaliparaj population

IV Southwestern Region, consisting of:
- Sarbhon, surrounded mainly by the Anavil population.

The camp leaders were drawn from various parts of Gujarat and were empowered to take all crucial decisions during the no-tax campaign and this gave them a strong sense of involvement. They reported directly to Sardar and also kept in close touch with the local leaders. Their day usually began very early in the morning at about 3 a.m. and ended only when they were tired. They handed out handwritten or printed patrikas (leaflets), warned the villagers of the Government's attacking party's movements and carried messages between the camps as well as to the headquarters. They rarely made speeches, but distributed Sardar's speeches in leaflets. 'Never before had I heard such brilliance in his language', said Mahadev Desai, 'It is from the speeches of Vallabhbhai in Bardoli that the lovers of Gujarat discovered how rich their language was', said Narahari.[19] The local workers were assisted by about 1,500 volunteers in various camps. Most of these were students from the Ashrams and sons of local leaders. These were to help the peasants during adverse circumstances and do the other works of distributing patrikas and organising evening Bhajan Mandals. His experience of Kheda satyagraha made him engage the rural womenfolk in the campaign. For spearheading their activities, Sardar and the other workers brought the women members of their own families. Maniben

Patel (Sardar's daughter), Sharda Mehta (wife of Sumant Mehta, the Sarbhon camp leader), Bhaktiba (wife of Gopaldas Darbar, the Bamni camp leader), Shardaben Shah (wife of Fulchand Shah, the Sialda camp leader), were some of the important women workers.

Vallabhbhai secured the support of almost every segment of the social system. No key group was left out, lest the Government should use it to sabotage the movement. Vallabhbhai also understood how to use the strength of caste organisation. For instance, the Lewa Patidars of 18 villages in Sarbhon Division passed a resolution of 2 April 1928 that they would not buy, hire or accept as gift any forfeited land and would take stern measures against any member who paid the revenue dues.[20] The leaders of artisan castes, such as barbers (hajams), cobblers (mochis), and the tailors (darjis) had also passed resolutions of non-cooperation against those who paid land revenue.[21] The Kaliparaj community had already passed a similar resolution on 21 February 1928. Even the Village Councils, which had nothing to do with caste divisions, stressed the importance of unity and remained united to take measures against any individual who co-operated with the Government.

This movement was led throughout by Vallabhbhai from 12 February 1928 to 6 August 1928, when the settlement of the dispute was accepted by both parties. Neither Jawaharlal Nehru nor any other leader of the Congress had organised and brought to a successful conclusion such a prolonged and well-managed Satyagraha movement. In fact J. Nehru had no idea how to manage a mass movement. It needed great organising capability and immense patience and perseverance apart from the capacity for hard work. Nehru limited his efforts to making speeches to crowds as well as to any important assembly of Congress leaders and to inviting the Government to arrest him and put him in jail where he could start writing a book. Independence did not come from such activities. One is not wrong in saying that Jawaharlal Nehru usurped the position of supreme leader of India from Vallabhbhai purely with the help of Gandhiji.

25

VITHALBHAI

From 6 April 1926, when Lord Irwin assumed the Viceroyalty, Vithalbhai Patel enjoyed the privilege of numerous intimate talks with him on the question of India's future and her relations with Britain, such as perhaps no other Indian ever had either with Lord Irwin or any other Viceroy. This was possible because Vithalbhai was President of the Viceroy's New Delhi Legislative Assembly. He represented Gujarat from where he was elected in 1924, and held this position while the Bardoli Satyagraha was in full swing. Lord Irwin wrote to the Bombay Governor, Leslie Wilson, telling him to use Vithalbhai to influence his younger brother, Vallabhbhai, for any possible settlement of the dispute. We now know that that effort failed. Later on 6 September 1928 and 29 October 1928 Lord Irwin, agitated and perturbed by the strength and consequences of the Bardoli Satyagraha, wrote two letters to the Governors of all the Provinces warning them of the dangers ahead. This was the time Lord Irwin was searching for a solution to bring about more peaceful conditions in India. The Bardoli settlement was effected on 8 August 1928. The much-hated Simon Commission had landed at Bombay on 3 February 1928 and the reasonable and successful boycott of the Commission by the Congress members of the Central Assembly and the Provincial Assemblies had all added to the pressure to make peace in the troubled land. Prior to that and the Bardoli campaign in 1927, Vithalbhai's constituency, Gujarat, went through the disaster of excessive rains and the resulting flooding. All the seven rivers of Gujarat, Vishwamitri, Shedi, Vatrak, Dhadhar, Sabarmati, Meshwa and Khari, swelled and burst their banks and carried away everything in their path. Villages on their banks suffered the most. During the four days of this downpour, men, women and children had to hang on the tops of trees or run up to the roof of taller and stronger houses. Their cattle were mostly swept away, or if they were tied to strong posts they drowned under the swirling currents. District towns also suffered as they became marooned. The houses collapsed, walls buckling and sending the roofs tumbling down. Rail and telegraph communications ceased functioning and thus large areas were cut off, which made relief work extremely difficult. This was the situation which Vithalbhai, Vallabhbhai and Dadubhai and other social workers faced.

From 25 to 29 July 1927, between 42 and 54 inches of rain fell in an area 200 miles in length and 50 miles wide, covering Ahmedabad, Kaira, Broach, Panch Mahal and Surat districts of Gujarat. Congress relief organisation did alleviate the immediate problems, but the sheer size of the tragedy exposed the inadequacy of non-official organisations.

Only the government could rehabilitate the homeless and rebuild the rain-damaged houses and public buildings. Dadubhai, Jairamdas Desai and Bhimbhai Naik, who were members of the Bombay Governor's Legislative Council, worked hard on the Governor Sir Leslie Wilson to get Rs.14,500,000 out of the Famine Relief Fund. This was set apart from the general land revenue every year. They also persuaded the Government to give ordinary loans to farmers under the Agriculturists Loan Act and Takavi Grants. This was a distribution of relief to peasants and farmers by way of easy loans with which to purchase the necessary agricultural equipment, bullocks and building material for their houses. Sir C.V. Mehta, the finance member of the Bombay Government, held relief conferences at Nadiad and Anand in collaboration with Vallabhbhai and Dadubhai. He praised their efforts to help even before the Government could start their relief work.

At the time of the Gujarat flood, Vithalbhai was in the UK, where he had gone on a legislative and parliamentary fact-finding mission. He wanted to study how the Speaker of the Parliament in London conducted business. Being a perfectionist, he wanted to follow the procedures and conduct the proceedings in Delhi Assembly, of which he was the President, in a similar fashion. He was anxious to acquaint himself thoroughly with Parliamentary traditions, conventions and procedures. This was with a view of seeing how far he could go, while keeping strictly within the bounds of the Constitution, in promoting the political advance of India.

On his return to India, as he set foot at Bombay, he asked Dadubhai who had come to receive him at the Port: 'What news is there here?'. Dadubhai replied that excessive rain on four days, 25 to 29 July, had created havoc in Gujarat. He, Vallabhbhai and other Congress workers were doing as much as they could towards the relief of the population. He stressed that Vithalbhai should come to Nadiad as soon as the Parliamentary Session in Delhi finished, which would be on 27 December 1927.[1]

In the Bombay Council session held at Poona on 10 and 11 October, Dadubhai made several speeches describing the flood havoc in Gujarat and especially Kaira, which was his constituency. He asked the Bombay Government to release more money and materials, not only to bring immediate relief but also to aid reconstruction of fallen houses and public buildings. Once the session ended, on 16 October, Vithalbhai and Dadubhai went back to Nadiad, to help Vallabhbhai in his efforts to help the suffering people. On 19 October, they visited Dakor and the surrounding mal track.[2] During the last week of October a meeting of all the leading relief workers of Gujarat was held at Nadiad under the presidency of Vallabhbhai, to consider a scheme for the reconstruction of houses in the flood-stricken area. Vithalbhai and Dadubhai were present at this meeting. In the meantime the Viceroy was coming to Bombay for a State visit in the week starting 28 December. Vithalbhai persuaded the Viceroy to visit Kaira District and tour round the distressed areas. Lord Irwin agreed to have dinner with him at Ahmedabad and attend a tea party at Nadiad. On 12 November Vithalbhai wrote to Lord Irwin: 'For several years I have been a staunch advocate of total prohibition and on principle I ban all alcoholic drinks from my table. I hope your Excellency will not mind if I observe that rule on this occasion also?'. In his reply, dated 16 November, Lord Irwin said: 'As regards the observance of alcoholic prohibition at your dinner, I am of course entirely in your hands and would not dream of doing anything but respect the principles of my host'.

In his letter dated 30 November to Colonel Harvey the private secretary to the Viceroy, Vithalbhai wrote: 'His Excellency will be glad to know that Mr Vallabhbhai Patel, President of the Ahmedabad Municipality and the chief relief worker in Gujarat, has consented to attend the dinner even though he is a staunch non-cooperator'. In his letter to Lord Irwin dated 3 December, he wrote: 'Your Excellency will be glad to know that, besides the members of the

Bombay Legislative Council from Gujarat, your Excellency will meet a few prominent relief workers at my Nadiad tea party. These relief workers are orthodox non-cooperators, having no faith whatever in the Council programme. They are believers in the mass-movement and have consistently refused, for the last several years, to have anything to do with functions held in honour of Government officials. Your Excellency will have some real idea of the damage caused by the floods to houses and agricultural land when we visit villages in the Kaira District'.[3]

On 11 December 1928, the Viceroy of India, for the first time in the history of the Raj, stepped down from the train onto the soil of Nadiad. An account of the Viceregal tour is best left to the following Associated Press despatch of 11 December.

'His Excellency the Viceroy alighted from his saloon at 9am at Nadiad Station. He was received by Collector and Hon'ble Mr V.J. Patel. Collector then presented to Viceroy principal officials and non-officials; among the latter were Mr Vallabhbhai Patel, Darbar Gopaldas Desai and Rao Saheb Dadubhai P. Desai. Viceroy then accompanied by Collector, Hon'ble Mr Patel, Mr Vallabhbhai Patel, Executive Engineer, Assistant Collector and Rao Saheb Dadubhai Desai left for Dabhan. On arrival at Dabhan, His Excellency left his car and was conducted on foot through part of village to see some of the fallen houses. Party then left for Sandhana where, on arrival, His Excellency drove through village to see houses damaged by floods. From there party left for Matar. While crossing Vatrak River by temporay bridge to Wasna, His Excellency was shown portions of river bank where fields had been washed away. On arrival at Wasna His Excellency drove through village and then left his car in order to walk through fields on which sand had been deposited and irrigation wells had been demolished. Party next proceeded to Kaira where on arrival they had brief rest at Collector's bungalow, then drove through Kaira town. On way His Excellency left his car and proceeded on foot to see damage suffered by town walls and houses in Rabari Wada and locality of Ahmedabad gate. His Excellency then returned to Nadiad at 1 p.m.

In the afternoon Her Excellency Lady Worsley also joined the party and drove through Nadiad town to have view of damaged houses. They then went to Bilodra where on arrival Their Excellencies left their car and proceeded on foot to village site where they walked round part of village to see damages caused by floods to lands, wells and houses. They then left for Vina. On arrival car first drove towards fields on northern side of village. His Excellency then left his car and proceeded on foot to see fields damaged by floods, accompanied by Collector and Hon'ble Mr Patel, but as it was getting late, His Excellency enquired of nonofficial workers and villagers extent of damage to houses and fields. At every village visited by His Excellency he was greeted by villagers and non-official relief workers. Khaddar dress and Gandhi caps were in evidence at every place. The party then left Vina for Nadiad where Their Excellencies and party drove to District Local Board Hall to attend a tea party given by Hon'ble Mr Patel. This party was attended by members of Bombay Legislative Council from Gujarat and principal relief workers, also by some prominent men from Nadiad. Among relief workers Messrs Vallabhbhai Patel, Laxmidas, Mohan Lal Pandya, Ravishankar, Shankarlal Parekh, Narhari Parikh, Chimanlal Dave, Imam Saheb, Maganlal Gandhi, Darbar Gopaldas and several others were present. The members of Legislative Council present were Rao Saheb Dadubhai Desai, Haribhai Amin, Gordhanbhai Patel, R.B. Bhimbhai Naik, Dr Dixit, Mukadam, Jairamdas Desai, Dr Mansuri, Amrital Sheth, Jivabhai Patel, Shivdasani. Among prominent men from Nadiad were Gopaldas V. Desai, M. Samalbhai Desai, T.S. Parekh, President of the Nadiad Municipality; the Collector and Superintendent of Police were also present. After tea the Viceroy had a brief conversation with the members of the Legislative Council and relief workers individually and collectively. He then left for his saloon at 6 p.m., after having passed a delightful afternoon and expressed his satisfaction at the wonderful work done by the non-official agency to relieve the distress caused by the floods. In every village His Excellency was greeted by the non-official workers who presented him with a petition detailing grievances of the locality concerned; Rao Saheb Dadubhai presented a petition for the whole district. His Excellency promised to consider these petitions and pass them on to the Governor of Bombay with whom he said he would discuss the whole matter. His Excellency gave special interviews in his saloon at Nadiad to Darbar Gopaldas, President of the District Local Board and a leading non-co-operator, and also to the President of the Municipality.'

E.O.M., P.A. to the President, Legislative Assembly; 11–12–1927: 'By this tour of his, not only did the Viceroy get a better idea of the damage caused by the floods and of the sufferings of the poor consequent on them, but the humble and ignorant peasantry of Gujarat, too, realised the value of their representation in the Legislature. The otherwise inaccessible gods of Simla and New Delhi appeared to them to be humble enough to visit their humble huts. (By the way, we might remind our readers that 20 years after this event, Vithalbhai's brother persuaded Mountbatten, as Vithalbhai had persuaded Irwin, to visit this part of the country). The humble peasantry felt highly honoured by the visit to their humble huts, through mud and dust and turbid waters, of the all-powerful representative of His Imperial Majesty. Was that not a proof positive of the power of the people and the value of democratic institutions? This was the first occasion when the people of a remote constituency could – through their chosen representative in the Legislature – induce the virtual ruler of the whole of India to come to them and see for himself the wretched plight to which they had been reduced. This visit of the Viceroy gave the people of this region, for the first time, the opportunity to place before the Head of the British administration in India their multifarious grievances and the crying need for several long-overdue reforms'.[4]

Later, on 4 January 1928, Lord Irwin wrote to the King Emperor in London as follows:

'Your Majesty,

When I last had the honour of writing, Sir, we were on the point of leaving Delhi again for Bombay in order to fulfil various engagements there and entertain the King and Queen of Afghanistan. We spent two or three days en route to Bombay in the Ahmedabad District that had suffered very severely from rain and floods during the monsoon, and to the relief of which Your Majesty has been good enough to make a contribution. We spent some days in visiting different districts, that had been affected, where we were shown dilapidated and practically demolished villages and various points where flooded rivers had eaten away great tongues of land and deposited five and six and seven feet of sand on what had been good agricultural soil. I have no doubt Your Majesty will have heard direct from Sir Leslie Wilson about the general effect of the damage that has been wrought. The thing that struck me most particularly was the extent to which brick houses in the villages had been destroyed, not by flood, but merely by the force of driving rain loosening and washing away the mud mortar between the bricks until there was nothing left to hold the wall together. The suffering of the people must have been very great. In several places one was shown trees in the middle of villages up which people had had to cling and stay there two or three days till the water subsided. Your Majesty will be pleased to hear that the various philanthropic agencies have worked in very close collaboration with Sir Leslie Wilson's Government, and I think doing all that is possible to repair the harm. As was of course to be expected, the villagers and the local politicians who are organising relief were loud in their requests for much more generous assistance than has been found possible. This I am afraid, must be held to have been unavoidable, and I am satisfied that Sir Leslie Wilson is doing everything in his power to meet the difficulties of the situation. In spite of the fact, that our visit there followed very closely upon the first storm that had been aroused by the announcement of Parliamentary Commission and in spite of the fact also that Ahmedabad was in the bad days of non-cooperation rather a storm centre. It was, Sir, very gratifying to note the general atmosphere of friendliness that seemed to prevail among all classes of the people. On the last afternoon of our visit, the President of the Assembly, Mr Patel, in whose constituency we were and who himself, as Your Majesty knows, is a member of the Congress party, invited me to a tea party, where he had collected to meet us all the most prominent swarajists and congressmen of the district. Several of them had hitherto refused to meet any official person and it was encouraging to see that they were willing, not only to meet us, but to do so on terms of great cordiality. The truth, I think, is that the agitation against the Statutory Commission is purely political, and finds little or no echo in the minds of the ordinary masses of the people. I don't think, Sir, that there is anything very new to report about the general political situation in this regard. Most of the political bodies have been holding their annual congresses during Christmas week, and have been using a good deal of strong language, as is always the case. I am reluctant to make rash prophesies but all those who are most competent to form opinions concur in thinking that there is a good hope that with time many of those who are now in the ranks of opposition will wish to turn to courses of greater sanity. A good many bodies have already professed their determination not to boycott the Commission, and I think this is bound to have an effect gradually, upon others who will be unwilling to lose the opportunity to be heard. Much will depend, Sir, upon the personal effect that Sir John Simon can create when he gets out here, and upon the decisions that he may reach as to the precise procedure that he will propose to follow as affecting the mutual relations of his Commission with the suggested Indian committee.

I should like if I may to repeat my expression of good wishes to Your Majesty and her Majesty the Queen for 1928 and many future years, and I have, with my humble duty, the honour to remain, Your Majesty's devoted and obedient servant, IRWIN'.[5]

It should be noted that in the Gujarat flood relief work, Gandhiji was absent in the hills of South India recuperating from a near nervous breakdown. This had been due to the failure of his two agitations; one in 1918, the Kaira Satyagraha and in 1922 the non-event of the Bardoli agitation for which he was imprisoned and later released. Subhas Bose writes in his book: 'By middle of 1927 the leadership of the Congress was on the whole found wanting, Mahatma Gandhi was suffering from acute mental depression and was living in retirement of active politics. Motilal Nehru had left for Europe owing to professional reasons. In the circumstances, the responsibility of leadership was vested in Mr Srinivas Ayenger.'[6] As mentioned earlier, it was Dadubhai who encouraged and pepped up Gandhiji in 1929–30 with the idea of a salt satyagraha which brought him back to full mental health.

When you read the two letters from Vithalbhai (of 9 March 1930 and 11 May 1933, see Appendix 4) you may possibly think, what a cheek this little man has to criticise the great Mahatma. But if you check the following facts, you would perhaps think otherwise.

Vithalbhai's connections at the highest positions in the Congress were long before Gandhi and Jawaharlal and Sardar came on the scene. As far back as 1918 he was the Chairman of the Reception Committee of the Congress session in Bombay. Gandhiji became Congress President for the first time in 1924. Pandit Nehru first entered into a high position, as joint secretary, in 1923. Even Motilal Nehru first became President at the 1919 Amritsar Congress with Vithalbhai as joint secretary. In fact Vithalbhai was the first office bearer of the Congress amongst all the Congress leaders we know. He had the vision that one day Congress would represent all of India and worked towards that end.

In 1924 while he was a member of the Bombay Legislative Council, where Dadubhai was also a member since 1920, he was elected to the newly constituted Central Legislative Assembly in Delhi. On his going to Delhi, Dadubhai assumed the leadership of opposition from Gujarat. On 22 August 1925, Vithalbhai was elected President of the newly constituted Central Assembly, in which office he was expected to represent all interests. He had to resign from the Congress Working Committee, to which he was again elected in 1930 only after he resigned his Presidency to participate in the Salt Satyagraha on 25 April 1930. From 22 August 1925 to 25 April 1930, being the President of the Central Legislative Assembly, he could not participate in the proceedings of Congress and its working committee. During that time Gandhiji acquired full control of Congress. Vithalbhai, the only person capable of confronting Gandhiji, was not there until 25 April 1930. On 28 August 1930 he was arrested, then released on health grounds 5 January 1931. He went straight to hospital in Bombay and his illness prevented him from attending the Congress Working Committee. That Committee met at Karachi from 1 to 2 April 1931 and gave Gandhi an unanimous vote to go alone to London as the sole representative of the Congress at the Round Table Conference. If Vithalbhai had been present he would not have agreed to this.

Gandhi left on 28 April 1931, accompanied by Mahadev Desai, Devdas Gandhi, Pyarelal, Mira Ben and Mrs Sarojini. Vithalbhai had left for treatment in Vienna on 24 February 1931. From there, after undergoing treatment, he went to London (against medical advice) to help and assist Gandhi. As soon as he reached London he could clearly see that the British strategy was to involve Gandhiji in minor issues, particularly the communal problem, so that a division would occur among the Indian representatives. As a result they would start fighting among themselves, forgetting their main objective which was to unitedly ask for Dominion status. Gandhi, who had come there as the sole representative of Congress and being one of the two signatories of the Gandhi-Irwin Pact, wanted to get to grips with the main constitutional problem without losing time.

He should not have been treated as one of the many. However, the very decision of the Congress Working Committee, arrived at in the absence of Vithalbhai, to select the Mahatma as their sole representative at this second Round Table Conference was a thoroughly unwise one. Alone in an assembly of 107 men, with all kinds of nondescripts, flunkeys and self-appointed leaders arrayed against him like a solid phalanx, he would be at a great disadvantage.[6] Moreover, he would have nobody at his side to back him up in the fight that he would have with reactionary Moslem leaders. (Vithalbhai was not an officially appointed Congress delegate so he could not enter the conference and sit beside the Mahatma. He could only advise him outside the conference chamber.) The second Round Table Conference consisted of 107 members, of whom 65 were from British India, 22 from the Indian States and 20 from the three British political parties; while the Minorities Committee of the conference was composed of 6 Britishers, 13 Moslems, 10 Hindus, 2 from the depressed classes, 2 from Labour, 2 Sikhs, 2 Christians, 1 Parsi, 2 Britishers domiciled in India, 1 Anglo-Indian and 3 women – a total of 44. The Moslems, who were a quarter of the population of India, had the largest representation and there was only one nationalist Moslem among them.

Vithalbhai suggested to the Mahatma that, if any points of conflict arose, he should ask that they be referred to the League of Nations. Gandhiji was not in a mood to listen to Vithalbhai. 'I and my God' was his response to Vithalbhai's appeal to reason. The Mahatma appeared to have gone to London, not for the purpose of negotiating a treaty with the British Government, but in order to preach the gospel of non-violence and truth to the materialistic West. Vithalbhai despaired and the failed Round Table Conference concluded on 1 December 1931. Gandhi left London on 4 December and arrived at Bombay on 28 December, by the SS *Pilsna*. Vithalbhai also arrived in Bombay on the same ship.

Vithalbhai again left India on 5 March 1932 for further treatment in Vienna. On 9 March 1932 he wrote the following letter while aboard the SS *Ranchi* at Aden: 'Brother Dadubhai; all the work has come to nought, and for that I consider Gandhi as responsible. He never accepts any advice and except satyagraha he does not know anything else. In the circumstances it is our duty to the people of India, that when I regain my good health, we should openly follow the road, which we feel is the right road for freedom struggle, and in that I hope you and all other friends will help me. Please give my regards to everyone and please do write to me. Yours, Vithalbhai.'

During the years that he was President of the Central Assembly, though he had to resign his membership of the Congress Working Committee, he was one of the most prominent of the leaders and he tried to back Gandhiji with all his power of persuasion. As President he came in close and frequent contact with the Viceroy. The Viceroy being the executive head of the Government and its administration, Vithalbhai had to consult him often on the legislative conduct and proceedings of the Central Legislative Assembly. He also had to discuss the disputes and differences between Government benches and the opposition in the Assembly. The political skill of Vithalbhai was such that gradually he came to have a hold on Lord Irwin who considered him as a well-meaning friend. In this way he was successful in winning him over to his way of thinking on Indian political problems. He became a link between the Government and the Congress. Although the Viceroy was constantly surrounded by his advisers who lost no opportunity of impressing upon him the necessity of constantly keeping before himself the official point of view. The personal integrity of Lord Irwin was impeccable and he was not opposed to the legitimate aspirations of the people of India.[7] Bardoli settlement occurred in August 1928, prior to that the Simon Commission landed at Bombay on 3 February 1928. On 26 December 1927 the Madras Congress had already announced the boycott of the Simon Commission. Then again the All-parties Conference met at Lucknow on 28 to 30 August 1930 and declared in favour of Dominion self-government. Meanwhile the Calcutta Congress, on 28 December 1928, had already changed its goal to that of complete independence.

Gandhi wrote in his *Autobiography*: 'I must regard my participation in Congress proceedings at Amritsar (1919) as my real entrance into Congress politics. My attendance at the previous Congress was nothing more perhaps than an annual renewal of allegiance to the Congress. I never felt on those occasions that I had any other work cut out for me, except that of a mere private, nor did I desire more.' Vithalbhai, however, was Joint General Secretary of the Delhi Congress (1918) and the Amritsar Congress (1919). He was a very loyal office holder of the Congress and during the twenties he forcefully promoted the Congress cause to Lord Irwin, the Viceroy, in his letters and conversations.

26

JAWAHARLAL NEHRU – SOME OPINIONS AND JUDGEMENTS

A – EXTRACTS FROM 'JAWAHARLAL NEHRU IN THE HISTORY OF THE CONGRESS' BY PATTABHAI SITARAMAYA

In pursuance of an AICC resolution, Swami Shraddhanand, Motilal Nehru and Pandit Malavya went to the Punjab in the last week of June 1919 to inquire into the happening in Punjab. Then Andrews went there and returned. Both Motilal and Pandit returned and then Motilal went there again. Then Jawaharlal went with Andrews.[1] Jawaharlal was arrested and convicted in May 1922 in connection with the boycott of Prince's visit and also for the boycott of British cloth.[2] In April 1923 J. Nehru released from jail.[3] J. Nehru – at his insistence resignation of some members from the Congress Working Committee.[4] 6 May 1923 – C.W.C. meeting at Bombay – J. Nehru resigned (25 May 1923).[5] 'J. Nehru has become the President of Allahabad Municipality.'[6] 'December 1925 Cawnpore Congress had an easy time except for certain labour demonstrations and minor trouble from certain delegates which were brought under control by sturdier men like J. Nehru'.[7] 'The International Congress against imperial and colonial oppression – Jawaharlal Nehru at the time was in Europe and he represented India and sent up a report from Brussels where it was held. The A.I.C.C. expressed its appreciation of his services.'[8] Madras sessions of Congress 1927 declared: 'This Congress declares the goal of the Indian people to be complete independence'. This resolution had for some time become a hardy annual. It received an added impetus by the arrival of Jawaharlal Nehru from Europe and espousal of the cause by him.[9] The Simon Commission was being boycotted. 'Lucknow experienced several wanton and unprovoked police charges on unarmed and peaceful gatherings, on the occasion of the visit of the Commission. Even in 1928 Jawaharlal was not spared by the U.P. police.'[10] A remark by Jawaharlal in Lucknow, 30 August 1928, that the Talukdars like the Maharajah of Mahmudabad and Raja Rampal Singh were unnecessary men in Society[11] refers to Jawaharlal's view as advocate of complete independence.[12] At the post-Bardoli Congress, held in Calcutta on 29 December 1928, Jawaharlal Nehru and Subash Chandra Bose submitted similar amendments to the Congress Resolution proposed by Mahatmaji.[13] Jawaharlal as one of the signatories of a letter to All Parties Conference (held at Lucknow prior to the Congress), asking for complete independence instead of Dominion status.[14] Subhas Bose, in his book 'The Indian Struggle', wrote that Jawaharlal Nehru lacked the essential quality of leadership namely the capacity to make decisions and face unpopularity if need be. He was a great disappointment, but there was no help for it. What had been expected of him had to be accomplished by lesser men.[15] From the above it can be clearly seen that Nehru had not done any extraordinary work. All local and provincial workers did the same as Nehru was doing. He never did anything extra to deserve the presidency of the Indian National Congress.

In July 1927, Catherine Mayo published her book 'Mother India', which later became quite famous.[16] She was criticised for leaning towards the functioning of the British Raj, but it did provide a factual résumé of the political situation in India. She drew her conclusions from available official as well as public records based on facts. So one can say that she described the true political climate in India for 1927. She mentions Gandhi on several pages and Dadubhai is mentioned twice. However, she does not mention Jawaharlal Nehru simply because then he was a political nonentity. Even Vallabhbhai is not mentioned because he became an All-India leader only after Bardoli in 1928–1929, while Dadubhai had existed as a leading Bombay Province nationalist leader taking up cudgels against the Government as elected representative in the Bombay Provincial Legislative Council since 1920. So no doubt attention was paid to his popular public activities.

At the 1929 Lahore Congress presidency contest – in the provincial voting ten provinces voted for Gandhi, five for Vallabhbhai and three for Jawaharlal Nehru. Gandhiji was duly elected, but he resigned. It became necessary under the constitution to elect a substitute. Accordingly a meeting of the A.I.C.C. was held in Lucknow on 28 September 1929. Here Gandhiji saw the wisdom of installing on the Gadi of the Congress a younger man, who would inspire confidence in the younger folk of the country. The attendance at Lucknow was not large and Jawaharlal Nehru was elected with the support of Gandhiji. Thus Vallabhbhai was left out.[17] Thus the die was cast by Gandhiji at the request of Motilal Nehru and Jawaharlal became the youngest President of the Congress. The Presidency catapulted a man who had no experience or expertise of civil disobedience, into a national figure, who again with Gandhiji's help and blessing became the first Prime Minister of India, who led it on the ruinous path of a selfish idealist, engrossed in his own personal aggrandisement. This was the second time that the Mahatma preferred Jawaharlal to Vallabhbhai. If this was not a Gandhi-Nehru conspiracy, what else was it? Even the death of Gandhiji proved it abundantly when Nehru went to the microphone with the words: 'Father of the Nation is no more'. Till then no one ever thought of the words 'Father of the Nation'. 'Motilal pressed Jawaharlal's claim on Gandhiji'. 'But for Gandhiji, Jawaharlal could not have been elected at the Lahore session. He climbed to this high office not by the main entrance or even a side entrance but by a trap door'.[18] This fits with what Dadubhai told the writer: 'Motilal earnestly requested Gandhiji to let Jawaharlal (39 years old) be the President during my lifetime. Gandhiji agreed and let go Vallabhbhai's legitimate claim'. Dadubhai was there at this A.I.C.C. at Lucknow. 'But the Mahatma took a clever step in supporting the candidature of Pandit Jawaharlal Nehru and his election opened a new chapter in his public career. Since then Pandit J.L. Nehru has been a consistent and unfailing supporter of the Mahatma.'[19]

Jawaharlal Nehru, in the preface to his autobiography, begins with: 'This book was written entirely in prison … the reader I must warn him that this account is wholly one-sided and inevitably egotistical; many important happenings have been completely ignored and many important persons who shaped events have hardly been mentioned … those who want to make a proper study of our recent past, will have to go to other sources' (2 January 1936).[20]

B – VITHALBHAI'S ELECTION AS PRESIDENT OF LEGISLATIVE ASSEMBLY IN 1925. EXTRACT FROM 'BOOK 2, *VITHALBHAI*' BY GORDHANBHAI PATEL:

In pursuance of the provisions of the Government of India Act, 1919, the Legislative Assembly was called upon, for the first time during the 60 years existence of the Indian Legislature, to elect its own President. The Assembly was composed of a block of nominated and European phalanxes on the one side and the elected representatives on the other side. Hitherto the occupant of the presidential chair had been either the Viceroy or his nominee. The office of President was looked upon as a strategic point in the machinery and framework of the Government of India Act. Experience had shown that the chair of the Assembly possessed immense real power. The total membership of the Assembly came to 143. However, about 120 members were expected to be present at the time of the ballot. Vithalbhai's Swarajists Party had 44 members. Opposing Vithalbhai were the pro-government 12 nominated members, 8 unofficial European members and 24 official members. The position was thus far balanced. This official block was going to vote against Vithalbhai. They were supposed to support the candidacy of Rangachariar. Jinnah was totally against Vithalbhai and he took all his Muslim members to go against him. However, all the Bombay members, except Jinnah, were for Vithalbhai. Vithalbhai's canvassing power was employed in full swing and it brought the votes of Purushottamdas, N.M. Joshi, Dumasia, Harchandrai, Harisingh Gour, Raju, Malaviya and Setalvad. The Government procured the solid support of Jinnah's men, the European group, nominated members and some liberals and independents. In short, the Congress vote alone was not enough to win this election. However, in an exciting contest Vithalbhai secured 58 votes against Rangachariar's 56. The will of the people and the strength of the Congress had succeeded against heavy odds. The gods, for the first time, seemed to smile on India in revolt. An avowed congressman, one who a few days before had been violently attacked by the Anglo-Indian press and the bureaucrats all over the country, was elected to the Presidential Chair of India's Parliament. A congressman as President was a definite landmark on the road to legislative democracy. Vithalbhai occupied the Presidential Gadi, not because of his wealth or social position, but because of his intrinsic merit and devoted public service. A commoner, a peasant now sat on the exalted chair, which had for years together been the exclusive preserve of the Peers of Britain – the Viceroys of India.

On Vithalbhai occupying the chair Sir Alexander Muddiman, as leader of the House and Home Member of the Government of India, warmly welcomed him and promised him full Government support. He said: 'I trust that the relations that have existed between the Chair and the House during the tenure of office of your distinguished predecessor will continue. In our personal relations, as leader of the House, it will frequently be my duty to visit you in your room and discuss the scope of the business before the House and I trust that the same cordiality and the same harmony will prevail as has prevailed in the past.' Motilal Nehru accorded him a warm welcome and expressed his wish and desire to claim him back in the Swaraj Party on completion of his term. He said: 'All I can say at the present moment is that you have filled us with high hopes amd that we are confident that you will fulfill them worthily.'

Jinnah said that Vithalbhai was now on trial, but he felt sure that he would do his utmost to fulfill the expectations they had formed of him.

So this day, 22 August 1925, became one of the most momentous days in the progress of India towards self-governance.[21]

C – EXTRACTS FROM SUBHAS BOSE'S 'THE INDIAN STRUGGLE, 1920–42'

'Even at the Lahore Congress, in December 1929, the Mahatma had no plans for launching an anti-government campaign of any sort. Though he moved the Resolution on independence which was unanimously adopted by the Congress. Not till February 1930, after much heart searching, did he make up his mind to start a civil-disobedience movement in the country; begining with a campaign to manufacture salt. But though the Congress did not give a bold and intelligent lead to the country during the whole of 1929, the unrest did not abate in any way.'[22]

'The All-India Congress Committee is a body of about 350 members representing the different provinces of India. Every year it elects an executive of 15 members, called the Working Committee.'[23]

'Early in January 1930, Gandhiji's first order went out. January 26th should be observed all over India as the Day of Independence. On that day a manifesto prepared by the Mahatma and adopted by the Working Committee of the Congress was to be read from every platform and accepted by the people. The manifesto was at once a declaration of independence and a pledge of loyalty to the Indian National Congress and to the sacred fight for Indian Liberty.'[24]

'Simon Commission Report issued 7 June 1930. Labour Party came to power in June 1930 and they issued the Simon Report.'[25]

'On 12 November 1930, the first session of the Round Table Conference was held in London. Ramsay Macdonald opened it as Chairman.'

'The net result of the first session of the Round Table Conference was the offer to India of two bitter pills – Safeguards and Federation. To make the pills palatable, they were sugar coated with "Responsibility". To make matters worse, the anti-nationalist Muslims who were present at the Round Table Conference declared that they would agree to responsible government with federation and safeguards only if the communal question was decided to their satisfaction. The proposal of federation was one of the cleverest moves adopted by the British Government at this stage and it is a pity that elderly politicians like Sir Tej Bahadur Sapru and M.R. Jayakar did not see through the game at once. Though Mr Srinivas Sastri and Mr M.A. Jinnah did at the beginning feel suspicious towards the idea of bringing in the conservative elements (Indian Princes), which can act as deadweight to checkmate the radical forces in British India. The first Round Table Conference was adjourned "sine die".'

'Karachi Congress of December 1931, undoubtedly represented the pinnacle of Mahatma's popularity and prestige. I travelled with him for some days and was able to observe the unprecedented crowds that greeted him everywhere. I wonder if such a spontaneous ovation was ever given to a leader anywhere else? He stood out before the people not merely as a Mahatma but as the hero of a political fight. The question that stirred me at the time was as to how he would utilise the unique position he had been able to attain? The first shock came when the news was announced that the Working Committee on 2 April had selected Mahatma Gandhi as the sole representative of the Congress at the Second Round Table Conference and that he had accepted that decision. The decision alone was thoroughly a wrong one. Alone in an assembly of about one hundred men arranged against him, he would be at a great disadvantage, moreover he would have nobody at his side to back him up in the fight that he would have with reactionary Muslim leaders.'

'The second move of the Mahatma was a positive blunder. In private and in public, he began to say that his going to the Round Table Conference depended on his ability to solve the Hindu-Muslim question beforehand. He also began to say that if the Muslims made a united demand on the question of representation, electorate, etc. in the new constitution, he would accept the demand. The effect of these statements was a most tragic one. After the Delhi Pact the reactionary Muslims had been somewhat overawed by the strength and power of the post-Bardoli and Dharasana Campaign and they were in a mood to come to terms with that body on a reasonable basis. The first statement of Mahatma immediately changed their mood and made them feel that they held the key position. Mahatma had a conference with the reactionary Muslims in Delhi. They, led by Jinnah, made a fourteen point demand. One of the demands was a separate electorate. That evening when I (Subhas) met him, the Mahatma was depressed. He asked me if I had any objection to a separate electorate. I replied that separate electorates were against the fundamental principles of nationalism and that I felt so strongly on the subject that even Swaraj on the basis of separate electorates is not worth having. Soon after this the Mahatma issued a public statement saying that he could not accept the demands made by the communalist Muslim leaders, since the nationalist Muslims were opposed to it.'

Mahatma sailed on S.S. *Rajputana* and arrived in London on 12 September 1931, via Marseilles, to attend the second Round Table Conference. The Conference was composed of 107 members. Of these few, if any, shared Gandhi's views so he was at a grave disadvantage. By the last meeting, on 1 December 1931, the Round Table Conference had failed to reach any satisfactory conclusions. Gandhiji landed back in Bombay 28 December 1931 by S.S. *Pilsna*. Vithalbhai also travelled by S.S. *Pilsna* to Bombay.

D – LEGACY OF GANDHI-NEHRU ALLIANCE

The headquarters of the Ministry of Industry was in the 'Udyog Bhawan' and it was there that the 'Permit Raj' resided. This system injected for the first time the seeds of 'Bribes Culture' into the body of the Central Government administration. Prior to that, bribing of Government servants was unknown. The very thought of bribing a Government servant was abhorred by the inhabitants of British India. Thanks to Nehru's ideological following of Soviet Russia, the first Five-year Plan was enacted and passed in the Indian Parliament. From now on, even if you wanted to manufacture a wrought-iron nail, you had to go to Delhi (never mind that you may be 1,500 miles away) to ask for permission from Udyog Bhawan!

Nehru in his ignorance did not realise that a Government, or its Planning Commission, cannot allocate resources adequately and efficiently without the information on demand and prices that only a free market can give. This was the real cause of the abject failure of the Soviet Union which in the end had to turn to a free market economy (in the 1990s).

From the actions and letters of Vallabhbhai one can safely surmise that he would never agree to a Permit Raj. He was a practical man, seasoned by the hereditary peasant instincts of the Desais. Vallabhbhai openly said that: 'My only culture is agriculture'. In managing the absorption of 565 native Princes into the fabric of independent India, he had amply shown the practicality of his vision. In one of his letters to Dadubhai, he mentions that once the integration of States was done, he would give a thought to the financial and political management of the future progress of India.[26] Alas he died before he could start, and with his death the door lay open for Nehru to experiment with the motive power provided by his own whims and inexperienced self. The death of Sardar left Nehru with the powers of a dictator, which he really became. During the reign of Prime Minister Nehru, I have asked the opinions of quite a few secretaries of Central Government Ministries, and privately among themselves, all called Nehru – 'The Great Mogul'! From then on his word was law. No minister could challenge him, all the Secretaries of Ministries were afraid lest he demoted them. Almost every day, the Permanent Secretaries of the Ministries received a note from the Prime Minister requiring the files on various subjects to be sent to him. When the files returned, in some of them, were directions or quibbles from Nehru. His sole interest was to remain in power and to that purpose the work of all the ministries was modelled. The very mention of his name struck terror in the Secretaries. He was the remote emperor who ruled by the pen.[27]

After Vallabhbhai's death in 1950, he went less and less to the Parliament to answer questions. Only on State occasions he would go to make a bombastic speech and have himself photographed and publicised as a true servant of the poor and downtrodden.

E – 'INDIA WINS FREEDOM' BY MAULANA ABUL KALAM AZAD

NEHRU'S BLUNDER ON CABINET MISSION PLAN

26 April 1946 – Maulana Azad issues a statement proposing to Congressmen that they elect Jawaharlal as President. Gandhiji had already decided on this.

6 July 1946 – Working committee makes a draft of resolution accepting the Cabinet Mission Plan, for the AICC meeting at Bombay. AICC meets in Bombay, accepts mission plan and endorses Nehru's election as President.

10 July 1946 – At Bombay Nehru tells the press: 'Congress would enter the constituent assembly completely unfettered by agreements and free to meet all situations as they arise.'

27 July 1946 – Muslim League meets in Bombay, passes a resolution rejecting the Cabinet Mission Plan citing Nehru's utterances as evidence of unreliabilty of Congress. Asked for Pakistan and rejected the Cabinet Mission Plan.

8 August 1946 – CWC meets at Wardha and issues on 10 August a statement correcting Nehru's statement. Jinnah however held Nehru's statement represented the real mind of the Congress. Once the British left, the Congress would go back to the position taken up in Jawaharlal's statement.

12 August 1946 – Jawaharlal was invited by the Viceroy to form an interim government at the centre. 'His Excellency the Viceroy, with the approval of His Majesty's Government, has invited the President of Congress to make proposals for the immediate formation

of an interim government and the President of the Congress has accepted the invitation. Pandit Jawaharlal Nehru will shortly visit New Delhi to discuss the proposal with His Excellency the Viceroy.' The same day Jinnah issues a statement rejecting the CWC's 10 August resolution and rejects Nehru's invitation to join the interim government.

15 August 1946 – Nehru met Jinnah at his house. Nothing came out of the discussions and the situation rapidly deteriorated. Meanwhile on 9 August 1946, the Congress Working Committee appointed a parliamentary sub-committee consisting of Sardar Vallabhbhai Patel, Dr Rasendra Prasad and Maulana Azad, to select candidates for election to the new Assembly.

16 August 1946 – Mob violence of an unprecedented nature broke out in Calcutta. Hundreds were killed and thousands were injured. Property worth crores was destroyed. Processions were organised by the Muslim League which began to loot, kill and commit acts of arson. 16 August 1946 was a black day not only for Calcutta but for the whole of India. A peaceful solution by agreement between Congress and the Muslim League was now impossible. Maulana writes: 'This was one of the greatest tragedies of Indian history and I have to say with the deepest of regret that a large part of the responsibility for this development rests with Jawaharlal. His unfortunate statement, that the Congress would be free to modify the Cabinet Mission Plan, reopened the whole question of political and communal settlement. Mr Jinnah took full advantage of his mistake and withdrew from the League's earlier acceptance of the Cabinet Mission Plan.

Jawaharlal had earlier made a mistake of same magnitude in 1937, which had strengthened the position of the Muslim League. When the first elections were held in 1937 under the new Government of India Act 1935, the Congress gained a thumping majority in most provinces, while the Muslim League had suffered a major setback throughout the country, except in Bombay and the United Provinces. In Bombay the League had won a number of seats, but it was in the United Provinces that the League attained its greatest success, mainly on account of the support given by the Jamiat-Ul-Ulema-I-Hind. The Jamiat had given their support under the impression, that after the election, the Muslim League would work in co-operation with the Congress.

Chaudhari Khaliquzzaman and Nawab Ismail Khan were then

Sardar Vallabhbhai Patel

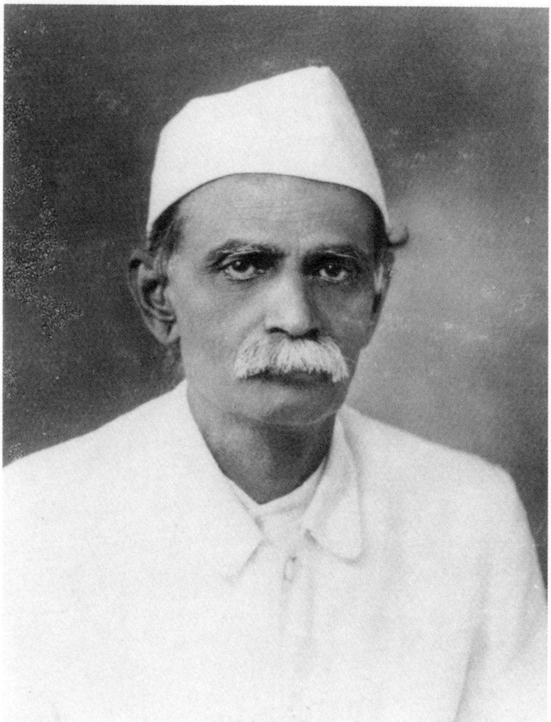

Dadubhai Desai

Mr. Fanshawe Mr. Mowbray, M.P. Sir James Lyall Lord Brassey (President) Mr. Pease Mr. Haridas Veharidas
Sir W. Roberts H.H. the Maharajah of Darbhangah Mr. Wilson, M.P.

THE MEMBERS OF THE ROYAL COMMISSION ON OPIUM NOW RETURNING FROM INDIA

The Royal Opium Commission

Girdhardas Desai

1918 Willys Knight car with Dadubhai at the wheel, driving Mugatram Maharaj.

Vithalbhai Patel in the garden of Dadubhai Desai's bungalow, 1930.

Dadubhai Desai, on the right, with Maharaj Singh, Governor of Bombay, circa 1940.

The Author (4th from left, front row) and the Congress Medical Mission to Malaya, 1946. Congress President Maulana Azad (centre of back row).

2
3
4
1
5
6
7
UNITY AND PEACE.
Family Group Photos of Bhausaheb Desai family Desai of Nadiad.
1 Rao Bahadur, Viharidas, Ajoobhai Desai Alias Bhausaheb 1st Non official President of Nadiad Municipality 1876.
2 Rao Saheb Haridas Viharidas Desai Diwan of Wadhawan Wankaner Idar & Junagadh, Native State of Saurashtra 1870 To 1895 and Member of Royal Opinion Commission C 1893 and Friend of Swami Vivekannand. B-1840 - D-1895.
3 Anana Saheb, Mangaldas Viharidas Desai, Vice President Nadiad Taluka Local Fund, 1874 Assistant Revenue Commissioner Kutch State 1876-82 and long time in huriditary Desaigiri Service.
4 Sardar Rao Bahadoor Bahechudas, Viharidas Desaialleas Mansaheb - President of Nadiad Municipality 1884-1888 Member of Legislative Council - 1888 Diwan of Junagadh state 1896-98 1903-1906.
5 Sardar Prurushottamdas Viharidas Desai Alias Dayasaheb President of Nadiad Municipality 1898 to 1902 M.L.C. Bombay 1907 to 10.
6 Sardar Gopaldas Viharidas Desaiallies Nana Saheb Assistant Revenue Commissioner Bhavanagar State and Private Secretary to Nawab of Junagadh state and Social Worker First President of Hindu Ahanthashram Nadiad 1909.
7 Desai Giridhardas Magaldas allies Tatyasaheb. Diwan of Lathi & Bajana State 1898 - 1902 President Nadiad Municipality 1915-18 Chairman Nadiad. Municipality Municipal School Board 1905 to 1912 Chairman Dist. School Board. His NICK Name given By his grand father Bhausaheb In the Member of Tatya Tope who has Been Given Shelter In his Home in 1857.

Four generations of the Desai family.

1946 The author at Congress Medical Mission to Malaya.

Viharidas, Dadubhai, Gandhi, Vallabhbhai, Purshottamdas, Vithalbhai, Ajubhai.

Sardar Vallabhbhai Patel with Mahatma Gandhi in Bombay.

Courtesy of GandhiServe Foundation. Copyright: Kanu Gandhi/GandhiServe

Jawaharlal Nehru and Sardar Vallabhbhai Patel circa 1949.

Built In 1750 A.D. By Shankardas V Desai
{Diwan Of Lunawada }

Shankerdas Desai's Haveli

23rd Light Dragoons were commanded by Lt. Col. Sir John Floyd - in the war against Tipu at Seringapatam 1792 and 1799. Later named 19th in 1803/4 they were employed in taking possession of Peshwa lands in Gujarat and were stationed in Nadiad.

Shiva Temple built circa 1985 in memory of Dadubhai Desai in Majusar, Baroda District. (Gifted by the Author's wife, Saroj Desai, née Amin).

leaders of the Muslim League in the United Provinces (UP). They assured me that they would not only co-operate with the Congress, but would fully support the Congress programme. They naturally expected that they would have some share in the Government; if the ministry consisted of seven members only, two would be Muslim Leaguers and the rest would be Congressmen. After discussion with me, a note was prepared to the effect that the Muslim League would work in co-operation with Congress and accept the Congress programme. Both Chaudhari Khaliquzzaman and Nawab Ismail Khan signed this document and I left Lucknow for Patna as my presence was necessary for the forming of the ministry in Bihar. After some days I returned to Allahabad and found to my great regret that Jawaharlal had written to Chaudhari Khaliquzzaman and Nawab Ismail Khan stating that only one of them could be taken into the ministry. Neither of them was willing to come in alone, they therefore expressed their regret and said they were unable to accept Jawaharlal's offer.

This was a most unfortunate development. If the League's offer of co-operation had been accepted, the Muslim League Party would for all practical purposes merge with the Congress. Jawaharlal's action gave the Muslim League in the UP a new lease of life. All students of Indian politics know that it was from the UP that the League was re-organised. Mr Jinnah took full advantage of the situation and started an offensive which ultimately led to Pakistan. I tried to persuade Jawaharlal to modify his stand. I told him he had made a great mistake in not bringing the Muslim League into the Ministry. I also warned him that the result of his action would be to create a new lease of life in the Muslim League and thus create new difficulties in the way of Indian freedom. Jawaharlal did not agree with me and held that his judgement was right. He argued that with a strength of only 26, the Muslim Leaguers could not claim more than one seat in the Cabinet. When I found Jawaharlal to be adamant, I went to Wardha and sought Gandhiji's advice. When I explained the whole situation to him, he agreed with me and said he would advise Jawaharlal to modify his stand. I have to place on record that when Jawaharlal put the matter in a different light, Gandhiji submitted to Jawaharlal and did not press the matter as he should have done. The result was that there was no settlement in the UP. Mr Jinnah took full advantage of the situation and turned the whole League against the Congress. After elections many of his supporters had been on the point of leaving Jinnah, but now Jinnah was able to win them back to his fold.'[28]

F – FURTHER PROOF OF JAWAHARLAL'S INEXPERIENCE AND UNDESERVED POSITION AS THE PREMIER LEADER OF INDIA

Maulana Azad was elected as the President of the Congress in 1939. According to the Constitution of the Congress, the President is elected for one year only. A new President should have been elected in 1940, but the war intervened and then the 'Quit India' movement and individual satyagraha campaigns obliged the Government to declare Congress an unlawful organisation and imprisoned the leaders. So Maulana remained the President for seven years, from 1939 to 1946. Now the situation was normal and the negotiations with the Sir Stafford Cripps Mission had started. The consensus was that Sardar Patel should be unanimously elected as President. Acharya J.B. Kripalani was, at the time, the general secretary of the Congress and he saw that the Party wanted Sardar to be President, because he was perceived as a great executive, leader and organiser. The Party was also conscious of Sardar's successful '1942 Quit India' exertions which were not matched by Jawaharlal. Based on these considerations, 12 of the 15 provincial congress committees nominated Vallabhbhai.[29] No provincial congress committee nominated Jawaharlal. However, as soon as Nehru's name was proposed, through the hidden hand of Gandhi, Kripalani handed Patel a fresh piece of paper with the latter's withdrawal written out on it. This way, Nehru could be elected unopposed.[30] Vallabhbhai showed the paper to Gandhi, who said to Nehru: 'No provincial congress committee has put forward your name, only the working committee has.' To this remark, Jawaharlal responded with complete silence.[31] This confirmed that Jawaharlal did not intend to take second place. Accordingly, Gandhi asked Patel to sign the statement prepared by Kripalani; Vallabhbhai did so at once.[32]

So Patel gave in to Gandhi's wishes as he had done in 1929 and again in 1939. The die for the future of India was now cast. We all know what that future turned out to be – establishment of Pakistan a certainty, loss of Kashmir to Pakistan, future prosperity of India undermined by the Planning Commission, and he allowed China to take over Tibet.

Maulana wrote:[33] 'The next point which I had to decide was about the choice of my successor. I was anxious that the next President should be one who agreed with my point of view and would carry out the same policy as I had pursued. After weighing the pros and cons, I came to the conclusion that the election of Sardar Patel would not be desirable in the existing circumstances, taking all facts into consideration. It seemed to me that Jawaharlal should be the new President. Accordingly, on 26 April 1946 I issued a statement proposing his name for the Presidentship and appealing to Congressmen that they should elect Jawaharlal unanimously. I acted according to my best judgement, but the way things have shaped since then has made me realise that this was perhaps the greatest blunder of my political life. I have regretted no action of mine so much as the decision to withdraw from the Presidentship of the Congress at this critical Juncture. It was a mistake which I can describe, in Gandhi's words, as one of 'Himalayan' dimensions.

My second mistake was that when I decided not to stand myself, I did not support Sardar Patel. We differed on many issues but I am convinced that if he had succeeded me as Congress President, he would have seen that the Cabinet Mission plan was successfully implemented. He would have never committed the mistake of Jawarharlal which gave Jinnah the opportunity of sabotaging the plan. I can never forgive myself when I think that if I had not committed these mistakes, perhaps the history of the last ten years would have been different.'[34] We all know the consequences of electing Jawaharlal as President of the Congress. The result was that on 6th August 1946 the Viceroy invited the President of Congress to form an interim Government at the centre. Thus Nehru became the parliamentary leader of India, a position which he clung on to till his death. Sardar Patel was automatically forced to become his subordinate. The hidden hands of Gandhiji had contrived this situation, because immediately after Maulana's statement to step down, Gandhiji declared his support of Jawaharlal to succeed as Congress President. Sardar Patel embarrassingly accepted the second rank; of course fully reliant on his tight control of the entire Congress organisation, he could easily call an election contest and win it, but in the interests of India he did not want division and recriminations in the hitherto united and single-purpose Congress. Sardar took this humiliation from Gandhiji in his stride, but never forgave him for the rest of his life. Gandhiji also knew that the game was up. From now on they both went their different ways. While Nehru's intimacy with Gandhiji went on growing, any difference he had with Sardar was immediately reported to Gandhiji, who would call Sardar to reconcile with Nehru.[35] Even with Gandhiji's help, Nehru could not gain control of the Congress machinery. That machinery was in the safe hands of Sardar. Sardar had a full knowledge of all the Provincial Congress Committee Presidents and members and workers. He was in constant telephone contact with them. It was the same with all the Provincial Chief Ministers. To preside over and control the party machine came naturally to him and as a result the loyalty of the rank and file was assured to Sardar.

M.O. Mathai writes: 'That was the type of work Nehru shunned. He also left the field open for Patel to be the Chairman of the Congress Central Parliamentary Board until Independence. This gave Patel the hold on the party machine.'[36] Mathai writes further: 'Power was Nehru's mistress and he did not like Patel to flirt with her; but he put up with it in the interest of a semblance of unity and harmony.'

On 2 September 1946, Sardar joined the interim Government as Deputy Prime Minister in charge of Home Affairs and Information and Broadcasting. Immediately afterwards a new Ministry of States was contemplated. It was Nehru's intention to be in charge of it and he had selected H.V.R. Ayengar to be the secretary of the States Ministry. Mountbatten realised that Nehru was not suited for this job. He believed that Nehru had his head in the clouds while Patel had his feet on the ground.[37] He not only wanted Sardar to be the Minister of States but also wanted V.P. Menon as the Secretary of the ministry. Mountbatten talked Nehru out of the new Ministry. The decision about the new Ministry lay with the Prime Minister Designate and not with the Governor-General. But Nehru allowed himself to be talked out of the new Ministry. Of course unwillingly, Nehru bowed down to the organisational strength of Sardar.

Maulana writes: 'Jawaharlal's nature is however such that he often acts on impulse. He is generally open to persuasion but sometimes he makes up his mind without taking all facts into consideration. Once he has done so, he tends to go ahead regardless of what the consequences may be'.[38]

G – THE 2004 INDIAN ELECTION

It is thanks to Vallabhbhai, Vithalbhai and Dadubhai, who more than anyone else helped to put Gandhiji on his pedestal, that the Indian Congress though in almost terminal decline got back to power. History will show that sanctifying Gandhi's name has caused more damage to India than the benefits it bestowed.

In India on 13 May 2004, one of the greatest election upsets of all time occurred when Sonia Gandhi and her Congress Party swept to power, defeating the BJP Government which showed and guided India to the path of prosperity. It had fostered a growth rate of 8 per cent, taken India into the very centre of global trade in goods and services and computer technology, and also gone some way in restoring normal and cordial relations with Pakistan and the Western democracies.

The (London) *Times* wrote in its editorial: 'Voters have handed victory to a party that has appeared more and more a prisoner of its past ... has only grudgingly accepted the opening of India's markets and the end of old-fashioned socialism and State control. Congress, which ruled almost without a break for the first fifty years of independence, looks set to return to office. With it comes the return of the Nehru-Gandhi dynasty which has led every Government headed by the 119-year-old party ... a party that six years ago was in terminal decline ... the danger now is two-fold: that a triumphant Congress will see no need for change and will revert to old-fashioned socialism in the misguided belief that this will help the poor; and that the BJP, stunned by its defeat, will revert to the hardest of hard nationalist sectarian lines.'[39]

'In India one third of voters are still illiterate and Gandhi being the most famous political logo available, the Congress party has worked assiduously to maintain brand loyalty. The contents this time around may be made in Italy, and be politically untested, but it says Gandhi on the tin, and that for voters is enough.'[40] So Sonia Gandhi received more votes than her rivals.

Born in Turin as Sonia Maino into a working-class, Roman Catholic, Italian family, she led a liberal Western-style life. She did not become an Indian citizen until her late thirties in 1983. In 1968 she had married Rajiv Gandhi, son of Indira Gandhi and grandson of Jawarharlal Nehru. Indira was assassinated in 1984. Rajiv then succeeded her as Prime Minister and later he too was assassinated in 1991. The sheer force of the Gandhi name has helped to propel Sonia Gandhi and the Congress party back to power. Now a fourth generation of political Gandhis is emerging, in the shape of Sonia's children – Priyanka and Rahul. Note that none of this family are related to Mahatma Gandhi.

APPENDIX 1

CREATION OF NEW VILLAGES

Proposal by Ajoobhoy Purbhodas Dessoy to the Kaira collector:

Bombay Castle
1st November 1819
Sir,
With reference to my address dated yesterday on the subject of the Cultivation of Wastes. I now do myself the honour to submit a translation of a paper of proposals for the establishment of three Villages, within the bounds of Certain Villages within district of Aleenah, each new Establishment to have attached to it land to the extent of five thousand Beegas.

2nd After the submission I have already taken the liberty of making of my Sentiments on the Subject of the light to be appropriate to wastes. I will not advert further to this point in this address – than shortly to observe that where such a field for improvement presents itself, as the proposals now Submitted, show the existence of the Right Hon'ble the Governor in Council will, I doubt not, feel disposed to reconsider his decision on this head before finally resolving not to adopt the only measure which can effectually render such extensive wastes beneficial to the State and to our Subjects.

3rd In respect to the proposals themselves they do not promise such extensive advantage as that which is likely to result from the Establishment of a village on the meadowland of Neriad – but everything consider that in the inferiority of the soil, the turbulence of the neighbourhood – the great distance from a market and the

smaller rates of Bugotie, even in established villages – the terms offered are, comparatively, as fair in every respect as those which I recommended to be granted to that proposed new village – the Pussaita solicited is conformable to Custom, and it is the most flattering method of rewarding and perpetuating the services of individuals, who do a service to Government, in the way proposed, by rendering produce and promoting the population of land previously waste, and of no available value to the State or to its Subjects. But the terms on which people can be induced to bring wastes, which now yield nothing, into cultivation especially as they only operate for a few years can be of no consideration, compared to the great object of effecting such a desirable improvement. These terms it should be kept in view because no sacrifice on the part of Government a little forbearance avail that they solicit while they promise to return advantages which, if they could not otherwise be secured, would not be dearly purchased by a temporary sacrifice.
4th Two of the persons who offer to undertake the tasks submitted, are members of the Dessoy family of Neriad. They possess capital and not being employed in the affairs of their own district, it is desirable to engage them in undertakings that will occupy their attention, and prevent their again resorting to machinations to oppose the Government, nothing is so likely to enlist their attachment to the Government, as permitting them to engage themselves in this way, while in no way can their money be applied more advantageously for their own interests and those of the community. One of the other persons is a man of considerable enterprise and of exemplary good conduct, while Veerchand Laldas is a shroff who possesses some capital. These last engage to establish one village between them.
5th Such offers are a compliment to the British Government, since it is the security of property, under its strict administration of Justice which, giving confidence to the people, alone emboldens them to such undertakings that the want of faith in our predecessors and the want of any tribunal, an interested farmer accepted for the redress of grievences, never would have been contemplated under their auspices.
6th If I may venture to predict what these proposed Establishments are likely to yield in a given time, I would say that at the end of 8 years, what now produces nothing would give at least from 25 to 30,000 Rupees per annum and that even then there would be

great scope for further improvement. But whatever may be the result in this respect, I consider it my duty to recommend that a fair trial be given to the parties, whose tender is submitted, as the best likely method I can devise of tendering those wastes beneficial.
7th Of the villages to which the lands belong I may remark, that they cannot attend their cultivation to these lands and that they will yet have considerable waste tracts if those in question are withdrawn from their limits.
I have the honour to be, signed A. Robertson, Collector.
1st September 1819.
Proposals for establishing three villages in the Boundaries of Lasoondra, Ravallya and Chetarssoomba of the Alinah district.

Each village to have 5,000 beegas of land attached to it. These we will bring into cultivation, establishing the villages, collecting cultivator dues, in return for which we request a lease or a purvanah.

For the first three years the land cultivated to be free from assessment, to enable us to build wells for drinking water and to make advances for stock etc which will be necessary on establishing the villages, after the expiration of three years the following rates to be collected from all cultivated land:

1	year per beega	1 Rupee
2	ditto	1 1/3 ditto
3	ditto	2 ditto
4	ditto	2 2/3 ditto

Such land as may be of inferior quality being allowed for.

On the 8th year a panchaiet shall settle and fix the khatav of the cultivators. For our trouble in this business we solicit 100 beegas may be granted to us as pasaita property beyond which we shall look for no emolument and when the village shall be fully established we shall pay any revenue which according to the produce may be fixed by Government.

The following pussaitas must be given to ravaneas 125 beegas and to the different village craft 100 beegas.

The land that the well for drinking water may be upon to be granted by Government.
Signed: Dessay Ajoobhoy Perbhudas and Dessoy Samaldas, Desoybhoy.
True translation, signed A. Robertson, Collector

The explanations afforded by Captain Robertson have so completely removed the material objection which occurred when his proposal of the 22nd April 1818 for granting 3,000 beegas of meadowland in the neighbourhood of Neriad to Dwarcadas Shankerdas for establishing a new village came first under services that the Government into no longer hesitates to authorize the measure and from the testimony which Captain Robertson has borne to the character of Dwarcadas we have particular pleasure in giving our sanction to the Complement intended to be paid by the 17th articles to the founder by directing that the village shall bear the name of Dwarcapoora.

The Governor in Council is pleased to accede to Captain Robertson's recommendation in favour of the proposals offered by Dessoy Ajoobhoy Perbhoodas and others for establishing three new villages within the bounds of certain villages in the District of Alinaiy, each village to consist of 5,000 beegas.

1st November resolved that Captain Robertson be accordingly authorized to conclude the necessary details for giving effect to these arrangements which it is hoped will ultimately be attended with the great advantages which may with so much reason be anticipated from them.

Ordered that a copy of Captain Robertson's letter of the 22nd April 1818 be transmitted with his letter of September the 17th.[1]

APPENDIX 2

REVENUE SURVEY AND ASSESSMENT FOR KAIRA

Confidential Revenue Department
Bombay Castle
18th February 1911

Memorandum No. 1667 – The undersigned presents compliments to the Commissioner, N.D., and in forwarding a copy of the correspondence ending with Mr Barrow's letter No. 2942, dated 20th June 1910, on the subject of the future treatment of estates held under the Bhagdari and Narvadari tenures, is directed to state that on full consideration the Governor in Council accepts generally the views stated in Mr Barrow's letter and has decided not to issue any instructions such as those contemplated in the draft orders accompanying Government memorandum No. 3710, dated 23rd April 1910.

R.D. Bell, Under Secretary to Government.

No. 3710, dated 23rd April 1910

The undersigned presents his compliments to the Commissioner, N.D., and in forwarding copies of draft orders on the subject of the treatment of estates held under the bhagdari and narvadari tenure, is directed to state that before finally issuing the orders, Government will be glad to receive any suggestions or criticisms which Mr Barrow may desire to submit on them after consultation with such officers or unofficial gentlemen as he sees fit.

R.D. Bell, Under Secretary to Government.

Some Suggestions from Purushottamdas Desai:

The Resolution which Government propose to issue on the subject of the treatment of estates held under the bhagdari and narvadari tenure, declares that it is doubtful whether the recognition by the Collector of an alienation of an unrecognised sub-division is legally valid. In this connection I would suggest that steps should be taken to clear this point by amending the law.

The Resolution attempts to regulate the powers of interference by the Collector, which from the history of the operation of section 3 appears very necessary.

I think it is equally necessary to have a register prepared of the recognised shares and recognised sub-divisions of narva lands. These terms are used in the law, but I am not aware of any practical clear definitions of them. With the increase of heirs, sub-divisions of the bhaga must necessarily take place, and these sub-divisions according to our custom are each and all independent of one another. The practice of dividing the bhaga or narva and taking possession by every member of his own share, is more common now than it was before. The falo or jama is also similarly divided and instead of all the sub-shares being held jointly and severally responsible for the jama each sub-sharer has possession of his proper share of the land and is held responsible for a proportionate share of the jama. Under these circumstances it will appear essentially necessary to prepare an authentic register of such sub-divisions wherever they may have taken place by common consent. This will facilitate the work of the Collectors to a very great extent.

In the next place I would respectfully suggest that a provision should be made to encourage transfers among the members of the narvadars themselves. This will secure the object of the Act and prevent the tendency of narva lands going outside the families. When, as above mentioned, narva lands have undergone several sub-divisions amongst different successors of the original family of a narvadar, the term dismemberment should, I think, be ordinarily interpreted to mean the passing of a portion of the narva land out of the family.

In several villages the building site (Ghaban) is included in the narva and is subjected to sub-divisions along with the arable land. The divisions of building site land are not generally made rateably with the other land but is based on convenience of the sharers, the inequalities being settled by cash compensation. Whereas agricultural land is divided precisely according to shares and the division of the falo is based entirely on this class of land only, although, under the settlement, the jama is supposed to have been calculated on both classes of land. For this reason, it will appear advisable in the interests of the narvadars to exclude the building site land from the operation of section 3.

In paragraph 5 of the draft it is declared inadvisable to interfere where the original transaction is of long standing. I am humbly of the opinion that it would be better both for the Collector and the parties to the transaction if the period be prescribed. Twelve years would appear reasonable.

The last sentence in paragraph 6 is rather unnecessary. When reasons are clearly defined for the guidance of the enquiring officer, it would be improper to add that he may also interfere for any other reasons, for it will not secure an uniform practice and the officer will not find his position much improved.

Narvadars will feel very grateful for the very generous spirit in which the orders in paragraph 9 are intended to be framed. Wherever the jama is in excess of the assessments, complaints have not ceased to exist. So long as the narvadars had the enjoyment of the privileges and perquisites associated with the narva, they had little ground for complaint. But at this period all these advantages have been gradually wiped out and it is no wonder therefore that the narvadars should complain against the excess as very unjust.
Nadiad, 24th May 1910, Purushottamdas V. Desai.

Remarks on the draft orders relating to Bhagdari and Narva tenures submitted by Sardar Davar K.E. Modi of Surat.

Bhag and narva property was given full and formal recognition at the time of the Original Revenue Survey and the Revenue Records from these times onwards form the best evidence. The High Court has decided that there cannot be repeated recognitions – and in my humble view it is not the perverseness of the bhagdars that is to blame so much as the undoubted obstinacy and unwillingness of certain collectors that is at the bottom of the little mischief that is found to exist. The Collectors must no longer be encouraged to put their own construction upon the phrase 'it shall be lawfull'. They should be brought under the regulative influence of the Commissioner; and especially as there is no means left for cancelling the phrase, except a recourse to fresh legislation, which under present circumstances would seem to be out of the question.

I fully approve of the instructions which are intended to be issued regarding the working of the Bhagdari Act V of 1862.

I would suggest that the attention of the Collectors should be drawn to the fact that not infrequently the recognised bhagdar attempts to oppress his sub-sharers who may be poor by not allowing such sharers to alienate their shares at a fair and reasonable value, and forcing them to sell the shares to him at much below the real value. In such cases the sub-sharer may be allowed to bring all the facts before the Collector, who should use his discretion and allow the sub-shares to be alienated to outsiders.

In the Punjab the alienation of land has been prohibited by the legislation passed only a few years ago, but if I am not mistaken, provision has been made for allowing alienation where the Revenue Officer considers it necessary.

The recognised sharer attempts to oppress the sub-sharer in another way also, namely, by not paying the land revenue due, and allowing the share to be confiscated. Of course, the other bhagdars may be paying the revenue to prevent confiscation, but in some cases the chief sharer would manage to secure the land to himself. Such cases are rare and if they are brought to the notice of the Collector, he would no doubt be able to see that no undue advantage is taken by any person.

With regard to the observation of Government that in some cases the jama may be excessive, my own experience of the narvadari villages of the Kaira District is that the jama may be excessive only in very rare cases. The difficulty with the sub-sharers arises only when the lands comprised in the shares for which they are liable are not all in their possession, and when the persons holding the lands do not contribute their due quota. In such cases an arrangement should be made by the Revenue authorities doing proper justice to all. Such arrangements were often made at the time of the original and the revised surveys, and in some cases the difficulties were removed by practically introducing the survey system, making each person responsible for the jama of the land actually held by him.

APPENDIX 3

OPIUM TRADE IN INDIA

BOMBAY CASTLE
31st January 1821
Resolved that the following advertisement be published by hand bills and in next Saturday's Courier announcing the sale of mature opium at this Presidency in the 24th of April next –
GOVERNMENT ADVERTISEMENT Notice is hereby given,
That on Wednesday the 24th of April, at eleven o'clock in the forenoon, will be sold by public auction at the Sale Room in the Bunder, the quantity of about fifteen hundred Bengal Chests of mature opium, the produce of the Year 1819–20. Conditions of the sale.
2nd The opium to be sold by the one pecul Chest of lbs 133½ in Lots of five chests each; one Rupee to be paid down to bind the bargain, and a deposit of 10 per Cent on the price of each Lot in money, or public securities, to be made by the purchasers before the expiration of five days, in default thereof the Lot or Lots, to be resold, and all losses and expenses attending such resale, to be paid by the first purchasers, and any profit arising therefrom to belong to Government.
3rd The opium to be paid for and cleared out within 2 months from the day of sale and in case any opium shall not be paid for and cleared out, the abovementioned deposit of 10 per cent, and the earnest money, will be forfeited, – – – the opium advertised for a ready money sale, all losses and expenses attending such Sale to be borne by the first purchasers and any profit accruing from it to belong to Government.

4th The following papers may be seen at this office at any time between the hours of 10 and 3 o'clock on the ?? April and following days previous to the day of sale:
No. 1 – Warrantees of the opium now as advertised for sale.
No. 2 – Reports of the examination of the opium.
No. 3 – Account of the weight of the opium when packed.
No. 4 – Statement of the average weight in Bombay of 6 Chests.
5th – On the day of sale the above mentioned documents will be laid on the table, and Samples of the opium to be sold, will be exhibited for inspection of the Merchants.
6th – Individuals under the Presidency of Fort William, who may be desirous of purchasing any portion of the opium in question, are at liberty until the 5th of March next to send to the Board of Customs, Salt and Opium at that Presidency, proposals to that effect, stating the number of lots which they may wish to purchase, and the price they may propose to give for all, or each, in Bombay Rupees, and accompanying their tenders with security for the due observance of the conditions of the sale in money, or Company's paper, or other security approved by the Board, to the extent of 10 per Cent on the price of each lot; any deposits made as security for such tenders will be returned. Certificate from Bombay, that the opium purchased by the party has been purchased under his tender.
7th – The proposals so received will be transmitted to Bombay, and ultimately entrusted under an assurance of secrecy to the charge of the officer appointed by the Government to supervise the sale, who will purchase the opium, if the selling price falls within the terms of the tender – – – several tenders have been received, the advantage over the rest to the highest tenderer or tenderers, to the extent of his or their tenders, the benefit eventually of a lower price than what he or they may offer, according to the following plan.
Clause First – in case one or more tenderers shall undertake for the purchase of the whole quantity of Opium to be exposed for sale, at an uniform price, then the Lots shall be put up at the amount of such prices, and if no higher bid be offered, the sale shall be concluded in favour of such tenderer, or tenderers.
Clause Second – if there be several tenders embracing in the aggregate the whole quantity of opium for sale, but not at an uniform price, the sale shall be commenced by putting up the Lots successively at the lowest amount that may be so tendered, if there be no Bid beyond this, the sale of the whole quantity of opium shall be concluded with

all the tenderers at that rate if there be an advance of price bid, the officer appointed to superintend the sale shall bid up by an advance of one Rupee per Chest until there is no higher bidder, or until the amount of the highest tender shall be reached. If no one outbid him, the lot shall belong to the highest tenderer, and so on with the following Lots in succession so long as there shall be any unsatisfied tender at a rate exceeding the amount bid.

These lots will of course be bought in on account of the persons making such tenders, the remaining Lots, in so far as bidders may be found at rates exceeding the unsatisfied tenders still held by the superintendent of the sale, will be sold by the usual free Competition.

Clause Third – If tenders be received comprising more than the entire quantity of opium to be sold, the Superintendent shall strike off the excess from the lowest tender and put up the lot at the lowest of the rates offered in such numbers or portions of the highest tenderers as may comprise the whole and proceed in the sale in one or other of the modes above specified as the case may be.

Clause Fourth – If the tenders do not comprise the whole of the opium to be sold, the Superintendent of the sale shall not bid on behalf of the Tenders until the number of chests not tendered for shall be disposed of. These he will sell by open competition to the highest bidders, without however disclosing the number tendered for, and if on completing the sale of the Lots so left untendered for, it shall appear that the average price which they may have fetched, does not exceed the rate specified in the lowest tender, all the tenderers shall have the quantity for which they may have tendered at such average price, if the average price fetched by the said Lots exceeds the rate tendered, supposing all the tenders to be made at uniform rates, or at the rate of the lowest tender, if the tenders be made at various rates, then the Superintendent will proceed by putting up the Lots in the manner specified in these 1st or 2nd Clauses, as the case may be.

8th – In case of equality in the amount of two or more tenders, the priority will be determined by the time at which they were respectively given in by the Merchants to the Board of Customs, Salt and Opium, in whose office they will be regularly registered as received.

9th – Individuals under the Presidency of Bombay who may be desirous of purchasing any portion of the Opium which will be put up of Sale at the Second Bombay Sale, are at liberty, until the 3rd of February next, to send to the Secretary to Government in the Revenue Department at this Presidency, proposals, to that effect, stating the number of lots which they may wish to purchase, and the price they may propose to give for all or each in Sicca Rupees, and accompanying their Tenders with security for the due observance of the sale, in money, or Company's paper, or other security approved by the Government, and these tenders so received will be transmitted to Bengal and acted upon in every respect as is provided in the case of Bengal tenders for Bombay opium in paragraphs 6th, 7th and 8th of this advertisement.

Bombay Castle 27th January 1821
Published by order of the Right Honourable the Governor in Council.
Signed – James Farish, Secretary to Government.
Minutes 27th January – Ordered that Copies of the Preceding Advertisement be transmitted to the Supreme Government Resident at Indore and Accountant General a Copy being transmitted to Mr Secretary Simson with the Hon'ble the Governor.

Wrote the following letter to the Secretary to the Supreme Government: 'Sir, I am directed by the Hon'ble the Governor in Council to request You will inform His Excellency the Most Noble Governor General in Council that an advertisement has been published under this date announcing the sale of a quantity of Mature Opium not exceeding 1500 Bengal Chests the period for the sale has been fixed for the last week in April which is considered to be as early as it will be practicable to hold the Sale in the present season.
2nd A clause has been added to the advertisement in conformity with the Suggestion Conveyed in the 4th Paragraph of Your letter of 24th November last announcing that the same accommodation will be allowed to the mercantile community of Bombay in regard to the purchase of opium at the Second Calcutta Sale as is allowed by the advertisement of the 23rd November to the merchants of Bengal in regard to the mature opium to be sold at this Presidency the 3rd of February has been fixed as the latest date for receiving tenders for the purchase of Bengal opium.
Bombay Castle, 27th January 1821.
I have the honour to be, J. Farish, Secretary to Government.[1]

All this opium was to be sold for the sole purpose of its export to China. There payment would be received from the Chinese in Portuguese gold coins. These would be exchanged for Indian rupees at the Hong Kong treasury.

(The original documents are reproduced in Appendix 5.)

APPENDIX 4

LETTERS WRITTEN BY SOME OF THE MAJOR CHARACTERS MENTIONED IN THE TEXT

(Where the original letter was written in Gujarati, an English translation has been added)

Correspondence is included from the following:

Vithalbhai J. Patel

1 10 May 1926 to Gandhi
2 31 May 1926 to Gandhi
3 1 June 1926 to Gandhi
4 28 July 1926 to Gandhi
5 5 July 1929 to Lord Irwin
6 12 July 1929 to Lord Irwin
7 21 October 1929 to Dadubhai
8 3 December 1929 to Dadubhai
9 12 December 1929 to Dadubhai
10 6 March 1930 to Dadubhai
11 16 March 1930 to Dadubhai
12 12 April 1930 to Lord Irwin
13 20 April 1930 to Lord Irwin
14 23 April 1930 to Lord Irwin
15 24 April 1930 to Lord Irwin
16 25 April 1930 to Lord Irwin
17 25 April 1930 to Lord Irwin
18 25 April 1930 to Lord Irwin
19 9 March 1932 to Dadubhai
20 14 April 1932 to Dadubhai

21 9 May 1933 Bose-Patel Manifesto
22 11 May 1933 to Dadubhai
Sardar Vallabhbhai Patel
23 16 January 1930 to Dadubhai
24 20 January 1930 to Dadubhai
25 31 May 1940 to Dadubhai
26 30 November 1941 to Dadubhai
27 11 November 1945 to Dadubhai
28 9 May 1946 to Dadubhai
29 5 June 1946 to Dadubhai
30 11 May 1947 to Lord Mountbatten
31 15 May 1947 to Lord Mountbatten
32 3 July 1947 to Maharajah of Kashmir
33 5 July 1947 Future of States
34 7 November 1947 to Dadubhai
35 23 December 1947 to Ayengar
36 23 December 1947 to Nehru
37 24 December 1947 to Nehru
38 29 December 1947 to Nehru
39 1 July 1948 to Dadubhai
40 25 July 1948 to Dadubhai
41 21 September 1948 to Dadubhai
42 9 August 1949 to Nehru
43 16 August 1949 to Nehru
Lord Irwin
44 18 July 1929 to Vithalbhai
45 26 July 1929 to Vithalbhai
46 13 April 1930 to Vithalbhai
47 15 April 1930 to Vithalbhai
48 21 April 1930 to Vithalbhai
49 23 April 1930 to Vithalbhai
50 26 April 1930 to Vithalbhai
Mahadev Desai (Gandhi's secretary)
51 21 March 1930 to Dadubhai
Gandhi
52 25 July 1926 to Vithalbhai
53 25 July 1926 to Vithalbhai
54 23 May 1944 to Dadubhai
55 24 October 1944 to Dadubhai
56 11 April 1946 to the Author

Jawaharlal Nehru
57 28 July 1930 to Gandhi
58 23 December 1947 to Vallabhbhai
59 11 August 1949 to Vallabhbhai
Manilal Gandhi (Gandhi's son)
60 24 October 1953 to the Author
Vivekananda
61 30 August 1895 to Mother Hale
62 2 March 1896 to Haridas Desai
63 undated to Diwanji
Miscellaneous
64 30 April 1930 Invitation to a Meeting in Borsad
65 30 April 1930 Shivabhai Ashabhai to Dadubhai
66 5 December 1929 Dadubhai's Delegate's Certificate to the Indian National Congress
67 13 August 1939 the Author joins the Indian National Congress

1 Vithalbhai to Gandhi, 10 May 1926, from Bombay

Dear Mahatmaji,

When I accepted the office of President of the Legislative Assembly I had made a resolution within myself that I would devote the savings from my salary towards the furtherance of some object calculated to promote the national welfare. It was not possible for me for various reasons to save anything worth the name within the first six months. Since the last month, however, I am glad to say that I am quite out of the woods, and can, and do, save a substantial amount. I find that on an average, I require Rs.2000 per month for my expenses. The amount of my net salary, excluding income tax, is Rs.3625. I propose, therefore, to set apart Rs.1625 per month, beginning from the last month, to be utilised hereafter in such manner and for such purpose as you may approve. I have, of course, some ideas in this matter, and I will in due course discuss them with you. But whether you agree with me in those ideas or not, the amount is at your disposal.

I enclose herewith a cheque for Rs.1625 for the month of April.

I trust you will not decline to take this responsibility.

I am, yours sincerely,

2 Vithalbhai to Gandhi, 31 May 1926, from Sukhdale Simla

My Dear Mahatmaji,

I enclose herewith a cheque for Rs.4325, Rs.1625 being my contribution from my salary for the month of May, and Rs.2700 representing the balance I had in hand out of the amount of Rs.3200 actually collected for the purse of Rs.5000 which my colleagues of the Bombay Corporation had subscribed on the expiry of my term of office as President of the Bombay Corporation. I had already explained to you personally when I last met you at Sabarmati why this balance, which in normal circumstances I had intended and announced to spend for such purposes of the Swaraj Party and the Bombay Municipal Nationalist Party as I considered proper. I now propose to remit to you to be devoted to the fund to be started from my monthly contributions out of my salary.

I learn that you propose to proceed shortly to England, and perhaps you will have no time to consult friends and settle the object on which, and the manner in which, the fund should be expended. If that be so, the fund may be allowed to accumulate until your return, and I shall be regularly remitting my monthly contribution to whomsoever you name.

The Private Secretary to the Viceroy writes to me to say that His Excellency desires to have another talk with me and will write to me later as regards the time and date as soon as His Excellency is free from his other engagements.

I hope Devidas is picking up. Will he come to Simla at all, or is he accompanying you to England?

With kind regards,

3 Vithalbhai to Gandhi, 1 June 1926, from Sukhdale, Simla

(In connection with the above, there is an episode, which, in spite of its unpleasantness, has to be recorded. Motilal Nehru and Vithalbhai had worked for years as brothers and comrades in arms. Motilalji wished that Vithalbhai should give half his salary to the Party funds of the Swarajists. Vithalbhai, at one time, had favoured the idea. On second thoughts, however, he thought that, as the Speaker and a non-party man, it was not right for him to make any contribution to the Party funds. He did what he thought was the correct thing to do when he sent his contribution to Mahatmaji, instead, Motilalji appears to have acquiesced in the arrangement, but not quite willingly. In fact, some sort of estrangement between Motilalji and Vithalbhai had begun to appear since the time the Tatas appeared on the scene. This incident added fuel to the smouldering embers. It is difficult to believe that Motilalji could not see the logic of Vithalbhai's reasoning, but so it was, and though apparently everything was all right between them, since this occasion there was a definite rift in the lute in regard to the relations between Vithalbhai and Motilal Nehru. Correspondence between Vithalbhai and Mahatmaji on these matters throws abundant light on the whole of this situation, and I therefore take the liberty of quoting it in full).

My Dear Mahatmaji,

It has pained me much to read Panditji's letter to you, a copy of which Mahadev was good enough to send me under your instructions.

It is my misfortune that with the best will in the world I am often misunderstood both by my friends and foes alike. The fact is that the question as to what I intend to do with the savings from my salary was never seriously discussed with me either by Pandit Motilal or any other Swarajist leader. It is no doubt true that suggestions were made on odd occasions from time to time more in a loose manner than with any degree of seriousness – one of the suggestions being that as soon as it was possible for me to do so, I should contribute half my salary to the party funds. Panditji is quite right in saying that I favoured that suggestion; but he knows too well that neither he nor I considered the question whether it was proper for the Speaker to make any contributions to the funds.

The matter, however, did not take any definite shape till Mr. Srinivas Iyengar on the occasion of the Swarajists walk-out made a concrete proposal that it would please Panditji if I agreed to contribute to the Swaraj Party funds half of my salary from the month of April. I resisted that proposal as soon as it was made, and pointed out to Mr. Iyengar that the propriety of such a course was not free from doubt, and the Panditji himself would not insist on my adopting that course. I do not know how Mr. Iyengar could have given Panditji to understand that I had agreed to his proposal. In order to remove any misunderstanding I personally discussed the various alternatives with Panditji before I left Delhi; but, as we could not agree on any particular suggestion, we decided to leave the matter to you. I am now quite clear in my mind that it is not right for me, as Speaker of the Assembly representing all parties, to make any contributions from my salary towards the fund of any one Party and I have no doubt that you will have no difficulty in determining the object, or objects, on which this fund should be expended. I know I have offended Panditji by refusing to join the walk-out of the Swarajists in spite of his strong views in that behalf, but time alone will show who is right and who is wrong.

With kind regards. Yours sincerely, V.J. Patel

4 Vithalbhai to Gandhi, 28 July 1926, Sukhdale, Simla

My Dear Mahatmaji,

Your letter with a copy of the draft reply to my letters enclosing cheques representing my contributions from time to time out of my salary. Many thanks.

Perhaps you are aware that my term of office will expire with the dissolution of the Assembly, and it is my intention to seek re-election with a view to enable the Assembly to establish a convention similar to the one that obtains in the United Kingdom. If the Assembly chooses to re-elect me, I propose the same arrangement regarding my contribution from my salary for a period of three years. I am not sure about the wisdom of publishing our correspondence at this stage. Such publication, I am afraid, is bound to be construed in some quarters as an attempt on my part to influence the election in my favour. You are probably aware that I am, unfortunately, not without mean political rivals who are always ready to twist and turn anything that they can get hold of to my prejudice, regardless of thc effect of such a course on national interests. Don't you think that, in the circumstances, it is better to delay the publication of the correspondence till January next, when the election will be over, and it will be definitely known whether I am out of office, or whether a term of three years is ensured me. There will not then be the slightest objection to the publication of the correspondence at that stage. If you, however, do not agree with this view, I shall return the draft reply with one or two small alterations, which I propose to suggest for your consideration. I have already received my pay bill for the month of July and, therefore, enclose herewith a cheque for Rs.1625 representing the amount of my contribution for that month.

I had a letter from Devdas, and it seems that he is quite happy at Mussoorie and does not feel inclined to move from there for another couple of months. I do not, therefore, propose to disturb him in his plans.

With kind regards. Yours sincerely, V.J. Patel

5 Vithalbhai to Lord Irwin, 5 July 1929, from Simla

My Dear Lord Irwin,

I hope this finds you and Her Excellency comfortably settled in 88 Eaton Square.

As regards your great mission, you are fully aware of my views, and I should like to emphasise what I told you when we last met that if by any formula the British Government make it worth the while of Congress leaders to agree to take part in a Round Table Conference in London, half the battle is won. My only apprehension is that you are not in full possession of the exact views of the Congress leaders in this respect, and there is, therefore, the danger of the formula not being acceptable to them. I wish you had seen them before you left or it was possible for me to accompany you.

Do remember me to your good old father and your sister and tell them how troublesome, sometimes, but how very good I have been to you on the whole.

Always at your service, Yours sincerely,

6 Vithalbhai to Lord Irwin, 12 July 1929, from Simla

My Dear Lord Irwin,

I am writing this because when you left Simla you were good enough to tell me that if there was anything that in the prosecution of your mission you, in my opinion, ought to know, I should not hesitate to communicate with you.

Since your departure speculations are rife as to what you might or might not do in London, and it has been freely mentioned that you have, supplied to you by individual leaders of one or two parties in the Assembly, their respective statements of conditions which in their opinion would be regarded as a sufficient gesture on the part of the British Government to enable the representatives of the people of India to consent to take part in a Round Table Conference. These statements, I am further told, are in the nature of a draft declaration to be made by the British Government. In this conection, I cannot help regretting that it was not possible for you before you left to have a heart-to-heart talk with the leaders of the party that really matters, that is the only party which is in a position to deliver the goods to any appreciable extent – I mean the Congress Party in the Assembly and the country. If you knew what happened ten years ago, I am sure you would agree that every endeavour should be made on this occasion to secure the co-operation of those Congress leaders who believe in the British connection, and I know there are yet a very large number of them. For this purpose, it is very necessary that the British Government should take one or two of them into their confidence, say Mahatma Gandhi or Pandit Motilal Nehru or both, and have their previous consent to the terms of the proposed announcement, and I hope they would not permit consideration of prestige to stand in the way of their doing the right thing at the right moment.

If you will read the pamphlet enclosed herewith, you will be in a position to understand the attitude of the Congress in 1919 and realise what a great mistake the British Government had made on that occasion in adopting the policy of rallying the moderates and ignoring the Congress. Ten years ago, as the Leader of the Congress Deputation in England, I was in a position to assure the Joint Select Committee that no one in India desired separation from Britain. Today, on the other hand, there is a party in the Congress itself advocating independence. As one in the thick of the fight, I know that Mr. Montagu took into his confidence liberal politicians of India and relied upon their support to his scheme treating the Congress leaders as irreconcilable with the result that India has not yet settled down to constructive work and the party of separatists has grown up in our midst. I only hope that the mistake of 1919 will not be repeated on this occasion. I have already assured you that my services are at your disposal in this matter.

Yours sincerely,

7 Vithalbhai to Dadubhai, 21 October 1929, from Delhi

Tele : Address :—

"PRELEGAS"

PRESIDENT LEGISLATIVE ASSEMBLY

DIEU ET MON DROIT

Delhi

21-10-29

My dear Dadubhai,

I leave for Bombay on the 6th morning & shall be staying at the Sardar Griha.

I propose to visit some places in Gujarat & if you will see me in Bombay we shall fix up the programme.

Yours

V J Patel

8 Vithalbhai to Dadubhai, 3 December 1929, from Delhi

Tele : Address :—

"PRESLEGAS"

PRESIDENT LEGISLATIVE ASSEMBLY

New Delhi

3-12-29

My dear Dadubhai

Let me thank you most heartily and also all the members of your family for the grand hospitality and very good time you gave me during my stay in Nadiad - I wish I could have stayed on for a few days more but as you are aware I have several things on hand which I must attend to.

Please let me know when you & Mrs. are coming to Delhi. I feel lonely after having passed such happy days in the company of your family. I would, therefore, like you to come here without delay.

Please remember me to Borampi.

Vithalbhai Pranjivan.

Yours

V J Patel

9 Vithalbhai to Dadubhai, 12 December 1929, from Delhi

Tele : Address :—

"PRELEGAS."

PRESIDENT LEGISLATIVE ASSEMBLY

20, Akbar Road,
New Delhi, 12th December 1929.

My dear Rao Saheb

I received your letter of the 10th December, and I am disappointed that you are not coming soon. I wish you could immediately start and come over and leave the party to join you at Delhi on their way to Lahore. Do come.

Yours

Rao Saheb Dadubhai P. Desai,
Esq.,B.A.,
Member of the Bombay
Legislative Council,
<u>Nadiad.</u>

10 Vithalbhai to Dadubhai, 6 March 1930, from Delhi

Tele. address 'Prelegas'
President Legislative Assembly
New Delhi
6 March 1930

Brother Dadubhai,

I cannot understand why you are silent for so many days. I am sticking to the Presidential chair under your advice, but how long; I need your advice badly, so please come here as soon as you can.

Let me know in precise details, about what is going on at Sabarmati and also your own assessment of it. I personally feel that a grave mistake is being committed but no one is able to speak up. Whatever it is, but I need your advice about what I should do. It is imperative, to come to a final decision.

Yours, Vithalbhai.

(Dadubhai's long silence was due to his frequent meetings with Gandhi at Sabarmati Ashram to discuss confidentially the scheme for the salt campaign. See Chapter 17.)

Tele : Address :—

"PRELEGAS."

PRESIDENT LEGISLATIVE ASSEMBLY

[illegible]

[illegible]

[illegible]

11 Vithalbhai to Dadubhai, 16 March 1930, from Delhi

President Legislative Assembly
New Delhi

My dear Dadubhai,

Thanks for your letter. I must have a long talk with you before I decide upon this final step that I propose to take. Many friends have advised me to continue for some time in my present position but I feel so miserable that I do not know what I shall do at any moment. It is true that Gandhi has made a great mistake and lost a golden opportunity and his selection of salt law for Civil Disobedience does not appeal to me at all. But if that is to be done under these circumstances is a question which worries me day and night. Please tell me when you are coming.

Yours, V.J. Patel.

(The lost golden opportunity refers to Gandhi's non-attendance at the First Round Table Conference; see letter 13.)

Tel: Address:—

"PRELEGAS."

PRESIDENT LEGISLATIVE ASSEMBLY

New Delhi

16.3.30

My dear Dadubhai,

Thanks for yr letter. I must have a long talk with you before I decide upon the final step that I propose to take. Many friends have advised me to continue for some time in my present position but I feel so miserable that I do not know what I shall do any moment. It is true that Gandhi has made a great mistake & lost a golden opportunity & his selection of salt law for civil disobedience does not appeal to me at all. But what is to be done under these circumstances is a question which worries me day & night. Please tell me when you are coming.

Yours

V J Patel

[illegible]

12 Vithalbhai to Lord Irwin, 12 April 1930, from Simla

Holcombe, Simla, 12 April 1930
My Dear Lord Irwin,

I have now received Dr. Sapru's reply to my letter. As he is in the midst of the performance of the funeral rites and the Shradh of his mother who died only a few days back, he regrets he is unable to run up to Simla to discuss the question of my resignation with me personally. The next best thing that he does under the circumstances is to emphasise in his letter certain considerations against the step which I propose to take and (to) express a hope and belief that I might yet reconsider my decision which would be to him a matter of great regret and to friends one of embarrassment. All the reasons urged by Dr. Sapru except one were present to my mind all these days and were fully considered by me. The only new argument urged by him against my resignation and which had not occurred to me so far has been expressed by him in his letter in the following words:

'You can, while holding office, use your great position and influence to bring about peace and reconciliation and I would earnestly urge it on you to work in that behalf. I am afraid once you take this step, your utility as a possible mediator will be greatly affected, if not entirely gone'.

Although the path of a peacemaker is full of difficulties, as you know to your cost, I have always placed my services at your disposal for that purpose and considering our intimate relations, it does not matter whether I am in office or out of it, you have a right to call upon me, no matter where I am, to play the part of mediator if and when, in your opinion, occasion for it arises. In any case, I should have stayed on if I were convinced that there was any immediate chance of negotiations opening up; but from the way in which things are moving, I cannot help feeling that both sides are drifting apart further and placing themselves in irretrievable positions making the task of reconciliation more and more difficult. It is not my purpose at present to apportion blame to either side. I merely look at the question from the point of view of the decision I have to take.

I do not know how your mind works and what your plans are. But as far as I am concerned, I feel certain that delay on my part in taking the final step is being misunderstood in the country, though I am prepared to continue even if my services were really required within the next few days by Your Excellency for the purpose referred to in Dr. Sapru's letter. And let me assure you once again, whether I continue or I do not, that my services are at your disposal as hitherto whenever you require them.

With kind regards. Yours sincerely,

13 Vithalbhai to Lord Irwin, 20 April 1930, from Simla

Holcombe, Simla, 20 April 1930
My dear Lord Irwin,

I have received your letter of the 15th April from Peshawar, and am deeply sorry that you do not see much chance of things taking such a turn in the near future that you would have to call upon my services on the way indicated by Sir Tej Bahadur Sapru in his letter to me. The only comment I have to offer in that connection is that further delay would simply complicate matters and make your task more difficult. I have always made it clear to you that Congress and Gandhi alone were in a position to deliver (the) goods to any appreciable extent, and a Round Table Conference in which Congress leaders could not be persuaded to participate was not worth much, if (worth) anything at all. It was for this reason that since the day you landed in India I was endeavouring (as) best I could to bring you and them together, and although I have so far failed in the result, I am not yet without hope that before long you would realise the strength behind the Congress and find a way to enlist their support to the conference. I repeat my assurance that my services are at your disposal for that purpose whenever you choose to requisition them. I feel sad, however, that your great name should in the meantime be associated with a campaign of wholesale arrests and imprisonment of hundreds of Congress workers who, if India were a free country, would have, I know, made excellent administrators.

Regarding the question of my resignation, you had asked me to let you know my final decision privately. As I have often told you, the Chair of the Assembly has not been a bed of roses to me. In my anxiety to uphold and, may I say, enlarge the authority of the Chair and the dignity of the House and its rights and privileges, I have come in constant conflict with Government and they would have, but for certain reasons of which you are not aware, made short work of me long ago. I know I have silently suffered persecution and harassment in a variety of ways for my independence and for doing what I thought, under the circumstances, was in the best interest of the Assembly and the country, and I would have resigned long ago had it not been for our mutual regard and the encouragement I was receiving from you now and again. The thought that as the first elected President of the Assembly I owed a duty to the constitution and my country that I should endeavour to make the office a success as far as possible was also present in my mind in continuing in the Chair in the midst of all these difficulties. I know you will believe me when I say that nothing will be more painful to me than a feeling that it should be necessary for me to tender my resignation when such a good friend as you, for whom I have such high admiration and regard, is at the helm of affairs, but I am sure you will agree with me that one's duty to one's country is greater than all other considerations put together. I have fully considered the question from every point of view, and I have come to the conclusion that under new conditions my usefulness as President has ceased to exist and I should be serving the interest of my country better at this juncture by giving my open and active support to the Congress movement and endeavouring to the best of my capacity to keep it non-violent. I reached this decision finally on the day on which Pandit Jawaharlal Nehru, the President of the Congress, was arrested and sentenced. I had already explained to you at some length during my last interview with you at Delhi my reasons for the step I proposed to take, and your last letter supplies me with additional reason why I should not delay my resignation much longer. I propose, therefore, to submit to you my formal resignation within the next two or three days.

I have to dispose of in consultation with you one or two matters before I resign, and I should be obliged if you can find time for this purpose.

Always at your service, I remain, Yours sincerely, V.J. Patel.

14 Vithalbhai to Lord Irwin, 23 April 1930, from Simla

Holcombe, Simla, 23 April 1930
My Dear Lord Irwin,

After I left you yesterday and thinking over the conversation we had, I feel we should further clarify our respective ideas as what exactly I should say in talking to Gandhi and Panditji in order to pave the way for opening up negotiations. I consider this very essential as I am anxious that I should say or do nothing which might subsequently be put down to my mishandling the situation. I have no doubt you will also feel as I do and we must therefore meet once again before I leave Simla.

Will it be possible for you to have a cup of tea with me in my poor hut either today or tomorrow or the day after at 4p.m.? You have never visited my Simla house and I shall feel highly honoured if you can agree to do so before I leave. There will be no third person and we shall have a quiet and useful talk for our mutual guidance.

I hope to send you my letters by tomorrow evening.

Yours sincerely,

15 Vithalbhai to Lord Irwin, 24 April 1930, from Simla

Holcombe, Simla, 24 April 1930
My Dear Lord Irwin,

I confess to a feeling of disappointment to read your letter of 23rd of April 1930. Of course, our conversation during my last interview had left me in the impression that you would be prepared to treat with Gandhi and Motilal in the near future if I brought any terms from them, and my clear recollection is that we discussed what those terms should be if they were to be acceptable to you. It now transpires that I have misunderstood you, and it is quite clear from your letter that you have also misunderstood me, and we both must regret that this should be so, particularly as it was my last interview with you in my official capacity. I was really so pleased when we parted that I felt the situation was not beyond hope. But the general trend and stiffness of your letter leaves me sad and with a feeling that you have not yet realised the gravity and seriousness of the situation. I feel it all the more because this was my last endeavour in the interests of peace in my official capacity and it has met with this unfortunate fate. Perhaps my country-men have not yet purged their sins fully and still more sacrifices and sufferings are in store for them. In these circumstances, the only course open to me is to state frankly what I feel in my letters to you and leave matters there. I hope to be able to complete them by tonight to enable me to place them in your hands by tomorrow morning.

Yours sincerely, V.J. Patel.

16 Vithalbhai to Lord Irwin, 25 April 1930, from Simla

Holcombe, Simla, 25 April 1930
My Dear Lord Irwin,

I have, since I last saw you, prepared two documents which are enclosed in separate covers herewith, and whilst they contain in brief my frank statement, I assure you I have weighed every word in them and put myself under considerable restraint in the choice of expressions.

I propose to leave Simla on Sunday afternoon, and I hope I have your permission to do so.

Wishing you and Lady Irwin the best of luck.

Yours sincerely, V.J. Patel.

17 Vithalbhai to Lord Irwin, 25 April 1930, from Simla

To His Excellency Lord Irwin, Viceregal Lodge, Simla
Holcombe, Simla, 25 April 1930

While I tender my resignation of the office of the President of the Legislative Assembly for reasons which I personally explained to you at some length at my interview with you on the 3rd of April and have briefly stated in another letter herewith, I consider it my duty not so much in the capacity of the President, with the sands of my official life running out, but rather as a true and devoted friend, to lay certain considerations before you at this juncture when I believe you are perplexed and puzzled lest one false step on your part might make the situation beyond redemption.

India is determined to be free, and no obstacle will be too great for her to overcome. Englishmen will never understand how it is and why Indians regard jail, which is intended for criminals, as a place of pilgrimage, and a public man who in his endeavour to secure freedom for his country has not gone to jail is at a discount. Suffering without retaliation for the cause of the country has become a matter of religion with most Indians. The process of suffering will go on till freedom is won.

Since you assumed the Viceroyalty of India, I have enjoyed the privilege of having numerous talks with you on the question of India's future and her relations with Britain as perhaps no other Indian has. From the day you landed in Bombay I began to acquaint you with the true situation. On that day, I had a long conversation with you and I told you how the great Non-co-operation Movement of 1920 was started and how it had very nearly achieved its object but ultimately failed. I also told you then that though the movement for the time being had failed, Congress was still the most representative institution in India, Gandhi was still a living force in Indian politics and was merely biding his time and that he was the man in India with the largest following and the one man who was essentially fitted to lead a mass movement. I urged upon you the absolute necessity of taking the earliest opportunity to get in touch with him and with his co-operation take steps to settle India's problems once and for all. You were then just a stranger to this land, and therefore did not rightly express any view or commit yourself to any opinion.

Subsequently you came in touch with your so-called constitutional advisers and your civil service who naturally had your ears. You also met a large number of public men of various schools of political thought in the country. The only people who did not come near you were the Congressmen – followers of Gandhi. Later, in our conversations, you more than once doubted whether Gandhi really counted in the political arena and whether the Congress had not lost much of its following in the country. I thought you were discounting my advice and that you were being wrongly advised. I then told you that Gandhi would before long lead a mass movement in India and that it would be your misfortune to resort to repressive methods much against your own inclination. I knew I was all alone in tendering such advice to you and that you would not accept all that I was telling you.

In 1927, when I was in England, I told the same thing to His Majesty, the King Emperor, and also to Lord Birkenhead and other leading public men of England. Talking about further constitutional reforms with Lord Birkenhead, I told him that nothimg short of immediate establishment of full responsible government would meet the requirements of the situation and that any delay in doing so would further complicate matters and seriously endanger the relations betweeen the two countries. Difficulties regarding defence of India were pointed out to me, and I told him 'where there was a will, there was a way', and if England would be prepared to give a loan of the requisite number of officers on such terms and conditions as may be agreed upon for a period of, say, five years, the so-called difficulties about defence would disappear. I also warned him that if India's problem was not settled to the satisfaction of the Congress without delay, England must be prepared to face the revival of the Non-Co-operation and Civil Disobedience Movement of 1921 on a much larger scale in 1930.

On my return from England, I repeated all this to you. Two or three months later, I learnt with pain and no less surprise that the British Government had appointed an all-White Commission called the Simon Commission. I felt that all my advice had fallen on deaf ears. The overwhelming majority of my countrymen decided to boycott the Commission and I thought of resigning my office to enable me to stand shoulder to shoulder with my countrymen in the boycott agitation. You, on being consulted, in the capacity of a personal friend and not as the Viceroy of India, advised me not to do so, and I accepted your advice and issued a letter to the Press explaining my position. The boycott movement made tremendous strides and was a grand success. You then for the first time realised that after all there was something in what I was saying to you all along. You thereupon thought of going to England to acquaint the British Government with the situation in India as you understood it and to have some declaration made to placate the boycotters.

My political opinions and my public activities before I accepted office are well known. I never believed that reason, persuasion or argument had any place in Britain's dealings with subject races. She never yields gracefully and out of mere generosity or merely because of the righteousness or justice of the cause, and whenever she does so, it is only when circumstances make it absolutely impossible for her to do otherwise. In this view, every agitation calculated to bring irresistible pressure to bear on the British Government, every activity which was likely seriously to embarrass the British administration in India, and every movement designed to create conditions which might make it difficult, if not impossible, for the British rulers to carry on in this country, had my fullest support. And today, after years of intimate connection with your Government in my official capacity, I am in a position to declare that those opinions have not varied in the slightest degree, or rather,

I am confirmed in the views I held before I accepted office. It is for you and the British Government, therefore, to consider what all this means.

It is no doubt true that my mentality began to undergo change when you decided to go to England to find a way out of the impasse resulting from the boycott of the Simon Commission, and I felt that perhaps you were destined to help India to realise her destiny and unite the two countries by a bond of real friendship, and I saw in your efforts a possibility for India to come into her own without further sufferings and sacrifices. I believed you meant well, though I did not fully realise your limitations and your difficulties. In any case, I was anxious that your efforts should not be wasted, and therefore I wanted you to take one very necessary precaution. On the 25th of May, last year, when you were about to leave Simla for England, we discussed the subject matter of your mission at some length, and I told you on that occasion that you were making a great mistake in not ascertaining from Gandhi and Pandit Motilal Nehru what sort of declaration would satisfy the Congress. You told me that you knew their views, and, in particular, of Pandit Motilal Nehru, through a common friend and that in any case it was too late for the purpose. I cannot help feeling that considerations of prestige and your hesitancy to believe that the Congress had so great a hold on the country and that Gandhi was really so powerful as I was representing (him to be) to you, prevented you from accepting my advice.

Whilst you were in England I wrote to you two letters and I had two from you. In my first letter I emphasised what I had told you on the 25th of May, that if by any formula the British Government could make it worth the while of the Congress leaders to agree to take part in a Round Table Conference, half the battle was won, and I added that my only apprehension was that you were not in full possession of the exact views of the Congress leaders in that respect and that there was, therefore, the danger of the formula not being acceptable to them.

In my second letter, I expressed my regret that it was not possible for you before you left India to have a heart-to-heart talk with the leaders of the party that really mattered, the only party which was in a position to deliver the goods to any appreciable extent – I meant the Congress Party in the Assembly and the country. I then made a definite suggestion in that letter that the British Government should take one or two of these leaders into their confidence, either Mahatma Gandhi or Pandit Motilal Nehru, or both, and have their previous consent to the terms of the proposed announcement and hoped they (the British Government) would not permit considerations of prestige to stand in the way of their doing the right thing at the right moment.

In your letters you assured me that you would do your best to find a way of peace out of our difficulties and that you were not likely to under-estimate the importance of doing everything that was possible to make it easier for all sections of opinion to come together. You returned to this country by the end of October, and made the announcement on behalf of His Majesty's Goverment. You were good enough to send me a copy in advance and when I met you in Delhi a couple of days before the announcement was made, I told you at once that the annoucement would put the Congress on the horns of a dilemma. If they accepted it, they would run counter to the Calcutta Congress Resolution and their declarations from time to time; if they did not accept it, they would at once lose the sympathy and support of Liberals and others who, I have no doubt would accept the announcement unconditionally. Speaking for myself, I was inclined to accept the Round Table Conference, given a satisfactory personnel and general amnesty to political prisoners. I was so inclined, not so much because I believed that I and my Congress friends would get all that we stood for as a result of the Round Table Conference, but because, in my judgement, in the event of a failure of the Conference and the resulting disappointment in the country, the Congress could start mass movement with greater justification and under more favourable auspices and also because I was so very much impressed with your sincerity. In any case, of one thing I was certain, namely, that a Conference without Congress leaders was (to my mind) unthinkable and futile. I therefore suggested to you to have a meeting with Gandhi and discuss the announcement with him. In my letter dated 2nd December 1929, I wrote to you as follows: 'I should like to repeat what I have so often made clear that the acceptance of the announcement by other political parties in the country means very little if the Congress Party is not reconciled to it. If the Congress at Lahore commits itself to the goal of independence and declines to participate in the proposed Round Table Conference, it would, in my opinion, be a bad day both for England and India. It is, therefore essential that every endeavour should be made to prevent the Congress from doing so. I have also made it clear to you that the only person who is yet in a position to save the situation is Mahatma Gandhi, and I must impress upon you once again to do all that lies in your power to strengthen his hands and satisfy him. In my interview with you in Bombay I had told you that you should say or do something which could be regarded as a sufficient justification by Mahatmaji and his colleagues to ask the Congress to stay its hands.'

A meeting was accordingly arranged on 23 December at the Viceroy's House, Delhi, when Gandhi and Pandit Motilal Nehru on behalf of the Congress asked for a definite assurance from you that at the Round Table Conference the British Government would support a scheme of immediate establishment of Dominion form of Government in India as a condition precedent to the Congress participating in the Conference. As you could not agree to give that assurance, the Conference fell through. For the moment, however, I felt that Gandhi was somewhat unreasonable in demanding such an assurance when he was dealing with a Viceroy who was sincerely trying his best to find a solution, and I told him so. Subsequent events both in India and in England, e.g the speech of Earl Russell, your own address to the Legislative Assembly on the 25th of January last, the numerous prosecutions of public men for mere expressions of opinion not involving any incitement to violence, and last but not least, the manner and method by which your Government forced on India Imperial Preference, treating all declarations about the reality of Fiscal Autonomy made by responsible British statesmen as mere scraps of paper and in utter defiance of the advice tendered by the President of the Legislative Assembly that the threat held out to the assembly by Government should be withdrawn before voting took place because it was in violation of the spirit of the Fiscal Autonomy Convention and also cut at the root of freedom of vote guaranteed by the Government of India Act, have disillusioned me completely; and Gandhi, to my mind, stands vindicated.

The Congress met and declared Complete Independence as its immediate objective; and Non-Cooperation and Civil Disobedience as the weapons with which to attain it. Gandhi gave his ultimatum to you and has now started the movement of Civil Disobedience. The response is spontaneous and countrywide. Hundreds of my countrymen of the first rank have already courted imprisonment, thousands and thousands are prepared to follow them, and even to lay down their lives, if necessary, in the cause of the country. The British Government repressed a somewhat similar movement in 1921, by all sorts of means, fair and foul, imprisoning thousands of Congressmen. But that movement has left behind a wonderful awakening and a desire for freedom among the masses throughout the country. That awakening and that desire are now an asset in this movement, and though you might temporarily suppress it, it is bound to have its ramifications in unfathomable but dangerous directions.

I have a feeling that every action of yours in this connection, e.g. the appointment of the Simon Commission, your unwillingness to take Congress leaders into your confidence before you made your announcement, etc, was based on the wrong advice that Congress and Gandhi had not that hold on the country and the following which I always represented they had. I know it is not your fault. Any other man, however well-meaning, as you are, surrounded by people some of whom are by no means friendly to the Congress and the country and others hopelessly out of touch with the realities of Indian political life and who could not under the circumstances be expected to give the right advice, would act similarly as you have done. Events of the last few days, I am confident, must have been an eye-opener to you, and at this juncture I desire to tender my final advice. I would ask you to lay aside, in the larger interests of our respective countries, all considerations of prestige and invite Gandhi for a settlement. I shall be told that Parliament was the ultimate authority and therefore no other authority had any power to give any undertaking which would commit Parliament. I have never been able to understand this argument. It is no doubt true, technically, Parliament is the supreme authority. But there is nothing to prevent the British Government to give an undertaking that, as far as they are concerned, they were prepared to make certain proposals to Parliament. It is such an undertaking that Gandhi demands. It is on the basis of such an undertaking that the Conference would meet and discuss such outstanding questions as would be still left open, such as the number of British troops and officers that should remain in India under the control of a responsible Minister and the period and other terms and conditions of such an arrangement, the question of foreign affairs in the meanwhile, and the question of Indian States. Barring these three matters, on which agreement could be reached at the Conference, no other question regarding the administration of India should be open for discussion at the Conference. The Conference must take the form of a meeting of the plenipotentiaries of both countries to discuss and arrive at an agreement on these and kindred questions.

It is true that the Congress has now adopted complete independence as its object (objective?) but I am not without hope that if without further sacrifice and delay India is offered complete responsible Government within the British Commonwealth of Nations, she would be prepared to accept it, and perhaps such responsible Government is more to her advantage in her present condition than isolated independence. As I stated to the Assembly on the 21st January 1930, I have always maintained, and still maintain, the change in the Congress creed notwithstanding, that the relations between Great Britain and India can only be finally adjusted on the basis of India's right to Dominion Status being acknowledged without any reservation, and the method of giving effect to that decision being examined in some joint and equal Conference between the plenipotentiaries of the two countries, and that the greater the delay in finding a solution of the problem on these lines, the lesser the chances for a favourable atmosphere for the purpose and its general acceptance in this country. As you are aware, I have missed no opportunity during the last four years that I have been in the Chair of the Assembly to press this view as strongly as I can upon your attention. No doubt, such a settlement would have been more welcome before the last Congress, but (for?) at this stage it was bound to leave in the country a party advocating complete independence and denouncing those who accept the settlement. This, however, would be a matter of domestic concern to be fought out by the two parties in India. But I must utter a word of warning. If this movement is suppressed, and the solution of the problem such as I have suggested is further delayed, all those Indians who would thereafter talk of Dominion Status for India would be condemned as traitors, and the possibility of having India as a self-governing unit in the British Commonwealth of Nations would be lost for ever

I fully appreciate the difficulty of the position in which you have found yourself, and I know that no one wishes more than you that the affairs of India may again be speedily guided into smoother waters. May I, therefore, hope that you will take due note of the recent manifestations of the determination of the people of India to attain freedom at any cost and use your great influence with the British Government accordingly? But if for any reason you find yourself unable to persuade the British Government to accept in substance the suggestion I have made, my advice is that you should tender the resignation of your high office rather than allow your great name to be associated with a campaign of repression designed to suppress the legitimate aspirations of the 320 million human beings. You have so far endeavoured to serve India well and you would have served her even better if you had been correctly advised. You would serve her best by resigning if you find that the situation is beyond you and you have to choose between repression and resignation. But I know you hold a unique position in the Councils of the Empire today. You have a rare opportunity. You sincerely believe in solving India's problem. Your influence with all parties in England is great, and you enjoy in abundant measure the confidence of the Secretary of State for India and the British Government. If, therefore, you take courage and rise to the occasion, you will serve both India and England as no man has served in the past. If you fail, it must be India's good-bye to England.

18 Vithalbhai to Lord Irwin, 25 April 1930, from Simla

To His Excellency Lord Irwin, Viceregal Lodge, Simla,
Holcombe, Simla, 25 April 1930

I hereby tender my resignation of the Office of President and also of the Membership of the Indian Legislative Assembly. In doing so, I take the opportunity of giving your Excellency some idea of the difficulties and obstacles the first elected President had to encounter in the discharge of his duties and also stating briefly the reasons which have impelled me to tender my resignation.

I have been in the Chair of the Assembly since August 1925. Strict impartiality, and more than that, absolute independence have guided my conduct throughout. Neither a desire for popular applause nor a fear of bureaucratic frowns have I allowed to influence my conduct at any time. I may have made mistakes; but I can say with clear conscience today that on no occasion have I been actuated by any personal or political feeling, and in all that I have said and done I have, according to my poor judgement, endeavoured to consult the best interests of the Assembly and the country.

By unflinching adherence to these two principles in the discharge of my duties under circumstances however difficult, I brought down on my head the wrath of the bureaucracy. It is, no doubt, true that they tolerated my adherence to these principles up to a point; but in matters that really mattered to them, it was a different story. King's Government must be carried on, and even the Speaker of the popular Assembly is expected to behave and to make it easy for the bureaucracy to carry on. I gave them no quarters and refused to be a part and parcel of the administration or be subservient to them on any matter, however vital from their point of view, and in the result, harassment and persecution was my lot at least for the last three years. The Chair had been a bed of thorns for me throughout. They went to the length of organizing and carrying out a social boycott of the President of the Assembly. They condoned – to use a milder term – all sorts of attacks in the press, and otherwise, on the impartiality of the Chair in the most unbecoming language imaginable. I could not retaliate nor could I speak out, and I had to bear all this in solemn silence all the time. The only relief I had was when on occasions I spoke out my mind to some extent to Your Excellency in private.

The authority of the Chair and the dignity of the House were matters of no concern to them, or rather it was their special concern, on occasions, to endeavour to undermine them and lower the Chair in the estimation of the public. As if this was not enough, a clique of underlings determined on a campaign of vilification, abuse and misrepresentation of the President was allowed to thrive, doing its work unhampered. One of the items of its programme was to prejudice Your Excellency against me. How far they have succeeded in that object, it is not for me to say.

Certain correspondents of newspapers in India and in England had always free access to this clique and received at its hands every encouragement and inspiration. Columns of these newspapers were at the disposal of the clique for its campaign against the President, with the result that to the ordinary white man, not only at the Headquarters of the Government of India but throughout the country, the occupant of the Assembly Chair became an eye-sore, so much so that his exit from the Chair would be hailed with a sigh of relief and even delight by him.

In these circumstances, it should not surprise Your Excellency to learn that I had been shadowed and my movements had been constantly watched. It seemed to me as if there was a deliberate and organised conspiracy to persecute me in order that I might, in sheer disgust, tender my resignation and thereby supply a handle to the enemies of India to demonstrate that Indians are unfit to hold such responsible positions. It was an open secret that the Government of India and their officials had no love for me and tolerated me in that Chair because there was no way by which they could remove me except by a direct vote of censure. But they were never sure of getting a majority in the House to pass such a vote and perhaps you would not lightly allow such a motion to be tabled.

In the midst of all these difficulties, I carried on, because I believed that I was serving my country by doing so. Fortunately, when matters came to a crisis, I had won and they had lost. A man with weaker nerves would have resigned long ago or become subservient to them. I did neither, but stuck to my post and laid down precedents and conventions and gave rulings which, I venture to think, might do credit to any Assembly in the world.

My tenure of office had throughout been a period of one continuous struggle between the Chair and the Assembly on the one hand and the Government on the other, and in spite of many limitations imposed upon me and the Assembly by the Constitution, I had always endeavoured to uphold and enlarge the authority of the Chair and the dignity, the rights and privileges of the House against the powerful bureaucracy, and I believe I have, to a certain measure, succeeded. These five years have been to me so strenuous, so full of worries and anxieties that it has seriously impaired my health. My only solace is in the feeling that I still retain the confidence of my people.

It is not my purpose to blame any particular individual or individuals. My complaint is against the system under which all these horrible things which I have just described are possible, and the sooner such a system is put an end to the better for all concerned.

Notwithstanding all the harassment and persecution, I should have certainly continued to occupy the Chair if by so doing I had thought that I would better serve my country. But I am convinced that, under changed conditions, my usefulness as President of the Assembly has entirely ceased to exist.

Owing to the boycott of the Assembly by the Congressmen in obedience to the mandate of the Lahore Congress, followed recently by the resignations of the leader of the Opposition, Pandit Madan Mohan Malaviya, and a band of his loyal followers as a protest against the manner and method by which Government of India forced down the throat of an unwilling Assembly the principle of Imperial Preference, the Assembly has lost its representative character, and when speaker after speaker got up on the Tariff Bill discussion and said that, by the attitude adopted by the Government of India, namely that the Assembly must accept British Preference or the mill industry of India must go to wreck (rack) and ruin, they would be compelled to vote against their conviction and not on the merits of the Government proposals, I felt (wondered) whether it was worth while any longer presiding over an Assembly where it was not possible for the President to safeguard even the freedom of the vote supposed to have been guaranteed by the Government of India Act. It goes without saying that the Assembly would hereafter exist merely to register the decrees of the Executive, and I should be doing a disservice to my country if I continued to lend false prestige to such a body by presiding over it any more.

Apart from these considerations, in the grave situation that has arisen in the country, I feel that I would be guilty of deserting India's cause at this critical juncture if I were to continue to hold the office of the President of the Assembly. On the 21st of January 1930, in explaining my position, as President of the Assembly, in reference to the resolution of the Lahore Congress I had used these significant words: 'Whilst, therefore, I am quite clear that it would be wrong and indeed dangerous for any President to act on the mandate of any political party in or outside the House, I am equally emphatic that, circumstanced as India is, a situation might arise when in the larger interests of the country the President of the Assembly might feel called upon to tender his resignation with a view to a return to a position of greater freedom.'

I have no doubt in my mind that such a situation has now arisen in the country. My people have been engaged in a life-and-death struggle for freedom. The movement of non-violent Non-co-operation and Civil Disobedience initiated by the Indian National Congress under the leadership of Mahatma Gandhi, the greatest man of modern times, is in full swing. Hundreds of prominent countrymen of mine have already found their place in His Majesty's jails;

thousands are prepared to lay down their lives if necessary, and hundreds of thousands are ready to court imprisonment in the prosecution of that great movement. At such a juncture in the history of the struggle for freedom of my country, my proper place is with my countrymen with whom I have decided to stand shoulder to shoulder, and not in the Chair of the Assembly.

As Your Excellency is aware, I was endeavouring in my humble way for the last four years that you have been at the helm of affairs in India to prevent such a situation from developing. I had all along pleaded that the crisis could be averted only by Dominion Status without reservation, and the method of giving by the frank and full recognition of India's claim to complete effect to that decision being examined by some joint and equal conference between the plenipotentiaries of the two countries. In another letter (kept?) herewith I have stated in some detail the result of my endeavours on these lines. That letter, therefore may be treated as part of this.

I confess I felt for a time that better days were in sight and India would soon secure her legitimate place as a free and self-governing unit in the British Commonwealth of Nations without further sufferings and sacrifices. But the recent events both in England and India have completely disillusioned me, and I have now come to the deliberate conclusion that all talk about the so-called change of heart on the part of the British Government and change of spirit in the day-to-day administration of the country and (the?) Dominion Status being in action in India is merely an eye-wash, is as unreal as the Fiscal Autonomy Convention and is not to be found anywhere translated into action in any shape or form. In these circumstances, I have no doubt whatever that there is no desire on the part of the British Government to recognise the justice of the claim made by the Congress and satisfactorily (to) settle India's problem to the lasting benefit of India and Britain alike. On the contrary, there has been abundant evidence in the recent actions of the Government in all parts of the country that, true to their traditions, they have launched on a policy of ruthless repression designed to crush the legitimate aspirations of a great people. I am convinced, therefore, that Mahatma Gandhi stands fully vindicated in the attitude he has taken up – that he was not prepared to advise the Congress to participate in the Round Table Conference in London unless there has been a full and frank recognition of India's claim to complete Dominion Status without any reservation and unless it was made clear that the Conference was to meet to explore methods of giving effect to such decision. In such a situation the honourable and patriotic course open to me is to sever my connection with the Government of India, which I hereby do by tendering my resignation, and take my legitimate place in the fight for freedom side by side with my countrymen. I only hope my indifferent health will not prevent me from actively participating in the movement, but in any case I shall be giving my moral support to it by this resignation.

In the end, I desire to place on record my sincere appreciation of your friendly feeling towards me and of the advice you gave me from time to time and of your uniform courtesy and kindness (throughout?).

Two instances, in particular, of your special regard for me I shall always remember with gratitude. During my term of office, my constituency was in serious trouble on more than one occasion – (1) in 1927, owing to unprecedented floods; on that occasion Your Excellency at my request visited the flood-stricken area and moved about from village to village under the most trying conditions and expressed to my people your personal sympathy which they needed so much at that time; and (2) in 1928, owing to unjustifiable enhancement of land revenue in the Bardoli Taluka; there too, Your Excellency at my request used your good offices with the Government of Bombay to settle the trouble which was about to result in a serious crisis.

I now close with an assurance to Your Excellency that, although my official connection with you ceases from today, my personal regard for you shall continue as hitherto, and with a hope that we might some day meet in our unofficial capacity and without reserve exchange notes on our respective actions in our official capacity.

19 Vithalbhai to Dadubhai, 9 March 1932, from Aden

P.& O.S.N.Co.
SS *Ranchi*, Aden
9.3.1932

Brother Dadubhai,

All the work has come to naught and for that I consider Gandhi as responsible. He never accepts any advice, and except satyagraha he does not know anything else.

In the circumstances, it is our duty to the people of India, that when I regain my good health, we should openly follow the road which we feel is the right road for freedom struggle, and in that I hope you and all other friends will help me.

Please give my regards to everyone and please do write to me.

Yours, Vithalbhai

Note

This letter discloses the exasperation of Vithalbhai. He was certain, that if Gandhi had followed his advice, he would have succeeded in obtaining Dominion Status at the Second Round Table conference. See further details in Chapter 25 and Appendix 5, Document 18.

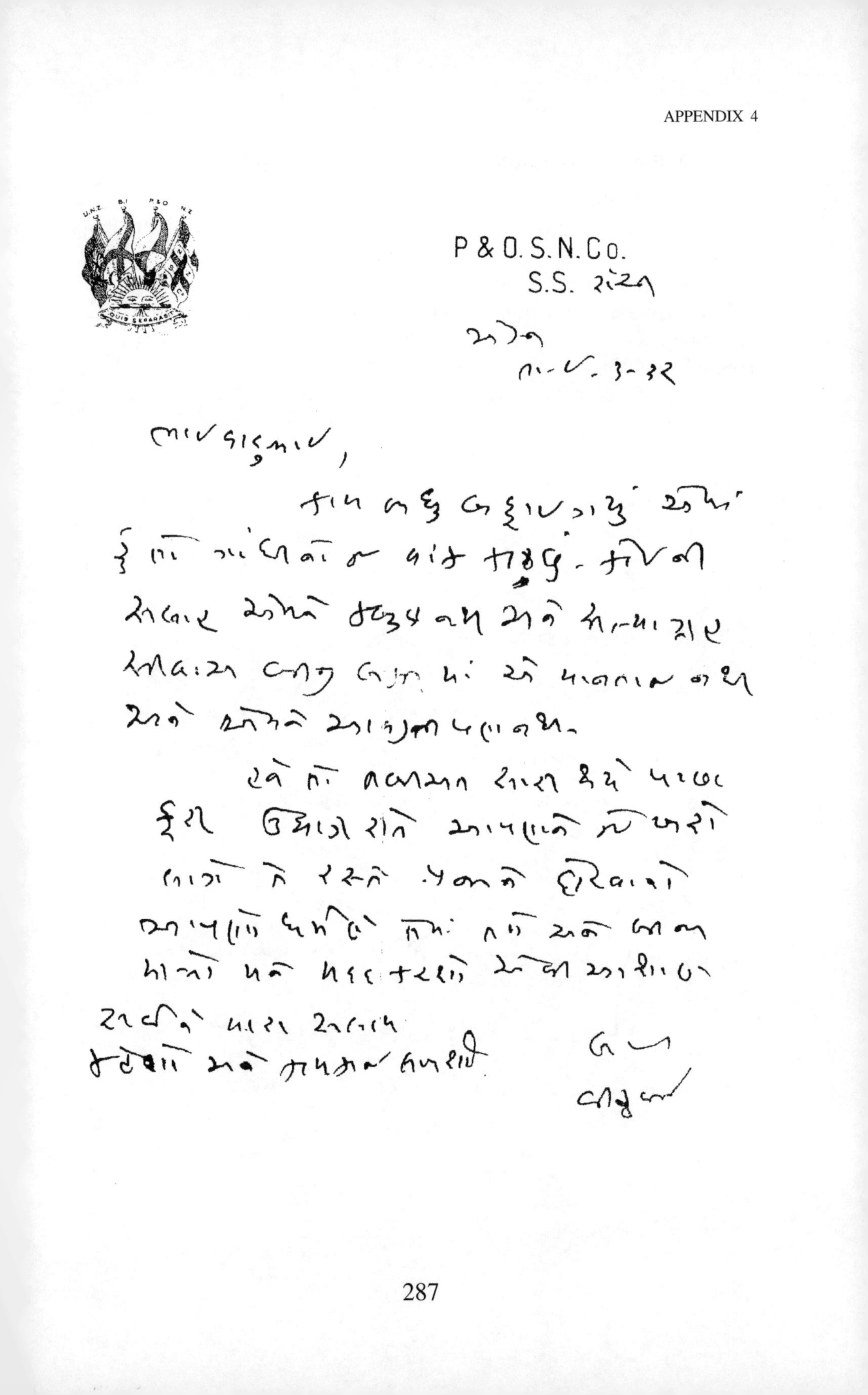

P & O.S.N.Co.
S.S. [illegible]

એડન
૧૦-૮-૩-૩૨

[illegible],

[illegible]

[illegible]

[illegible]

20 Vithalbhai to Dadubhai, 14 April 1932, from Vienna

Brother Dadubhai,

It seems my health is getting better recently, but on reading the news from India, I become anxious and unsettled.

Once I get a little better, I am planning on getting working.

From time to time please write to me what is happening there (in India)

Yours Vithalbhai

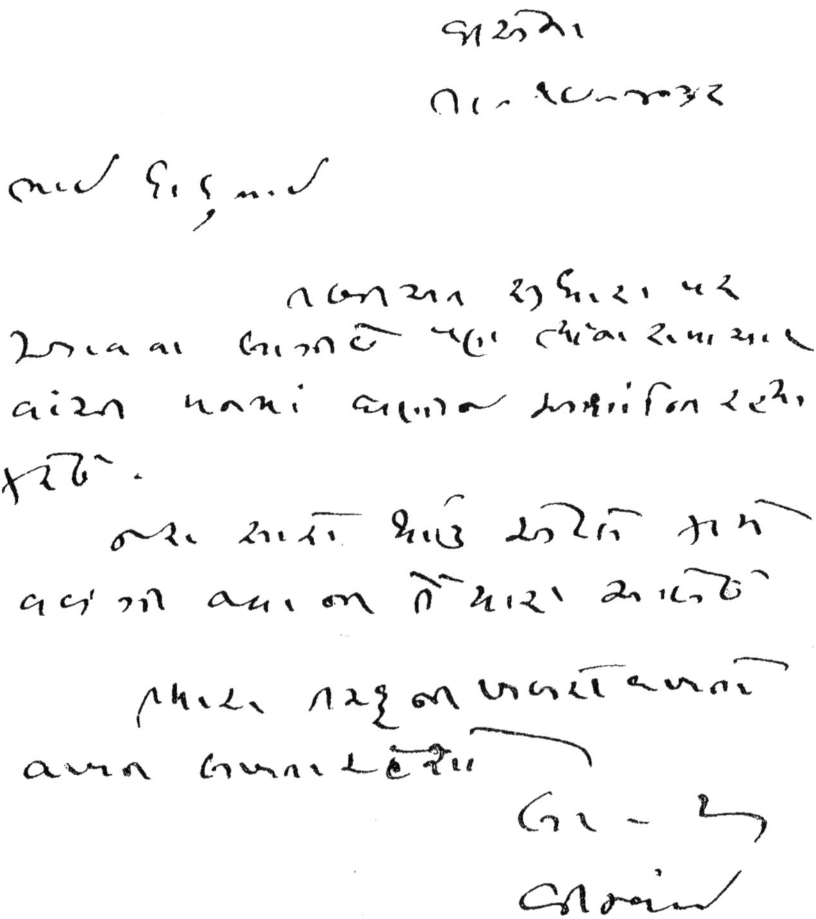

21 Vithalbhai on the Bose-Patel Manifesto, 9 May 1933, from Vienna

The Bose-Patel Manifesto

(Vienna, May, 1933).

THE events of the last thirteen years have demonstrated that a political warfare based on the principle of maximum suffering for ourselves and minimum suffering for our opponents can not possibly lead to success. It is futile to expect that we can ever bring about a change of heart in our rulers merely through our own suffering or by trying to love them. And the latest action of Mahatma Gandhi in suspending the civil disobedience movement is a confession of failure as far as the present method of the Congress is concerned. We are clearly of opinion that as a political leader Mahatma Gandhi has failed. The time has therefore come for a radical reorganisation of the Congress on a new principle and with a new method. For bringing about this reorganisation a change of leadership is necessary, for it would be unfair to Mahatma Gandhi to expect him to evolve or work a programme and method not consistent with his life-long principles. If the congress as a whole can undergo this transformation, it would be the best course. Failing that a new party will have to be formed within the Congress, composed of all radical elements. Non-co-operation cannot be given up but the form of Non-co-operation will have to be changed into a more militant one and the fight for freedom to be waged on all fronts.

V. J. PATEL
SUBHAS CHANDRA BOSE
9-5-33.

(Later, after Vithalbhai's death, Subhas on 29 April 1939 formed a party within the Congress for the purposes mentioned in the above Manifesto and called it 'Forward Bloc'.)

22 Vithalbhai to Dadubhai, 11 May 1933, from Vienna

Sanatorium Himmelhof
Dr. Leo Mautner
Wien
XIII Himmelhofgasse 35
11.5.1933

Brother Dadubhai,

Reccived your letter. Your letter to me at New York was received the day I left and Roberts redirected it to me. Please write and acknowledge to Roberts.

Where and when the invitation from God will come, nobody knows, but when and where it comes I am ready. If I can get the strength of walking I wish to come back to India. My health has deteriorated completely. I am forbidden to get up from bed. How many months it will take I don't know. Doctors believe that this is the result of American tour. They think that long rest will do the trick.

Now only if Mahatma Gandhi steps out of public life, will his credibility remain intact. He does not know how to wrestle against the British. His habit of fasting, really advertised that India is not fit for independence.

Please do write to me as usual. Subhasbabu is here and visits me daily, his health is now much improved. Yours, Vithalbhai.

Note

Gandhi was preparing to start his fast on the issue of representation of the untouchables. Vithalbhai did not approve, he felt it would be better to have proper negotiations. Vithalbhai now decided it was time for Gandhi to retire from politics. Just two days before writing this letter he had issued, with Subhas Bose, the Bose-Patel Manifesto.

HIMMELHOF
DR. LEO MAUTNER
WIEN
XIII. HIMMELHOFGASSE 18

23 Vallabhbhai to Dadubhai, 16 January 1930, from Ahmedabad

President: Shree Vallabhbhai J. Patel	1000–7–28
Secretaries: Shree Jivanlal A. Diwan	Telegram 'Congress', Tel 174
Shree Manilal V. Kothari	Gujarat Provincial Committee
	Community Improvement Hall
	Ahmedabad
	16.1.1930

Dear Brother Dadubhai,

Received your letter. After visiting Matar and Mahemdabad, I am struck with fever. Mamlatdars have increased the land revenue assessments, fresh investigation of Matar affair is started, but nothing similar is being done about Mahemdabad. In both the Talukas, the current year's land revenue demand should be postponed; but without putting up a fight who will listen? That is why I feel we should fight. I have written through Maxwell a letter to the Governor, I am waiting for his reply. Viceroy has come so perhaps it will take time. A conflagration has to be started if the answer is not favourable. This time I am thinking of only one year's land revenue non-payment campaign.

You let me know when you are coming back.

This week I am going to close my house here.

Vande Mataram from Vallabhbhai.

Note

The Bardoli Satyagraha Settlement came on 6 August 1928 and after that Sardar intended to start similar satyagrahas in Kaira District. Both these letters mark the beginning of such movements, with Dadubhai's co-operation. The background to these letters, and the events which followed, are shown in Chapter 19. Dadubhai participated in, and then carried on his own shoulders (in the absence of Sardar), this movement from May until October 1930. At that point he was arrested and sent to prison. With the rest of the leaders he was released on 25 January 1931.

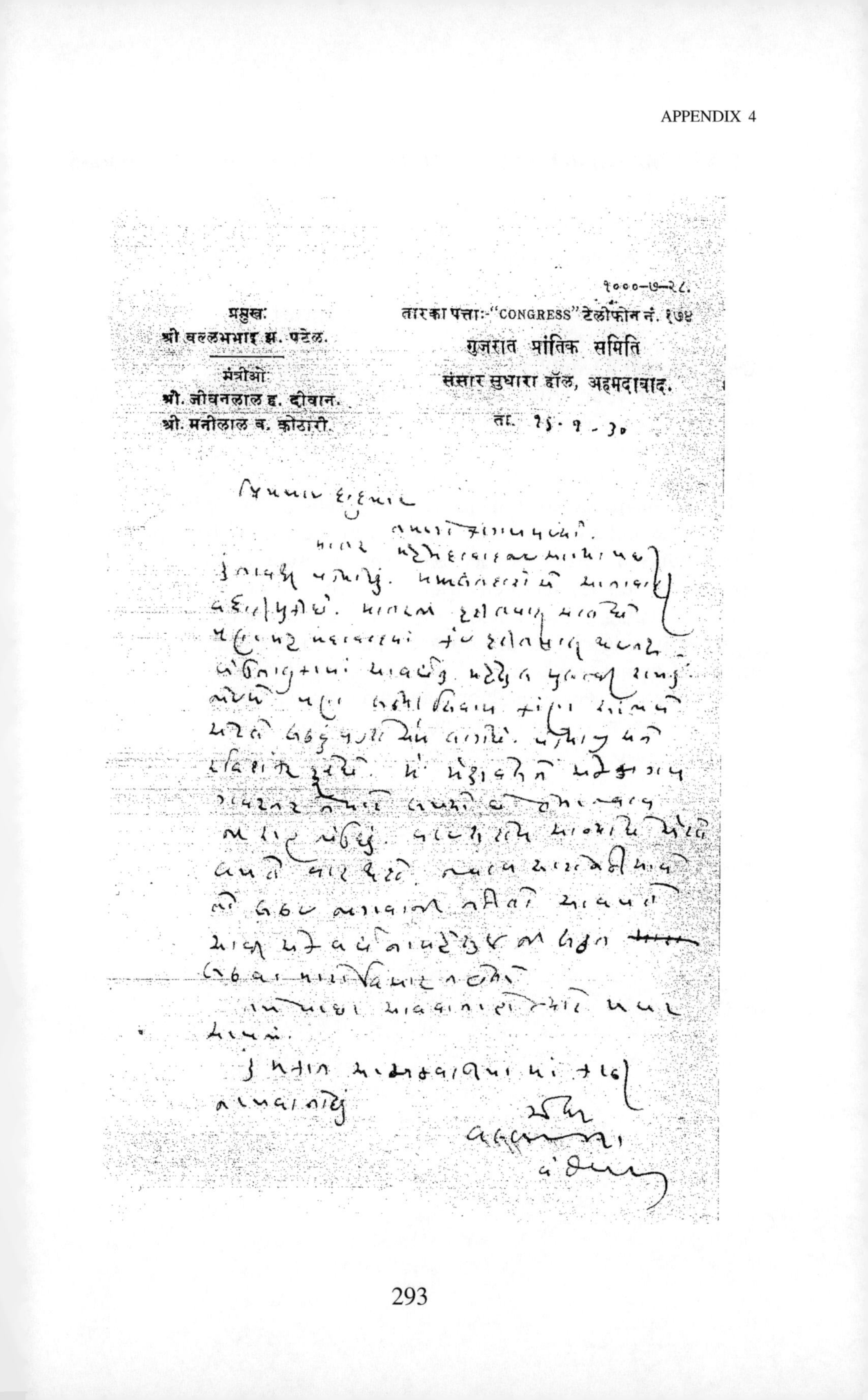

१०००—७—२८.

प्रमुख:
श्री वल्लभभाइ झ. पटेल.

मंत्रीओ:
श्री. जीवनलाल ह. दीवान.
श्री. मनीलाल व. कोठारी.

तारका पत्ता:-"CONGRESS" टेलीफोन नं. १७४

गुजरात प्रांतिक समिति

संसार सुधारा हॉल, अहमदावाद.

ता. ૧૫-૧-૩૦

[illegible]

24 Vallabhbhai to Dadubhai, 20 January 1930, from Ahmedabad

President: Shree Vallabhbhai J. Patel
Secretaries: Shree Jivanlal A. Diwan
Shree Manilal V. Kothari

1000–7–28
Telegram 'Congress', Tel 174
Gujarat Provincial Committee
Community Improvement Hall
Ahmedabad
20.1.1930

Dear Brother Dadubhai,

Received your letter. Government's reply has come stating that the Governor Saheb himself is making enquiries and afterwards he will give me a detailed reply. Also, now the Collector has started Mahemdabad inquiry too, and yesterday the previous orders of revenue from seven villages are rescinded. Everything is now postponed and fresh inquiries will be instituted. At both places the Mamlatdars have confounded the issue. The one at Matar has acted like a butcher. He has perpetrated extreme atrocities. As the entire matter is being re-examined, I hope the cultivators will get justice.

After having closed my house, I have no intention of setting up house elsewhere. Whenever I will come to Ahmedabad I will either stay at the Ashram or Doctor Kanunga's place. Mainly my intention is of living in Bardoli, and now how long is this life remaining outside is also unpredictable. Up to 2.2.1930 I will be in Ahmedabad and after that will go to Bardoli.

Vande Mataram from Vallabhbhai.

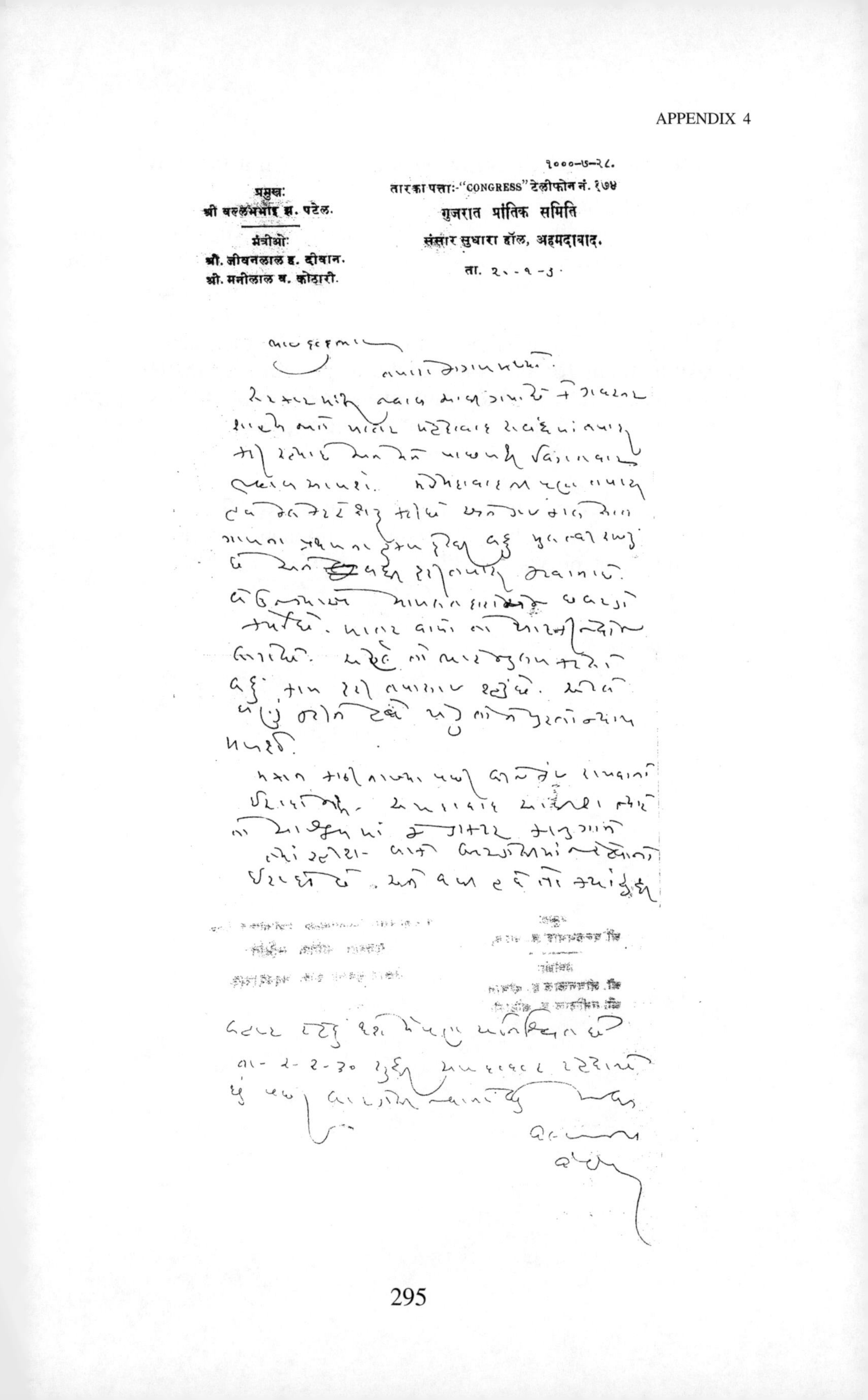

१०००-७-२८.

प्रमुख:
श्री वल्लभभाई झ. पटेल.

मंत्रीओ:
श्री. जीवनलाल ह. दीवान.
श्री. मनीलाल व. कोठारी.

तारका पत्ता:-"CONGRESS" टेलीफोन नं. १७४

गुजरात प्रांतिक समिति

संसार सुधारा हॉल, अहमदाबाद.

ता. २०-१-३०.

[illegible]

[illegible]

25 Vallabhbhai to Dadubhai, 31 May 1940, from Bombay

Brother Dadubhai,

Received your letter. Bhai Jeenabhai's and Maneklal's letters were also received by me. I have directly written to them. Please meet them and they should vote for Maganbhai. That is my opinion and that is why I have forwarded my strong opinion. I understand their dilemma. There is no social offence in their action. I am requesting them for the good of humanity. In this matter I have no axe to grind, you, they and everyone knows that. So please meet them and persuade them to our viewpoint.

Vallabhbhai's Vande Mataram

(This letter, written in Gujarati, clearly shows Sardar's way of thinking and his actions to persuade opponents of his views. It also shows that he was working closely with Dadubhai.)

वल्लभभाई पटेल

टेलिफोनः २४१०१ तारः *Powerfarm*
६८ मरीन ड्राईव
बंबई १

૧૦.૩.૫૦

[illegible]

[illegible]

લિ.
વલ્લભભાઈ [illegible]

26 Vallabhbhai to Dadubhai, 30 November 1941, from Wardha

Dear Brother Dadubhai,

Tomorrow from here I am going to Bombay. After three or four days will go to Bardoli. Bapu will also come to Bardoli. He will stay with me for a month. He will come via Bhusawal on the tenth, Mahadevbhai will also come. As it is near, whenever convenient you will be able to come and we can meet.

One representative of Anand Institute has to be appointed on the Rural Development Board. For that post I have suggested your name.

I hope you are in good health. Hope all the family is well.

Vallabhbhai's Vande Mataram.

(Gandhi stayed with Sardar in his Bardoli cottage on various dates in 1936, 1939, 1941 and 1942.)

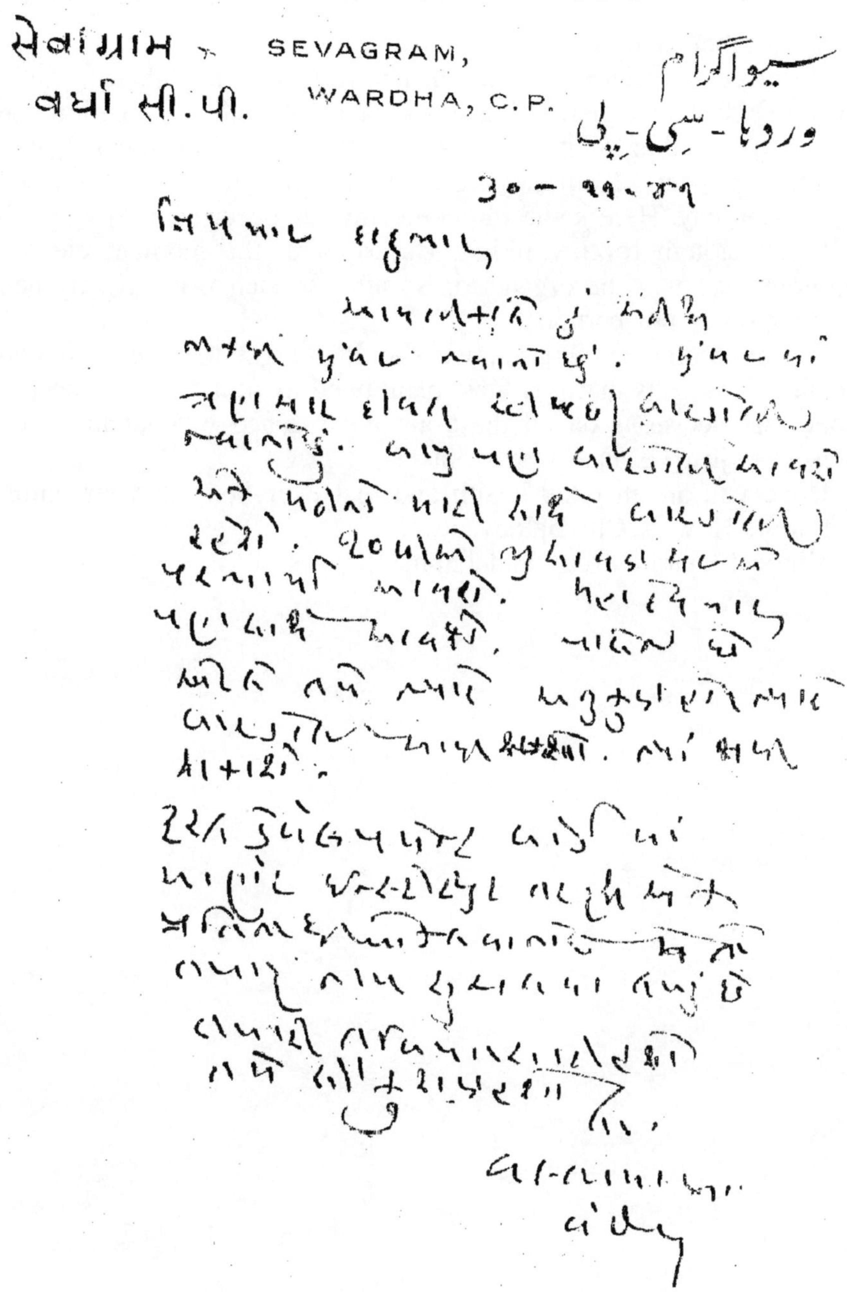

सेवाग्राम SEVAGRAM, سیواگرام

वर्धा सी.पी. WARDHA, C.P. وردھا - سی - پی

૩૦-૧૧-૪૧

27 Vallabhbhai to Dadubhai, 11 November 1945, from Bombay

Dear Brother Dadubhai,

Received your letter of the 9th. I have heard talks about creating an university in Gujarat. There are talks of colleges creation too. As I am attending to improve my health, I have not given thought to these projects. I am staying here till 19th and after that I will go to Bombay. Here some improvement has occurred to my health, but not enough for my liking. But right at the moment election programme has to be organised. So after I reach Bombay, my next destination is not certain.

When I come to Gujarat, we should all get together and plan about the subjects that you have mentioned in your letter. I sincerely hope that decisions on all these are not reached without me being present – just because I was outside.

Hope you are in good health and that everybody in your family are well. How is Chi Baldev now?

Vande Mataram from Vallabhbhai.

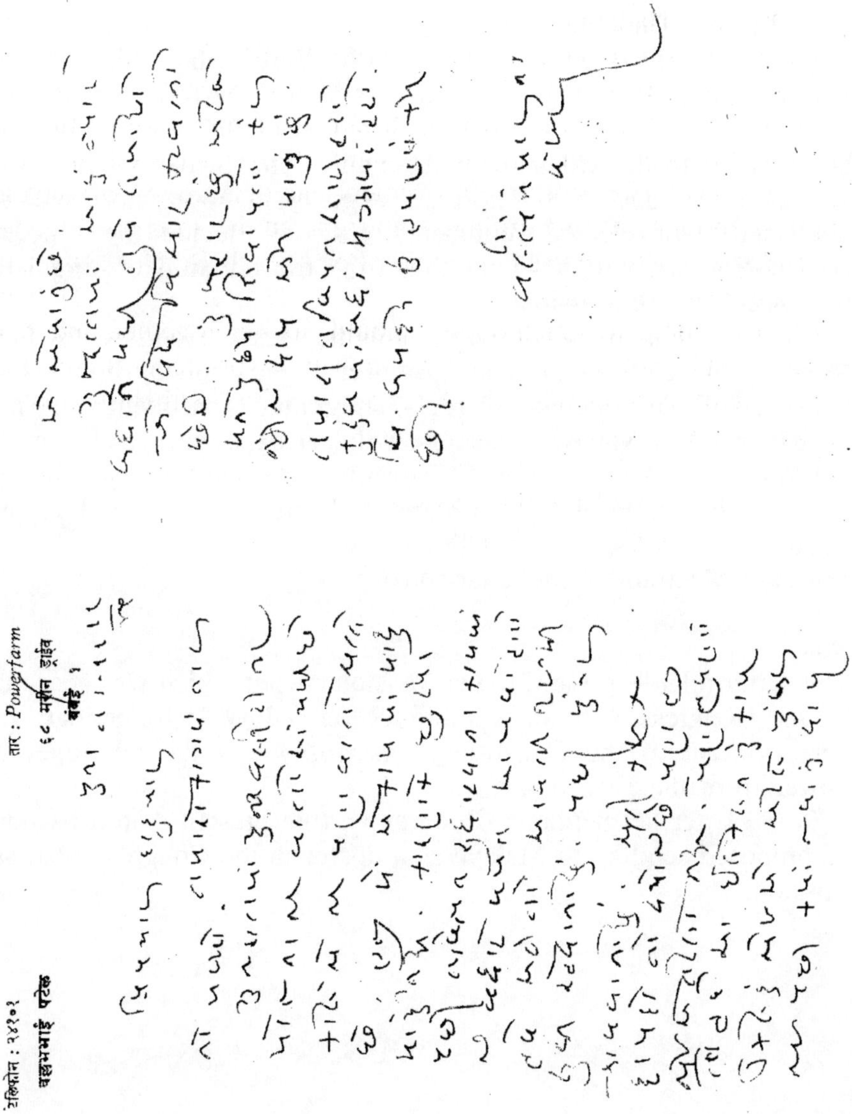
टेलिफोन : २४३०३
वल्लभभाई पटेल
तार : Powerfarm
६८ मरीन ड्राइव
बंबई १

28 Vallabhbhai to Dadubhai, 9 May 1946, from Simla

Dear Brother Dadubhai,

I have received your letter of 25th. Here it has taken longer than expected. It is difficult to predict as to how long it will take.

Creation of provinces and the formation of the constitution will be assigned to the Constituent Assembly. The British Government will have no hand in it. The present government structure will be abolished. Our elected representatives will decide the type of constitution we will have, at that time the creation of linguistic provinces will be possible.

Chi. Chittaranjan had a desire to join the Malaya Congress Medical Mission. He came a bit late, however I telegraphed Bidhan and he accepted Chittaranjan by reply telegram. Subsequently he has already reached Malaya. There he will get experience and worldly wisdom.

Hope you are in good health and with my good wishes for your family.

Vande Mataram from Vallabhbhai.

Note

This letter relates to the Cabinet Mission Award which was accepted by the Congress Working Committee on 6 July 1946. Sardar was very hopeful of the Constituent Assembly and the take-over of power from the British.

In the letter he mentions Chittaranjan (the present Author) whom he proposed sending to Malaya as a doctor in the Congress Medical Mission.

29 Vallabhbhai to Dadubhai, 5 June 1946, from Bombay

Dear Brother Dadubhai,

Received your letter. This time there is good opportunity for getting public works in Gujarat. Gujarat has good and solid representation in the Cabinet. Gujarat ministers are also very strong and whatever good work needs to be done should be carried out.

Morarjibhai is there and Dinkerbhai, Vaikunthbhai and Gulzarilal are our men. Maharshira representatives are complaining about Gujarat representation.

My work with the Cabinet Mission is not finished. To complete that I will go to Delhi on the 7th inst. I hope that work will be successful in a few days.

Chi. Chittaranjan has written a letter to me from Malaya. There he seems to be getting good experience.

Hope everybody in your family is in good health.

Vallabhbhai's Vande Mataram.

Note

In this letter he weighs in for his own constituency and power base. He also mentions the Report of the work of the Congress Medical Mission (submitted by the present writer), which had given free medical treatment and medicines to all the inhabitants of Malaysia i.e. Malays, Chinese, Indians and all others. When the mission's work ended after six months, the Selangor Unit which the present author was running, had treated over 18,000 patients.

टेलिफोन : २४२०२
वल्लभभाई पटेल

तार : Powerfarm
६८ मरीन ड्राइव
बंबई १

30 Vallabhbhai to Lord Mountbatten, 11 May 1947

To Lord Mountbatten; 11 May 1947.

1/ I am not quite sure if the cumulative effects of appointments to the posts of Trade Commissioners and other similar posts overseas made since October 1946 have attracted your attention. As far as I have been able to gather the previous appointments were as follows:

1. Trade Commission, New York	Mr. S.K. Kripalani ICS (now vacant)
2. Deputy Trade Commissioner, New York	Mr. I. Shaffi
3. Trade Commissioner, Canada	Mr. Ahuja
4. Trade Commissioner, Mombassa	Sardar Sahib Sagar Singh
5. Trade Commissioner, Teheran	Mr. Hassan
6. Trade Commissioner, Alexandria	Mr. Rahim
7. Trade Commissioner, Paris	Mr. S.S. Bajpai
8. Trade Commissioner, UK	Sir David Meek
9. Trade Commissioner, Sydney	Mr. R.R. Saxena

2/ Recent appointments have been as follows:

1. Trade Commissioner, UK	Mr. Ikramullah ICS
2. Dep. Trade Commissioner, UK	Mr. A.S. Lall
3. Indian Supply Mission, UK	Mr. Habibullah
4. Economic Adviser to Indian Military Mission, Berlin	Dr. Mukhtar
5. Personal Assistant to the above	Prof. Abdul Majid
6. Trade Commissioner, Milan	Mr. G. Ahmed IP
7. Trade Commissioner, Sydney	Mr. A.D. Azhar (vice Mr. R.R. Saxena)

3/ The above list will make it quite clear that the representation of non-Muslims in these appointments has been very inadequate. In fact the impression one gathers is that it has been largely ignored. I presume the Commerce Department obtained your approval to these appointments, but while dealing with individual cases it is of course impossible for you to have realised the cumulative effect of these appointments in regard to communal representation. I feel that something should be done to retrieve the position. I understand that some appointments are still to be made: New York, Singapore, Rangoon and Iraq. It is possible other posts e.g. Switzerland, Japan,

South American countries, may also be created. I would request you that in filling these appointments, this aspect of the matter be borne in mind.

31 Vallabhbhai to Lord Mountbatten, 15 May 1947

To Lord Mountbatten, 15 May 1947.

1/ I have seen your Private Secretary's note on the case relating to criticism of the action of the Chief Commissioner, Delhi, which I had recorded on two files. I find that you would like to discuss it with me at our next interview which comes off on 17 May. In order to save time, I feel I should let you know other cases in which I have had to take serious objection to the Chief Commissioner's attitude or his way of administration so that you might be familiar with the background.

2/ The first time that I had to take a very serious view of his attitude was when he made a reference to Government containing a sarcastic mention of my instructions that the Delhi administration should be more liberalised and asking me to issue instructions to the Provincial Congress Committee of Delhi that they and their volunteer organisations must obey the orders in force for the maintenance of peace in Delhi and not defy orders, for example, the one issued under Section 144 against carrying of lathis and big sticks. In this case the facts were that the Congress volunteers who were engaged to keep order on the occasion of a meeting of the AICC held with permission of the Chief Commissioner had acted on provocation from some Scheduled Caste demonstrators and the local police, despite requests from the volunteers to disperse the Scheduled Caste demonstrators who had formed an assembly contrary to the orders of the District Magistrate, looked on and did nothing.

3/ The second instance was in January 1947 when while forwarding his recommendations regarding a successor to Mr. Robinson, Senior Superintendent of Police, Mr. Christie not only mentioned that he had communicated to the Government of the Punjab, without any authority from me, my views on the adjustment of over-representation of Muslims in the police force in Delhi with a view to restoring proportion more in accord with population but also made a gratuitous reference to the absence of Moslem Officers at the head of the main branches of district administration. There was no occasion for this remark at all because the Punjab Government had recommended only three Europeans and one Indian Christian and no Muslim.

4/ During the Assembly session I noticed several cases in which

the Chief Commissioner had delayed the supply of information; indeed, in some cases the replies to questions which had to be prepared after receiving material from the Chief Commissioner were submitted to me at the last minute. I then called for a statement of cases pending in the Chief Commissioner's office and noticed that there were avoidable delays in a very large number of cases.
5/ Even on 2 May 1947 the Chief Commissioner referred to Government a case in which the police proposed to take action under Section 107 Cr.P.C. against two parties of members of the Scheduled Caste on the ground that both belonged respectively to the parties sponsored by two Hon'ble Members of the Cabinet, namely, the Law and the Labour members. The position that the law must take its course and the authorities responsible must use their discretion in such cases irrespective of whose followers the persons concerned were, was, to my mind, so obvious as to suggest to any person with a sense of responsibility that he should take his own decision. I had to state this principle and say that a reference to the Central Government was unnecessary.
6/ From the above, I am sure you will appreciate that my conclusions with regard to the Chief Commissioner were based on a careful study of his administration during the last several months.

32 Vallabhbhai to the Maharaja of Kashmir, 3 July 1947, from Delhi

VII. 2

Vallabhbhai Patel to Maharaja of Kashmir[1]

NEW DELHI,
3 July 1947

My dear Maharaja Sahib,

Rai Bahadur Gopaldas [a prominent Hindu of Lahore] saw me today and conveyed to me the substance of your conversation with him. I am sorry to find that there is considerable misapprehension in your mind about the Congress. Allow me to assure Your Highness that the Congress is not only not your enemy, as you happen to believe, but there are in the Congress many strong supporters of your State. As an organization, the Congress is not opposed to any Prince in India.[2] It has no quarrel with the States. It is true that recent events resulting in the arrest of Pandit Jawaharlal Nehru[3] and the continued detention of Sheikh Abdullah have created a feeling of great dissatisfaction amongst many Congressmen who wish well of your State. Pandit Jawaharlal Nehru belongs to Kashmir. He is proud of it, and rest assured he can never be your enemy.

It is unfortunate that none of the Congress leaders has got any contact with Your Highness. Personal contact would have removed much of the misunderstanding, which probably is based largely on misinformation gathered through sources not quite disinterested.

Having had no personal contact, my correspondence has been with your Prime Minister since the arrest of Sheikh Abdullah, and my efforts have been to persuade him to have a different approach to the problem, which in the long run would be in the interest of the State.

It is necessary to assure you that in your domestic affairs the Congress has no intention whatever of interfering. If it had not been so, the Constituent Assembly would not have been able to attract a vast majority of Princes who have joined it, and I have no doubt that the rest will also join with very few exceptions who have no choice owing to peculiar circumstances, for instance Bahawalpur, Kalat, etc.[4] In the Negotiating Committee, your Prime Minister was present, and our decisions were unanimous in the four meetings[5] that he attended. In these meetings, all the Princes got complete satisfaction from us about their special rights, privileges, etc. which they enjoyed.

I fully appreciate the difficult and delicate situation in which your State has been placed, but as a sincere friend and well-wisher of the State, I wish to assure you that the interest of Kashmir lies in joining the Indian Union and its Constituent Assembly without any delay. Its past history and traditions demand it, and all India looks up to you and expects you to take that decision. Eighty per cent of India is on this side. The States that have cast their lot with the Constituent Assembly have been convinced that their safety lies in standing together with India.

I was greatly disappointed when His Excellency the Viceroy returned without having a full and frank discussion with you on that fatal [fateful] Sunday[6] when you had given an appointment which could not be kept because of your sudden attack of colic pain.[7] He had invited you to be his guest at Delhi, and in that also he was disappointed. I had hopes that we would meet here, but I was greatly disappointed when His Excellency told me that you did not avail of the invitation.

May I take the liberty of suggesting that it would be better if you even now come to Delhi, when you will certainly be his guest? We want an opportunity of having a frank and free discussion with you in an atmosphere of freedom, and I have no doubt that all your doubts and suspicions, of which I have heard form Gopaldas, will completely disappear. In free India, you cannot isolate yourself, and you must make friends with the leaders of free India who want to be friends with you.

Yours sincerely,
VALLABHBHAI PATEL

[1]See Appendix VII. 1, note 1.

[2]In his statement of 5 July, Patel repeated that the Congress were "no enemies of the Princely Order". See Appendix VII. 3.

[3]Nehru was arrested by the Kashmir authorities on 20 June 1946 for defying an order prohibiting his entry into the State. He had gone to Kashmir in connection with defending Sheikh Abdullah in a sedition trial. See No. 594, *TP*, VII, 1021-2.

[4]See Enclosure to Appendix VII. 10.

[5]The earlier meetings had concentrated on the modalities of discussions to be held between the States Negotiating Committee and the corresponding committees of the British India portion of the Constituent Assembly. See No. 326, *TP*, IX, 575-7. Also see No. 276, notes 1 and 2, Vol. I, Part I, 478. In the fourth meeting held after announcement of 3 June Plan Mountbatten urged the States to join either of the successor Dominion Constituent Assemblies. He confirmed that such an action of the States would be "a matter of free choice", and that the question of any State deciding to join neither Constituent Assembly was "hypothetical", at that stage. See Enclosure to No. 27, Vol. II, 65-71.

[6]22 June 1947.

[7]Nehru had described the attack of colic as an "old trick". See No. 319, para 5, *TP*, XI, 592.

33 Vallabhbhai's Statement on the Future of States, 5 July 1947

Statement by Vallabhbhai Patel[1]

L/P&J/10/81

FUTURE OF THE STATES

Sardar Vallabhbhai Patel's Assurance

Following is the full text of Sardar Vallabhbhai Patel's statement on the Indian States, made on 5th July:

"It was announced some days back that the Government of India had decided to set up a department to conduct their relations with the States in matters of common concern. This Department has come into being today and the States have been informed to this effect.

On this important occasion, I have a few words to say to the Rulers of the Indian States, among whom I am happy to count many as my personal friends. It is the lesson of history that it was owing to her politically fragmented condition and our inability to make a united stand that India succumbed to successive waves of invaders. Our mutual conflicts and internecine quarrels and jealousies have in the past been the cause of our downfall and our falling victims to foreign domination a number of times. We cannot afford to fall into those errors or traps again. We are on the threshold of independence.

It is true we have not been able to preserve the unity of the country entirely unimpaired in the final stage. To the bitter disappointment and sorrow of many of us, some parts have chosen to go out of India and set up their own governments. But there can be no question that despite this separation, the fundamental homogeneity of culture and sentiment, reinforced by the compulsive logic of mutual interest, would continue to govern us. Much more would this be the case with that vast majority of States which, owing to their geographical contiguity and indissoluble ties—economic, cultural and political—must continue to maintain relations of mutual friendship and co-operation with the rest of India. The safety and preservation of these States, as well as of India, demand unity and mutual co-operation between its different parts.

When the British established their rule in India, they evolved the doctrine of Paramountcy, which established the supremacy of British interests. That doctrine has remained undefined to this day but in its exercise there has undoubtedly been more subordination than co-operation. Outside the field of Paramountcy there had been very wide scope in which relations between British India and the States have been regulated by enlightened mutual interests. Now that British rule is ending, the demand has been made that the States should regain their independence.

I do not think it can be their desire to utilise this freedom from domination in a manner which is injurious to the common interests of India or which militates against the ultimate paramountcy of popular interest and welfare, or which might result in abandonment of that mutually useful relationship that has developed between British India and the Indian States during the last century. This has been amply demonstrated by the fact that the great majority of Indian States have already come into the Constituent Assembly. To those who have not done so, I appeal that they should join now. The States have already accepted the basic principle that for defence, foreign affairs and communications they would come into an Indian Union. We ask no more of them than accession on these three subjects, in which the common interest of the country are involved. In other matters, we would scrupulously respect their autonomous existence.[2]

This country, with its institutions, is the proud heritage of the people who inhabit it. It is an accident that some live in States and some in British India, but all alike partake of its culture and character. We are all knit together by bonds of blood and feeling, no less than of self-interest. None can segregate us into segments; no impassable barriers can be set up between us. I suggest it is, therefore, better for us to make laws sitting together as friends than to make treaties as aliens.

I invite my friends, the Rulers of the States, and their States and their people to the Councils of the Constituent Assembly in this spirit of friendliness and co-operation in a joint endeavour inspired by a common allegiance to our Motherland, for the common good of us all.

There appears to be a great deal of misunderstanding about the attitude of the Congress towards the States. I should like to make it clear that it is not the desire of the Congress to interfere in any manner whatever with the domestic affairs of the States. They are no enemies of the Princely Order but, on the other hand, wish them and their people, under this aegis, all prosperity, contentment and happiness. Nor would it be my policy to conduct the relations of the new Department with the States in any manner which savours of domination of one over the other; if there would be any domination, it would be that of our mutual interests and welfare. We have no ulterior motive or selfish interests to serve. The common objective should be to understand each other's point of view and come to decisions acceptable to all and in the best interests of the country.[3]

With this object, I propose to explore the possibility of associating with the administration of the new Department a standing committee representative of both the States and British India.

We are at a momentous stage in the history of India. By common endeavour, we can raise this country to new greatness, while a lack of unity will expose us to fresh calamities. I hope the Indian States will bear in mind that the alternative to co-operation in the general interest is anarchy and chaos which will overwhelm great and small in common ruin if we are unable to act together in minimum of common tasks.

Let not future generations curse us for having had the opportunity but failed to turn it to our mutual advantage. Instead, let it be our proud privilege to leave a legacy of mutually beneficial relationship which would raise this sacred land to its proper place amongst the nations of the world and turn it into an abode of peace and prosperity."[4]

34 Vallabhbhai to Dadubhai, 7 November 1947, from Delhi

Dear Brother Dadubhai,

Received your letter of 16th, previous letters are also received. I could not answer to you because I am weighed down by intense work. At the moment I am engaged in cleaning up centuries of rubbish of the native states.

Work of incorporating Junagadh State is nearly complete.

Problem of Kashmir is daunting.

Hyderabad problem is even more daunting.

A lot of smaller states have to be tackled and integrated.

Problems with Pakistan have also to be solved.

Once all the above problems are solved and peace pervades in the entire country of India, we have to start work for the future reconstruction of the economy of the country.

With God's help every problem will be solved.

I hope you are keeping good health and that your entire family is well.

Vallabhbhai's Vande Mataram.

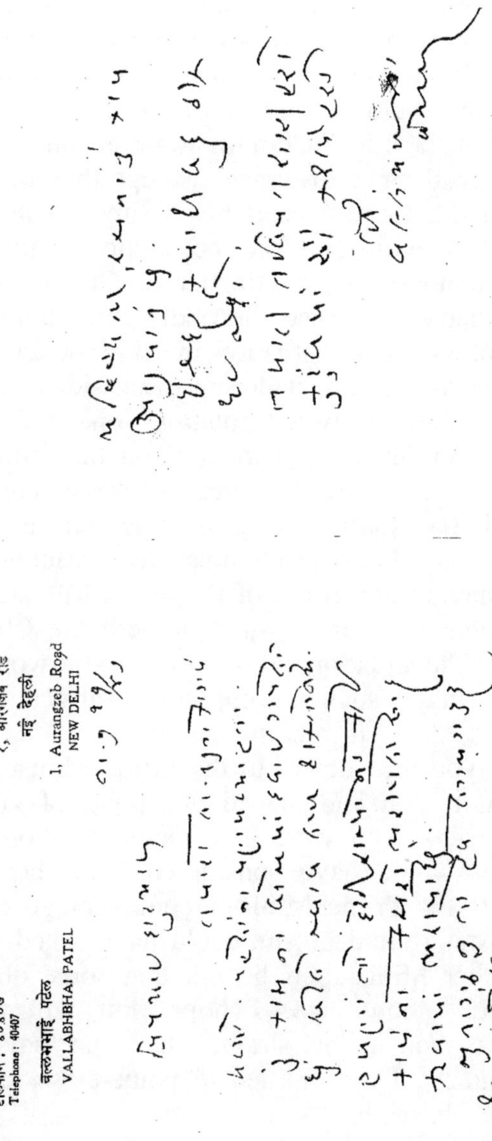

टेलिफोन : ४०४०७
Telephone : 40407

वल्लभभाई पटेल
VALLABHBHAI PATEL

१, औरंगजेब रोड
नई देहली
1, Aurangzeb Road
NEW DELHI

35 Vallabhbhai to Ayengar, 23 December 1947

To H V R Ayengar,

I learnt yesterday that you had been to Ajmer presumably to acquaint the Prime Minister with the true situation there. I was somewhat surprised to hear of it because I thought that as a senior and experienced officer you would see the implications of it. In the first place, the position of the Chief Commissioner is somewhat analogous to that of the head of a province, except that in all matters and not merely in the Central field he is subordinate to the Central Government. He would, therefore, be entitled to resent any inquest by any person other than a Minister of Government or the Secretary of the Ministry concerned. Secondly I had already issued a statement to the press on the situation in Ajmer-Merwara in so far as I had been able to appraise it during discussions, with the Chief Commissioner at Jaipur and two deputations, one in Delhi and the other at Jaipur. I told Jawaharlal about it on the 19th. I do not know if he told you about it, but a summary of the statement was broadcast from All-India Radio and also appeared in the Evening News of the same day. In these circumstances, your visit was bound to be taken as having arisen out of the Prime Minister's dissatisfaction with the statement that I issued or with the Chief Commissioner's handling of the situation. As an official you would, of course, appreciate how much such an impression affects the prestige of Government and the local administration.

Of course, I realise that you are subject to the Prime Minister's orders, but I still feel that if you had placed this point of view which, of course, as an official you were in a better position to realise, the Prime Minister would have considered twice before acting on his suggestion. If the Prime Minister could not go and still he wanted some Minister should go, he could have asked me or Gopalaswami or any other Minister, if he felt that some other Minister other than myself should go. I hope you will not misunderstand my writing to you in this strain; I feel that, having regard to our previous contacts, I am entitled to point these facts to you on a purely personal basis.

36 Vallabhbhai to Nehru, 23 December 1947

To Jawaharlal Nehru,

I am surprised – perhaps 'shocked' would be a more appropriate description – to hear that you sent Ayengar to Ajmer-Merwara.

I had already reported to you about the Ajmer situation, of which I had received (information) from Shankar Prasad who met me at Jaipur at my request. I had also given a detailed account of the happenings in Ajmer to the Press on the same day. Although it did not appear until the 20th, its summary had appeared in the Evening News (New Delhi) on the 19th. In these circumstances, the visit could have had only one significance in the eyes of the local public, namely, that it was to get an 'independent' account of the happenings as you were not quite satisfied either with the account I gave or with the local handling of the situation. The former interpretation would be almost tragic, while the latter would imply no confidence in an officer of the standing and seniority of the Chief Commissioner who could be subordinate only either to a Minister or the Secretary to Government concerned. Apart from this, Shankar Prasad is one of the ablest officers of the United Provinces, whose efficiency and honesty and impartiality are beyond reproach. I will not be surprised if this has disheartened Shankar Prasad already and of course affected his prestige. In any case if you were not satisfied with the report, you could have sent Gopalaswami or some other Minister for personal enquiry and report.

I quite appreciate that there was a move to discredit the local administration on the part of Messrs. Kaul and Bhargava. I hope Ayengar's visit has disillusioned you about them. If so, some thing will have been gained, though the whole proceeding is such as fills me with considerable distress.

I can only express the hope that we have seen the last of such 'visits of inspection'.

37 Vallabhbhai to Nehru, 24 December 1947

To Jawaharlal Nehru (draft),

Thank you for your letter of 23 December.

It was common knowledge between us that our approaches on certain vital problems were different but as on the conclusion or final decision there was no difference, we pulled on together so long in the common interest of the country, particularly as the stakes involved were very heavy.

The stand that you have taken in your letter of yesterday involves, in my humble opinion, issues on which there appear to be differences of vital character between us. You seem to feel that my action in explaining what I consider to be the probable consequences of any action taken by you regarding matters which fall within my ministerial responsibility or in venturing to question the propriety or soundness of any action which ignores or affects such responsibility results in restraining or constraining your liberty or your freedom which you consider necessary for the due discharge of your responsibility. I am afraid I cannot subscribe to this view.

I shall maintain that your sending Ayengar to Ajmer was not right and its reactions on the public mind as well as on the mind of the officer concerned cannot but be far from desirable. The other matters referred to in your letter are, I think, not relevant.

I have no desire to restrain your liberty or direction in any manner nor have I ever done so in the past. It is also not my desire to hustle you or to embarrass you in any manner, but when it is clear to us that on the fundamental question of our respective spheres of responsibility, authority and action there is such vital difference of opinion between us, it would not be in the interest of the cause which we both wish to serve to continue to pull on longer.

On the other question also I do not think that the matter of my approach was wanting in courtesy, but as I have already written to Gopalaswami, I will not say anything more.

The question of your resignation or your abdicating your functions does not arise at all. I am at one with you in that the decision may be taken with dignity and goodwill and I will strain every nerve to help you in doing so but will not, I am sure, want me to continue long as an ineffective colleague. Under the restrictions (of) ministerial responsibility which you consider legitimate and which, judging from the stand you have taken in Gopalaswami's case also, would include even another minister's encroachment, under your direction, on such responsibility, it would be impossible for me to function.

38 Vallabhbhai to Nehru, 29 December 1947

To JAWAHARLAL NEHRU,

Thank you for your letter dated 23 December 1947.

I agree that the matter had better be discussed at a Cabinet meeting and find that one had already been convened.

About Ajmer, I enclose a copy of a letter which Shankar Prasad had written to (V) Shankar and which was received by him today (Serial No. 12). You will notice that Ayengar's visit has had adverse reaction locally and has considerably upset Shankar Prasad himself. I am glad you agree that Shankar Prasad is an able and competent officer. I should go a little further and say that officers of his calibre are rather rare. We can ill-afford to keep such officers discontented for no fault of theirs. I am also sending a copy of the letter which Shankar is sending to Shankar Prasad under my instructions (Serial No. 13), but I hope, if you visit Ajmer, you will succeed in removing the impression both from his mind as well as from that of the local people that there was any kind of inquisition at all, or that there was any lack of confidence on our part in Shankar Prasad's impartiality or efficient conduct of affairs.

I learn from Shankar Prasad's letter that Ayengar visited certain places and saw some people in Ajmer. I do not know if Ayengar has presented you with any report on his visit to Ajmer. If he has done so and if you have no objection, I should like to have a copy of the report for my information.

39 Vallabhbhai to Dadubhai, 1 July 1948, from Delhi

Dear Brother Dadubhai,

I received your letter of 15th.

What you suggested about Junagadh, I have informed it to the Regional Commissioner.

Regarding Rajkot, I have talked to Menon and also informed Dhebarbhai. My health is improving and I will be going back to Delhi on 6th.

I also received your letter of 9th. You wrote about the capital of Saurashtra, but in that matter I am unable to take any action, as my name seems to be getting involved in the process. Otherwise, like Somnath, I would love to rekindle the ancient history.

Yours, Vallabhbhai's Vande Mataram.

टेलिफोन : ४०४०७
Telephone : 40407
वल्लभभाई पटेल
VALLABHBHAI PATEL

१, औरंगज़ेब रोड
नई देहली
1, Aurangzeb Road
NEW DELHI

કેમ્પ: દહેરાદૂન,
૧.૭.૪૮

પ્રિય ભાઈ દાદુભાઈ,

તમારો તા. ૨૫મીનો પત્ર મળ્યો. જુનાગઢ વિષે તમે લખ્યું હતું તે બાબત રીજીઓનલ કમીશનરને લખેલું છે.

રાજકોટ વિષે મેનનને વાત કરી છે ને ઢેબરભાઈને પણ કહ્યું છે. મારી તબીયત ઠીક સુધારા પર છે. ને હું તા. ૬ઠ્ઠીએ દિલ્હી જવાનો છું.

તમારો તા. ૯મા નો કાગળ પણ મળ્યો હતો. સૌરાષ્ટ્રની રાજધાની વિષે તમે લખ્યું તે બાબત હું કાંઈ કરી શકું એમ મને લાગતું નથી. કારણકે એમાં મારૂં પોતાનું નામ આવતું જણાય છે. બાકી સોમનાથની જેમ

(પાછળ)

પુરાણો ઈતિહાસ તાજો કરવો એ મને ગમે ખરૂં.

લી.
વલ્લભભાઈના
વંદેમાતરમ્

શ્રી. દાદુભાઈ દેસાઈ,
દેસાઈવગો,
નડીઆદ

40 Vallabhbhai to Dadubhai, 25 July 1948, from Delhi

Brother Dadubhai,

Chi Sadhuram's and your letter are received. I am glad to know that his annual state payment question is solved. Work of creating Mahagujarat is going on at full speed. Now only Baroda remains to be merged. Now all big and small states have been annexed to India. Saurashtra has been consolidated and now it can be merged with India anytime. Once the Baroda problem has been solved, that will also be merged. Then we shall deal with the small island of Diu. Administration of Kutch is to be taken over by the central government. The whole state is backward so we have to help develop Kandla as a port. It is intended to make it like Karachi and settle there the refugees who have come from Pakistan. You must have known that we have lifted and closed the Virmgam customs port. Except Hyderabad all States have merged. Some small states remain which will be merged without trouble. Hyderabad problem has complications, so it will take some time to solve. I do not think the problem is insurmountable.

My health is better now, but still I cannot undertake long journeys. I must live carefully so I cannot come to Nadiad. Beneficial rain must have come there, that is what I believe.

You and your family be well. Vallabhbhai's Vande Mataram.

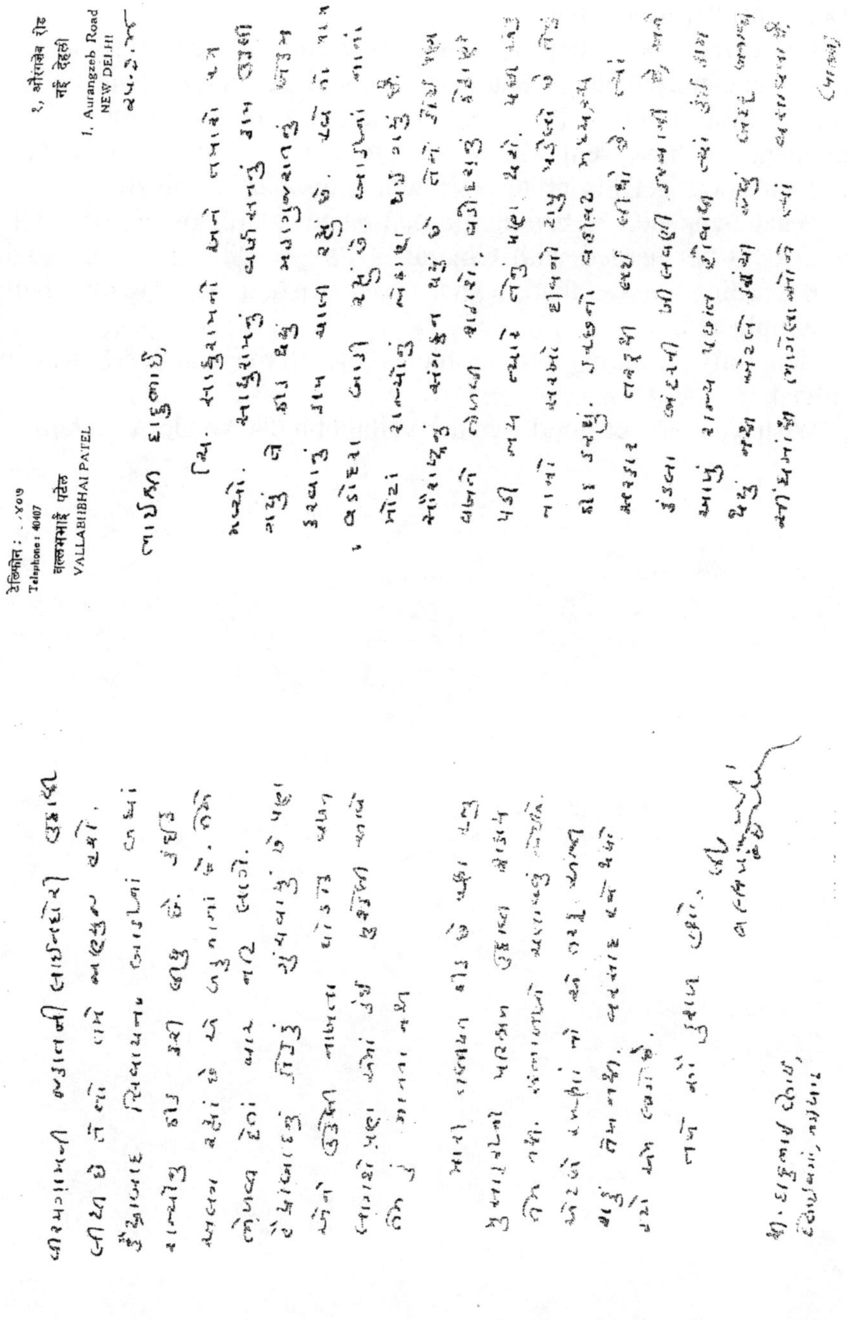

टेलिफोन : ४०४०७
Telephone : 40407
वल्लभभाई पटेल
VALLABHBHAI PATEL

१, औरंगजेब रोड
नई देहली
1, Aurangzeb Road
NEW DELHI

41 Vallabhbhai to Dadubhai, 21 September 1948, from Delhi

Dear Brother Dadubhai,

I received your letter. Junagadh problem will be solved in time. In the end the whole of Saurashtra should be merged with Gujarat. So all these things will be settled once and for all together. At the moment we have sent Mr. Masani to Brazil as our representative and once we get his report, we will think further about it.

What happened regarding Baroda State is welcome. After all it is also to be merged with Gujarat.

Regarding Hyderabad, what you wished is already being accomplished.

Generally speaking the problems of all the smaller States are solved.

Wish you are in good health. Vallabhbhai's Vande Mataram

टेलिफोन : ४०४०७
Telephone : 40407

वल्लभभाई पटेल
VALLABHBHAI PATEL

१, औरंगजेब रोड
नई देहली
1, Aurangzeb Road
NEW DELHI

૨૧.૯.૪૮

પ્રિય ભાઈ દાદુભાઈ,

તમારો કાગળ મળ્યો છે. જુનાગઢનું પણ બધુ આખરે ઠીક થઈ રહેશે. આખરે તો આખું સૌરાષ્ટ્ર ગુજરાતમાં ભેળવવું જોઈશે. અત્યારે એ ઝઘડાનો ઉકેલ એની બરાબર થઈ જશે. હાલમાં દેશમાં આપણા તરફથી મેં સાહેબને મોકલ્યા છે તેમનો રીપોર્ટ આવશે ત્યાર પછી શું કરવું તે વિચાર કરશું.

વડોદરાનું જે થયું તે ઠીક થયું છે. હવે તો એને પણ ભોગવવા દેવાનું છે.

હૈદ્રાબાદનું પણ તમે ઇચ્છતા હતા તેમ ફેંસલો આવવા રહ્યું છે. આખરે બધાં રાજ્યોનો વારો

(પાછળ)

૨

ઉકેલ થઈ ગયો છે

તમારી તબીયત સારી હશે

લી.
વલ્લભભાઈના
વંદે

શ્રી. દાદુભાઈ દેસાઈ,
દેસાઈવગો,
નડીઆદ

42 Vallabhbhai to Nehru, 9 August 1949

To JAWAHARLAL NEHRU,

1/ I have seen the minutes and decisions of the Cabinet meeting held on Saturday, 6 August 1949, relating to the amendments proposed by us for incorporation in the new Constitution in so far as the provisions relating to the States are concerned. I am rather upset by the decisions relating to the privy purse payments, guarantees in respect of rights and privileges given to the rulers and regarding entries in the Legislative list (in so far as this matter relates to the Indian State Forces). What I learn from Vellodi about the trend of discussions in the Cabinet not only distressed me, but filled me with apprehensions and anxiety. I could not imagine that, after such repeated discussions over the question of privy purse, after our taking approval from the Cabinet to the many proposals for merger and integration which we put forward to Cabinet from time to time after solemn agreements having been reached between the Governor-General and the Rulers on these matters, there should have been so much misapprehension and even ignorance. Every decision and every policy that we have pursued in regard to States has not only been approved but acclaimed by the Assembly whenever any matter concerning the States has come up. It is, therefore, difficult for me to understand that my Cabinet colleagues should shirk the responsibility which devolves on them to ensure that all these agreements and arrangements are fully honoured not only by ourselves but by successor Governments and that they should regard a constitutional guarantee in regard to the continuance of privy purse as being unpopular in the Assembly.

2/ The question of merger and integration of States has been discussed in the Assembly a number of times. White papers have been circulated among members. During the last Budget session, we circulated a memorandum covering practically the whole field of our arrangements with the Rulers and the States and we specially dealt therein with the question of privy purse, pointing out the savings which we had effected as a result of these settlements. The covenants between the Rulers and the Governor-General had been placed on the table of the house. As far as I remember, there was seldom any reference to the privy purse settlements except perhaps a passing one. These arrangements were generally applauded as eminently satisfactory ones. Frankly speaking, therefore, I cannot

understand the fears regarding their acceptance by the Assembly.
3/ As regards the privy purse, I have said a number of times in the assembly, and we have made it clear in our published documents that the privy purse fixed by us makes a reduction of several crores in the expenditure which used to fall on the revenues of these States, i.e. the Civil List and other allowances of Rulers. We have also to remember that the total expenditure on privy purse running to about 2 or 5 crores is comparatively an insignificant price to pay for the consolidation and unity of India which we have achieved. We have entered into solemn undertakings and agreement with the Princes about the privy purse, and I do not think that we can, in good conscience, leave it to future Parliaments to do as they like with these amounts. These are commitments which have been consecrated by the signature of the Head of State on behalf of the people of India with the full approval of the Cabinet, and it is our moral duty to ensure that these commitments are fully honoured both now and in the future. This can only be possible if we guarantee these payments under the constitutional provisions. Any other alternative would not be satisfactory and would not satisfy those who have accepted in good faith our pledges and our promises. We are, therefore, in honour bound to include these guarantees in the Constitution.
4/ As regards the privileges and rights conceded to the Rulers, these are again part of the same commitments and carry the same moral obligations on our part. I think it would be correct to say that the Princes attach considerable significance to these rights and privileges. It is a question of self-respect and honour for them, and I do not think that having taken from them everything else that mattered, we should show any niggardly attitude in these matters.
5/ You will recall that we had given the Rulers our assurances that they would continue to remain as they were except for accession of three subjects. There were, therefore, nothing to compel or induce them to merge their identity. If they had chosen to keep out of these arrangements, they could have continued to draw the heavy Civil Lists they used to draw before and in a large number of cases the Rulers would have enjoyed unrestricted use of their State revenues. Few people have any idea of the numerous ways in which they have squandered away the revenue of the States. There were, in fact, a large number of cases, no limits to their privy purse and if they had continued to rule a few years more they

would have squandered away a considerable amount of the country's wealth. There were a few honourable exceptions, but you could count them on the tips of your fingers. Thus the capacity for mischief on the part of Rulers in this respect was far greater than one could imagine. Even now the amount of harm that could be caused to the country by going back on our solemn promises would be very substantial. You may also be aware that in the Deccan States even under the award of Dr. Rajendra Prasad, Dr. Pattabhi Sitaramayya and Shri Shankararao Deo, the scales of privy purse were more liberal than ours. In many cases where the Civil Lists were fixed under agreements between Rulers and representatives of the people, the amounts settled were higher than those which we have now given. Lastly, even the amounts which we have settled, where they exceed 10 lakhs, are liable to be reduced to the latter figure after the lifetime of the present incumbents.

6/ We have also to consider these two matters from another point of view. Under the draft Constitution, agreements reached by the Rulers prior to the coming into force of the new Constitution would not be justiciable. The covenants under which we have guaranteed the privy purse and the rights and privileges of rulers will not, therefore, be within the jurisdiction of the Supreme Court. They will be subject virtually to the rule of Paramountcy, to which they are subject now. In these circumstances, a constitutional guarantee is the only thing that can provide some sort of a safeguard for the Princes. The only alternative would be to make these agreements justiciable. But if we do so, you and I, and even successor Governments, will have a perpetual cause for regret. I would, therefore, once more urge upon you and my Cabinet colleagues to reconsider the matter and to accept our proposals which had been reached in full agreement with the Drafting Committee. If the Chairman of the Drafting Committee or any of my colleagues feels any hesitation in sponsoring these proposals before the Constituent Assembly, I am quite prepared to interrupt my stay in Bombay and to come to Delhi merely for the sake of sponsoring these proposals. I consider it a matter of faith and honour, and I feel it would be moral cowardice on my part if I refrained from discharging this obligation.

7/ Regarding the Indian State Forces, it would not be proper to make a transitional provision, again because the provision in the covenants are by no means transitional. What we hope to do is gradually to persuade the Princes to integrate their forces fully with the Indian Army. Even within the course of one or two years, we have succeeded in substantially reducing the position of the Princes in relation to the State Forces. In another one or two stages, we may be able to integrate them fully, but for obvious reasons it is not possible for us to say so. Otherwise, we would be charged with breach of faith. Making a transitional provision, such as the Cabinet has suggested, would bring about the same position that we wish to avoid, namely, the Princes would feel that we are departing from the arrangements which had been solemnly agreed to in the covenants, but even from now on, we are contemplating their termination in the period of transition. On the other hand it would be much more appropriate to retain the item in the list in accordance with the provisions of the covenants, and subsequently to allow it in actual practice to fall into desuetude. If the pace is as fast as we expect, it may even be possible to do away with this entry under the easier means of amendment to the Constitution provided for the first five years.

8/ So I hope you will appreciate the depth of feeling and the mental strain under which I have written this letter. I would be grateful if you would kindly read it to my Cabinet colleagues so that they may be able to appreciate the same. In the meantime, I am asking Menon to prepare a detailed note relating to these three matters and request the Cabinet to reconsider their attitude on these matters.

43 Vallabhbhai to Nehru, 16 August 1949

Letter to Jawaharlal Nehru,

Thank you for your letter of 11 August 1949. I have also seen the minutes of the Cabinet Meeting on the same subject. So far as I am concerned, if there is a provision in the Constitution honouring the guarantees and obligations which we have incurred, that would serve my purpose. At the same time, I do not see how we can avoid bringing these facts to the notice of the party. The party might well ask us to enlighten it on the nature and extent of the obligations which we are honouring. We shall then have to reveal these details. My object in saying this is not to emphasise that these details should be mentioned in the Constitution. Actually in that matter, I agree it would be unnecessary to do so, but my purpose is only to say that we shall have to face the party on this issue, whether we like it or not.

Binding Government in perpetuity is by no means a novel thing. Many agreements are entered in the name of Government and its successors, which means binding ourselves in perpetuity.

It has been a very sad experience to me to have spent the independence anniversary away from you. I know that in these critical times, my place is by your side. I only hope and pray that the period of my absence from Delhi would be as short as possible. I was particularly unhappy when I heard about the refugees bothering you in such an unseemly manner. It is a disgrace to all of us and quite contrary to the very elements of decency in public life. I wish I were in Delhi at the time to share your burden. You have treated these refugees with much greater consideration than they deserved.

I have had a talk with (K.M.) Munshi about the compensation clause. Theoretically, Rajaji's position is correct, in that the Supreme Court would not like the idea of being dragged in before legislation is enforced. I have, therefore, told Munshi that the alternative draft which he brought would be adequate. There is still a certain amount of discrimination against the Zamindari property, but that we could justify on the ground of this abolition of Zamindari is either a fact already or is going to be a fact in the near future. It is necessary to ensure that whatever has been done is not undone on technical grounds. Apart from this, we can also contend that the Zamindars are only intermediaries and all their rights to land flow from the recognition of their status as such by the State. The land belongs to the State, and therefore, the Zamindars are not entitled to full rights of and compensation for ownership. I think, if put this way, there will not be any difficulty in the party, particularly now, when lands other than Zamindari are outside the scope of this discriminatory treatment.

Ayengar, when he was here, discussed with me the proposals regarding the Services and Public Service Commission. The proposals regarding the Services were approved by the Cabinet long ago. They are, in so far as the Secretary of State's services are concerned, the logical consequence of the specific agreement which we have entered into with His Majesty's Government and the only way in which we can implement that agreement is by having constitutional guarantees. At one stage, you thought that we might reduce the emoluments of the Services, particularly of the higher posts. This, I am afraid, can be achieved by voluntary agreements rather than by any imposition, which would open us to the charge of breach of faith on our past commitments. I hope, therefore, there would be no difficulty in regard to the Services. The objection to leaving it to Parliament are quite obvious. Parliament can make or unmake laws, whereas it is not so easy to interfere with constitutional provisions.

As regards the Public Service Commission, the Cabinet has come to some decisions. The Drafting Committee's proposals mean some departure from these decisions, in as much as the draft provisions specify the tenure of the Members of the Public Service Commission and the procedure for removal, resignation, etc., which, according to the Cabinet decision, should have been left to parliamentary legislation. However as the articles are drafted, I think we need have no objection, because the Constitution gives us power to suspend a member pending an enquiry and provides for a judicial enquiry.

Golvankar came and called on me today. I had a general talk with him explaining to him what the pitfalls were which the RSS should avoid in the interests not only of itself, but of the country at large. I particularly emphasised completely eschewing destructive methods and adopting a constructive role, and warned him against the suicidal policy of the Savaricar group, of which Godse (Gandhi's assassin) was the exponent. I found him quite receptive and full of undertaking. I have a feeling that he will not give us any trouble and will now adapt himself to the new requirements.

I wonder if you would be coming this side at all during my stay here, but if you can get away and come here, it would be so nice. I know you must be troubled with many things, as I am troubled here. In any case, there is a further accentuating circumstance, namely, the distance from the actual scene in which events are being shaped. Perhaps, a mutual exchange of ideas would set the minds of both of us at ease.

44 Lord Irwin to Vithalbhai, 18 July 1929, from London

88 Eaton Square, SW1,
Dear Mr. Patel,

Thank you very much for your letter, Lady Irwin and I had quite a good voyage, although rather rough as far as Aden, and rather hot after that.

You may rely on me to do my best to find a way of peace out of our present difficulties, and I hope that you, on your side, will use whatever influence you have, if anything is done at this end, to get the Congress leaders to meet it half-way.

I spent two days with my father at the beginning of the week, and found him wonderfully well. It was a great pleasure to see him again. V sincerely,

45 Lord Irwin to Vithalbhai, 26 July 1929, from London

88 Eaton Square, SW1,
Dear Mr. Patel,

Thank you for your letter of 12th July, and for writing frankly, as well as for sending me the pamphlet, which you enclosed.

I should very much have liked, had it been possible, to have been able to have some frank conversation of the kind you mention, but you will recollect I explained to you the reasons, before I left, that appeared to make it at that stage impossible.

Meanwhile you can rest assured that in anything that I may say to people here I am not likely to underestimate the importance of doing anything that is possible to make it easier for all sections of opinion to come together towards greater agreement than we have, unfortunately, been able to reach during the last year or two.

Yours sincerely,

46 Lord Irwin to Vithalbhai, 13 April 1930

Viceroy's Camp, India,
Dear Mr. Patel,

Thank you very much for your letter. I was sorry to hear that you had caught a chill on your way to Simla. I am afraid your health has been causing you a lot of trouble of late, and I hope you will be quite yourself again.

I am glad you advised Pandit Malaviya to come and see me before he left Delhi. I had a long talk with him. As you know, I believe that nothing but good can come out of frank personal discussion, even though the results may seem at the moment to be disappointing.

Yours sincerely,

47 Lord Irwin to Vithalbhai, 15 April 1930, from Simla

Viceroy's Camp, India,
Dear Mr. Patel,

Thank you very much for your letter of the 12th of April which has just reached me in Peshawar. I appreciate the difficulties of the position in which you have found yourself, and the thoroughness with which you have examined every aspect of the question. I do not however feel that I can take the responsibility of influencing your judgement by saying that I see much chance of things taking a turn in the near future that I would have to call upon your services in the way you indicate.

I am however grateful to you for the assurance you give me at the end of your letter that your services are at my disposal whenever I wish to avail myself of them, and you know that no one wished more fervently than I that the affairs of India may speedily again be guided into smoother waters.

Yours sincerely,

48 Lord Irwin to Vithalbhai, 21 April 1930, from Simla

Viceregal Lodge, Simla,
Dear Mr. Patel,

Thank you for your letter of the 20 April. Whatever view I may take of your decision, I do not think that I can usefully, or perhaps rightly, say anything more upon a matter that must in the last resort be one for your individual judgement, and therefore I do not feel able to contest your intention of submitting your resignation.

The situation that Mr. Gandhi has created naturally causes me very great concern, and I would do anything in my power to change it for the better. But as long as leaders of Indian opinion feel that progress will be achieved by open defiance of the law, I cannot pretend that I see much hope of reaching an understanding with them. Just as you, in your capacity as President, are bound while you hold the office to enforce the existing rules governing the work of the Assembly, so am I compelled to maintain the existing law against violation until it has been revised by those competent to do so. Those who have been arrested have only been so arrested after open breaches of the law, for the alteration of which they are fully entitled to press by every constitutional means, but which it is impossible for me to allow them with impunity to defy.

It is therefore with great regret that I learn of your decision actively to associate yourself with this movement. Moreover, knowing what I do of your feelings in regard to the general policy adopted by Congress towards the offer of His Majesty's Government, I cannot help being surprised that you should now be prepared to identify yourself with a course of action which in private conversation you had led me to believe that you, with me, deplored.

I have greatly appreciated the confidence you have been willing to repose in me through these difficult times. Some day perhaps we may see the result of what in different fashions, during the time we have worked together, we have each sought to promote. But I do not think this result will be nearer by the way of Civil Disobedience with all its inevitable consequences.

I shall be glad to see you at any time convenient, and will ask Cunningham to telephone.

Yours sincerely,

49 Lord Irwin to Vithalbhai, 23 April 1930, from Simla

Viceregal Lodge, Simla,
Dear Mr. Patel,

I have just got your letter. I am afraid you must have very much misunderstood the drift of our conversation yesterday if it suggested to you in any way that I was prepared to contemplate 'opening up negotiations' with Gandhi and Motilal. You, if I remember rightly, told me that you were going to see them and tell them that in your view the movement was mistaken and that it was possible that they might charge you with a message to myself. I told you in reply that of course if you wished to see me at any time, I should be glad to hear anything you could tell me; but as far as I was concerned, it was impossible to do anything, and it was impossible to expect any change for the better until those who were deliberately breaking the law, whatever might be their purpose, stopped doing so. That position I must make asolutely plain.

I think, in view of your imminent action, which as you told me yesterday will be accompanied by a strong attack on my Government, that my coming to your house for tea at this juncture would be inevitably and naturally misunderstood. So while thanking you for your thought, I fear I must ask you to excuse me. And in view of what I have said above, I am afraid we must both realise that at present there is nothing more that can be usefully said. Abstract constitutional discussions must clearly await the advent of smoother times.

Yours sincerely, Irwin

50 Lord Irwin to Vithalbhai, 26 April 1930, from Simla

Viceregal Lodge, Simla,
Dear Mr. Patel,

I have to acknowledge the receipt of your two letters dated April 25th, in which you submit your resignation of your office as President of the Assembly, and discuss at length the reasons that have led you to that decision.

Your letters make plain that your course of action is not one that could be influenced by reasoned argument, and it is evident that nothing is to be gained by a detailed reply. Nor is it necessary for me to vindicate the officers of my Government against charges which bear on their face their own refutation. You have however given an account of various conversations you have had with me during the time we were in official relations, and though I am not in a position to question the explanation of your motives and actions, I must claim to be the best interpreter of my own. One conspicuous example of a misunderstanding of events lies in your belief that it was at your request or in accordance with your advice that my Government discharged its responsibilities in connection with the movement for refusal of payment of land revenue in the Bardoli Taluka in 1928.

I regret that our official connection should be terminated in such circumstances, and can only hope that you and those with whom you are once again to be openly associated may come to realise how grave a wrong you do to India by rejecting the way of peace that lies open through free conference with His Majesty's Government, in order to encourage your countrymen to deliberate and dangerous defiance of the law.

Yours sincerely,

51 Gandhi's Secretary (Mahadev Desai) to Dadubhai, 21 March 1930, from Ahmedabad

Young India, Ahmedabad,
Dear Dadubhai Saheb,

On 24th at twelve noon you may please meet Vallabhbhai Saheb. Jailer must have written to you. Maniben wishes to come with you to see Sardar. She is staying at Dr. Kanuga's house.

Yours obediently, Mahadev Desai

(This occasion is referred to in Chapter 19. Sardar wanted to see Dadubhai in connection with the Land Revenue Satyagraha that Vallabhbhai had started with Dadubhai. He wanted to know about progress and to give his instructions on what to do while he was in prison. He also wanted to know how was the Salt Satyagraha going on.)

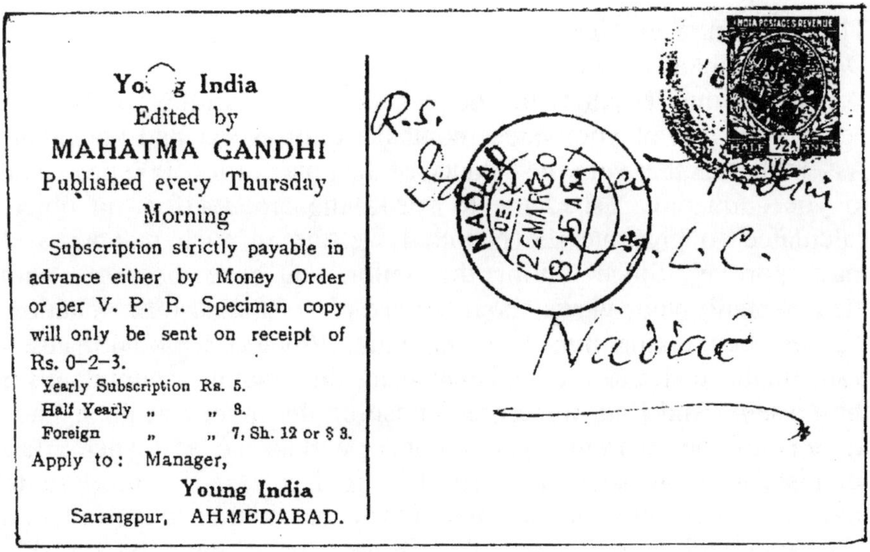

Young India
Edited by
MAHATMA GANDHI
Published every Thursday
Morning
Subscription strictly payable in advance either by Money Order or per V. P. P. Speciman copy will only be sent on receipt of Rs. 0–2–3.

Yearly Subscription	Rs.	5.
Half Yearly	„	„ 3.
Foreign	„	„ 7, Sh. 12 or $ 3.

Apply to: Manager,
Young India
Sarangpur, AHMEDABAD.

R.S.
NADIAD DELY 22 MAR 30 8.45 A.M.
Nadiad

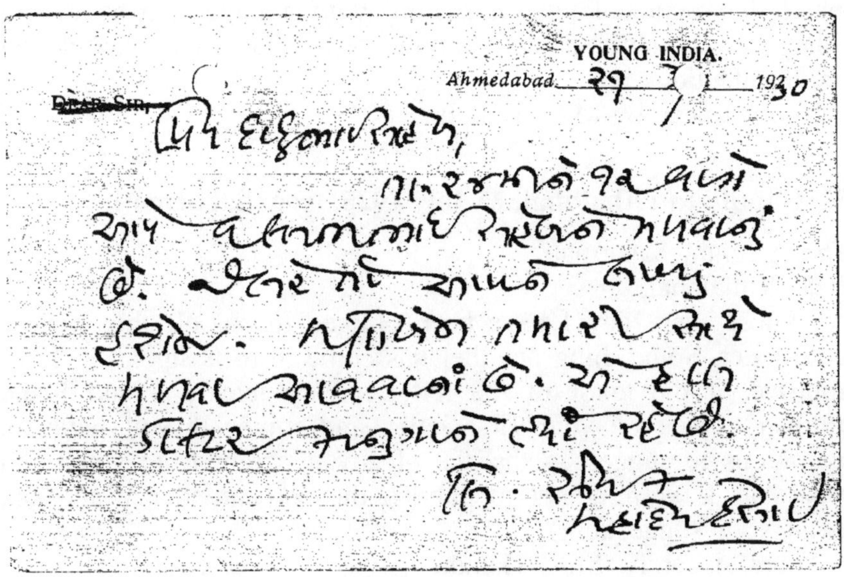

YOUNG INDIA.
Ahmedabad 21 3 1930

~~DEAR SIR,~~

52 Gandhi to Vithalbhai, 25 July 1926, from Sabarmati

The Ashram, Sabarmati,
Dear Vithalbhai,

I have your letters with cheques in all amounting to Rs.7575 being a portion of your three months' salary as the Speaker of the Assembly together with the balance of the purse of Rs.5000 presented to you. You have asked me to spend the amount for 'an object calculated to promote the National welfare in such manner as I may approve'. Since writing that letter, you have discussed with me personally your views about the use of your handsome donation. I have been taxing myself as to what I should really do, and I have finally come to the decision to let the amount accumulate for the present. And I am therefore depositing the money in the agency account of the Ashram for six months certain, so as to get a fair interest. And, as soon as party feeling has eased, I propose to invite the cooperation of a few mutual friends and then in consultation with you and them to use the money for some commendable national purpose.

Meanwhile, I tender my congratulations for the generous spirit which has actuated you in parting with a large portion of your salary for a public object. Let me hope that your example will prove infectious.

Yours sincerely, M.K. Gandhi

53 Gandhi to Vithalbhai, 25 July 1926, from Sabarmati

The Ashram, Sabarmati,
Dear Vithalbhai,

Almost every day I have been obliged to put off this enclosed little letter. Some thing or other has come in to postpone it. If you approve of the tenor of the letter, please telegraph and I shall publish copies of your first letter and mine. If you have any alterations to suggest – absence of any telegram from you I shall regard as a warning not to publish the correspondence and shall await your suggestions.

Yours sincerely, M.K. Gandhi

54 Gandhi to Dadubhai, 23 May 1944, from Juhu

Brother Dadubhai,

Received your loving letter. My whole life is based on experiments and has fructified on them. Please do not worry about me. I believe that God is behind all my experiments. I believe that as long as God wants to get work out of me, He will help me to survive. It is satisfying to me that you have controlled your mind and not come over here to see me.

Bapu's blessings,

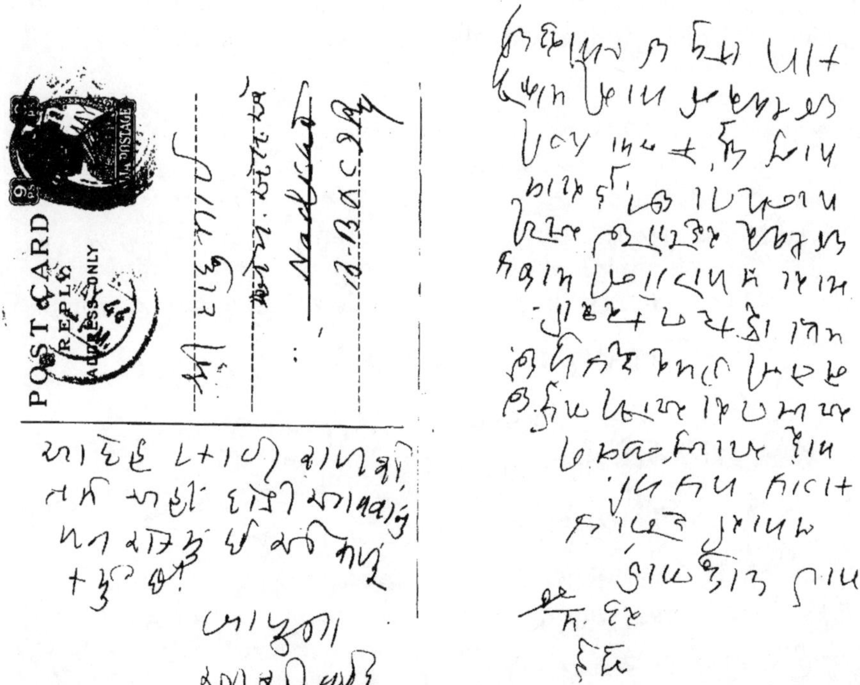

55 Gandhi to Dadubhai, 24 October 1944, from Sevagram

Brother Dadubhai,

Received your letter. It befits us, if women run the institutions of women. If they are going to make mistakes, they will surely learn from such mistakes. The Government is also telling us that they will give independence only after we learn how to govern. Accordingly, women whom we have crushed for long should be helped to be independent, and should have the right to make mistakes.

Blessings from Bapu.

(Dadubhai asked Gandhi if he could safely hand over executive duties of Vithal Kanya Vidyalaya to women workers.)

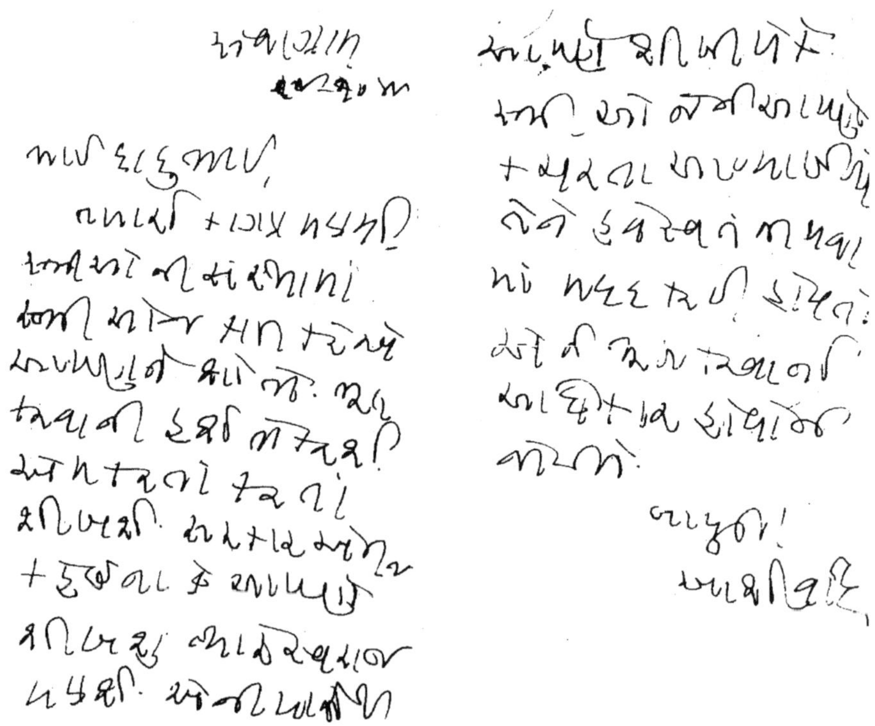

56 Gandhi to the present Author (dictated to Sushila Nayar) 11 April 1946, from Delhi

Dear Brother,

Gandhiji received your letter of 6 April 1946. He has directed me to write to you that you should stick to the truth under all circumstances and so also social service activity.

Sushila's Vande Mataram.

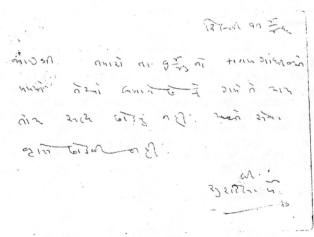

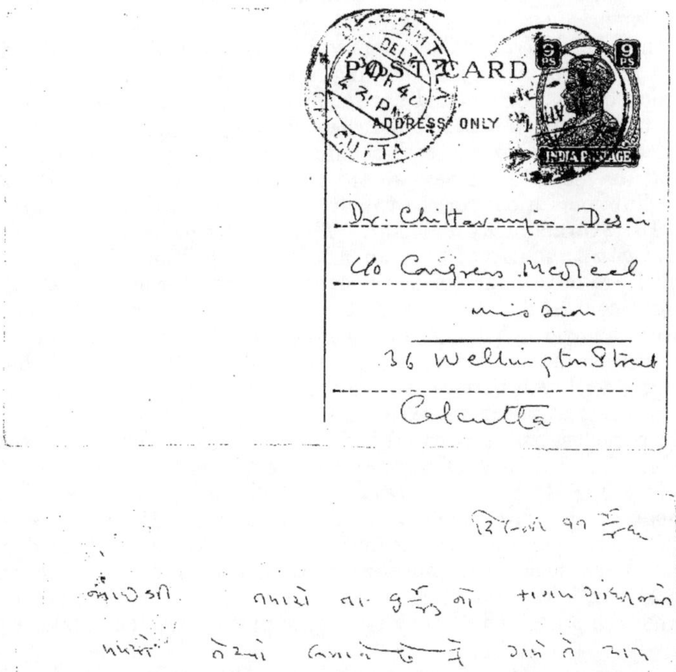

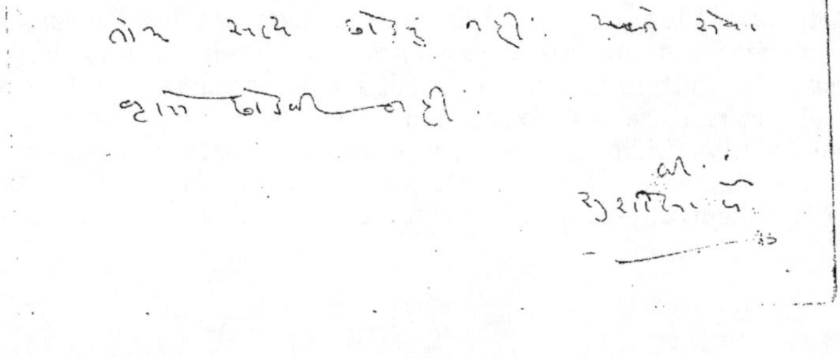

57 Nehru to Gandhi, 28 July 1930, from Naini Prison

(MSS EUR C152/25, Volume V, Part 2, p.626)

Pandit Jawaharlal Nehru's letter to Mr. Gandhi (with Pandit Motilal's endorsement) sent to Mr. Gandhi through the intermediaries, dated 28th July 1930.

Central Prison, Naini,
July 28*th*, 1930.

MY DEAR BAPUJI,

It is a delight to write to you again after a long interval even though it be from one prison to another. I would like to write at length, but I am afraid I cannot do so at present. I shall therefore confine myself to the matter in issue.

Dr. Sapru and Mr. Jayakar came yesterday and had a long interview with father and me. Today they are coming again. As they have already put us in possession of all the facts and have shown us your note and letter we felt that we could discuss the matter between us two and arrive at some decision even without waiting for the second interview. Of course if anything new turns up at the second interview we are prepared to vary any previous formed opinion. Our conclusions for the time being are given in a note which we are giving to Dr. Sapru and Mr. Jayakar. This is more or less brief, but it will I hope give you some idea of how our minds are working. I might add that father and I are in full agreement in regard to what our attitude should be.

I might confess that your point 1 regarding the "constitutional issue" has not won me over. Nor does father fancy it. I do not see how it fits in with our position or our pledges or with the realities of today. Father and I entirely agree with you that we can be "no parties to any truce which would undo the position at which we have arrived today". It is because of this that the fullest consideration is essential before any final decision is arrived at. I must confess that I do not see any appreciable advance yet from the other side and I greatly fear a false or a weak move on our part. I am expressing myself moderately. For myself, I delight in warfare. It makes me feel that I am alive. The events of the last four months in India have gladdened my heart and have made me prouder of Indian men and women and even children (!) than I have ever been. But I realise that most people are not warlike and like peace and so I try hard to suppress myself and take a peaceful view!

May I congratulate you on the new India that you have created by your magic touch? What the future will bring I know not, but the past has made life worth living and our prosaic existence has developed something of epic greatness in it. Sitting here in Naini jail I have pondered on the wonderful efficacy of non-violence as a weapon and have become a greater convert to it than ever before. I hope you are not dissatisfied with the response of the country to the non-violent creed. Despite occasional lapses the country has stuck to it wonderfully—certainly far more grimly than I had expected.

I am afraid I am still somewhat of a protestant regarding your 11 points. Not that I disagree with any one of them. Indeed they are important. Yet I do not think they take the place of independence. But I certainly agree with you that we should have "nothing to do with anything that would not give the nation the power to give immediate effect to them".

Father has been unwell for the last 8 days ever since he took an injection. He has grown very weak. This long interview last evening tired him out.

Yours affectionately,
(Sd.) JAWAHARLAL.

Please do not be anxious about me. It is only a passing trouble and I hope to get over it in two or three days. Love.

(Sd.) MOTILAL NEHRU.

P. S.—We have had another talk with Dr. Sapru and Mr. Jayakar. At their desire we have made some alterations in our note, but they do not make any vital difference. Our position is quite clear and I have no doubt whatever about it. I hope you will appreciate it.

(Here Nehru acknowledges the efficacy of the Salt Satyagraha to which he had contributed next to nothing. The efforts of Vithalbhai and Dadubhai led to its real success.)

58 Nehru to Vallabhbhai, 23 December 1947

To Sardar Vallabhbhai,

I have just received your two letters of today's date. First as regards Ayengar's visit to Ajmer. I told you that I intended going to Ajmer from Jaipur. Ayengar was going with me to both places and information of this was sent to the officers concerned. Quite apart from what the local authorities did, the recent occurrences in Ajmer were of primary importance and were likely to have far-reaching consequences. Next to Delhi itself, Ajmer is probably more important from this point of view than any other place in India. What happens in Ajmer might well affect our whole policy for better or worse. It was for this reason that I decided to pay a visit there, not so much from the local but the national point of view. Suddenly, owing to the death of my nephew, I had to cancel my visit. I thought this would have a bad effect in Ajmer as my visit had been announced and was eagerly looked forward to. That visit was intended to show to the country generally that we were anxious to do all in our power whenever such a situation arose and were taking a personal interest in it.

As I was not going, I asked Ayengar to proceed to Ajmer with my apologies and further to say that I would try to come later if that was necessary. I felt I owed that personal approach in the circumstances.

There was no question of sitting in judgement over any officer or official account. It was an approach to the public, especially the sufferers in the recent riots, in order to hearten them and lessen their fear. After such an occurrence I think it is very desirable for such personal approaches to be made both from the point of view of the officers and the public.

I think Shankar Prasad is a good and impartial officer – that has been my experience of him in the past. Why his prestige or reputation should suffer by my sending some onc to Ajmer, I do not quite see. In any event, the most important consideration is surely the effect on the public and not merely the reaction of an officer. We can hardly function on the purely official level when panic seizes the people or psychological conditions arise which may lead to disaster. The stakes are too high for us to get tied up in official red tape.

You will appreciate that I am also concerned with the prestige of our officers and am anxious that nothing should be done to injure it in any way. But the prestige of an officer or indeed our own prestige is after all a secondary matter when other vital issues are at stake. If we do the right thing with the public, our prestige will take care of itself, and so will the officers'.

An important question arises – Am I to be constrained in taking any action in regard to inspection or visit or like matters, which I consider necessary? That surely is an impossible position for me or any Prime Minister anywhere. Am I not to send a personal representative to any place either for a private inquiry or to convey a message? That would make me a prisoner without freedom to act in accordance with what I might consider the needs of the situation.

About your second letter, I am very sorry that what I wrote to you gave you pain. I am myself very unhappy about the trend of events and the difficulties that have arisen between you and me. It seems that our approaches are different, however much we may respect each other, and the issues that have arisen have to be considered very carefully and objectively by all of us. If I am to continue as Prime Minister I cannot have my freedom restricted and I must have a certain liberty of direction. Otherwise, it is better for me to retire. I do not wish to take any hasty step, nor would you wish to take it. We must, therefore, give full thought to the situation that has arisen, so that our decisions may be for the good of the country we have sought to serve these many years. If unfortunately either you or I have to leave the Government of India, let this be done with dignity and goodwill. On my part I would gladly resign and hand over the reins to you.

59 Nehru to Vallabhbhai, 11 August 1949

To Sardar Vallabhbhai

I have just received your letter of 9 August about incorporating in the new Constitution various decisions relating to privy purse payments and guarantees in respect of rights and privileges of the rulers etc.

I do not think that there was any desire on the part of the Cabinet to upset any undertaking taken on behalf of Government. The Cabinet was, however, a little surprised and taken aback by the fact that those privy purse payments free of income-tax, were for perpetuity. I confess that I had not realised this fact of perpetuity before. I am not sure in my own mind if any Government is capable of guaranteeing any payment in perpetuity. I doubt if this kind of thing has been done elsewhere except, perhaps, very rarely. It does not seem to me realistic because it is hardly possible, even through a constitution, to tie down the future in this way.

Nevertheless, because of the assurances given by Government, we have to abide by them, whatever the future might do. The practical aspect of this was that an inclusion of this long list of payments, free of tax and for perpetuity, in the Constitution would undoubtedly give rise to long and bitter debate in the party and in the Assembly. Public attention would be drawn to it in India and abroad. Whatever the ultimate result of voting, this debate will not be good from the point of view of either the Government or the Princes. The Princes would probably be bitterly criticised and they will feel that their position in regard to these guarantees was not very secure in spite of the constitution containing them. Looking at the temper of the party, I am rather doubtful if they would pass them as such. If they pass them, it would be by a fairly narrow majority.

The alternative is a specific article in the Constitution guaranteeing payment etc., of all obligations entered into by the Government in regard to the Princes etc. Without giving a list of all these, I think that this course would very largely meet your point of view and certainly it will be accepted as a fulfilment of our present duty to the Princes. It would avoid that particular publicity and bitter debate which a full list is sure to cause.

I have discussed this matter with a number of leading Members of the Constituent Assembly and all of them felt that giving a full list in the Constitution would make matters very difficult.

Anyhow we shall certainly discuss this matter fully in Cabinet and with Rajaji who, I understand, has had a talk with you. We shall not come to any final decision without reference to you. I do not want you to interrupt your rest and treatment and rush back to Delhi for this matter. We shall hold it up for the present and meanwhile will communicate with you.

60 Manilal Gandhi to the present Author, 24 October 1953, from Phoenix, Natal, South Africa

Brother Dr. Chittaranjan and dear Sarojben,

I am very grateful for your New Year's greetings. I pray the New Year brings you good health and prosperity. I am so happy that you remember me. I have not forgotten our short meeting which I often recall. I feel like coming back to see you, but that is in thc hands of God. Political atmosphere here is getting worse and can even mean death for me, and even that will not solve the problem. However, I will be happy to die doing social services. What else could be expected of us? I hope you are happy there. A lot of people have gone from here to the country where you live; you may meet some of them. I had lost your address so I am sending this letter to Sister Webster and hope you receive it safely.

Affectionately yours, Manilal.

MANILAL GANDHI
EDITOR: 'INDIAN OPINION.'

TEL. & CABLES: "GANDHI."
TELEPHONE: PHOENIX No 3.

P.O. P/BAG, PHŒNIX,
Natal.

તા. ૨૪-૧૧ ૧૯૫૩.

આદરણીય ડૉ. ચિત્તરંજન [illegible]

[illegible]

61 Vivekananda to Mother Hale, 30 August 1895, from USA

To Mrs. G. W. Hale

C/O MISS DUTCHER
THOUSAND ISLAND PARK
30th August [*July*] *'95*

DEAR MOTHER,

I was starting for Chicago, Thursday next [August 1], but your letter stopped me. The letter and the package have safely arrived.

Write to me or wire if you want me to come to Chicago. I will then start for Chicago next week, i.e. on Tuesday next [August 6]. I thought Sister Mary was at home. When are the other babies coming? My going to Europe is not yet settled finally. The babies have not written me a line—not one of them.

Oh, Mother, my heart is so, so sad. The letters bring the news of the death of Dewanji. Haridas Viharidas has left the body. He was as a father to me. Poor man, he was the last 5 years seeking the retirement from business life, and at last he got it but could not enjoy it long. I pray that he may never come back again to this dirty hole they call the Earth. Neither may he be born in heaven or any other horrid place. May he never again wear a body—good or bad, thick or thin. What a humbug and illusion this world is, Mother, what a mockery this life. I pray constantly that all mankind will come to know the reality, i.e. God, and this "Shop" here be closed for ever.

My heart is too full to write more. Write to me or wire if you like.

Your ever obedient Son,
VIVEKANANDA

P.S. We will think of the coming package [from the Maharaja of Khetri] in Chicago. How long will you be in Chicago? If it is only a week or so, I need not come. I will meet you in New York. If more than that, I come to see you.

Yours,
V.

62 Vivekananda to Giridharidas Desai, 2 March 1896, from New York

LXXXVII

To Shri Giridharidas Mangaldas Viharidas Desai

228 WEST 39TH STREET
NEW YORK
2 March 1896

DEAR FRIEND,

Excuse my delay in replying to your beautiful note.

Your uncle[1] was a great soul, and his whole life was given to doing good to his country. Hope you will all follow in his footsteps.

I am coming to India this winter, and cannot express my sorrow that I will not see Haribhai once more.

He was a strong, noble friend, and India has lost a good deal in losing him.

I am going to England very soon where I intend to pass the summer, and in winter next I come to India.

Recommend me to your uncles and friends.

Ever always the well-wisher of your family,

VIVEKANANDA

PS: My England address is: C/o E. T. Sturdy, Esq., High View, Caversham, Reading, England.

63 Vivekananda to Diwanji, from Khetri, September 1894

Khetri

Dear Diwanji Saheb.

Surely my letter had not reached you before you wrote to me. the persual of your letter gave me both pleasure and pain simultaneously, pleasure to see that I have the good fortune to be loved by a man of your heart power and position and pain to see that my motive has been misinterpreted throughout. Believe me that I love you and respect you like a **father** and that my gratitude towards you and your family is surely unbounded. The fact is this. You may remember that I had from before a wish to go over to **Chicago.** When at Madras the people there of their own accord in conjunction with H. H. of Mysore and Ramnad made every arrangement to send me up. And you may also remember that between H. H. of Khetri and myself there is the closest ties of love. Well, I as a matter of course, wrote him that I was going off to America. Now the Raja of Khetri thought in his love that I was bound to see him once before I departed especially as the Lord has given him an heir to the throne and great rejoicings were going on here and to make sure of my coming he sent his Private Secretary all the way to Madras to fetch me and of course I was bound to come. In the meanwhile I telegraphed to your brother at Nadiad to know whether you were there and unfortunately the answer I could not get. therefore the Secretary who, poor fellow, had suffered terribly for his master in going to and fro Madras and with his eye wholly on the fact that his master would be very unhappy if we could not reach **Khetri** within the **Jalsa,** bought tickets at once for Jaypore, on our way we met Mr. Ratilal who informed me that my wire was received and duly answered and that Mr. Vaiharidas was expecting me. Now it is for you to judge whose duty it has been so long to deal even justice. What would or could I do in this connection. If I woud have got down I could not have reached in time for the Khetri rejoicings, on the other hand my motives might be misinterepreted but I know your and your brother's love for me and I knew also that I would have to go back to Bombay in a few days on my way to Chicago. I thought that the best selection was to postpone my visit to my return. As for my feeling affronted at not being attended by your brothers is a new discovery of yours which I never even dreamt of or God knows perhaps you have become a thought reader. Jokes alone my dear Diwanji Saheb, I am the same frolicsome, mischievous but I assure you the innocent boy, you found me at **Junagad** and my love for your noble self is the same or increased a hundredfold because I have had a mental comparison between yourself and the Diwans of nearly all the states in **Dakshin** and the Lord be my witness how my tongue was fluent in your praise (although I know that my powers are quite inadequate to estimate your noble qualities) in every Southern court. If this be not a sufficient explanation, I implore you to pardon me as a father pardens a son and let me not be haunted with the impression that I was ever ungrateful to one who was so good to me.

Yours,
Vivekananda.

P. S. :- I depend on you to remove any misconception in the mind of your brother about my not getting down and that had I been the very devil, I could not forget their kindness and good offices for me.

As the other two swamies, they were my Gooroobhaies who went to you last at Junagad, of them one is our leader. I met them after three years and we came together as far as Abu and then I left them. If we wish I can take them back on my way to Bombay to Nadiad. May the Lord shower his blessings on you and yours.

Yours,
V.

64 Invitation to a Meeting in Borsad, 30 April 1930

Dear Shree . . . ,

Our District's Local Leaders have decided to call an Assembly of all Mukhis, Matadars and Rawanias who have tendered their resignations in the last and final fight for complete independence. The Assembly meeting has to decide what action should be taken following these resignations and decide whether to establish a Borsad Taluka Mukhi Matadar Mandal which could help in this fight for freedom. It is hoped that you will be able to attend this meeting.

The Assembly will be held at one hour past midday on 5 May 1930 in Borsad at Dasa Porvad Dharamshala. Abbas Tayabji Saheb as well as all the chief political workers of Borsad Taluka and of Kheda District and the leading citizens of those villages which have declared not to pay the land revenue until the Government releases the National Leaders, will be attending.

N.B. Those Mukhis who have not surrendered their seals of office, are requested to bring them to the meeting.

Satyagraha Chhavni, Borsad.

Lallubhai Laxmidas Patel, Secretary.

આમંત્રણ પત્રિકા.

ભાઈશ્રી ______________________________

મુ. ______________________________

બોરસદ તાલુકાના જે જે ગામના મુખી, મતાદારો તથા રાવણીયાઓએ પૂર્ણ સ્વરાજ્યની આ આખરની લડતમાં રાજીનામાં આપી સાચી વીરતા બતાવી છે. તે બધા ભાઈઓની એક સભા ગોઠવવાનું તાલુકાના કાર્યકર્તાઓએ નક્કી કર્યું છે. સભામાં રાજીનામાં આપેલા ભાઈઓએ હવે શું કરવું. બોરસદ તાલુકા મુખી મતાદાર મંડળ સ્થાપવા સંબંધી વિચાર કરવા તથા સ્વરાજ્ય યજ્ઞમાં કઈ અને કેવી રીતે તેઓ મદદ કરી શકે તે બાબતની સમજુત કરવામાં આવશે. તો આ સભામાં તમે હાજર રહેશો એવી વિનંતિ છે.

આ સભા તા. ૫-૫-૩૦ ને સોમવારે બપોરે એક વાગે બોરસદમાં દશા પોરવાડની ધર્મશાળામાં મળશે. આ પ્રસંગે પુજ્ય અબ્બાસ તૈયબજી સાહેબ અને જીલ્લા તથા બોરસદ તાલુકાના મુખ્ય કાર્યકર્તાઓ તથા તાલુકામાં રાસ તથા બીજાં જે જે ગામોએ આગેવાનોને જેલમાંથી સરકાર ન છોડે ત્યાં સુધી જમીન મહેસુલ ન ભરવાનો ઠરાવ કર્યો છે તે ગામોના આગેવાનો પણ હાજર રહેશે.

તા. ક.—જે મુખીઓએ પોતાનાં દફતર સરકારમાં ન સોંપ્યાં હોય તેઓએ પોતાનાં દફતર સોંપવા અત્રે સાથે લેતા આવવું.

સત્યાગ્રહ છાવણી
બોરસદ.
તા. ૩૦-૪-૩૦

લલ્લુભાઈ લક્ષ્મીદાસ પટેલ.

મંત્રી, સત્યાગ્રહ છાવણી-બોરસદ.

શ્રી બોરસદ પ્રીન્ટીંગ પ્રેસ બોરસદમાં પા. મનોરભાઈ ફુલાભાઈએ બોરસદ સત્યાગ્રહ છાવણીના મંત્રી લલ્લુભાઈ લક્ષ્મીદાસ પટેલ માટે છાપ્યું અને તેમણે બોરસદ સત્યાગ્રહ છાવણીમાંથી પ્રગટ કર્યું.

65 Shivabhai Ashabhai to Dadubhai, 30 April 1930, from Borsad

'Independence by Khadi thread'
Satyagraha Camp, Borsad District, Kheda
Shriyut Dadubhai Purushottamdas Desai, Nadiad

On 5th May Monday, we have organised a meeting of each town's Mukhi, Matadar and Rawania who have resigned their posts. We have also published a leaflet relating to this, which I am enclosing herewith.

Your presence at this meeting is very essential. We propose to set up a permanent council of these Mukhi-Matadars. In Borsad Taluka we have ten villages who have resolved not to pay the land revenue and we want to support them and suitably guide them for this purpose. In the final fight for independence, this Mukhi-Matadar Council is very important, hence on this special occasion we request your presence. Please respond to our request.

Shivabhai Ashabhai's Vande Mataram.

(At this time Sardar was in jail, until 26 June 1930.)

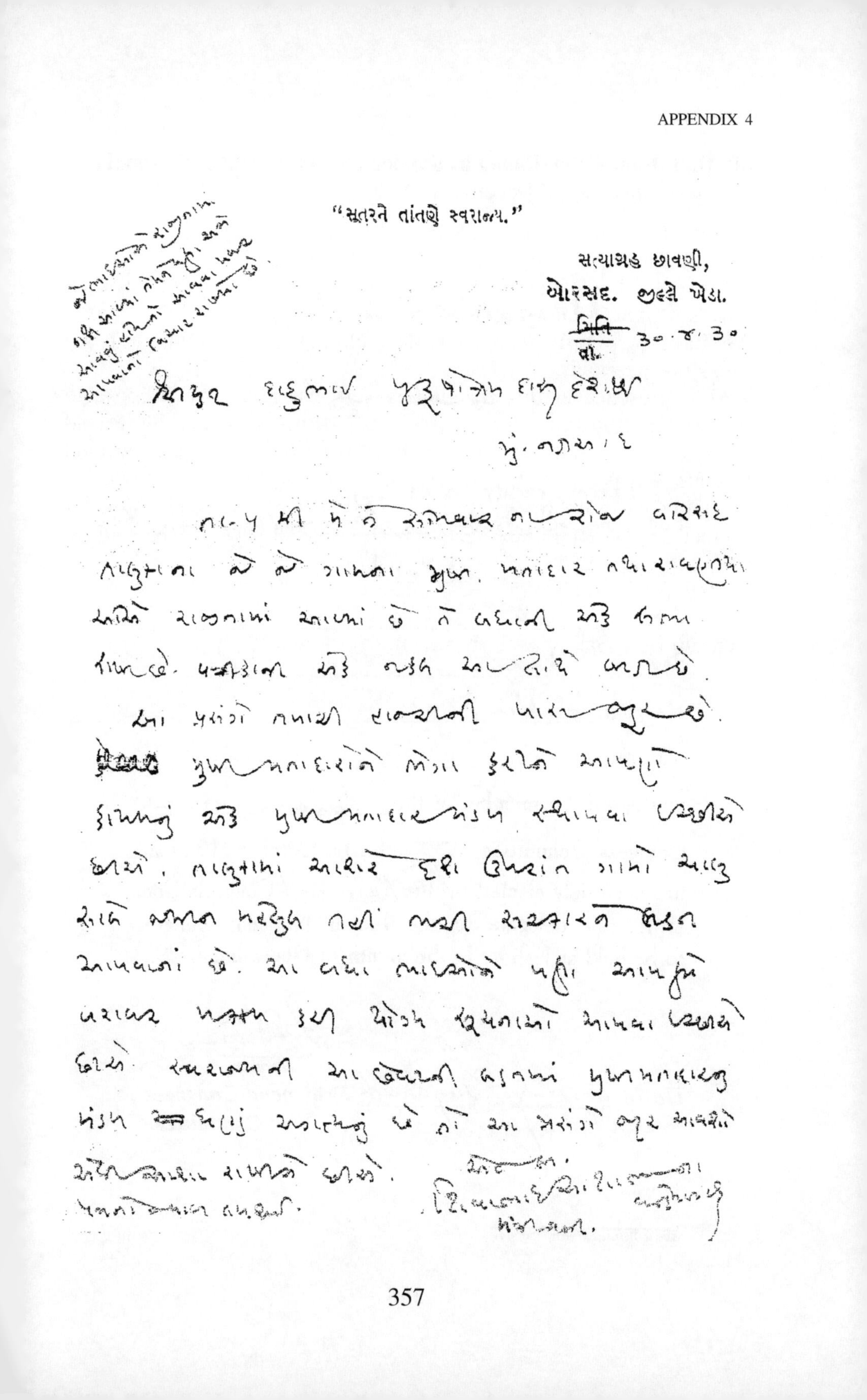

[illegible]

"સૂતરને તાંતણે સ્વરાજ્ય."

સત્યાગ્રહ છાવણી,
બોરસદ. જીલ્લે ખેડા.
~~મિતિ~~ ૩૦.૪.૩૦
તા.

ઠાકુર ઇન્દુલાલ પુરુષોત્તમદાસ દેસાઈ
મું. નડિયાદ

તા. ૫ મી મે ને રવિવારના રોજ બોરસદ તાલુકાના બે બે ગામના મુખી, મતાદાર તથા રાવણીયાઓએ સાથે રાજીનામાં આપ્યાં છે તે બધાની [illegible] [illegible].

આ પ્રસંગે તમારી હાજરીની ખાસ જરૂર છે. [illegible]

[illegible]

66 Dadubhai's Certificate as a delegate to an Indian National Congress meeting, 5 December 1929

Delegate Certificate.

No. 20

I hereby certify that :—

Full name Dadubhai Purshottamdas Desai

Occupation Landlord

Age 52

Sex Male

Religion Hindoo

Address Nadiad

was enrolled a member of the Kaira Dist

Congress Committee ~~On~~ before the 1st October, 1929 and has been duly elected by the Kaira Dist Congress Committee as a delegate to the Indian National Congress to be held at Lahore in the month of December 1929.

Secretary,

Dated 5-12-29 Gujarat Provincial Congress Committee.

Amrit Electric Press, Lahore.

67 The Author at the age of eighteen joins the Indian National Congress, 13 August 1939

Issued by B.P.C.C. Number 598–0
D'Girgaum Jilla Congress Committee
Mumbai
Shriyut Chittaranjan D. Desai

I have received with thanks your annual subscription of four annas for the membership of the Congress for the year 1939.

Signature: C.D. Desai, 13 August 1939

B.A. Khimji
Treasurer
Bombay Provincial Congress Committee.

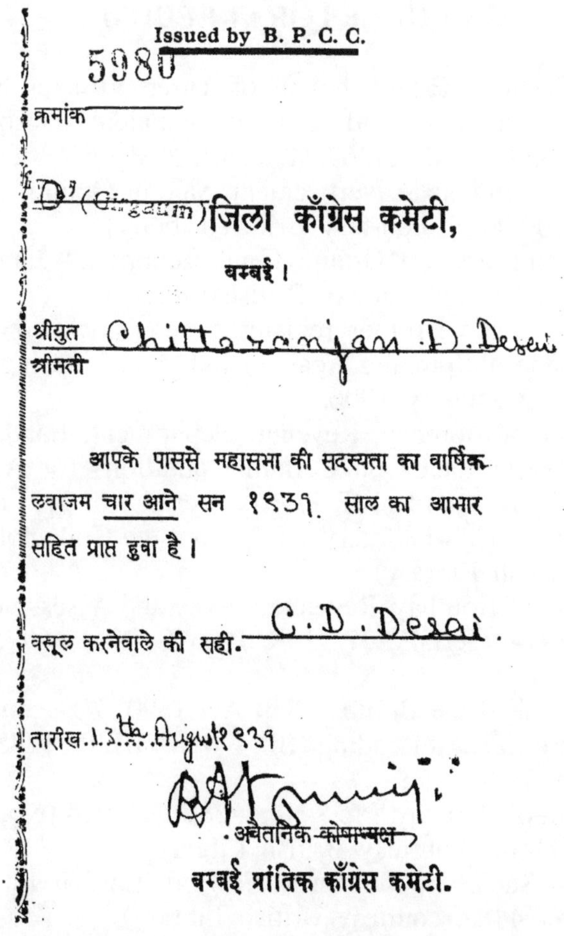
Issued by B. P. C. C.
5980
क्रमांक
D' (Girgaum) जिला काँग्रेस कमेटी,
बम्बई।
श्रीयुत Chittaranjan D. Desai
श्रीमती
आपके पाससे महासभा की सदस्यता का वार्षिक लवाजम चार आने सन १९३९ साल का आभार सहित प्राप्त हुवा है।
वसूल करनेवाले की सही. C. D. Desai.
तारीख 13th August १९३९
B A Khimji
अवैतनिक कोषाध्यक्ष
बम्बई प्रांतिक काँग्रेस कमेटी.

APPENDIX 5

FURTHER DOCUMENTS RELATING TO THE STRUGGLE FOR FREEDOM

1 Bombay Castle – Establishment of Three Villages by Dessoy Ajoobhoy Parbhudas and Dessoy Samaldas Desoybhoy; 1 November 1819 (10R P/367/71, courtesy British Library)
2 Bombay Government Advertisement, Sale of Opium; 31 January 1821 (10R P/368/9, courtesy British Library)
3 Royal Commission on Opium Final Report; 24 January 1895 (10R Volume XLII, courtesy British Library)
4 Dadubhai and his Brother register a new stock company, the Nadiad Swadeshi Spinning Weaving and Manufacturing Company Limited, on 8 January 1906.
5 Government of Bombay, Revenue Department, Lands – Kaira, Grant of Waste Lands on Certain Conditions for Agricultural Purposes; 7 May 1914 (10R P/9619, Serial No. 217; reproduces letter R–1215 of 23 February 1914, from the Collector of Kaira; courtesy British Library)
6 Government of Bombay, Revenue Survey and Assessment, Kaira; 20 May 1914 (serial 237, 10R P/0618, No. 4697, courtesy British Library)
7 A Bill to Amend the Bombay Salt Act 1890; 7 December 1922, with letter from Lord Reading (Bill No. XVIII, P/11245, courtesy British Library)
8 Government of Bombay, Press Note; 28 June 1924 (No. L.C./157-B, 10R P/11402, courtesy British Library)
9 Letter from Sir Leslie Wilson to Edward (Lord Irwin); 26 June 1928; (letter 448a, courtesy British Library)

10 Letter from Lord Irwin to Provincial Governors, 6 September 1928; (letter 71, 10R Mss EUR–152/22, courtesy British Library)
11 Letter from Lord Irwin to Sir Leslie Wilson, 28 October 1928 (letter 642c 10R Mss EUR–152/22, courtesy British Library)
12 Letter from Lord Irwin to Provincial Governors, 29 October 1928 (letter 645 10R Mss EUR–152/22, courtesy British Library)
13 Letter from Lord Irwin to H.M. the King; 11 March 1930 (letter 71, Mss EUR 152/1, courtesy British Library)
14 Letter from A. Master to Bombay Government, Home Department; 5 June 1930 (P/Conf/78, courtesy British Library)
15 Government of Bombay, Revenue Department, Resolution No. 5387/28; 22 July 1930 (Serial No. 26, 10R P/Conf/78, courtesy British Library)
16 Court Order sentencing Dadubhai to five months rigorous imprisonment, 13 October 1930 (courtesy British Library)
17 Patidar Marriage Circles (Gols)
18 Vithalbhai's statement on the failure of the Second Round Table Conference; 8 December 1931.

Document 1; Bombay Castle – Establishment of Three Villages by Dessoy Ajoobhoy Parbhudas and Dessoy Samaldas Desoybhoy, 1 November 1819

(A typed version of this document appears in Appendix 1.)

Bombay Castle ...... 1st November 1819.

Prinl Collector
For running up and recommending Schemes by Dessy Goabhoy Purshotoss, Dessy Jumuldars Dessyboy Jemadar Chitore Dossy & Purshund Lalchuse to Establish three Villages in waste Lands within the bounds of Certain Villages in the Attenate District

Sir,

With reference to my address dated yesterday on the subject of the Cultivation of Wastes, I now do myself the honor to submit a translation of a paper of proposals for the Establishment of three villages, within the Bounds of Certain Villages in the district of Atteenah each new Establishment to have attached to it, land to the extent of five thousand Beegas. —

2d. After the intrusion I have already taken the liberty of making of my sentiments on the subject of the right to reappropriate wastes, I will not advert further to this point in this address than shortly to observe, that where such a field for improvement presents itself, as the proposals now submitted, shew the existence of the Right Honble the Governor in Council will, I doubt not, feel disposed to reconsider his decision on this head before finally resolving not to adopt the only measure which

Colombo Castle ...... 1st November 1819.

which can effectually render such extensive wastes beneficial to the State and to our Subjects. –

3rd In Respect to the proposals – themselves they do not promise such extensive advantage as that which is likely to result from the Establishment of a Village on the meadow lands of Periad – but every thing consider – that is the inferiority of the Soil, the turbulence of the neighbourhood – the greater distance from a market and the smaller rates of Deyotie, even in established Villages – the terms offered are, comparatively, as fair in every respect as those, which I recommended to be granted to that proposed new Village – The Pegsaila solicited is conformable to Custom, and it is the most flattering method of rewarding and perpetuating the Services of Individuals, who, do a Service to Government, in the way proposed, by rendering productive and promoting the population of lands previously waste

Bombay Castle ...... 1st November 1819

waste, and of no available value to the state or to its subjects. But the terms on which people can be induced to bring Wastes, which now yield nothing, into Cultivation especially as they only operate for a few Years can be of no Consideration, compared to the great object of effecting such a desireable improvement. These terms it should be kept in view require no sacrifice on the part of Government, a little forbearance is all that they solicit, while they promise to return advantages, which, if they could not otherwise be secured, would not be dearly purchased by a temporary sacrifice.

4. Two of the persons who offer to undertake the tasks submitted, are members of the Desaye family of Neriad - They possess Capital and not being now employed in the affairs of their own district it is desirable to engage them in undertakings that will occupy their attention, and prevent their again devoting

Bombay Castle ...... 1st November 1819 -

to machinations to oppose the Government, nothing is so likely to enlist their attachment to the .. Government, as permitting them to engage themselves in this way, while in no way can their money be applied more advantageously for their own interests, and those of the Community. Khillon-ding, one of the other persons is a man of considerable enterprize and of exemplary good conduct while Purchund Laldass is a Shroff who possesses some capital - These last engage to establish one village between them .-

5. Such offers are a compliment to the British Government, since it is the security of property, under its ~~strict~~ administration of Justice which, giving confidence to the people, alone .. - emboldens them to such undertakings. That the want of ~~fourth~~ [faith] in our predecessors, and the want of any tribunal, an ~~interested~~ farmer excepted, for the redress of grievances never would have been

Bombay Castle ..... 1st November 1819

Contemplated under their auspices.—

6. If I may venture to predict what these proposed Establishments are likely to yield in a given time, I would say that at the end of 8 years, what now produces nothing, would give at least from 25 to 30000 Rupees per annum and that even then, there would be great Scope for further improvement—But, whatever may be the Result in this Respect, I consider it my duty to Recommend that a fair trial be given to the parties, whose tender is submitted, as the best likely method I can devise of rendering those wastes beneficial.—

7. Of the Villages to which the Lands belong I may Remark, that they cannot extend their Cultivation to these lands and that they will yet have Considerable waste tracts if those in question are with drawn from their limits.

I have

Bombay Castle .... 1st November 1819 –

Calicut zillah
North of Khemghe
Collector's office 1st
September 1819 –

I have the honor to be &c
(Signed) A. Robertson
Collector

Proposals for establishing three villages within the Boundaries of Lasomdra, Rewallya, and Chetmun–ba of the [illegible] district –

Each village to have 500 Beegas of land attached to it. –

These we will bring into cultivation establishing the villages, collecting Cultivators &c. In return for which we request a Lease or a Purwannah –

For the first three years the land cultivated to be free from assessment, to enable us to build tanks and wells, for drinking water, and to make advances for stock &c. which will be necessary on establishing the villages after the expiration of three years the following rates to be collected from all cultivated land –

Bombay Castle .... 1st November 1819

1st Years per Beegas ..... 1 Rupee

2d Do _ Ditto ..... 1 1/2 Ditto

3d Do _ Ditto ..... 2 Ditto

4th Do _ Ditto ..... 2 1/2 Ditto

such land as may be of inferior quality being allowed for —

On the 5th year a Punchaet shall assemble and fix the Khatas of the Cultivators —

For our trouble in this business we ask that 100 Beegas may be granted to us as Pasaita or heritable property beyond which we shall look for no other emolument and when the Village shall be fully established we shall pay any Revenue which according to the produce may be fixed by Government. —

The following Pasaitas must be given to 10 Raones _ 125 Beegas, and to the different Village craft 100 Beegas. —

The lands that the Well for

Bombay Castle ...... 1st November 1819.

drinking water may be upon to be granted by Government.—

(Signed) Dessy Apoobyjunthory

True Translation — Dessy Cannuldass Dessyboy

(Signed) A. Robertson — Imacour Cheloor Seng &

Collector — Veroshunk Lalldass

Kaira Collector

Explanation measures approved & the Establishment of the Village sanctioned.—

Minutes 1st Novr. The explanations afforded by Captain Robertson have so completely removed the material objection which occurred when his proposition of the 12th April 1818, for granting 3000, Beegas of meadow land in the neighbourhood of Neriad to Dwarcadass Santerdass for establishing a new village came first under review that the Governt. in C. no longer hesitates to authorize the measure and from the testimony which Captain Robertson has borne to the Character of Dwarcadass Santerdass we have particular pleasure in giving our sanction to the Complement intended to be paid by the 17th article to the Founder of

develop

Bombay Castle ..... 1st November 1819

Kaira Collector

directing that the village should bear the name of "Duarcapura". —

The Governor in Council is pleased to accede to Captain Robertson's recommendation in favor of the proposals offered by Dassoy Apoobhy Purboodas and others for establishing three new villages within the bounds of certain villages in the District of Nerriad each village to consist of 5000 Beegas. —

Minutes 1st Nov. Resolved that Captain Robertson be accordingly authorized to conclude the necessary details for giving effect to these arrangements which it is hoped will ultimately be attended with the great advantages which may with so much reason be anticipated from them. —

Ordered that a Copy of Captain Robertson's letter of the 22d April 1818 be transmitted with his letter of the 17th September

Copy of the report sent to the Collector of Northern Concan.

Read the following letter from the Post Master to Mr. acting Chief Secretary

Document 2: Bombay Government Advertisement, Sale of Opium; 31 January 1821

(A typed version of this document appears in Appendix 3.)

379
101

Bombay Castle 31st January 1821.–

Opium

Resolved that the following advertisement be published by Hand Bills and in next Saturdays Courier announcing the Sale of Malwa Opium at this Presidency in the 24th of April Next.–

...tisement announcing the Sale ...wa Opium at ...esidency in the ...pril next...

Government Advertisement.

Notice is hereby given,

That on Wednesday the 24th of April, at eleven O'Clock in the forenoon, will be sold by public Auction at the sale Room in the Bunder, the quantity of about fifteen hundred Bengal Chests of Malwa Opium, the produce of the Year 1819–20.

Conditions of the sale.

2nd. The Opium to be sold by the one pecul Chest of lbs. 133½ in Lots of five chests each; one Rupee to be paid down to bind the bargain, and a deposit of 10 per Cent on the price of each Lot in money, or public securities, to be made by the purchasers before the expiration of five days; in default thereof the Lot, or Lots, to be resold, and all losses and expenses attending such resale, to be paid by the first purchasers, and

Bombay Castle 31st January 1821.—

and any profit arising therefrom to belong [to]
Government.

3rd The Opium to be paid for and
cleared out within 2 months from the day of [sale]
and in case any Opium shall not be paid [for]
and cleared out, the abovementioned deposit
of 10 per Cent; and the earnest money, will [be]
forfieted, " " " the Opium advertised for a
ready money sale, all losses and expenses
attending such sale, to be borne by the first
purchasers and any profit accruing from
it to belong to Government.

4th The following papers may be [seen]
at this office at any time between the ho[urs]
of 10 and 3 O'Clock on the 1st of April and
following days previous to the day of sale.

No. 1.— Warrantees of the Opium now
advertised for sale.

No. 2.— Reports of the examination of the Opi[um]

No. 3.— Account of the weight of the
Opium when packed.

No. 4.— Statements of the average w[eight]
in Bombay of 6 Chests.

Bombay Castle 31st January 1821.—

5th On the day of sale the abovementioned documents will be laid on the table and Samples of the opium to be sold, will be exhibited for the inspection of the Merchants.

6th Individuals under the presidency of Fort William, who may be desirous of purchasing any portion of the Opium in question, are at liberty until the 5th of march next, to send to the Board of Customs, Salt and Opium at that Presidency, proposals to that effect, stating the number of lots which they may wish to purchase, and the price they may propose to give for all, or each, in Bombay Rupees, and accompanying their tenders with security for the due observance of the conditions of the sales in money, or company's paper, or other security approved by the Board, to the extent of 10 per Cent on the price of each lot; any deposits made as security for such tenders will be returned certificate from Bombay, that the Opium purchased by the party has been purchased under his tender.

7th The proposals so received will be

922

Bombay Castle 31st January 1821.

be transmitted to Bombay, and ultimately entrust[ed]
under an assurance of secrecy to the charge of the
officer appointed by the Government to superin[tend]
the sale, who will purchase the opium, if the
selling price falls within the terms of the ten[der]
* * * * * several tenders have been receiv[ed]
the advantage over the rest to the highest ten[derer]
or tenderers, to the extent of his or their tender
the benefit eventually of a lower price than
what he or they may offer, according to the
following plan.

Clause First – in case one or more tender[ers]
shall undertake for the purchase of the
whole quantity of Opium to be exposed
for sale, at an uniform price, then the
Lots shall be put up at the amount of
such price, and if no higher bid be
offered, the sale shall be concluded in
favor of such tenderer, or tenderers.

Clause Second. – if there be several
tenders embracing in the aggregate the
whole quantity of Opium for sale, but not
at an uniform price, the sale shall be

923
1012

Bombay Castle 31st January 1821.—

commenced by puting up the Lots successively at the lowest amount that may be so tendered it there be no Bid beyond this, the sale of the whole quantity of Opium shall be concluded with all the Tenderers at their rate. if there be an advance of price bid, the Officer appointed to superintend the sale shall bid up by an advance of one Rupee per Chest until there is no higher bider, or until the amount of the highest tender shall be reached. If no one outbid him, the lot shall belong to the highest tenderer, and so on with the following Lots in succession so long as there shall be any unsatisfied tender at a rate exceeding the amount bid.—

These lots will of course be bought in on account of the persons making such tenders; the remaining Lots, in so far as bidders may be found at rates exceeding the unsatisfied tenders still held by the superintendent of the sale, will be sold by the usual free Competition.

Clause third— If tenders be received comprising more than the entire quantity of

Opium

Bombay Castle 31st January 1821.

opium to be sold, the Superintendent shall strike off the excess from the lowest ten[ders] and put up the lot at the lowest of the rates offered in such number or portion of the highest tenderers as may comprise the whole and proceed in the sale in one or other of the modes above specified as the case may

Clause fourth — If the tenders do not comprize the whole of the opium to be sold the Superintendent of the sale shall not [bid] on behalf of the Tenders until the numb[er] of chests not tendered for shall be disp[osed] of. These he will sell by open competitio[n] to the highest bidders, without however disclosing the number tendered for; and if on completing the sale of the Lots so le[ft] untendered for, it shall appear that the average price which they may have fetched, does not exceed the rate specified in the lowest tender, all the tenderers sha[ll] have the quantity for which they may have tendered at such average price. If the average price fetched by the said Lots exceed

925

Bombay Castle 31st January 1821.—

the rate tendered, supposing all the tenders to be made at uniform rates, or the rate of the lowest tenders, if the tenders be made at various rates, then the Superintendent will proceed by putting up the Lots in the manner specified in the 1st or 2d Clauses, as the case may be.

8th — In case of equality in the amount of two or more tenders, the priority will be determined by the time at which they were respectively given in by the Merchants to the Board of Customs, Salt and Opium, in whose office they will be regularly registered as received.

9th — Individuals under the Presidency of Bombay who may be desirous of purchasing any portion of the Opium which will be put up of Sale at the Second Bengal Sale, are at liberty, until the 3d of February next to send to the Secretary to Government in the Revenue Department at this Presidency, proposals, to that effect, stating the number of lots which they may wish to purchase, and the price they may propose to give for all or each in Sicca Rupees, and accompanying their Tenders with security for the due observance of

Bombay Castle 31st January 1821.

of the sale, in money, or Company's paper, or other security approved by the Government; and the tenders so received will be transmitted to Bengal and acted upon in every respect as is provided in the case of Bengal tenders for Bombay Opium in paragraphs 6th 7th and 8th of the Advertisement.

Bombay Castle 27th January 1821. } Published by order of the Hon'ble the Governor in Council
(Signed) James Farish
Secretary to Government

Opium
Copies of the Advertisement transmitted to Bengal & to the Departments Concerned.

Minutes 27th Jany. } Ordered that Copies of the preceding Advertisement be transmitted to the Supreme Government Resident at Indore and Accountant General a Copy being also transmitted to Mr. Secretary Simson with the Hon'ble the Governor.

Wrote the following letter to the Secretary to the Supreme Government –

Opium
To Mr. Secretary McKenzie advising of the Publication of the Advertisement announcing the Sale here in April of 1500 Chests of Malwa Opium

Sir,

I am directed by the Hon'ble the Governor in Council to request You will inform His Excellency the Most Noble the Governor General in Council

Bombay Castle 31st January 1821.

in Council that an advertisement has been published under this date announcing the sale of a quantity of Malwa Opium not exceeding 1500 Bengal Chests the period for the sale has been fixed for the last week in April which is considered to be as early as it will be practicable to hold the sale in the present season

2d. A clause has been added to the advertisement in conformity with the suggestion conveyed in the 4th Paragraph of Your Letter of 24th November last announcing that the same accommodation will be allowed to the mercantile community of Bombay in regard to the purchase of Opium at the Second Calcutta Sale as is allowed by the advertisement of the 23rd November to the merchants of Bengal in regard to the Malwa opium to be sold at this Presidency the 3rd of February has been fixed as the latest date for receiving tenders for the purchase of Bengal Opium. –

Bombay Castle
27th January 1821

I have the honor to be &ca
(Signed) J. Farish
Secretary to Government

Document 3: Royal Commission on Opium Final Report, 24 January 1895

(Due to health problems Haridas Veharidas Desai was unable to proceed to England and instead submitted Memorandum III.)

FINAL REPORT

OF THE

ROYAL COMMISSION ON OPIUM.

PART I.

THE REPORT,

WITH ANNEXURES.

Presented to both Houses of Parliament by Command of Her Majesty.

LONDON:
PRINTED FOR HER MAJESTY'S STATIONERY OFFICE,
BY EYRE AND SPOTTISWOODE,
PRINTERS TO THE QUEEN'S MOST EXCELLENT MAJESTY.

And to be purchased, either directly or through any Bookseller, from
EYRE AND SPOTTISWOODE, EAST HARDING STREET, FLEET STREET, E.C., and
32, ABINGDON STREET, WESTMINSTER, S.W.; or
JOHN MENZIES & Co., 12, HANOVER STREET, EDINBURGH, and
90, WEST NILE STREET, GLASGOW; or
HODGES, FIGGIS, & Co., LIMITED, 104, GRAFTON STREET DUBLIN.

1895.

[C.—7723.] *Price* 1s. 6*d*.

272. The conclusions of the Commission as to Burma have been fully stated in the Section of our Report dealing with that Province. The Burmans are specially susceptible to injury from opium, and there is among them a popular sentiment against the habit. Special regulations have, therefore, been introduced which, short of universal prohibition, seem to us as restrictive as it would be expedient for any Government to attempt to enforce. Opium in Burma.

273. It only remains for us to give specific answers to the questions referred to us by Your Majesty as arranged in the Order of Reference. We cannot do this better than by reproducing the conclusions at which we unanimously arrived at the final meeting of the Commission at Bombay. To our regret, our colleague, Mr. Wilson, was prevented by illness from attending our deliberations. Every other member of the Commission, including our Native colleagues, was present. With the impression of our recent tour fresh in our minds, after a full discussion, but with no dissenting voice on the broader issues, we adopted the following resolutions:— The draft conclusions recorded at the close of the public inquiry.

I.—Whether the growth of the poppy and the manufacture and sale of opium in British India should be prohibited except for medical purposes, and whether this prohibition could be extended to the Native States?

I.—(a.) It has not been shown to be necessary, or to be demanded by the people, that the growth of the poppy and manufacture and sale of opium in British India should be prohibited except for medical purposes. A considerable minority, consisting of people opposed on principle to all stimulants, would support prohibition except for medical purposes, if relieved from anxiety as to the financial results, and as to the punitive and inquisitorial measures which repression would involve. The number who desire prohibition at all risks is exceedingly small. Prohibition except for medical purposes.

(b.) The authoritative extension of such prohibition to the Native States would be an interference on the part of the Paramount Power, for which we can find no precedent and no justification, and which would be resented by the Chiefs and their people. The growth of the poppy and the manufacture of opium have been prohibited in some Native States by orders passed by the Chiefs in accordance with Treaties or Agreements made with the Government of India; but such Treaties or Agreements rest upon an arrangement whereby a full and cheap supply of opium is secured for the internal consumption of these States and for the realisation by the Chiefs of an Excise Revenue from their people, and the Chiefs would cease to be bound by them if the supply were cut off or restricted. Extension of prohibition to the Protected States.

(c) The prohibition of the growth of the poppy and the manufacture and sale of opium in British India, except for medical purposes, involves the destruction of the export trade in Bengal opium from Calcutta to China and elsewhere, which would inflict a very heavy loss of public revenue on the Government and people of India. The existing Treaties, by which the import of Indian opium to China is permitted and regulated, have been deliberately accepted by the Chinese Government, and have been formally admitted by the Chinese Ministers on the last occasion of revision to contain all that they desire. In the natural order of things, it is for the Chinese Government to move first if it wishes to sacrifice the revenue which it derives and to annul the Treaty provisions legalising import on the ground that such an import is injurious to China. Whether the British Government bears part of the cost or not, it would not be right or fair to the people of British India for the British Discontinuance of the Bengal export trade.

Government to destroy, unasked by China, the Bengal opium trade; at any rate, it would not be right or fair for it to so act, unless there was convincing proof (1) that the trade stands on a different plane from the alcohol and is more pernicious and demoralising; (2) that its destruction would, in all probability, materially benefit China in a permanent way; and (3) that the Chinese Government is prevented from itself moving by fear of hostile action on our part. From the evidence before us, we do not think it proved that these reasons for unsolicited action by the British Government exist, and we agree in not recommending any action tending to the destruction of the trade. If at any future time the Chinese Government declares a wish to prohibit import, the question will be changed and we (the Commission) shall hold ourselves at liberty to reconsider it.

Extinction of the Malwa export trade.

II.—The nature of the existing arrangements with the Native States in respect of the transit of opium through British territory, and on what terms, if any, these arrangements could be with justice terminated.

II.—Existing arrangements with certain opium-producing Native States in respect of the transit of opium through British territory for the Bombay export trade are not, except in the case of Baroda, in the nature of Agreements, though in virtue of long established practice they may be held, perhaps, to have the force of Agreements. They consist of the prohibition of transit, except under a pass granted by a British officer, on payment of an Imperial transit duty. These arrangements rest in origin upon the power of regulation and taxation which the British Government has in consequence of these States being cut off from the sea by intervening British territory. The privilege of the transit of opium for export beyond the sea from Bombay on payment of a duty could not now be terminated with justice except by voluntary agreement, which, if obtained at all, would involve large pecuniary compensation, both to the State and private individuals, and also a heavy loss of public revenue to the Government of India.

Financial considerations.

III.—The effect on the finances of India of the prohibition of the sale and export of opium, taking into consideration (*a*) the compensation payable, (*b*) the cost of the necessary preventive measures, (*c*) the loss of revenue.

III.—The finances of India are not in a condition to bear the charges for compensation, the cost of the necessary preventive measures, and the loss of revenues would result from the adoption of a policy of prohibition.

Changes in system short of prohibition.

IV.—Whether any change short of total prohibition should be made in the system at present followed for regulating and restricting the opium traffic, and for raising a revenue therefrom.

IV.—(*a*.) The regulations for the restriction of the consumption of opium may be amended in various particulars. We are not prepared to make recommendations without careful study of details.

(*b*.) The Bengal monopoly seems to us the best system for regulating the production of opium in British India. Certain administrative reforms were recommended by the Commission of 1883.

(*c*.) We are not prepared at present to recommend any further development of the new regulations recently introduced into Burma. The operations of these new rules, which only came into force on January 1st, 1894, should be carefully watched before any further changes are introduced.

V.—The consumption of opium by the different races and in the different districts in India, and the effect of such consumption on the moral and physical condition of the people?

V.—(*a.*) We have made exhaustive inquiry into the consumption of opium in India and its effects. We find no evidence of extensive moral or physical degradation from its use. Consumption of opium in India and its effects.

(*b.*) Opium is extensively used for non-medical and quasi-medical purposes, in some cases with benefit, and for the most part without injurious consequences. The non-medical uses are so interwoven with the medical uses that it would not be practicable to draw a distinction between them in the distribution and sale of the drug.

(*c.*) The habitual use of opium as a stimulant by young people is generally condemned.

(*d.*) Opium-smoking is little practised in India; it is considered a disreputable habit.

(*e.*) The whole question of the effects of opium as medically considered must be worked out later in detail upon a careful collation of the large mass of evidence before the Commission.

VI.—The disposition of the people of India in regard to (*a*) the use of opium for non-medical purposes, and (*b*) their willingness to bear, in whole or in part, the cost of prohibitive measures.

VI.—The testimony laid before us has been unanimous that the people of India would be unwilling to bear the cost of prohibitive measures. Disposition of the people of India.

274. We desire to make a special reference to the Report which we understand to be in preparation by our colleague Mr. Wilson. The criticisms or suggestions which it may contain have not been submitted for our consideration. We regret that in the discussions which took place during the preparation of our Report we were not placed in possession of the views of our colleague.* Dissent from the general conclusions.

275. In conclusion, we desire to express our high appreciation of the services rendered by our Secretaries. Mr. Hewett met us on our arrival at Calcutta, and accompanied us throughout our tour in India. His duties were of a special and exceptional character, and were most efficiently performed. On our return to England Mr. Hewett began the drafting of our Report. On his departure for India, to take up an important appointment, the work was entrusted to Mr. Baines, to whom we are much indebted for the ability, patience, and knowledge of India which he has displayed in the execution of his task. Services of the Secretaries.

All which we humbly submit for Your Majesty's most gracious consideration.

(Signed) BRASSEY (*Chairman*).
J. B. LYALL.
LAKSHMESHWAR SINGH, OF DARBHANGA.†
W. ROBERTS.
R. G. C. MOWBRAY.
A. U. FANSHAWE.
A. PEASE.
HARIDAS VEHARIDAS.† DESAI

J. A. BAINES (*Secretary*).

London, 16th April 1895.

* The Maharaja of Darbhanga and Mr. Haridas Veharidas, not having been present during the preparation of the Report, are not to be held to have affixed their signatures to the 274th paragraph.

† Subject to the qualifying remarks contained in the separate Memorandum appended.

MEMORANDUM III.;

By Mr. HARIDAS VEHARIDAS. DESAI.

I am in some doubt as to how I can best put on record a few comparatively trifling particulars with regard to which I differ somewhat from the conclusions at which my colleagues have arrived, as I fear that any attempt on my part to dissect any portion of the Report and introduce into the body of it phrases expressing my own view, will not only spoil the harmony of thought and composition, but will, perhaps, not meet with the approval of my colleagues. I agree with almost all the decisions given on the chief points of reference. Thus, if the Right Honourable Chairman will permit me, I would venture to submit separately a few observations on those points where I think my own views require a little more elucidation.

2. Had the policy of the Government of India with regard to its relations with opium not been assailed from a moral point of view—had the people of India not been impressed with the idea that any reduction in the Indian revenue effected by the proposed abolition of the production and sale of opium would have to be met by fresh taxation—had they not been afraid that the inquiries by the Opium Commission would probably result in a further restriction to the supply and sale of opium which would deprive them of the privilege of conveniently using it in many ways;—and had a number of Christian Missionaries as well as a few others not been somehow or other strongly prejudiced against the use of opium except for purely and authoritatively medical purposes—I am confident that opium would have been shown before our Commission with greater justice to itself, as regards its capability of doing both good and harm, than what we have been able to learn of during our Inquiry. I believe it is fair to say that opium was introduced to us by both sides in a more or less exaggerated form with respect to its faults or otherwise.

3. Bearing this in mind, I should be disposed to pass over without too careful scrutiny the whole of the evidence which bears the marks of exaggeration, whether medical, military, or missionary. I would, on the other hand, lay great stress on the evidence given on behalf of the Native States, where opium is grown and also where it is not grown, and by the people in general, who have expressed their desire not to prohibit the production and sale of opium as proposed, and also their unwillingness to bear any tax to make up the loss in the Indian revenue that would be caused by the enforcement of the proposed prohibition of the product and sale of opium. So far as can be seen from the evidence before the Commission, the laudable endeavours of the disinterested and philanthropic associations at whose instance the Commission has been appointed have not been successful in making out a case against the use of opium in a manner that would necessitate such prohibition. But the evidence has shown us very conclusively that any further restriction against the use of opium would contribute towards the increase of the use of alcohol, which is admitted by all parties to be much more injurious and mischievous than opium, not to speak of its objectionable character in a majority of cases from a religious point of view. But it is greatly to be wondered at and regretted that this has not adequately drawn the attention of Government, inasmuch as they have adopted much more stringent measures against the use of opium than that of alcohol. For instance, it is illegal to sell or to keep more than from two to ten tolás of opium, while country liquors can be sold or kept up to a gallon without hitch or hindrance, and any quantity of European liquors can be imported as well as sold and kept even without a license. We have also evidence to show that the use of alcohol is spreading far and wide. It strikes the people of this country as unfair that before any attempt is made to relieve India from the effects of alcohol, which is comparatively a far more injurious and objectionable article, there should have been a movement, disinterested and sympathising as it is, to suppress the use, except for medical purposes, of a stuff like opium, which is admittedly far less harmful and objectionable so far as India is concerned. I would now leave it to the British people, noble-minded and sympathetic as they are, to see their way to adopting effective measures to check the exportation of European alcohol to India.

4. As regards the exportation of Indian opium to China. To abolish it would result in a great loss to Indian revenue. This loss the Indian people are unwilling and unable to make up by accepting the imposition of any additional tax. They have no voice to

check or reduce the expenditure made in India or in England to be borne by India, which is admittedly poor and already over-taxed, while its resources are constantly drained off to foreign countries without adequate and substantial return from them. It may also be mentioned that India is a dependency of England, while China is not that of India. Under these circumstances it cannot be for a moment imagined that those British people, who have disinterestedly taken up this cause for the good of India and China, would ever expect India, helpless as it is, to extend its generosity, at a great loss, towards China, in the manner proposed before the Commission. Again, viewing this point in another light, it is the Chinese Government that should take stringent measures against the importation of Indian opium, if it believes that it is either injured or ruined by accepting the drug from India. This it can well do now when it has been publicly announced before Parliament on behalf of the British Government that the Chinese Government are under no Treaty obligations to accept Indian opium, if they choose to refuse it. But if the Chinese Government, from past experience, still entertain any fears as to the *bonâ fide* carrying out of the authoritative announcement made before Parliament, I would suggest that an official communication might be sent from the British Government to the Chinese Government, informing the latter that any action on their part towards the stoppage of the importation of Indian opium into China, would be unhampered by the treaty obligations entered into by them with the British Government. I am, however, afraid China would not be prepared to do so, so long as it allows an extensive growth of opium on its own land, and also accepts importation of the drug from Turkey and Persia. Thus any attempt from outside for the benefit of China, would, if I have been able to see through the subject correctly, be ineffective, unless China takes the initiative in adopting the strictest measures, first against the cultivation of opium on its own land, and then gradually against the importation of the drug from foreign countries.

5. Though I am not prepared to agree altogether to the reasons stated in Section VII. of the Draft Report, in support of the Bengal Opium Monopoly, I feel inclined to acquiesce in its continuance so long as no better, or less objectionable, way of the manufacture and sale of opium has been brought to the notice of the Commission. But from the evidence before us I see reason to believe that the convenience and interests of the improvident and ignorant opium cultivators have suffered in the interests of the monopoly. The zeal of the officers engaged on the monopoly establishment, with some exceptions, appears to have been mostly directed to secure the interests of Government.

6. In addition to the recommendations made in the Draft Report therefore, I would propose that a general notification should be issued, and promulgated in such a manner as to make its contents fully and correctly known to the cultivators concerned, to the effect that they are not in any way bound to cultivate opium, that it is altogether optional for them whether to continue growing opium or to give it up, as it may suit them from time to time. It was objected to this during our Inquiry that such a notification would result in the decrease of opium cultivation, and consequently in a great loss to the opium revenue. But evidence was produced before the Commission to establish that the opium crop is the most paying of all other crops; and if that is the case, I fail to understand why fears should be entertained of a decrease in opium cultivation from any number of notifications of the tenor proposed. Such a notification would, in my humble opinion, be the only way of knowing the real wishes and convenience of the cultivators concerned as to growing opium. My proposal is based on the simple principle that when a cultivator pays fixed rent for his land, he ought to have, as a matter of right, full and unfettered discretion as to what kind of crop he should grow on the land. If any considerable number of cultivators within the opium monopoly district gave up the cultivation of opium, Government should either extend the limits of the territory now under the opium monopoly or find another part of the country where cultivators are willing to grow opium. But to make the cultivators of a particular part of the country grow opium against their wish is, as it were, to realise a revenue at their expense for the benefit of the rest of the British Indian subjects.

7. I am sorry to be unable to endorse the opinion expressed in Section VI. of the Draft Report as regards the Vaids and Hakims who practice in Brahmanic and Musalman methods of medicine. They are, I must admit, not surgeons, but very good physicians in their own way, and, so far as my own experience and knowledge go, not at all less careful in treating their patients than those practising according to European methods of medicine. These Vaids and Hakims, more or less, undergo a regular course of study in books of medicine which show the properties of different medical

R 4

stuffs, and describe the prescription and preparation of the same. These men may, in my humble opinion, be much more safely entrusted with dispensing opium than the common ignorant opium farmers or vendors under the present system. I am against the prohibition of the use of opium except for medical purposes, not because I think that no arrangement could be made to carry out prohibition, but because it appears to me to be neither desirable nor necessary that such a prohibition should be made under the present circumstances.

8. I think the system of local option against the free use of opium might be introduced in India as a tentative measure. The Government of His Highness the Gáekwád of Barodá has, of late, introduced this system in connexion with some undesirable caste customs. Government might legislate an enactment on this subject, and let those who choose to come under the law, apply for its enforcement, as was once the case for municipalities. Such an enactment would eventually lead to another—and a more beneficial one—for the check of the increasing use of alcohol.

9. As regards opium-smoking, I do not think orders such as have been already issued to check it will practically bring about the desired result. We have found from evidence that the practice of opium-smoking goes on all the same by simply arranging to be just beyond the technical scope of the restrictions made in such orders. The practice of opium-smoking is generally condemned; but nothing short of its abolition by law will, in my humble opinion, put an end to it. It is most desirable that it should be made penal. There were some cases before the Presidency magistrate of Bombay, where the accused were acquitted only because there were in a house, say, eight persons, and the quantity of opium used by them for smoking did not exceed the total of what each of them was allowed by law to possess. This is in my view plainly ridiculous. Under the present state of law, the opium-smokers can indulge in their vicious practice with impunity. To remove this difficulty a strict law should be made prohibiting opium-smoking in any form and under any circumstances, and thus frustrating the attempts of the lovers of opium-smoking as well as those interested in the opium trade to escape from its clutches.

10. Knowing as I do, as a Native of India, the feelings of the Natives in general regarding the habit of opium-smoking and its effects, I do not feel myself justified in entertaining any fears like those expressed in Section VI. As the evidence has shown that the habit of opium-smoking is confined to a very small number of people, and that it is disreputable, I feel the more convinced as to the necessity of prohibiting it by means of legislation, so that it may not gradually increase. This weighs with me so much that, with every deference to the views expressed in para. 195, I feel constrained to differ from them.

11. I do not see why the practice of opium-smoking can not be made illegal when gambling has been so treated. I do not find in the Bombay Act No. IV. of 1887 any restriction as to the number; but a qualification is made as regards the place of gaming. Such a qualification I would propose to remove in the case of opium-smoking. This meets the objection raised at our private sitting in Bombay against the practicability of my above proposal.

12. With regard to the estimated loss the opium-producing States would suffer, should the cultivation of opium in those States be discontinued. I may be allowed to bring prominently to the notice of the Right Honourable Chairman and my colleagues that the States concerned submitted these figures showing roughly estimated loss only because they were asked to do so. But almost all of them asserted that they would not be willing to undertake the abolition of the cultivation of opium in their territories for any amount of compensation, unless they were forced by Imperial orders to do so. Under these circumstances there remains no question of compensation.

(Signed) HARIDAS VEHARIDAS.

Junagadh,
24th January 1895.

Document 4: Dadubhai and his Brother Register a New Stock Company, 8 January 1906, 'The Nadiad Spinning, Weaving and Manufacturing Company Ltd.'

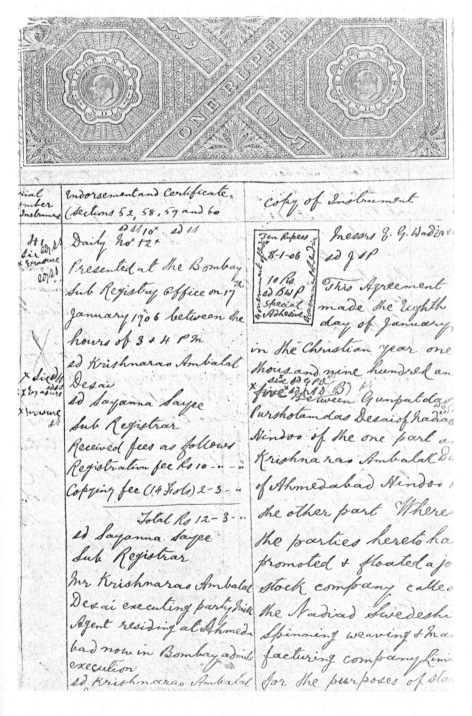

[Ser]ial [Nu]mber [of] Instrument	Endorsement and Certificate (Sections 52, 58, 59 and 60	Copy of Instrument
41 sd ss Sic x Erasure copy	sd ss 10x sd ss Daily No x 12x Presented at the Bombay Sub Registry Office on 17th January 1906 between the hours of 3 + 4 P.M sd Krishnarao Ambalal Desai sd Sayanna Sayee Sub Registrar Received fees as follows Registration fee Rs 10 - " - " Copying fee (14 Fols) 2 - 3 - " Total Rs 12 - 3 - " sd Sayanna Sayee Sub Registrar Mr Krishnarao Ambalal Desai executing party Mill Agent residing at Ahmedabad now in Bombay admits execution sd Krishnarao Ambalal	Ten Rupees 8-1-06 10 Rs sd BWP Special Adhesive (Government of India) Messrs E. G. Wadia & ... sd J S P This Agreement made the Eighth day of January in the Christian year one thousand nine hundred and six sd G P D five x sd A D (B) ss Between Gunpatdas Purshotamdas Desai of Nadiad Hindoo of the one part a[nd] Krishnarao Ambalal De[sai] of Ahmedabad Hindoo o[f] the other part Where[as] the parties hereto ha[ve] promoted + floated a jo[int] stock company called the Nadiad Swedeshi Spinning weaving + Manu[-]facturing company Limi[ted] for the purposes of sta[...]
x Sic sd ss x Erasure sd ss x Erasure sd		

Document 5: Government of Bombay, Grant of Waste Lands, 7 May 1914 and Letter R–1215 from the Collector of Kaira

Lands.
Kaira.
Grant of waste lands on certain conditions for agricultural purposes.

No. 4289.

REVENUE DEPARTMENT.

Bombay Castle, 7th May 1914.

Letter from the Collector of Kaira, No. R.—1215, dated 23rd February 1914 :—

"I have the honour to report that I find that large areas of cultivable lands are lying waste in this district. Recently an appreciable demand has arisen for such lands and I am inclined to give away these without insisting on heavy sums on account of occupancy price if the lands are required *boná fide* for agriculture.

"2. What this district suffers from is the dearth of population. The population went down after the famine of 1900, and there has been no recovery since. Plague and virulent malaria and subsequent years of scarcity have in fact caused in many tálukas a further reduction of population. Most of the land lies waste really because there are not enough people to cultivate the same, because no labourers even are available. There will be no increase in population so long as we are content to allow most of our waste to lie fallow, yielding only indifferent grass. These areas also gradually get overrun with bábul. These bábul forests and wide grass wastes become the refuge of pigs and wild animals, and on account of their ravages adjacent numbers are being given up more and more by cultivators. The numbers so thrown up in turn get overgrown with bábuls. This is another reason why the waste area is steadily on the increase in some tálukas. Again these bábul forests and large grass wastes harbour criminals, or help their escape and so make the detection of crime more difficult. Thus even from the point of view of suppression of crime, we must dispose of our wide waste areas. My policy is not to give away every bit of waste land for cultivation, but to reserve large compact and suitable blocks for grass, so that we can have a sufficient fodder reserve for emergencies, and to encourage agriculture in the rest, specially inviting outsiders so as to increase our population, infuse some new blood, and import fresh capital.

"3. As stated above, most of these waste lands at present either grow grass and are situated in grass areas or are covered with bábul jungles. Hence it is apprehended that in some cases the real object of taking up the land may turn out to be the profits of grass or bábul trade. As regards the grass lands, it is not likely that the holder will relinquish the occupancy as long as he does not lose in his grass business, which he is hardly likely to do, seeing that grass is often more paying than agriculture, taking into account the large amount of working expenses and trouble involved in the latter. But the prosperity of the táluka concerned, and for the matter of that of the whole district, depends, as explained above, not on the grass lands but on the extent of cultivation of the better sort in the district. Hence it is necessary to insist on the new occupants bringing the lands into cultivation within a certain fixed period on pain of forfeiture in case of failure.

"4. As regards the bábul areas, it will often be to the interest of the man concerned to clear the jungle with the least possible delay and then relinquish the land to save himself the necessity of paying the annual land revenue assessment due on the land and of spending a large amount of capital and labour on cultivation. This requires to be guarded against. It is contemplated to give out bábul lands as a rule without any occupany price, but on condition that the annual assessment is paid regularly. Against the cost to be incurred in rendering the land fit for cultivation, the occupant can get the benefit of the value of the bábul trees. But as stated before, to avoid the land being taken up solely on account of the trees, the further stipulation must be made that if the land concerned is not brought under cultivation within a fixed period, the man should pay at the end of that period the full value of the bábul trees as fixed at the time they were taken over by him and the land will further be liable to forfeiture by Government. Of course, he must also have paid the full assessment already during this period. In some cases the bábuls may be so thick and so valuable that the occupant cannot be given the whole of it gratis against the cost of rendering the land fit for cultivation. In such cases, a part of the value of the bábuls will be included in the occupancy price and he can have the benefit of the rest as in the former case.

"5. To secure the objects described in the last two paragraphs, I consider it desirable to insist on the condition that the man should bring under cultivation—

¼ area, say, within three years ;
½ within, say, five years ; and
whole within, say, eight years ;

A Rev 1085

allowing one-eighth of the total area for such fallow as may be needed for agricultural purposes.

"6. I also consider it indispensable to insist on the condition that the occupant should not be able to throw up by relinquishment parts only of the areas taken up by him, though he may be allowed to throw up the whole at any time if he thinks fit to do so. I have thought this condition necessary, firstly, in order to guard against the possibility of his directly evading, by relinquishment of part, the material condition regarding the bringing of the whole area into cultivation within a stipulated period, and, secondly, in order to prevent serious loss and difficulty being occasioned to Government by their being encumbered with inconvenient, unsuitable or inferior plots which it would not be to the interest of any other person to take up. I am also taking only a nominal price from him because in the large plots taken up under the agreement there will be good and bad lands mixed up alike.

"Then there is the bábul question to be considered in this same connection. It is necessary to give out the occupancy of bábul lands on the easiest possible terms in order to get rid of the inferior bábul forests, which only retard agriculture without any compensating benefit. I have explained above that in cases where the bábuls are not specially valuable or numerous, I propose to give them away for nothing as long as the man binds himself to bring the land under cultivation within a stipulated period; and unless we bind him not to relinquish a part only of the lands taken up, there is nothing to prevent him from throwing up plots from time to time as soon as he has cut and removed the bábuls and made enough profit out of them. Thus there will be no extension of cultivation—the lands will again be covered with fresh jungle and there will be no abatement of our difficulties.

"7. Again, a great majority of the applicants now coming forward are residents of foreign States, and in their case especially it is necessary to insist upon their furnishing sufficient security for the due payment of the land revenue. The value of trees in most cases is proposed not to be recovered unless and until the man fails to fulfil the condition regarding bringing the land into cultivation within the stipulated period. So a security clause is absolutely necessary.

"8. I am not, however, quite sure whether I can impose the above special conditions on an ordinary occupancy, under section 62 of the Land Revenue Code, without the special orders of Government. Under this section, as lately amended, it is lawful for the Collector 'subject to such rules as may from time to time be made by the Governor in Council in this behalf * * * to annex such conditions to the grant as he may deem fit.' No rules have yet been made by Government in this behalf since the amendment of the section. And I am advised that until such rules are made, the existing rules are to be followed.

"9. Now the lands concerned, *i.e*, the waste lands I propose to give out on special conditions as above detailed, are all surveyed assessed lands. The rules which are in my opinion applicable in their case, so far as they concern the present reference, are either rules 17 and 32 or rules 17 and 31. In the case of lands given out under the former set of rules, an agreement in form B suffices, while in the latter case a lease in form L is prescribed. No special conditions can be attached to the form B as appended to the rules, whilst I cannot be sure whether all the conditions I propose to insist upon can be embodied by me in form L, without the special orders of Government.

"10. In any case, believing that I was competent to embody my own conditions in a lease, I drew up a form of lease to suit my requirements and placed it in the hands of my Mámlatdárs. The result was that intending occupants were found to fight shy of a lease, as they desired to be invested at once with all the rights of a survey occupant on the old tenure, though they were quite willing at the same time to abide by my conditions as detailed above. I apprehended that if I persisted in insisting on a lease, a set back might occur at once in the matter of the disposal of waste lands, the demand for which has been exceptionally and incredibly brisk since I commenced giving out lands. I had therefore to dispense with the lease and to rest content with only an ordinary agreement, with the required conditions added thereto. I append two forms of agreement as drawn up by me to serve my ends. One is intended to cover cases of lands with valuable bábul and other trees, and the other of lands without such trees. I need hardly reiterate the necessity for the few special conditions embodied in the forms. I trust you will be so good as to move Government to accord very early sanction to the proposed forms, or such revised ones as they may think fit to prescribe after providing for the few essential conditions embodied by me.

"11. I must note here that in regard to the condition prohibiting part relinquishment up to a certain period, my attention has been drawn to the amended section 74 of the Land Revenue Code. This section, read in conjunction with the proviso, would seem to confer on an occupant the absolute privilege of relinquishing parts of his occupancy at any time, provided those parts are survey numbers or sub-divisions of survey numbers. If this be the strict interpretation, and it be held that under an agreement for occupancy I cannot legally insist even on special conditions being imposed on an occupant not being allowed to relinquish a part only of his whole holding, then the agreement will really be valueless and will not ensure the object aimed at. In that case, a lease is the only alternative and the intending occupants refuse a lease. All my conditions, it is true, can be safely embodied in a lease the form of which is sanctioned by Government. But a lease will not do for my present purposes, because as events have proved, the mere word 'lease' has the effect of driving away intending occupants, many of whom are illiterate and ignorant agriculturists, coming mostly from outside this district. Unless we can attract outsiders to our lands, there is no hope of increasing our population, bringing all our lands into cultivation and improving the material conditions of the district. The word 'lease' is associated in their minds with something temporary, and unless they feel they have the permanent occupancy they are not inclined to take up the land or spend money on improvements.

"So I am hoping that my view that section 74 does not apply in case of special agreements sanctioned by Government is correct.

"12. I beg to request that very early orders of Government may kindly be obtained on this reference, as the final agreements are pending the disposal of this reference."

Memorandum from the Commissioner, N. D., No. 714, dated 3rd March 1914:—

"Copy forwarded to Government in the Revenue Department for favour of early orders.

"2. The point is whether under section 62 of the Land Revenue Code the Collector, in disposing of unoccupied land on the ordinary survey tenure, is empowered to annex to the grant certain conditions which the somewhat peculiar circumstances of the district render necessary. He can annex such conditions as he may deem fit, but 'subject to such rules as may from time to time be made by the Governor in Council in this behalf.' In this instance, rules 29 and 31 appear to be applicable; the forms of agreement or lease already sanctioned will not suit the Collector's purposes, and he has accordingly prepared fresh ones which require the sanction of Government.

"3. With reference to paragraph 11 of the Collector's letter, the opinion of the Remembrancer of Legal Affairs may be taken. If even on an agreement specially sanctioned by Government it cannot be provided that the grantee shall not exercise the usual right of relinquishment of a portion of his holding, and if that can only be provided for by a lease, the taking up of the land, which is eminently desirable, will probably fall through."

Letter* from the Commissioner, N. D., No. 1185, dated 30th March 1914.

Memorandum from the Remembrancer of Legal Affairs, No. 988, dated 7th April 1914:—

"As the intending occupants are not willing to take a lease under rule 31 of the Land Revenue Code Rules, I am of opinion that an agreement under rule 32 embodying the special conditions proposed by the Collector is the appropriate course to be followed in this case. This will involve an amendment of rule 32 of the Land Revenue Code Rules. As, however, the forms of agreements will be used only in the Kaira district and only in disposing of waste lands, the amendment may, if Government approve, take the following form, viz. :—

To sub-clause (1) of rule 32 of the said rules the following further proviso shall be added:—.

'Provided further that no such agreement shall be necessary in the case of occupancies of lands in the Kaira district, if at any time the Collector deems it expedient to take an agreement in any of the forms contained in appendix J to these rules.'

"2. A consequential amendment will be necessary in rule 77; the amendment may be as follows :—

'For the sentence 'unless a lease has been executed in respect of the occupancy under rule 31, in which case it shall be in the form of such lease with such modifications, if any, as may be necessary' the following might be substituted :—

'Unless a lease has been executed in respect of the occupancy under rule 31 or an agreement has been taken in any of the forms contained in appendix J to these rules, in which case it shall be in the form of such lease or form, as the case may be, with such modifications, if any, as may be necessary.'

No amendment appears to be necessary in rule 36 (VI).

"3. If these proposals are approved by Government, the requisite draft notification will be furnished.

"4. In regard to the point raised in paragraph 11 of the Collector's letter, I am of opinion that, in view of the provisions of section 78 of the Bombay Land

* Not printed.

Revenue Code, as amended by Bom. IV of 1913, it would not be illegal to insert a condition prohibiting part relinquishment up to a certain period as proposed by the Collector.

"5. The forms of agreements, as slightly amended in red ink, appear to be in order."

Government telegram * No. 4215, dated 5th May 1914, to the Collector of Kaira.

RESOLUTION.—The proposals made by the Collector of Kaira are sanctioned and the draft agreements submitted by him are approved as revised by the Remembrancer of Legal Affairs, copies of whose memorandum No. 988, dated 7th April 1914, should be forwarded to the Collector of Kaira and the Commissioner, N. D., for information.

2. The Remembrancer of Legal Affairs should be requested to submit, for the approval of Government, the draft notification referred to in paragraph 3 of his memorandum.

C. W. A. TURNER,

Under Secretary to Government.

To

The Commissioner, N. D.,
The Collector of Kaira (with the two draft agreements),
The Settlement Commissioner and Director of Land Records,
The Remembrancer of Legal Affairs,
The Conservator of Forests, N. C.

* Not printed.

Document 6: Government of Bombay, Revenue Survey and Assessment, Kaira, 20 May 1914

Revenue Survey and Assessment.

Kaira.

Abolition of the concession in the shape of reduction of assessment in the Thásra táluka after the expiry of the existing period of the concession.

No. 4697.

REVENUE DEPARTMENT.

Bombay Castle, 20th May 1914.

Government memorandum No. 2232, dated 4th March 1911 :—

"The undersigned presents compliments to the Commissioner, N. D., and with reference to the orders contained in Government Resolution No. 10593, dated 22nd November 1910, is directed to forward the accompanying copy of Question No. 3 proposed to be asked by the Hon'ble Sardár Purshottamdás Vihäridás Desái at the next meeting of the Legislative Council, and of the reply to it and to request that he will be so good as to instruct the Superintendent of Land Records and Registration, N. D., to enquire into the condition of the Thásra táluka and submit a report after he has reported on the condition of the Mehmadabad and Mátar tálukas."

Question No. 3 put by the Hon'ble Sardár Purshottamdás Viháridás Desái.	Reply.
3. With reference to the statement (appendix L) laid on the Council table in reply to my question No. 1 asked at the meeting held on the 25th June 1910, does it appear advisable to Government to institute inquiries with regard to the judiciousness of the assessment rates especially in the Thásra táluka where lands have continued to be relinquished in spite of the concession continued since 1902?	The matter will be examined.

Government endorsement No. 2233, dated 4th March 1911 :—

"Copy, with a copy of the question and of the reply, forwarded to the Settlement Commissioner and Director of Land Records for information."

Government memorandum No. 10657, dated 25th November 1913 :—

"The undersigned presents compliments to the Commissioner, N. D., and in inviting his attention to Government Resolution No. 8879, dated 30th September 1913, is directed to request that he will expedite the submission of the report called for in Government memorandum No. 2232, dated 4th March 1911, regarding the fairness of the rates of assessment in the Thásra táluka of the Kaira district."

Letter from the Commissioner, N. D., No. 670, dated 25th February 1914 :—

"I have the honour to forward the report * on the condition of the Thásra táluka of the Kaira district called for by Government memorandum No. 2232, dated the 4th March 1911. The report submitted by Khán Bahádur P. R. Mehta has been reviewed both by the Collector of Kaira and the Settlement Commissioner, copies of whose remarks * accompany.

"2. The call for this report arose out of a question put by an Honourable Member in Council in 1911, implying that the rates of assessment were injudicious in Thásra 'where lands have continued to be relinquished in spite of the concession continued since 1902.' Now that the conditions have been carefully examined, Messrs. Mehta, Ghosal and Seddon are satisfied that no revision of the rates of assessment is called for, and I am of opinion that their unanimous conclusion may be accepted.

"3. Granted that the area of waste in the táluka is large, and that it is now in excess of that recorded in 1902, it may be maintained that the cause thereof must be sought for in a direction other than that of an excessively high assessment. Other causes, natural and artificial, have conduced to the growth of the waste area. From natural causes there has occurred since the last settlement a very large decrease in cultivating power—men and cattle have diminished in numbers, which made a falling off in the cultivated area inevitable; of late years all immigration, which might have helped to replace lost material, has been discouraged. Moreover,

* Printed as an accompaniment to this Resolution.

A Rev 1049—1

a very considerable portion of the area classified as waste is not waste, but grass land producing a yearly revenue for the State. The proportion of it which is culturable has hitherto been supposed to have remained unoccupied because there was no demand for it, but I find now that in this táluka since 1911 the grant of unoccupied land for cultivation has practically been prohibited with a view to the formation of large grass blocks, from the yearly leasing of which revenue was to be considerably increased. Papers now before me show that there is a no small demand for land in Thásra for cultivation; within the past few weeks, nearly 4,000 acres assessed at Rs. 5,893 have been sold for close on Rs. 40,000 without the grant of any concession in the shape of reduced assessment, while applications for some 3,200 acres more for Rs. 28,000 are now being dealt with. Held on the ordinary survey tenure the land will pay assessment every year to the State and will, it is expected, be brought under cultivation, but even if the occupants make a profit by the sale of grass grown upon a part of it, that will be immaterial to the State. This demand for land for cultivation is of itself a sufficiently clear indication that the assessment of the táluka is not 'injudicious.'

"4. The point on which there is a difference of opinion is the need for the continuance of the concession sanctioned for a further period of five years from the 1st August 1909 under Government Resolution No. 6921, dated the 16th July 1909, whereby the jiráyat lands of the táluka receive a remission of 16·6 per cent. Mr. Mehta advises the continuance of this concession until the expiry of the present settlement, that is to say, for another twelve years—fearing that its withdrawal would be followed by a further increase in the unoccupied area. Messrs. Ghosal and Seddon, on grounds which appear to me to be sufficiently convincing, are of opinion that continuance of the concession beyond the 31st July 1914 is unnecessary. I may note here that a year ago the Collector moved for the withdrawal of the concession already sanctioned on the Thásra grass lands, on the ground that 'the grass business has of late years been yielding high profits.' The reason appeared to me to be inadequate, and I was unable to submit the proposal for the sanction of Government. But I see no reason why the concession should be continued after the expiry of the five years for which it has been sanctioned.

"5. The cutting of a channel to carry off the overflow from the Shedhi river near the town of Thásra should not be a very difficult matter. The Executive Engineer for Irrigation should be directed to examine the locality and submit proposals for its effectual drainage."

RESOLUTION.—Government concur in the opinion expressed by the Collector of Kaira, the Settlement Commissioner and the Commissioner, N. D., that the concession for the Thásra táluka continued in paragraph 1 of Government Resolution No. 6921, dated 16th July 1909, for a period of five years from 1st August 1909 should cease with effect from 1st August 1914.

2. The attention of the Director of Agriculture and of Co-operative Societies should be invited to paragraph 19 of the Settlement Commissioner's letter.*

3. The proposals made in paragraph 18 of the letter * from the Settlement Commissioner and Director of Land Records and in paragraph 5 of the letter from the Commissioner, N. D., will be considered separately.

C. W. A. TURNER,
Under Secretary to Government.

To

The Commissioner, N. D.,
The Collector of Kaira,
The Settlement Commissioner and Director of Land Records,
The Director of Agriculture and of Co-operative Societies,
The Accountant General,
The Public Works Department of the Secretariat,
The Educational Department of the Secretariat,
The Financial Department of the Secretariat.

*. Printed as an accompaniment to this Resolution.

No. of 1914.

Copy forwarded for information and guidance to

Accompaniments to Government Resolution, Revenue Department, No. 4697, dated 20th May 1914.

No. 2441, dated 4th December 1913.

To—The Settlement Commissioner and Director of Land Records.

Sir,

In compliance with Government memorandum No. 2232, dated 4th March 1911, I have the honour to submit the following report on the Thásra táluka of the Kaira district. This report may kindly be read along with the reports on Mátar and Mehmadabad tálukas submitted last year and published as accompaniments to Government Resolution No. 8879, dated 30th September 1913.

2. During the course of this inquiry I visited 32 villages, selecting those in which the Padtar area was considerable or had increased since the revision settlement.

3. The revision settlement was introduced in this táluka in 1896 and the increase in assessment on the Government occupied area was from Rs. 1,74,448 to Rs. 1,89,933 or only 8·88 per cent.

4. Since the introduction of the revision settlement the condition of this táluka has engaged the attention of Government as will be seen from Government Resolutions noted in paragraph 7 of my report * on the Mátar táluka.

5. The remission in assessment of the jiráyat area of 16·6 per cent. (or 2 pies in the anna), sanctioned in Government Resolution No. 8933, dated 17th December 1902, has been continued, from time to time, up to the present year and amounts to about Rs. 17,000.

6. The population figures of the 85 Government villages are as under :—

1891 ...	... 74,596 souls.
1901 ...	... 56,934 „
1911 ...	... 55,232 „

7. The serious reduction in population is due to the famine of 1900 and several attacks of plague. Careful inquiry in the villages show that there has been very little emigration to other parts.

8. The most serious aspect of the reduction in population is the reduction in the number of Pátidárs by plague. In almost every village the number of Pátidárs' houses is reduced by more than half. Coupled with the well known fact that among Pátidárs the birth-rate is low, it cannot be expected that they will again make up their former number. This is a great loss to the táluka, as from the point of view of agriculture, ten houses of Dharálas or Mussalmáns or Garássias cannot make up for one house of the Pátidár.

9. The figures for live stock are as follows :—

Year.	Bullocks.	Breeding animals.
1872-73 ...	... 15,751	26,147
1892-93 ...	... 17,482	34,333
1901-02 ...	... 11,903	12,073
1908-09 ...	... 10,978	27,534

The reduction in live stock shows clearly the loss sustained by the táluka in material prosperity during the great famine of 1900. That period has, however, passed away and people now appear to have enough of breeding stock and it is one of the means of subsistance. Complaints are heard among the poor cultivators of the want of bullocks. This is, however, due to the fact that these people are afraid to borrow money to buy bullocks in these days of uncertain rainfall. There is plenty of grazing ground and almost everybody has a milch cow or buffalo or one or two calves.

10. Kaira exports to Bombay and the Military Dairy at Ahmedabad a large quantity of cream; but there is not a single separator working in this táluka. Only two villages, Kalsar and Dhunadra, export "máwa" (sweetmeat made by boiling down milk) to Bombay. However, ghee for sale is produced in small quantities in every village. The reason is that the animals are of poor description, not so valuable as are found in the Charotar and are not well fed on artificial food.

11. The unoccupied area has increased from 27,561 acres at the revision settlement to 37,257 acres in 1910-11 or 35 per cent. The increase is due to the decrease in population, to the reduction in the resources of the people and to the scarcity of, and increase in, the price of labour.

12. The unoccupied area generally consists of Mál land and Bolan land, *i. e.*, land subject to floods and which remains submerged in water during the rains for a longer or shorter period damaging the monsoon crop grown on it. Besides these two varieties there

* Printed as an accompaniment to Government Resolution No. 8879, dated 30th September 1913.

A Rev 1049—2

is the land which is too sandy (hungry soil) and has been given up because the cultivator does not find it profitable to cultivate it in these days. Such numbers are situated not in blocks, as the other two, but are interspersed in the whole village.

13. The táluka under report cannot be divided into distinct groups of superior and inferior villages. To describe a village as good or bad depends upon the fact of the proportion of Mál or Bolan lands in it. The Mál land has been described exhaustively in the survey reports of Kapadvanj and Thásra. In fact I was one of the officers who reported upon it at the time. It is therefore not necessary to allude to it any further in this place. It produces good grass. This year the contract for grass cutting is given out for Rs. 15,000, of which Rs. 10,000 are for the Thásra and Rs. 5,000 for the Kapadvanj villages.

14. As regards Bolan lands the villages situated on the Shedhi river are the greatest sufferers. It appears that of late years, in the villages between Thásra and Wangrole, this evil is increased owing to the outflow of water from the Wangrole Irrigation Tank. It is said that formerly the Shedhi water did not remain on the ground for more than three days. Of recent years it does not clear off after a week or more. Much of this land does not even produce grass fit for cutting. There appears to be no remedy for it. The Shedhi is a narrow river and the volume and force of floods are very considerable. It dries up in most places after the monsoon.

15. Of recent years, demand for land for cultivation has sprung up. It may be due to the high prices of cotton. Pátidárs and others from the adjoining congested tálukas are seeking for land in order to try their luck with cotton. Whatever may be the reason, the demand is genuine and should be met in a liberal spirit. In my humble opinion if Pátidárs or other good cultivators apply for blocks of 100 or 200 acres, they should be liberally assisted. There should be no gaggling for occupancy price, and the assessment for one or two years may be decreased. Above all, such applications should be promptly disposed of. The Padtar area is overgrown with Babul trees and Bordi thorns; besides there is the Dábh grass, a persistent weed and not good even as fodder, to be eradicated. It means hard labour and money to bring such lands under tilth and takes two years to do it.

16. In the village of Thásra, land situated on the village tank and on the Barchanda tank at the extreme end has gone out of cultivation of recent years. Nearly 600 acres are lying unoccupied. Last year one good rice number (survey No. 900) was transferred to another person for merely the survey assessment, whereas on the other side of the railway line in the same village an acre cannot be had for Rs. 500. So that there is demand for land in this village. The lands on the tanks have gone out of cultivation, because the floods in the Shedhi have increased of late years owing to the overflow from the Wangrole tank. But there is a demand for land and the unoccupied numbers will be taken up if some concession is made.

17. It may be mentioned that the Padtar area is sold annually for cutting grass, or for grazing to the villagers, and on inferior lands one anna per acre is charged to the village for grazing.

18. It affords grazing to the live stock which is a source of income to the people, besides yielding a good lot of manure required for the sandy soil of this táluka which would not be worth the trouble otherwise. Good Mál lands produce a large quantity of grass which affords employment to the people and their bullocks, which is another source of income besides agriculture.

19. The high price of cotton has induced people to extend its cultivation. The Roji (inferior perennial) was the only variety grown before. Kahanvi (Broach) is cultivated now. This is, however, essentially a wet táluka suited to rice, and I am afraid that except in high and dry fields cotton is not likely to make a headway. This year Cambodia cotton has been grown in several villages. It had suffered from the excessive rain of this year, but is now growing luxuriantly. It is, however, all leaf growth and no cotton. I also saw a few fields of Mathia (Khándeshi). This variety has also not done well. I have advised people to select fields for cotton which are on a higher level.

20. Inquiry made in the villages shows that the letting value of land is very low. This is but natural where there is so much waste area. As a rule, tenants cannot be had to take up land for cash rent. It is generally let on the Bhágbatai system.

21. Two large irrigation tanks have been completed lately, viz., the Vághroli tank (900 acres) and the Saiat tank (800 acres). Besides small tanks in 11 villages have been either repaired or extended. These improvements are highly beneficial.

22. I have no remarks to offer on the classification and other details of the survey. I find that the classification is correct. It may be mentioned that, as regards the distance from village scale, one uniform scale is applied in this táluka and it is a reducing scale.

23. This year was a good year for the rice crop. The rainfall was more than 50 inches against the average of 33 inches. Most unfortunately the rats have appeared and are destroying the cold weather crops. The position would have been serious if the rats

had appeared early in the season. It is, however, bad enough as there is no possibility of getting anything out of the cold weather crops of Sundhia and Kathol (juwár and pulses).

24. In conclusion, I am respectfully of opinion that nothing is required to be done beyond continuing the concession on the dry crop area. It appears certain that if the concession is withdrawn, more land will go out of cultivation. The táluka depends largely on the rice crop which has not done well of late years. It has not participated in the high price of cotton which is grown to a very small extent. I, however, find that the people are hopeful and in better spirit than the people of Mátar and Mehmadabad. All that is necessary is to follow a liberal policy in letting out the Padtar area. I beg to recommend that the concession on the dry crop area be continued up to the end of the current settlement (12 years). It is no use renewing it every few years. Sufficient time must be given to the táluka to recoup its vitality. The year 1911-12 was a famine year. This year there is the rat plague. The táluka cannot be expected to make any material improvement in a short time after such successive inflictions.

25. A statement * is herewith appended showing the Padtar area, population, etc., of the Government villages.

I have, etc.,
P. R. MEHTA,
Superintendent, Land Records and
Registration, N. D.

No. R.—217, dated 15th January 1914.

To—The Settlement Commissioner and Director of Land Records.

Sir,

I have the honour to return herewith Mr. Mehta's report on the condition of Thásra táluka forwarded to me under your No. 827-S.S. of 12th December 1913, and to state as follows.

2. We have already discussed this subject in conference, and decided that it is no longer necessary in our opinion to continue the remission concession in Thásra táluka. As I informed you then I was having the táluka records searched in order to get some more detailed information as to the actual condition of the táluka, and the figures so obtained would confirm our decision.

3. Mr. Mehta argues that there has been a steady decline in plough cattle, population and occupied area, even after the famine, and so unless we continue the concession more land is likely to be thrown up.

4. Firstly, as to the *cattle* statistics, Mr. Mehta's figures are not quite correct. Apparently Mr. Mehta has included in the figures for the year 1901-02 the plough cattle of three inám villages. According to táluka records, the number of plough cattle in 1901-02 was 10,219. This shows that by 1908-09 * there had been a slight increase and not a serious decline as estimated. I give below the detailed figures for the three periods as extracted from táluka records :—

* The last cattle census year.

Year.	Plough cattle.	Breeding cattle.	Young stock.	Total.
1892-93 ...	17,437	20,217	14,161	51,815
1901-02 ...	10,219	5,507	4,738	20,464
1908-09 ...	10,978	12,382	15,152	38,512

I must mention here, however, that these figures may not indicate the true facts. The census is taken in June, when on the one hand many professional graziers who annually bring large herds of breeding cattle to this district for grazing have not left the place yet, while, on the other hand, plough oxen are on their march through this táluka from Central Provinces to the different markets in Gujarát.

5. As to *population.*—There has, no doubt, been a heavy decrease, but I do not think this has anything to do with the assessment being high or low. There has been a general decline in population in parts of this district. Before famine the population was 74,596. There was a heavy decline in 1901 immediately after the famine. The population then was only 56,934. The figures for 1911 are 55,232 or a decrease of 1,702. I find that during this period through bad malaria and other causes the total number of deaths was 24,396 against 22,269 births. Thus the excess of deaths over births was 2,127 or more than the total decrease in population, suggesting that there was some immigration.

* Not printed.

As to the increase in *waste* area.—I give below a table showing all details of the three periods:—

Year.	Occupied.		Unoccupied cultivable waste.	Occupied.		Remarks.
	Inám.	Government.		Cropped.	Fallow.	
1892-93 ...	4,988	26,669	17,160	26,866	4,748	Of 26 Mál villages.
	22,304	43,003	6,540	62,247	3,135	Others.
Total ...	27,292	69,672	23,700	89,113	7,883	Total of the táluka.
1902-03 ...	4,663	23,021	22,397	18,403	9,270	Of 26 Mál villages.
	20,237	38,157	14,928	49,213	9,336	Others.
Total ...	24,900	61,178	37,325	67,616	18,606	Total of the táluka.
1912-13 ...	4,525	22,317	22,910 *	16,633	10,198	Of 26 Mál villages.
	20,830	35,383	16,168	49,409	6,798	Others.
Total ...	25,355	57,700	39,078	66,042	16,996	Total of the táluka.

* 14,392 Grass lands.
8,518 One-anna and free grazing lands.
22,910

6. I would impress on you the fact that the waste in Mál villages is only nominal. A perusal of the literature accompanying the Settlement Report will show that it has always been held that this Mál land is primarily suitable only for the growth of grass, Cultivation is not impossible, but is expensive, and for proportional capital expenditure the best profit is made from grass. Thus the policy adopted has always been to keep this as waste for the growth of grass. Applications from persons for plots out of this area for cultivation have been discouraged, because it was found that as a rule people spent some capital, but not enough in trying to render this land fit for agriculture and failed. Eventually the land was left fallow or given up and yielded neither crops nor good grass. Thus though the unoccupied area in Mál villages is still entered as such, it is nowadays being sold for grass cutting and is bringing in more or less a fixed revenue.

Thus of the 39,000 nominal waste in 1912-13, 22,910 acres are grass-reserves or given to villagers for grazing on reduced fees. This leaves 16,168 acres waste in the non-Mál villages. Out of this, about 2,000 acres are being leased to cultivators on annual leases. Instructions were issued two years ago that pending decision as to what lands were better suited for being reserved as grass lands, no area was to be leased on more than one year's lease. This leaves us with a true waste of about 14,168 acres in 1912-13 against 14,928 acres in 1902-03.

7. From figures collected I work out the following table:—

Year.	Average acres of Government and inám land occupied by one man.	Percentage of cropped land (Government and inám) as compared with total area.	Percentage of fallow land (Government and inám).
1892-93 ...	1·3	92	8
1902-03 ...	1·5	78	22
1912-13 ...	1·3	79	21

Thus in my opinion there has *not* been a steady decline in the prosperity after famine. The fact is admitted that there has been no marked improvement since the famine of 1900. For this the poverty and habits of the Dharalas are responsible and this has nothing to do with the high assessment. The land is poor and this fact has been taken into account in the classification and so in fixing the assessment. To get good crops out of this land it is necessary to spend capital and labour. The Dharala has no capital, he is not very energetic nor has he any initiative. So he prefers to work for the sowkárs, Pátidárs or others under their guidance. They supply the capital and brains, and the Dharalas do the manual labour and get a share of the crop. If we were to lower the assessment the Dharalas will not be able any the more to cultivate lands as full owners with any success.

8. The present condition is really due to the famine of 1900 having reduced the population. The land under cultivation had naturally decreased after the famine, and there has been no increase in population since, nor has there been an increase in the occupied area.

9. The assessment is not high, and I am sure this is not what is preventing outsiders from coming in, and as you remarked yourself we do not want to enter into a throat-cutting competition with neighbouring Native States or other tálukas in British districts and entice away their cultivators by reducing the assessments unnecessarily to below their true value.

10. The original settlement was made in the year 1864-65. In the revision settlement of 1894-95 the assessment was raised only by 8·88 per cent. We are giving concession at the rate of 16·6 per cent. This means that at present we are levying an assessment less than at the original settlement made 49 years ago. I think there can be hardly any justification for such a concession. The fact that at the revision settlement only an increase of 8·8 was settled shows clearly that full considerations had been given to the poverty of both the people and the land.

11. Lastly in my opinion the concession will really benefit more the sowkárs than the agriculturists. In Mál villages much of the occupied area has been reserved by the owners for grass at the cost of agriculture, as the proportional profit is greater. We too have been receiving applications from many for our grass lands (waste in Mál). All are willing to pay a good occupancy price. Thus by continuing the concession in these villages we are unnecessarily reducing our land revenue.

I have, etc.,
(Sd.) J. GHOSAL,
Collector of Kaira.

No. 827-S.S., dated 21st January 1914.

To—The Commissioner, N. D.

Sir,

I have the honour to submit herewith a report made by Khán Bahádur Mehta in obedience to the orders contained in Government Memorandum No. 2232, dated 4th March 1911, and dealing with the condition of the Thásra táluka, Kaira district.

2. Mr. Mehta visited a considerable number of the Thásra villages in November last, and of course he has known the táluka for many years. He had already dealt with the Mátar and Mehmadabad tálukas and Government have ordered that those tálukas should be resettled. But Mr. Mehta thinks that Thásra is in a better condition than Mátar and Mehmadabad, and that no fault need be found with the classification. Jiráyat lands in Thásra are receiving a remission* of 16·6 per cent. This concession will come to an end this year unless it is extended. Mr. Mehta would continue it till the end of the present settlement—about twelve years. He thinks it should not be withdrawn or more land may go out of cultivation. Beyond this, with prompt action in dealing with application for land, and the abandonment of attempts to get high occupancy price, Mr. Mehta thinks it is unnecessary to go.

* *Vide* Government Resolution No. 6921, dated 16th July 1909.

3. I have lately paid a visit to the táluka and I have consulted the Collector and the local authorities. Mr. Ghosal's letter is attached, and his views appear to me correct. We agree with Mr. Mehta's general conclusions, but would go rather further. I do not see any serious likelihood of harm following the withdrawal of the 16·6 per cent. concession, and I doubt whether it is really necessary to continue it. I propose to discuss the matter in some detail, and had better apologise beforehand.

4. There are, as Mr. Mehta quite correctly points out in his paragraph 12, three kinds of waste land—Mál land which may be left alone to grow grass, land which † is thrown up owing to the want of population and capital, and land spoilt by flooding.

† Or, as Mr. Mehta prefers to put it, which the cultivator does not find profitable.

The first kind is situated in certain particular villages—twenty-four in number. It pays well as grass land and there is no reason to reduce its assessment or to continue the present reduction. All the local authorities agree that the grass trade is a very profitable one. These "Mál" lands and their grass have often been discussed, and I can add nothing to what has already been said.

The second variety, no doubt, tends to be the inferior fields in each village. A small reduction or increase in assessment will make no serious difference. We must simply leave it alone till a demand for it springs up. I deal with this land at length in the succeeding paragraphs.

A Rev 1049—3

6

The third variety should be dealt with by constructing drains and by temporary remissions—not by reductions of assessment and no other action.

5. The population of the táluka was 71,761 in 1893-94, *i.e.*, when the revision settlement was being introduced; 74,596 in 1896-97, *i.e.*, just before the great famine; 56,934 in 1901 and 55,732 * in 1911. The first two figures are of course approximate, but are not likely to be seriously wrong; the second two are census figures.

* Not 55,232 as given by the Collector.

In 1894-95 there were 16,500 plough bullocks; in 1898-99, 16,590; in 1901-02, 10,191 † and in 1909-10, 10,920.†

† The Collector's figures include a few bullocks not used for the plough.

The area and assessment of Government waste lands were as follows :—

	Area.	Rs.
1894-95	23,673	36,196
1898-99	27,441	45,832
1904-05	39,393	71,325
1912-13	39,078	79,091

"Statistics are proverbially dangerous" as the late Mr. Wood wrote in connection with the subject in 1909. But it is clear that population decreased between 20 and 25 per cent. and plough cattle still more, as a consequence of the famine, and no recovery worth talking of has been effected. The figures for waste are a little doubtful, because it is difficult to discover the exact proportion to be deducted on account of land purposely left unoccupied for grass. It appears, however, that the genuine waste was about 4,000 acres in 1893-94 and some 15,000 in 1901-02, and that it is rather less now. On the other hand, Mr. Mehta states, and I have myself been told, that a demand for land is now beginning to spring up—not much more perhaps than a sign of the turning tide but something. There have been inquiries from the Charotar and from the Kahnam Country as to land available and fit for cotton.

6. I have given these few figures in the last paragraph because they seem to me to contain in themselves everything that is necessary for a complete understanding of the case as regards lands other than Mál lands and other than what is spoilt by flooding. Before the famine came a certain amount of land was cultivated in a certain way, by a certain number of people, and cattle and available capital. 20 per cent. of the people disappear, and of the means of cultivation more still. What remains is not sufficient to cultivate the land, and fields are thrown up. No natural increase has come to the population because of bad seasons and attacks of malaria, plague and cholera. The wealth which has poured into the cotton-producing districts of Gujarát has not come near Thásra. And the natural accumulation of capital has been checked by successive bad seasons, swarms of rats, and other misfortunes.

7. So long as the population does not grow, resources do not increase, and better methods of cultivation are not adopted, the waste land cannot be cultivated, whatever its assessment may be. The Thásra Dharalas are not the least likely to adopt improved methods of cultivation in the near future, nor do I suppose they will grow any more industrious or skilful just at present. They will doubtless increase in numbers as soon as they get a fair chance, and their condition will improve. We must either wait for this to occur, or we must get people from somewhere else. There appears to be no emigration from the táluka and hardly anybody finds his way to Ahmedabad or other centres of industry.

8. There is no reason to suppose that population and wealth will not return to their former level in time. If Thásra were part of a Native State, spasmodic and probably ill-regulated attempts would be made to attract cultivators from some other place. It hardly appears to me to accord with the dignity of Government to enter into a competition of this kind. And to my knowledge there is plenty of similar waste land in the neighbouring Savli, Baroda and Waghodia tálukas of the Baroda State.

9. In the villages round about Thásra most of the best land, especially if it is "Sanadia," is entered in the record of rights as belonging to the Thásra money-lenders. They let it out to Dharalas, who occasionally pay a money rent, but generally a half share of the produce. One can find two similar fields side by side, one cultivated and the other waste. Enquiries elicit facts showing that the waste field has been thrown up by a Dharala khátedár since the famine, while the other field belongs to a Bania who has let it for half the produce to a Dharala, perhaps the very man who has thrown up his own kháta. Asked why he has given up his own land, the man will say it is bad soil and gives no produce and the assessment is too heavy. Indeed it is bad soil from his point of view. He expects to be able to neglect it all the year, to scratch its surface and put some seed into it in June, to give it no manure and little weeding, and to gather a good crop. It is not the kind of land that will do this. But from the point of view of a man who would spend something on improving it, would till it well, weed it and manure it, and put a little skill and industry into the matter it may be quite a good field. It is no use to a Koli who has no capital or skill or industry, can pick and choose from other lands, can get 8 annas a day for

casual labour, and can make a little from the buffalo and cow that every Koli keeps at home. It is not the field for him, so he gives it up, and there is no one to take it in his place.

10. It is this kind of thing repeated for many hundreds of fields that increases the area of waste. As the labouring population grew less, the *sowkárs* competed for tenants, lowered cash rents for good lands and got the inferior ones cultivated on the old crop-sharing system. To pay a half share of the produce exactly suits the Dharala. He would rather pay it than a Government assessment. If he is not inclined to work or finds something better to do it does not matter; no taláti will worry him. If the season is bad and nothing comes up it troubles him very little; wages are high even in years of scarcity nowadays; almost the only serious calamity is a failure of grass and grazing.

11. Dharalas form the bulk of the population engaged in agriculture. But Pátidárs have an importance out of proportion to their numbers. And Pátidárs are not flourishing in Thásra. The causes are somewhat obscure, but plauge has been particularly virulent amongst these people. In the early days of plague Pátidárs were less ready to leave their houses than those who had nothing much to leave. And I am assured by an intelligent member of the community that a very considerable proportion of the grown up men remain unmarried owing to inability to afford a bride. However it may be, a reduction in Pátidárs means a more than proportionate throwing up of land. I may add that it does not appear that many Thásra Pátidárs are forsaking agriculture for other callings. This is the case in some places, but not in Thásra.

12. A few words are necessary as regards areas thrown up on account of flooding. It is surprising to find a large tract of excellent rice land, close to Thásra town, abandoned. This is owing to the flooding of the Shedhi river. Mr. Maconochie's picturesque description of this river would have been couched in stronger language had the Vanghroli tank been then constructed. The Shedhi now receives not only water from its former drainage area, but the overflow from the Vanghroli tank. It is therefore less able even than before to carry away in its narrow and tortuous bed all the flood water that it receives. The waters rise over its banks and make their way across country to the Vatrak river spoiling thousands of acres on the way. The local cultivators say that a drain should be cut from a point in the Shedhi in the village of Mithanu-Muvadu to one of the ravines (kotars) that lead to the Mahi. It seems a simple and obvious thing to do, and the best way of doing it should be investigated by the district authorities. There is a low ridge separating the Mahi from the centre of the táluka. I do not understand why no steps should be taken to remove an evil of this kind. It is not reduction of assessment that is wanted here, but a small engineering operation with remissions of land revenue till the flooding is prevented. The land affected in Thásra town alone is over 600 acres and in the jiráyat area cotton would have been tried before now but for this water nuisance.

13. If now the 16·6 per cent. reduction be not continued, what will be the result as regards lands now under cultivation or in occupation but growing grass? Mr. Mehta observes that more land will go out of cultivation. I very much doubt this. I do not deny that a field here and there may be thrown up. But nothing serious will be given up because we charge less than 9 per cent. more than the people paid forty years ago. Considering the enormous rise in prices since then, the real share of the produce taken is very much less now. We have now got down to an area of cultivation corresponding with agricultural population and the means of cultivation, and more land will not be thrown up so long as the assessment is a reasonable share of the produce. I cannot doubt that it is a more reasonable share now than it was under the old settlement, during which the táluka made quite satisfactory progress.

14. It must be remembered that if we continue the reduction of 16·6 per cent. on jiráyat lands we cannot very well pick and choose certain fields or certain villages. We shall have to give it in places where it is certainly not wanted. Mr. Ghosal suggested during our discussion abolishing the concession in the 24 Mál villages and keeping it up in the rest of the táluka. I do not think any case for such treatment is made out. There are poor cultivated fields in Mál villages just as elsewhere, and I do not know why they should not have a concession that is given to others.

15. Nor would it be safe to attempt regrouping or juggling with the classification. The grouping was done well and truly by Mr. Maconochie and it should be left alone. It has not been contended that it was based on survey settlement principles alone. That is clearly not the case. But there were other considerations and they still exist. The classification has not been attacked and Mr. Mehta says it is correct. This may be admitted, except for the invariable fault—a valuation too low for the very good lands and too high for the bad ones.

16. I am told that this year—a moderate year only, owing to the invasion of rats—some villages are paying $1\frac{1}{2}$ times and some villages twice the assessment on account of current demand and past arrears. Also that a similar demand was made last year. Considering the undoubted lack of resources and reduction of capital, and increase of indebtedness both to *sowkárs* and to Government for tagávi, and the fact that the harvest of 1911-12 was almost a total failure, I think this is a somewhat stiff demand, and perhaps rather too much. But if an expressive colloquialism may be permitted, the slight addition

of 16·6 per cent. to the assessment is "a mere fleabite" compared with this recovery of arrears. And I am informed that recovery was easily effected last year and is likely to present no difficulty this year too.

17. To sum up, I am of opinion that there is no necessity for any re-settlement of the táluka or any special change; that the increase of waste is a natural result of present conditions and cannot be helped; that there is no evidence that it is due to over-assessment; that the land will be gradually taken up again; that there is no real necessity for a continuance of the present 16·6 per cent. remission. On the other hand, I am inclined to think that the recovery of past arrears this year is on rather a drastic scale; and it would almost have been wiser, considering all the circumstances, to have been content with a little less. Clearly, too, the Shedhi flooding trouble should be fairly tackled. And finally, I agree with Mr. Mehta as to the methods of giving out land and as to haggling over occupancy price. Without competing with Native States in "cultivator catching" operations, there is no reason why energetic and adventurous people from other places should not be treated in a businesslike and liberal way if they want to try their luck with cotton growing in lands now lying waste and covered with babul. Could not a superior Revenue officer settle with such applicants on the spot with an eye to future returns and the permanent good of the táluka rather than immediate occupancy price? If papers are tossed about from office to office, men get tired of waiting and the season passes.

18. I have written somewhat severely about the Dharalas. I know these people fairly well, having lived for years just outside one of their villages. They are, without doubt, a most troublesome race, and if they have any good qualities it is not at all easy to discover them or draw them out. That being so, I should attach special importance to a spread of primary education. A few days ago I visited the Koli village of Muliad. There was no school nearer than Dákor, some three miles away, and I was soon surrounded by a crowd of dirty children growing up to be as ignorant and unsatisfactory as their fathers now are. The people told me that Dákor was too far for poor people to send their children and said that if there were a school at Ekalvelu—another Koli village a mile away—their children would be sent there. I think this might be managed, and I mention it as a mere example. No doubt there are many other similar cases.

19. I regret also to find that the co-operative movement has made no headway in this táluka. There is only one society, I am told, and that society seems to be far from flourishing. I wonder if anything could be done to stir things up a little. I am very well aware of the difficulties, but perhaps they could be gradually overcome. Indeed almost any village institution is to be welcomed as counterbalancing to some extent the deplorably deadening effects of our local board system.

I have, etc.,
(Sd.) C. N. SEDDON,
Settlement Commissioner and
Director of Land Records.

Document 7: Bill to Amend the Salt Act 1890; 7 December 1922 and Letter from Lord Reading

A BILL FURTHER TO AMEND THE BOMBAY SALT ACT, 1890 (BILL No. XVIII OF 1922).

The Honourable Sir IBRAHIM RAHIMTOOLA : Sir, I beg to move that a Bill further to amend the Bombay Salt Act, 1890, (Bill No. XVIII of 1922), be now read a first time. Sir, this is merely a formal piece of legislation which is required to put the employees of the Salt Department on the same footing as the employees of the Abkari Department. As pointed out in the statement of objects and reasons, desertions have been noticed among the employees of the Salt Department in the Northern Frontier and it is necessary to bring them under discipline on the same lines as provided in section 49A of the Bombay Abkari Act, 1878. The bill merely provides uniform discipline for the employees of both the departments, and I trust the Council will pass it.

First reading.

Rao Saheb D. P. DESAI (Kaira District) : Sir, I oppose the first reading of this bill. When I read the clauses of this bill, I thought that it was directed against the officials of the Salt Department. But when I read the statement of objects and reasons, I found that it was an indenture bill, that the labourers and employees who were to work on the salt works were to be tied down to certain agreements and proceeded against for breach of the agreements. Perhaps there may be some valid reasons for the breaches of the agreements on the part of employees, and since we find that similar breaches in the case of mill hands and employees are not taken cognizance of by the State, I do not understand why the poor men working on the salt works should be punished in this way if they break the agreements. Government may come forward and set right any grievances that there may be of these workers and come to a sort of compromise. Again, Sir, what I do not approve is that this Government should go out of its way to compel our people to do forced labour for the benefit of India Government, and so we should set our faces against any measure of this sort. With these remarks I oppose the first reading of this bill.

Mr. G. B. TRIVEDI (Thana District) : Mr. President, I also oppose the first reading of this bill. When I read about the bill, I made enquiries from people who stay near about Kharaghoda and I understand that the conditions prevailing there are not the same as those prevailing in Thana and other

H 615—1

Mr. J. B. KANGA : May I be permitted to speak, Sir ? I say that in substance both the sections mean the same thing, but the language of the proposed section, clause 2 of the bill, is certainly better than the language of section 49-A of the Abkari Act. I say so, Sir, for this reason. That section of the Abkari Act runs :

"Any Abkari officer who without lawful excuse shall cease or refuse to perform, or shall withdraw himself from the duties of his office, unless with the express written permission of the Commissioner......"

(The honourable member at this point was inaudible.)
There would be some such implication. Therefore the proposed section makes it clear that if he ceases or refuses to perform, or withdraws himself from the duties of his office.........

The Honourable the PRESIDENT : What is the language in the Abkari Act ?

Mr. J. B. KANGA : "Any Abkari officer who without lawful excuse"—'without lawful excuse' is put in first—"shall cease or refuse to perform, or shall withdraw himself from the duties of his office,"—'shall be punished' will come here—then "unless with the express written permission of the Commissioner." (At this point the honourable member was inaudible.) I, therefore, say that the proposed section removes all difficulties, and therefore the proposed section should be accepted. There it clearly lays down three conditions under which a man who ceases or refuses to perform, or withdraws himself from, the duties of his office will not be punished : (1) when he has obtained the express written permission of the Commissioner ; (2) when he has given to his superior officer two months' notice in writing ; and (3) when he has any other lawful excuse. I therefore submit that the proposed section should stand.

The Honourable the PRESIDENT : Well, after that the question is whether the honourable mover of the amendment (Mr. Gandhi) will drop his amendment.

Mr. C. M. GANDHI : In deference to the opinion of the Advocate General I beg leave to withdraw my amendment.

Amendment withdrawn by leave.

Rao Saheb D. P. DESAI (Kaira District) : Sir, I beg to move :

"In clause 2, clause (b) of new section 48-A, before the word 'imprisonment' add the word 'simple'."

Mr. B. G. PAHALAJANI (Western Sind) : I support the amendment, Sir, because according to the General Clauses Act, wherever the word "imprisonment" occurs, it may mean either simple or rigorous imprisonment. Therefore it is necessary that this Council should make it clear if it is to be simple.

Mr. C. M. GANDHI (Surat City) : Sir, I beg to oppose this. If we reserve that section for the purpose of acting as a deterrent on officers who are inclined to desert when they are required to be on duty, there should not be only simple imprisonment.

The Honourable the PRESIDENT : Are you replying, Rao Saheb Dadubhai Desai ?

Rao Saheb D. P. DESAI (Kaira District) : I have to reply, Sir. For such offences as cowardice rigorous imprisonment is not necessary. Rigorous imprisonment is only awarded in such grave cases as theft, extortion and such like offences. But here for simple desertion I do not think it is necessary to

[Rao Saheb D. P. Desai]

award rigorous imprisonment. The object of the bill would be served by awarding only simple imprisonment.

The Honourable Sir IBRAHIM RAHIMTOOLA : Sir, I hope the House will not accept the amendment. The punishment provided in this section is the same as in the Abkari Act. The word " imprisonment, " as the honourable member Mr. Pahalajani has pointed out, covers both simple and rigorous imprisonment. The discretion will rest with the magistrate who will award either simple or rigorous imprisonment according to the offence committed. He has the discretion of not punishing to the extent of the full three months, but can give a few days' imprisonment. Three months' imprisonment is the maximum penalty which has been authorised, and the discretion should, I think be left to the magistrate as to whether the punishment should be rigorous or simple ; that is on the same lines as the Abkari Act, and I hope the Council will not accept the amendment.

Amendment negatived.

Mr. S. K. BOLE (Bombay City, North) : I beg to propose another amendment that the words "simple or rigorous imprisonment" may be inserted so that the magistrate may not......

The Honourable the PRESIDENT : The honourable member may be reminded that the honourable member from Sukkur (Mr. Pahalajani) has drawn the attention of honourable members to the General Clauses Act where imprisonment means either simple or rigorous. The General Clauses Act has provided for it. So the amendment is unnecessary.

Mr. S. K. BOLE : I beg to move another amendment that, if the imprisonment is going to be rigorous, instead of " three months, " it should be " one month ". I therefore move that,

'In clause 2, clause (*b*) of new section 48-A, leave out the words "three months" and insert instead the words "one month".'

Amendment negatived.

Mr. B. V. JADHAV : I beg to move that the word " three " should be left out and the word " two " inserted in its place. The section requires two months' notice for enabling a revenue officer to resign his post. It means to say if an officer refuses to work without a proper excuse he is to be put in jail for three months as a punishment ; but if he chooses to give notice, two months' notice will be quite sufficient, and therefore it is not necessary that he should be in jail for a longer period than two months.

The Honourable the PRESIDENT : You mean three months' imprisonment ?

Mr. B. V. JADHAV : In line 10 the words are " three months " ; so I think the punishment should not exceed two months. I, therefore, move that

" In clause 2, clause (*b*) of new section 48-A, leave out the word 'three' and insert instead the word 'two'."

Mr. DIPCHAND T. OJHA (Karachi City) : Mr. President, in support of the amendment moved by my honourable friend Mr. Jadhav I would say that it is a pity that the first amendment was lost regarding imprisonment for one month. Now we are coming to two months' imprisonment as against three and I hope we shall all be ready to compromise on the situation. Supposing, Sir, for the sake of argument, a magistrate convicts and sentences him to rigorous imprisonment, which may be for the full period, that is, two

[Mr. Dipchand T. Ojha]

months, don't you think it would be very hard for the man to undergo the rigorous imprisonment, even for five days or ten days subjected as he would be to so many hard rules and regulations of the jail at present ? Nowadays we are all tired of these imprisonments and we all know, sir, that the treatment dealt-out to the prisoners in the jails nowadays is extremely hard and we are hearing so much about it........

Mr. M. A. HAVELIVALA : I rise to a point of order. Can the honourable member go into all these matters while dealing with this amendment ?

Mr. DIPCHAND T. OJHA : Well, Sir, I need not refer to others. In order to support my contention and convince my honourable colleagues that they should not vote for the proposition of three months' imprisonment, I merely quote certain instances to show whether or not imprisonment even for ten days or fifteen days or a fortnight, would not be very hard having regard to the present hard and drastic regulations and rules of the jail and whether we think, Sir, that under the present rules and regulations of the jail, even five days' imprisonment accorded to a prisoner would or would not meet the ends of justice. Why, Sir, therefore, should we go to two months' or three months' imprisonment and see the man in jail under the present rules and regulations of the jail ? I, therefore, say that it is a pity that the first amendment was lost and that we should all compromise in the matter and provide that not more than two months' imprisonment should be awarded—whether simple or rigorous I do not say—if we have any feeling for our fellow creatures.

The Honourable Sir IBRAHIM RAHIMTOOLA : Sir, when the sense of the House was ascertained as to whether the bill should be referred to a select committee, it was found that the honourable members were prepared to pass all the three readings now. After this, to bring forward these amendments, one after another, is hardly a consistent attitude. The point is this that the Abkari Act, provides a maximum penalty of three months and the discretion whether it should be simple or rigorous vests in the magistrates. The provision of that Act has been in operation for ten years and we have not heard a single complaint against the manner in which it has been worked. I do hope, Sir, that the Council will reject this amendment and accept the original clause as it stands, which is exactly what it is in the Abkari Act.

Question put that the word 'three' in clause 2, line 10, do stand part of the clause.

Motion carried.

Clause ordered to stand part of the bill.

Clause 1 (Short title) ordered to stand part of the bill.

Preamble ordered to stand part of the bill.

The Honourable Sir IBRAHIM RAHIMTOOLA : Sir, I beg to move that the bill be now read a third time and passed.

Third reading.

Question put and agreed to.

Bill read a third time.

The Honourable the PRESIDENT : I declare that the bill is now read the third time and passed.

Pro. No. 13

LEGISLATIVE DEPARTMENT.

No. 96 OF 1922.

To

THE RIGHT HONOURABLE VISCOUNT PEEL,

HIS MAJESTY'S SECRETARY OF STATE FOR INDIA.

Delhi, the 7th December, 1922.

SUBJECT:—*The Bombay Salt (Amendment) Act, 1922.*

MY LORD,

IN conformity with the provisions of section 82 (1) of the Government of India Act, I have the honour to forward herewith an authentic copy of the Act noted above which has been passed by the Bombay Legislative Council and to which I have signified my assent.

2. In accordance with the instructions contained in your predecessor's despatch No. 61, dated the 21st December, 1869, a copy of the papers relating to the Act mentioned in the accompanying list is enclosed.

I have the honour to be,

MY LORD,

Your Lordship's most obedient, humble Servant,

(Sd.) READING.

Document 8: Government of Bombay, Press Note, 28 June 1924

PRESS NOTE.

Subject.—Appointment of a Committee to consider the question of bringing the process of the revision of land revenue assessment under closer regulation by statute.

At the last session of the Legislative Council a Resolution was moved by Mr. R. G. Pradhan, M.L.C., and adopted by the Council with certain modifications, recommending the appointment of a Committee consisting of official and non-official members of the Council, with a non-official majority, to consider the question of bringing the process of the revision of land revenue assessment under closer regulation by statute, as suggested by the Joint Parliamentary Committee on the Government of India Bill, 1919, and to report on the nature and form of the legislation that should be undertaken towards that end. In pursuance of this Resolution a Committee consisting of the following gentlemen has been appointed to make proposals to Government and to report before the end of March 1925, on the nature and form of the legislation required :—

The Honourable Revenue Member of the Executive Council (Chairman),
The Commissioner, N. D.,
The Commissioner, C. D.,
The Commissioner, S. D.,
The Secretary to Government, Finance Department,
The Joint Secretary to Government, Public Works Department,
The Settlement Commissioner and Director of Land Records,
Mr. G. A. Thomas, I.C.S., M.L.C.,
Khan Bahadur Shah Nawaz Khan Ghulam Murtaza Khan Bhutto, O.B.E., M.L.C.,
Mr. Mahomed Ayub Shah Mahomed Khuhro, M.L.C.,
Syed Muhammad Kamil Shah, M.L.C.,
Rao Saheb D. P. Desai, M.L.C.,
Mr. H. B. Shivdasani, M.L.C.,
Mr. R. G. Pradhan, M.L.C.,
Mr. R. D. Shinde, M.L.C.,
Mr. B. K. Dalvi, M.L.C.,
Khan Bahadur Ismail Saheb Madarsaheb Bedrekar, M.L.C.,
Mr. Lalji Naranji, M.L.C.,
Moulvi Rafiuddin Ahmad, Bar.-at-Law, M.L.C.,
Sardar G. N. Mujumdar, M.L.C.,
Mr. D. R. Patil, M.L.C.,
Mr. R. G. Soman, M.L.C.

Mr. Thomas will act as Secretary to the Committee. The first meeting of the Committee will be held at Poona on 19th July 1924.

No. L.C./157-B.

REVENUE DEPARTMENT.

Bombay Castle, 28th June 1924

Forwarded to—

the Commissioner in Sind (with a request that the Press Note may be published in the *Sind Official Gazette*),
the Commissioners of Divisions,
the Settlement Commissioner and Director of Land Records,
all Collectors, including the Deputy Commissioner, Upper Sind Frontier,
the Secretary, Legislative Council,

[P. T. O.

L Rev 198

the Accountant General,
the Private Secretary to His Excellency the Governor,
the Director of Information,
the Oriental Translator to Government,
the Legal Department,
the Finance Department,
the Public Works Department,
the Honourable Mr. C. V. Mehta,
Mr. F. G. Pratt, I.C.S., M.L.C.,
Mr. G. W. Hatch, I.C.S., M.L.C.,
Mr. H. L. Painter, I.C.S., M.L.C.,
Mr. G. A. Thomas, I.C.S., M.L.C.,
Mr. G. Wiles, I.C.S., M.L.C.,
Mr. V. M. Griffiths, M.L.C.,
Mr. F. G. H. Anderson, I.C.S.,
Khan Bahadur Shah Nawaz Khan Ghulam Murtaza Khan Bhutto, O.B.E., M.L.C.,
Mr. Mahomed Ayub Shah Mahomed Khuhro, M.L.C.,
Syed Muhammad Kamil Shah, M.L.C.,
Rao Saheb D. P. Desai, M.L.C.,
Mr. H. B. Shivdasani, M.L.C.,
Mr. R. G. Pradhan, M.L.C.,
Mr. R. D. Shinde, M.L.C.,
Mr. B. K. Dalvi, M.L.C.,
Khan Bahadur Ismail Saheb Madarsaheb Bedrekar, M.L.C.,
Mr. Lalji Naranji, M.L.C.,
Moulvi Rafiuddin Ahmad, Bar.-at-Law, M.L.C.,
Sardar G. N. Mujumdar, M.L.C.,
Mr. D. R. Patil, M.L.C.,
Mr. R. G. Soman, M.L.C.,
Editors of Newspapers,
all Registered Libraries,
the Non-Official Members of the Legislative Council other than those specified above.

By order of the Governor in Council,

H. K. KIRPALANI,
Acting Deputy Secretary to Government.

Document 9: Letter from Sir Leslie Wilson to Lord Irwin, 26 June 1928

No. 448a.

To H. E. THE RIGHT HON'BLE SIR LESLIE WILSON, P.C., G.C.I.E., C.M.G., D.S.O., Governor of Bombay.

Govt. House, Ganeshkhind,
June 26th, 1928.

MY DEAR EDWARD,

I am writing this to keep you in touch with the latest developments with regard to Bardoli, as it is probable that we shall have to approach your Government, within a few days, with regard to some suggestions we may make as to the idea of arriving at some settlement. I feel that it is necessary to do this before my Government comes to any final decision as to any possible way of meeting the situation, because both you and the Secretary of State, who sent me a cable on the 21st instant, have approved of the policy which we have been following up to the present; and, as any settlement may affect future settlements in other parts of India, I have already told my Government that I do not feel justified in making any offer without the agreement of the Government of India.

2. There is no doubt that Bardoli has become an all-India question. It is now openly stated to be such, and you may remember the telegram published by Dr. Ansari on the 19th instant, to the effect that the people of Bardoli are not fighting against the unjust enhancement of local land revenue. This, by itself, removes the dispute from the narrow question as to whether Government was, or was not, right in the amount of re-assessment in the Taluka.

3. I have, however, not the slightest doubt that Government was generous in this re-assessment, and as to Government's decision being confirmed by any competent authority. In fact, we have known for some time of the possibility of trouble over the Bardoli re-assessment, and, for that reason alone, took particular care on the very generous side. As I have told you before, Bardoli has been prepared for a test case for many years, and, if we give in to the demands now made in Bardoli, it will be a victory for the Congress men on this subject of land revenue all over India. Naturally, the most gross mis-statements are being made as to Government's action, and we have a complete reply to every one of them. We have kept very strictly to the penalties under the Land Revenue Code, and have, in fact, been very lenient to the agriculturists themselves, and, at the moment, have only forfeited and sold a very small portion of land belonging to rich landlords, which is cultivated by tenants.

4. The Indian Merchants' Chamber have taken up the case very strongly, and, as they were a responsible body, I have, at considerable length, replied to letters addressed to me by the President, Mr. Mody, in answer to his question as to what the policy of Government is with regard to Bardoli, so that the Chamber can advise their Member of the Legislative Council, Mr. Lalji Naranji, as to whether he should, or should not, resign his seat as their representative. After two very long letters, the Chamber still seemed unsatisfied, and I therefore suggested a conference with them, with the result that Mr. Mody, Sir Purshottamdas Thakurdas, and Mr. Lalji Naranji met myself and representatives of Government last Friday. We had a three hours' talk, and I saw Purshottamdas for an hour later in the afternoon.

5. The result of the conversation is very evident to me, and they are obviously anxious for a settlement so long as that settlement will let Mr. Vallabhbhai Patel retire from the dispute without loss of prestige to him. You must understand that the majority of the members of the Indian Merchants' Chamber are Gujeratis, and many of them are deeply interested in land in Gujerat.

6. It was suggested that a settlement might be arrived at by Government agreeing to a re-enquiry *de novo* by a Government officer. I said that I did not think there were insuperable difficulties to this, that Government was perfectly convinced of the justice of the re-assessment, and was willing to prove their case to anyone, but, of course, could not agree to any enquiry by

581

independent individuals. I pointed out, however, that any such enquiry must take place on the spot, with particulars acquired in the villages themselves, and consequently no new enquiry could start until next cold weather, as it was impracticable during the monsoon. This meant that no report could really be received until about May next. I also said that Government could not assent to any such enquiry until the land revenue had been paid up, to which they would not agree, as this would let down Vallabhbhai Patel, who has made them all swear that, under no conditions, will they pay up the newly assessed revenue. They talked of the difference between the old assessment and the new assessment being paid into the Imperial Bank, and held as a kind of Trust until the report of the new enquiry had been received, but this appears to me entirely irregular, and shows complete distrust of Government. It would suit their case because they would go round to the agriculturists and tell them that they need only pay the old assessment, saying nothing about the difference between that and the new, while some individuals would guarantee the amount of the difference; but this is illegal, apart from the fact that Government could not accept such a suggestion, because Government can only receive amounts due for land assessment from the occupants of the land. The whole proposal is designed to save Vallabhbhai Patel, but I do not think Government can think of any such suggestion, and the only proposal it could consider is that the difference should be paid to the credit of Government. I am not quite sure that I would not be prepared to go so far as to agree to the difference being paid to revenue deposit, and not credited to revenue receipts until the new report is received. This would show the agriculturists who had refused to pay that they have got to pay, and, even if some people paid up on their behalf, they could only do so as accredited agents, and each agriculturist would definitely have to appoint, in writing, someone as his agent to pay for them.

7. As this question has assumed such undue importance with regard to the somewhat minor question which was originally at issue—as to whether the re-assessment was fair or unfair—it will probably not be dropped by the Congress workers if no settlement is arrived at, in which case we must see it through. There is a lot of wild talk of possible bloodshed, but I have had the Commissioner down here for two days, and we have worked out such a plan of campaign as will, so far as we can possibly foresee, prevent any clash between the army of volunteers which Patel has now got in Bardoli, and the police. So far as we have agreed, at the moment, to this plan of campaign for the monsoon period, we propose to continue to issue notices of forfeiture of land of those who have not paid, but not to declare the land waste and sell it. The tenants are already cultivating the land, and we propose to let them continue to do so, informing them, however, that the crops which they cultivate will be the property of Government, and liable to seizure for payment of land assessment when they are ripe. There will also be no trouble about the land

forfeited and sold, because the purchasers are allowing the old tenants to continue to cultivate, and are giving them very easy terms, but, at the same time, informing the tenants that the crops, when grown, will be their property. There will consequently be no cause, during the monsoon, for any trouble arising, such as an attempt by the Satyagrahaists to prevent cultivation, and this army of Vallabhbhai Patel's will have to remain throughout the monsoon in the Taluka totally unemployed, at considerable cost to the organisers of this civil disobedience. At the moment, I understand the army is costing them over Rs. 1,000 a day, and is, in fact, doing nothing.

8. I put this at some length, as I want you to understand the situation at the moment, so far as I can put it in a letter, particularly in view of the fact that we shall very likely be communicating officially with your Government at an early date. I naturally should like to see a settlement, but I am sure that neither you nor the Secretary of State would care for one which could be acclaimed as a complete victory by the other side, and to give in on the question of the payment of the newly assessed revenue would, to my mind, be fatal. We have already rumblings of much future trouble in other districts which are due for re-assessment, and if it were once thought that the agriculturists had only to refuse to pay the newly assessed rate, and to avoid such payment until re-enquiries had been made, a perfectly impossible situation wou'd be created for the future. I do not imagine that there will be much trouble in getting the assessment from the crops after the monsoon, as I think, by that time, the enthusiasm will have been much damped by the monsoon and by time.

9. Needless to state, I am being very bitterly attacked, and am having some little difficulty with the Gujerat members of my Government; but I think they will agree to the decision of the majority, and my Muhammadan members, and, of course, my European members strongly support me. In fact, I think I ought to tell you that my European Revenue Member, Hatch, who is acting for Rieu, is rather inclined to refuse to attempt any settlement. I do not agree with him, because I cannot help feeling that, if Government make a suggestion which proves to any moderate-minded man that it is willing to put to a fair test its decision as to the re-assessment, the case of Government will be much strengthened. The main point at issue is, I must repeat, that those who have refused to pay the enhanced assessment must do so, one way or the other, as part of the settlement.

10. There will be various other questions outstanding which Vallabhbhai Patel will want settled in his favour, such as the return of the forfeited land, but nothing can be done in this by Government, as the lands no longer belong to Government, but to the private individuals to whom they have been sold.

11. If, at any time, any other point of view on any of the questions affecting Bardoli have been put to you about which you may feel not entirely

583

confident that we have acted quite correctly, I feel sure that you will let me know, for I am fully aware that every effort is being made, both directly and indirectly, to put Government in the wrong. As you can imagine, I am having a very worrying time about this; but I am glad to say that the prospects as to an end of the mill strike seem considerably improved.

Yours very sincerely,

(Sd.) LESLIE WILSON.

Document 10: Letter from Lord Irwin to Provincial Governors, 6 September 1928

391a

No. 533b.

*To H. E. THE RIGHT HON'BLE THE VISCOUNT GOSCHEN OF HAWKHURST, G. C. I. E., C. B. E., V. D., Governor of Madras.

*" " " " " " SIR LESLIE WILSON, P. C., G. C. I. E., C. M. G., D. S. O., Governor of Bombay.

*" " " SIR MALCOLM HAILEY, G. C. I. E., K. C. S. I., Governor of the United Provinces of Agra and Oudh.

*" " " " GEOFFREY DE MONTMORENCY, K. C. S. I., K. C. I. E., K. C. V. O., C. B. E., Governor of the Punjab.

†" " " " MONTAGU BUTLER, K. C. S. I., *Kt.*, C. B., C. I. E., C. V. O., C. B. E., Governor of the Central Provinces.

†" " " " LAURIE HAMMOND, K. C. S. I., C. B. E., Governor of Assam.

Viceregal Lodge, Simla,

September 6*th*, 1928.

[Private.]

MY DEAR————

I have been thinking a good deal over recent events at Bardoli, and I should like to put you privately in possession of the way my reflections have been moving, [for I can feel no doubt that the Bardoli episode, and its settlement are likely to have permanent reactions in other parts of India.]

[To Bombay.]

[I can feel no doubt that the Bardoli episode, and its settlement are likely to have permanent reactions in other parts of India. The terms offered by the Bombay Government and finally accepted by those organising the movement of non-payment had the full approval of the Government of India, and I think in the circumstances, they were inevitable. But we should, I suspect, delude ourselves if we thought that the settlement was likely to leave the situation unchanged.]

[To Madras, United Provinces, Punjab, Central Provinces and Assam.]

391*b*

I suppose that Land Revenue Administration has always been the danger point of administration, and I fancy that this will be more and more true as time goes on. Land-revenue payers are bound to develop a political self-consciousness, and as they do so are likely to scrutinise more jealously any enhancement of revenue they may be called upon to pay. There is here an obvious field for the political agitator, who will certainly not be slow to avail himself of any opportunity that offers for the organisation of a mass movement, on an issue of immediate interest to large numbers of persons, which may embarrass Government.

In any such effort he will no doubt seek to make the most of any comparisons, whether fair or not, that can be drawn between the contribution to national revenues of the income-tax payer and land-revenue payer, that will serve to promote in the mind of the latter a feeling of injustice. You will know all this much better than I—and indeed it is very evident how much combustible material there is lying about. Our purpose must be to prevent it catching fire.

I must confess that I myself entertain some sympathy for the land-revenue payer, as compared with the man who pays income-tax. The principles by which the latter is taxed are clearly defined by Statute, and if he differs from the income-tax authorities about the interpretation of these principles, he can demand a reference to the High Court.

The land-revenue payer is in very different case. For reasons that are familiar to us all, it has not been possible to give effect to the recommendations of the Joint Parliamentary Committee that the principles of his assessment should be more closely regulated by Statute. And, at the later stage, if he claims that the recognised principles of land-revenue assessment have been unjustly applied, he has no redress other than a system of appeal to the executive authority. The existing system of appeal and review is no doubt very elaborate, but the point I am concerned to make is that the fact that the whole business is entirely in the hands of the executive exposes a very dangerous flank to popular agitation, as compared with the income-tax payer who can seek redress against the alleged misinterpretation by the executive through the High Court. For these reasons, *i. e.*, because (1) I feel that the question is going to assume increasing importance; (2) it seems so attractive a field for anti-Government agitation; and (3) I feel certain that sooner or later Government will have to introduce some modification into what is now a purely executive process; I think that the course of wisdom is that we should without delay apply our minds to the examination of what it may be possible to do, in order to prevent the emergence of difficult situations, such as that with which your / the Bombay Government has recently been confronted.

A suggestion has been made that fresh attempts should be made in all Provinces—other than those with a permanent settlement—to incorporate the main principles of assessment in Statute.

[To Punjab.]

[I know you have recently had a Bill in your Council dealing with this matter, which you told me you were still considering.] Such Statutes might include a provision by which a prescribed number of assessees might be given a right to approach a judicial or some *ad hoc* tribunal against a decision passed by the highest revenue authority to whom appeal is now permitted, where the assessment is challenged on the ground that either (*i*) the pitch of assessment, or (*ii*) the pitch of enhancement, or both of these have been arrived at by methods or are based on considerations which are foreign or contrary to the rules or law regulating settlements in a Province, and the judicial or other tribunal might have the power to direct a re-enquiry if it holds that the complaint is just. The value of this suggestion seems to consist in removing the incentive to mass action by giving to parties, who may not have faith in the impartiality of the various members of the hierarchy of revenue experts, or the Local Government, access to an independent tribunal. This is a purely tentative suggestion, but it will serve to illustrate the kind of thing passing through my mind. I recognise of course the natural objections that may be taken to any such proposal; but I am by no means certain that they are conclusive.

We have considered the general problem as carefully as we can here, and have authorised Sir Muhammad Habibullah to communicate officially with Local Governments, drawing their attention to the problem and inviting them to permit their Revenue Members to attend a General Conference on this

391*d*

subject at some early and mutually convenient date. The object of this letter is to tell you rather more completely than is possible in an official communication the reasons that convince me personally of the desirability of trying to put our heads together over the matter, and of the anxiety that I feel in regard to it. I hope therefore very much that when the official letter reaches you, you will endeavour to spare your Revenue Member for such joint deliberations as I foreshadowed, and will discuss the matter in advance with him from the kind of point of view I have sought to indicate.

Yours $\frac{\text{ever}^*}{\text{sincerely}\dagger}$,

(Sd.) IRWIN.

Document 11: Letter from Lord Irwin to Sir Leslie Wilson, 28 October 1928

487

No. 642c.

To H. E. THE RIGHT HON'BLE SIR LESLIE WILSON, P.C., G.C.I.E., C.M.G., D.S.O., Governor of Bombay.

Viceregal Lodge, Delhi,
October 28th, 1928.

MY DEAR LESLIE,

Thank you very much for your letter of 11th October about the letter which I propose to send to Governors regarding Bardoli. The point you raised in paragraph 2 of your letter is an important one and I have had it examined by the Home and Legislative Departments, with the result that we have added a paragraph at the end of the letter. I send you a copy of the addition for your information. The question whether a compaign of the kind we are thinking of could be declared unlawful is one of the points on which the opinion of Governors is definitely being asked.

I saw the *Times of India* article you speak of. I do not know whether you could warn the Editor of the danger likely to follow on irresponsible articles of this kind, but if you found a chance of doing so, I think it might be useful.

Yours ever,

(Sd.) IRWIN.

[ENCLOSURE TO THE ABOVE LETTER.]

Copy of addition to the letter to Governors.

In page 3 of the draft to Governors after the words "as soon as a definite campaign of non-payment of taxes or revenue is launched it would be feasible to declare the organisation unlawful", add the following :—

It would of course in every case be a question of fact whether such a declaration could be made. In the Bardoli case on the facts reported to us we held that such a declaration would be justifiable. It seemed to be clear that in Bardoli there was a definite combination of persons amounting to an association within the meaning of section 15 (*1*) of the Act. The objects of the Association appeared to be—

(1) to prevent the landholders from paying the land revenue due from them;

(2) to prevent the execution of coercive processes, such as the seizure of moveable property; and

(3) to prevent the cultivation by the new owners of lands which had been forfeited for failure to pay land revenue.

The view taken here was that the pursuit of any of these three objects could reasonably be held to constitute either interference with the administration of the law, namely, the Bombay Land Revenue Code, or with the maintenance of law and order, and that therefore the organisation could be declared an unlawful association. It could not of course be said in advance that any and every association which advocates or organises non-payment of taxes could properly be declared an unlawful association. This would depend on the methods employed; but it seems doubtful whether any association of this kind could work effectively without bringing itself within the scope of section 16 of the Act.

Document 12: Letter from Lord Irwin to Provincial Governors, 29 October 1928

No. 645.

To H. E. THE RIGHT HON'BLE THE VISCOUNT GOSCHEN OF HAWKHURST, G. C. I. E., C. B. E., V. D., Governor of Madras.

" " SIR MALCOLM HAILEY, G. C. I. E., K. C. S. I., Governor of the United Provinces of Agra and Oudh.

" " " GEOFFREY DE MONTMORENCY, K. C. S. I., K. C. I. E., K. C. V. O., C. B. E., Governor of the Punjab.

" " " MONTAGU BUTLER, K. C. S. I., *Kt.*, C. B., C. I. E., C. V. O., C. B. E., Governor of the Central Provinces.

" " " LAURIE HAMMOND, K. C. S. I., C. B. E., Governor of Assam.

Viceregal Lodge, Delhi,

October 29th, 1928.

MY DEAR———,

I have already written to you about the question whether the land revenue law in the different Provinces is satisfactory, and that matter is no doubt being taken up by your Government officially. There are however some further points, arising out of the Bardoli trouble, which I have been discussing with Leslie Wilson and on which I should greatly value your opinion. For it is disquieting that a re-assessment, which is an ordinary incident of administration, should give rise to a movement of opposition to Government which becomes of All-India importance, and which, unless Leslie Wilson had succeeded in getting a settlement on his terms, would probably have involved for its suppression a long process of attrition, during which strong feeling would have been roused against Government all over the country.

The conditions in Bardoli of course, arising from its political history and connections, were very special. Nevertheless it does not seem to have been immediately realised in the lower ranks of the administration that a disputed or unsatisfactory re-assessment might in those special conditions provied occasion for a movement of this sort. That danger has now been made plain to everyone, and the lesson for other parts of India is that wherever local conditions suggest the possibility of working up a popular movement against Government in connection with the land revenue, all the processes in the re-assessment, beginning with the selection of the Settlement Officer and ending with the final orders of Government, require the most careful attention of the Government.

The above relates to the first stage, namely, the actual re-assessment, and the orders passed upon it. The second stage was the development of the movement to refuse payment. It appears that when organized opposition in Bardoli first began to show itself, the local officers were not sufficiently alive to the situation, and the movement was allowed to grow without adequate steps being taken to counter it, and without Government even receiving full information of what was going on. A movement like this must obviously be dealt with at the very beginning; if it is allowed to develop, it soon becomes formidable.

Leslie Wilson is so much impressed by this aspect that he suggests that the existing powers of Government for checking an organised movement of non-payment of revenue or taxes are not adequate and that something more is required. I am inclined to the view that the ordinary provisions for the collection of land revenue or other taxes, reinforced by the normal provisions of the criminal law and the power conferred by the Criminal Law Amendment Act, Part II, to declare an organization of this sort unlawful if vigorously applied in the beginning should suffice, and I am not convinced that the situation necessitates the taking of fresh powers. The Criminal Law Amendment Act enables a Local Government to declare an organization to be unlawful if it has for its object interference with the administration of the law, and it would seem that as soon as a definite campaign of non-payment of taxes or revenue is launched, it would be feasible to declare the organization unlawful. It would of course in every case be a question of fact whether such a declaration could be made. In the Bardoli case on the facts reported to us we held that such a declaration would be justifiable. It seemed to be clear that in Bardoli there was a definite combination of persons amounting to an association within the meaning of section 15 (*3*) of the Act. The objects of the Association appeared to be—

(1) to prevent the landholders from paying the land revenue due from them;

(2) to prevent the execution of coercive processes, such as the seizure of moveable property; and

(3) to prevent the cultivation by the new owners of lands which had been forfeited for failure to pay land revenue. The view taken here was that the pursuit of any of these three objects could reasonably be held to constitute either interference with the administration of the law, namely, the Bombay Land Revenue Code, or with the maintenance of law and order, and that therefore the organisation could be declared an unlawful association. It could not of course be said in advance that any and every association, which advocate or organises non-payment of taxes could properly be declared an unlawful association. This would depend on the methods employed; but it seems doubtful whether any association of this kind could work effectively

491

without bringing itself within the scope of section 16 of the Act. I should be glad to know what you think about this. But the important thing seems to me that the powers we already possess should be promptly invoked.

Yours $\frac{\text{ever}}{\text{sincerely}}$,

(Sd.) IRWIN.

Document 13: Letter from Lord Irwin to H.M. the King, 11 March 1930

To HIS MAJESTY THE KING-EMPEROR.

The Viceroy's House, New Delhi,
March 11th, 1930.

Your Majesty,

I had intended to write last week to give Your Majesty some account of the progress of affairs here, but I postponed it in the hope of being able to give a rather more definite indication of how things promised to shape themselves. Your Majesty may have seen in the papers a reproduction of Mr. Gandhi's notorious communication to myself. This had been freely advertised in anticipation of delivery for some time past, and I am told that the emissary, whom Mr. Gandhi conceives to have been sent to him by Providence for this very purpose excited some curiosity when he appeared on his errand. I did not see him myself, as the letter was delivered to my Private Secretary, but he informed me that the emissary was a blend of football professional and a rather raw college undergraduate. He appeared in homespun Gandhi cap, college blazer amd football shorts. However, all this was the lighter and less important side. The communication itself, if Your Majesty has not seen it, was clearly one which offered no hope whatever of accommodation, although it was couched in courteous terms and in form suggested the possibility of exchange of views. The whole atmosphere of it was such as to preclude any expectation of the writer being the least inclined to abandon his courses of unreason. It seemed to me that the only appropriate course was to send a very curt and stiff reply which would make it pretty plain that Government could not bargain or parley in regard to a considered and announced intention of law-breaking. Meanwhile Mr. Gandhi has announced his intention of starting off on his march tomorrow, and his march is calculated to take him five days. We have considered the whole situation very fully, and I am quite satisfied that, though it will have regrettable repercussions on our Moderate friends, we cannot afford to let the would-be law-breaking forces gather momentum, and that therefore, if and when Gandhi reaches the point of breaking the law, we shall have to arrest him. The only exception to this necessity that I can possibly foresee would be that, if his march had been such a fiasco and the whole thing were so ridiculous as merely to be exciting derision, one might be able to leave it alone. But I do not anticipate that this is at all likely to be the kind of setting in which the play will be acted.

The Bombay Government arrested one of the Patel brothers two days ago, the brother of our Assembly President. So far as I can judge, this has been quite a good thing. He was Gandhi's right-hand man in organisation, and was supposed to be going to lead the movement when Gandhi himself had been withdrawn. The adjournment was moved in the Assembly yesterday to protest against his arrest, but I am glad to say was defeated by a very handsome majority, which is all to the good.

The Chamber of Princes had a full week's Session the week before last, at which they began by passing a Resolution of warm congratulation to Your Majesty on recovery of health. When they got to their detailed business they applied themselves for the most part to an examination of the doctrine of Paramountcy, and the grounds on which intervention by the Paramount Power was covered by their respective treaties and engagements. I do not think the discussions did much good, as the subjects are hardly susceptible of being

110

thrashed out merely by the instrument of formal speech. But I do not think they did much harm either; and, although I think the Princes were unwise to criticise the exercise of paramountcy as freely as they did, inasmuch as this encourages the reply from the British Indian politician: "Well, if you don't want paramountcy you must have democratic control from below", I fancy the Princes were happy at being able to speak freely and give expression to what undoubtedly are grave doubts in some of their minds. I rather hope, Sir, that it may be possible for me to have another conference with some of the Princes when we get to Simla on a good many of the matters that, though important to them, will have no chance at all of being discussed at the Conference in London. The upshot of all these different talks is I think that I can assure Your Majesty that the Princes are quite happy and well satisfied that their case is now being fairly considered and heard.

We hope to get our business in the Legislature finished in about another fortnight's time, after which I expect to go up to the Frontier for a short trip, returning to Simla in time for Easter. Your Majesty will remember that British troops re-occupied Wana in Waziristan last November, and I am rather anxious, if I can, to go up to these parts and see how it is all settling on the spot. Lady Irwin, while I am doing this—which she would not in any case be able to do—is going to rush home for a month, leaving here in the first days of April.

With an expression of my humble duty to Your Majesty, and to Her Majesty the Queen,

I have the honour to be,

Sir,

Your obedient and devoted servant,

(Sd.) IRWIN.

Document 14: Letter from A. Master to Bombay Government, 5 June 1930

(Dadubhai's speech as Chairman of the Reception Committee is reported in the *Patrika* of 4 June 1930.)

Confidential.

Serial No. 26

Indian Press Ordinance.

Security from the Keeper of the "Tribhuvan Printing Press", Nadiad.

No. M.A.G. (C)—3, dated the 5th June 1930.

From—A. MASTER, Esq., I.C.S., District Magistrate, Kaira;

To—The Secretary to Government, Home Department, Bombay.

I have the honour to request that Government may be moved to issue a notice in writing requiring the printer Shah Muljibhai Durlabhdas of Nadiad under section 3 of the Indian Press Ordinance Act, 1930, of *Kheda Samachar Patrika* dated the 4th June 1930 printed at the Tribhuvan Printing Press, Nadiad, to deposit a sum of Rs. 2,000 either in money or in equivalent thereof in securities of Government of India.

2. In *Kheda Samachar Patrika* the matter described in section 4 of the Act is published. A copy of its issue of 4th June 1930 is appended herewith, wherein the article headed "Paying revenue to savage Government is a great sin" encourages the people not to pay land revenue. Its translation is appended hereto. Its printer Muljibhai Durlabhdas has made a declaration on 15th May 1929 under section 4 of the Press and Registration of Books Act XXV of 1867 as the keeper of the Tribhovan Printing Press. Its printer Muljibhai Durlabhdas and its publisher Vithaldas Maganlal Kothari have not made declarations under section 5 of the Press and Registration of Books Act XXV of 1867 in order to avoid the obligations of the Act.

Endorsement by the Commissioner, Northern Division, No. C.N.J.P.—438, dated the 9th June 1930.

Forwarded with accompaniments to Government with a recommendation that Shah Muljibhai Durlabhdas of Nadiad, keeper of the "Tribhuvan Printing Press", Nadiad, may be required to deposit security as proposed by the District Magistrate.

---

(1) Translation from the *Kaira Samachar Patrika* dated 4th June 1930 :—

CHALLENGE OF WAR TO GOVERNMENT BY THE KAIRA DISTRICT.

Paying revenue to savage Government is a great sin.

The satanic spirit of Government is transgressing limits day after day. It has also transgressed limits in commission of atrocities. In order therefore to strongly support the movement of independence and to effectively challenge the cruel and destructive policy of repression adopted by the Government, a conference of the agriculturists of this district was held on the 31st May in a pandal which was specially constructed in the Santa Ram Maharaj temple at Nadiad under the presidentship of Mr. Jivanlal Divan. The meeting-place had been adorned with buntings and boards on which quotations containing maxims had been painted. Though the conference was to begin its work from 2 p.m. cultivators from distant villages had begun to pour in from 12 noon. About 1,300 agriculturist delegates from various villages of the district and about 2,500 visitors had attended, which included about 200 ladies. Among the invited guests, there were Prof. Swaminarayan, Mr. Bhailal Sarabhai, Mr. Jivanlal Vrajray Desai, Mr. Kunverji Mehta and others. The President entered the pandal at the time fixed for the opening of the conference, which then commenced its work by singing the chorus of "Raghupati Raghav Raja Ram" and a song sung by ladies. At the completion of the song Mr. Dadubhai delivered his speech in his capacity of the chairman of the Reception Committee. He said that the non-co-operation movement had been initiated by this very district and that the first sacrifice in the present war of independence had been made by this district. There is greater veneration for Gandhiji in this district than for any one else. This district cannot tolerate in any way his internment by Government. It would not be regarded as improper if this District taken any step for his release. The necessity for convening this conference had been specially felt in order to express resentment at this policy of repression adopted by Government, The duty of not paying revenue has devolved upon all persons. A decision should therefore be arrived at after serious consideration.

* * * * * * *

H 175 CON

2

After completion of the address of the chairman of the Reception Committee, Mr. Shankerlal Parikh, the Secretary of the Conference, read out messages of sympathy and for wishing success of the conference from Mr. Bhikhabhai Naik, Mr. Ganesh Vasudev Mavalanker, Mr. Vaman Mukadam, Mr. Dinkerray Desai and others.

On the completion of the above programme, Mr. Jivanlal Divan ascended the dais and the current of his speech poured forth. The text of this speech will be published in another issue of the *Patrika*.

The following seven resolutions were passed by the conference, after the President resumed his seat. Delegates from different Talukas had discussed them. The resolutions included those regarding non-payment of Land Revenue, wearing pure (genuine) khaddar, prohibition of liquor, etc., one resolution said that those Government servants who had not resigned should do so now. After the above resolution was placed before the conference, Naranbhai Somabhai, a Talati in Matar Taluka, declared resignation of his post. After the passing of the resolution regarding non-payment of Land Revenue, one old agriculturist got up and zealously declared : " I will not pay now even a pie." Mr. Madhubhai, the Secretary of the Kapadvanj Taluka Samiti, who had received a serious injury during the first raid at Dharasana, said a few words. In the end, after expressing thanks to the President, a national song was sung and the conference came to a close, and all dispersed.

(2) *Decision of the Kaira District.*

1. Mr. Bhailal Dahibhai of Palaj has given an invaluable sacrifice of his life in the battlefield of Dharasana for the sake of the freedom of this country. This sacrifice of life by him has taught a priceless lesson to the public by realizing the truth of the principle of " living by death ". This conference prays that God may grant complete peace to the soul in heaven of this man who had no addiction (charm for) to material life. May God grant patience and peace to his family for enabling it to tolerate separation from that heroic son.

2. Our District has till now given as much self-sacrifice as it could in this great non-violent war for complete self-Government—a war which commenced with the internment of Sardar Vallavbhai, who is the soul of agriculturists in this District and sanctified by the sacrifices of innumerable leaders and volunteers. Government have transgressed limits by removing and imprisoning in jail Mahatma Gandhiji who is the greatest man in the world and who is the rescuer of 33 crores of the Indians. This District therefore believes that it is the essential duty of every resident of this District to join the struggle. Considering this sacred duty, we, the agriculturists of the Kaira District, after understanding the seriousness and risk involved in the step which we propose to take, take a vow that until Mahatma Gandhiji and Sardar Vallabhbhai are liberated and until they permit us, we shall not pay Land Revenue. We shall tolerate with full understanding and willingness all difficulties including beating, jails, destruction of property and death.

3. This conference hopes that all Government servants of this District especially those Talatis, Mukhis, Matadars and Ravanias who have not yet resigned, will discharge their duty towards the country by immediately resigning. The conference congratulates Mr. Durlabhji Desai, the former District Deputy Collector, Kaira, . . . Collector of Ahmedabad, on their having resigned their posts.

4. The Conference believes that during the time of the present war Government servants of various departments, who stick to their services, become instrumental in the oppressive administration of the Government and so it is proper that the people should socially boycott them, for the sake of fulfilling the vows taken by the public and for the protection of public interests. It therefore requests all villagers, castes and Panchas and Mahajans of the District to warn the Government servants with whom they have relations, to severe their connection from the Government, and if they do not respect the warning, proper steps should be taken to effectively boycott them.

5. The volunteers of this District have graced the non-violent war, by giving sacrifices of their sacred lives and blood in leading a raid against the salt pans of Dharasana for violating the salt laws and in mutely suffering the cruel and destructive charges by lathis at the hands of stone-hearted Government servants and mercinary " gundas " in the presence of the Collector and the Commissioner. This conference offers its greeting for the self-sacrifices of all these persons, and expresses its contempt for the inhuman and cruel behaviour of Government servants.

6. This conference believes that it is the pious duty of every Indian to free India from her economic dependence, to put on khaddar, and to boycott foreign cloth and British goods.

7. It is a great sin from religious point of view to drink or distil liquor. Government get a source of great income from this vice. This conference hopes that the people of this District will protect religion and save themselves from economic loss by its complete prohibition.

3

Opinion of the Remembrancer of Legal Affairs, No. 148-P., dated the 17th June 1930.

The article which contains an account of the Conference held at Nadiad is objectionable under section 4 (1) of the Press Ordinance. The account states *inter alia* that a resolution was passed stating that the agriculturists of the Kaira District have taken a vow not to pay land revenue and it contains other instigations also. The keeper of the Press where the *Patrika* was printed has made a declaration under section 4 of the Press and Registration of Books Act and action against him can be taken under section 3 (3) of the Press Ordinance.

No. 2297-Poll., dated the 25th June 1930.

From—C. B. B. Clee, Esq., Deputy Secretary to Government, Home Department, Bombay;

To—The District Magistrate, Kaira.

With reference to your letter No. M.A.G. (C) 3, dated the 5th June 1930, I am directed to forward herewith for action under section 25 of the Indian Press Ordinance, 1930, a notice (in duplicate) which Government have issued under section 3 (3) of the same Ordinance requiring the keeper of the Tribhuvan Printing Press, Nadiad, to deposit with you security to the amount of two thousand rupees as keeper of the Press. I am to request that you will be so good as to cause it to be duly served and inform Government in due course whether the deposit is or is not made.

Endorsement from the Deputy Secretary to Government, Home Department, Bombay, No. 2298-Poll., dated the 26th June 1930.

Copy, with a copy of the notice, forwarded with compliments to the Commissioner, Northern Division, with reference to his endorsement No. C.N.J.P. 438, dated the 9th June 1930.

GOVERNMENT of BOMBAY.

To

Shah Muljibhai Durlabhdas,
Keeper of the Tribhuvan Printing Press, Nadiad.

Whereas a declaration under section 4 of the Press and Registration of Books Act, 1867, in respect of the Printing Press called the Tribhuvan Printing Press situated at Municipal House No. 1552-Ward No. I, Nadiad, was made by the Keeper of the said printing press before the Honorary Magistrate, First Class, Nadiad, on the 15th May 1929, that is to say, before the commencement of the Indian Press Ordinance 1930;

Any whereas it appears to the Governor in Council that the said printing press is used for certain of the purposes specified in section 4, sub-section (1), of the Indian Press Ordinance, 1930;

Now, therefore, you Shah Muljibhai Durlabhdas being the keeper of the said printing press are hereby required in accordance with the provisions of section 3, sub-section (3) of the Indian Press Ordinance, 1930, to deposit with the District Magistrate, Kaira security to the amount of two thousand rupees in money or the equivalent thereof in securities of the Government of India.

By order of the Governor in Council,

C. B. B. CLEE,

Deputy Secretary to the Government of Bombay,
Home Department

Witness my hand and seal
this 24th day of June 1930.

APPENDIX 5

Document 15: Government of Bombay, Revenue Department Resolution, 22 July 1930

Confidential.

Civil Disobedience Movement.
Measures for counteracting — against the payment of land revenue.

GOVERNMENT OF BOMBAY.

REVENUE DEPARTMENT.

Resolution No. 5387/28-Confl.

Bombay Castle, 22nd July 1930.

Letter to the Government of India, Home Department, No. O-B dated 17th June 1930 :—

"I am directed by the Governor in Council to inform the Government of India regarding the state of the land revenue collections in those districts of Gujarat in which the movement for the refusal of the payment of land revenue has been most intensively carried on, and to explain some of the measures which the Government of Bombay have decided to adopt for meeting the situation.

"2. The campaign for the non-payment of land revenue has been strongly organised in the districts of Ahmedabad, Kaira, Broach and Surat. A statement is attached showing the land revenue arrears overdue at the beginning of June, and the percentage these arrears bear to the total land revenue demand of each taluka. The statement defines fairly clearly the areas in which contumacy now prevails. In five talukas of the Ahmedabad District the arrears range from 35 to 52 per cent. of the demand, but to a very considerable extent these are due to real difficulty on the part of the cultivators to meet their liabilities. In many parts the last season was poor and, although liberal concessions have been made as usual under the operation of the Land Revenue Suspension and Remission Rules, it is believed that the difficulty in completing the land revenue collections in the Ahmedabad District is due to a large but not easily definable extent to economic conditions.

"3. In the Kaira District the difficulty in collecting land revenue in the talukas of Matar and Mehmedabad on account of the poor condition of the cultivators was such that the Government of Bombay decided to suspend the collection of the entire land revenue demand including the demand on account of 'unauthorised' arrears carried forward from previous years. The only demand now being made in these talukas is on account of local fund cess. Throughout the rest of the district, despite strong agitation, the collection of the land revenue has been successful except in the talukas of Borsad and Nadiad. Contumacy in these talukas is restricted to about 20 villages, and the total amount at stake is about one lakh of rupees. The hostile attitude of the cultivators in some instances is intense; their attachable property has been removed to Baroda territory to the extent that only earthen vessels are commonly used for the purposes of eating and drinking.

If measures are not successfully undertaken to collect the outstanding arrears, it is likely that next year the refusal to pay land revenue will spread considerably in the Kaira District.

"4. In the Broach District contumacy on an extensive scale is confined to Jambusar Taluka where 47 per cent. of the land revenue remains uncollected.

"5. In the Surat District the Bardoli Taluka is the worst affected and the hostile attitude of the inhabitants is such that, even in cases of serious crimes such as murder, all assistance and information is refused to the authorities. Contumacy is widespread in the Valod Petha and the Chorasi Taluka and is appreciable in other parts.

"6. In order to collect the outstanding revenue, the Government of Bombay intend now to utilise the coercive powers which they possess under the provisions of the Bombay Land Revenue Code, such as the attachment of moveable property and the arrest of defaulters. The matter which they wish specially to bring to the notice of the Government of India is the policy which they propose to enforce in respect of the forfeiture and sale of the holdings of defaulters. To understand the position fully, it is necessary to refer to circumstances connected with the agitation in the Bardoli taluka two years ago. At that time considerable areas of land belonging to defaulters were forfeited and sold, and the purchasers were given a definite assurance that the sale was a final transaction. Later, when an arrangement in the nature of a compromise was proposed, it was laid down as a condition by those who represented the cultivators that the forfeited lands should be restored to their original owners. This was a condition which Government could not fulfil, but they consented to use their influence and bring pressure to bear on the purchasers of the forfeited lands in order to induce these purchasers to restore the lands to their original holders on refund of the purchase price. This was actually done and, for the immediate end in view, with success.

H 80 CON

"7. There is a disposition in some quarters not confined to the Congress party to regard the present position in Gujarat as being of such a nature that it can only be ameliorated by something in the nature of a compromise, agreement or settlement between Government on the one hand, and those who now advocate the non-payment of land revenue as a political weapon on the other. If the situation were viewed in this light, it may be admitted that, if lands are now forfeited, their restoration would be one of the conditions laid down by the other side prior to giving their consent to any such compromise. If the lands are forfeited and sold, it is clear that Government could not, on a second occasion, consent to bring pressure to bear on the purchasers of the forfeited lands for their restoration. On the other hand, if lands are merely forfeited and not sold it is certain that they will be cultivated by the original holders and, though Government will be able subsequently to attach the crops grown and to treat them as stolen property if they are removed by the cultivators, the struggle to restore the authority of Government will merely be prolonged for another five or six months. In the opinion of the Governor in Council it is essential that the defiant attitude of those who refuse to pay land revenue should now be definitely attacked and broken, on the clear understanding that there will be no reversal of the coercive measures undertaken. In the Bardoli taluka two years ago the agitation was based on an economic dispute. On the present occasion Government are attacking contumacy adopted as a political weapon, and propose, accordingly, not to use coercive measures in areas, such as the five talukas of the Ahmedabad District, where the last season was bad. But in parts of the Borsad and Nadiad talukas of the Kaira District, in the Jambusar Taluka of the Broach District, and in the Bardoli taluka and other parts of the Surat District the Government of Bombay propose to make a beginning with the forfeiture and sale of the lands of contumacious defaulters. They have accordingly instructed the Collectors of these districts to make a cautious beginning and to confine forfeiture and sale at the outset to selected and exemplary cases. The Collectors have been given full discretion to sell the forfeited lands with an assurance to purchasers that the sale will be a final transaction. Forfeiture will not necessarily be limited to so much of an occupant's holding as may be necessary to realise the outstanding arrears but the whole holding may be forfeited. The procedure of forfeiting and selling the holdings of contumacious defaulters will be extended as found necessary and desirable, but always within limits which will enable the land revenue staff in the affected districts to make the procedure a success.

"8. In view of the political aspects of the campaign for the non-payment of land revenue, I am to ask for the concurrence of the Government of India in the use by the Government of Bombay of their powers to forfeit and sell lands in the districts of Ahmedabad, Kaira, Broach and Surat in cases of contumacious default to pay land revenue, and for their assurance that they will support hereafter, if necessary, the Government of Bombay in refusing to yield to any agitation which may arise for the restoration of the forfeited lands.

"9. In this connection I am directed to report to the Government of India another measure which the Government of Bombay have decided to undertake in connection with the land revenue administration of the four disaffected districts in Gujarat. The Congress party, in pursuance of their campaign of civil disobedience, have been successful in instigating large numbers of village officers to resign their appointments. These village officers are village headmen (both stipendiary patels and patels appointed under the provisions of the Matadars' Act, Bom. Act VI of 1887), talatis and inferior village servants. Statements are attached showing the resignations up to date in each of the four districts. The talatis are stipendiary servants of Government and, although their zeal for Government work has been greatly affected, comparatively few have definitely resigned their appointments. Patels and inferior village servants have resigned in large numbers partly at least on an assurance from those advocating civil disobedience that in the final settlement with Government they will be restored to their appointments. If Government now proceed to fill the vacant appointments permanently they cannot, without breaking faith with those whom they appoint to fill the vacancies, consider subsequent proposals for the restoration, as part of a general settlement, to their appointments of those who have resigned. The position is therefore analogous to that connected with the forfeiture and sale of the lands of land revenue defaulters. After full consideration Government are of opinion that sufficient time has been given for the patels and inferior village servants who have resigned fully to consider and realise the consequences of their actions. They propose therefore not only to resume the lands assigned for the remuneration of those patels and inferior village officers who have resigned, but to give Collectors discretion to fill finally the appointments of stipendiary patels in clear cases where these have been active in the campaign against Government or where for similar reasons this action is considered necessary. This action will be taken on the clear understanding that it is final, and that Government will not subsequently consider proposals to bring pressure on those who have filled the vacant appointments to resign in favour of the original holders. In the case of patels appointed under the provisions of the Matadars' Act (Bom. Act VI of 1887) the position is that those who have resigned may have their life interest forfeited with the sanction of Government. The life interest of officiating patels may also be forfeited under the Act for disloyalty amounting to grave misconduct while the resignation of a Matadar involves the sacrifice of his life interest in the mata. In the case of those who resign their rights or appointments under the Matadars' Act, Government intend to allow their resignations to have full effect and, as in the case of stipendiary patels, not to consider subsequent requests that resignations should be cancelled wholesale as part of a general settlement between Government and the promoters of the civil disobedience campaign. I am to request that the Government of India will also give their concurrence to the policy to be pursued by the Government of Bombay in regard to village officers, including Matadars, who have resigned their rights and appointments in the course of the civil disobedience campaign."

Letter from the Government of India, Home Department (Political), No. D.—4166/30 dated 3rd July 1930 :—

"I am directed to refer to your letter No. O.B., Revenue Department, dated 17th June 1930, which contains a statement of the present position, and of the policy which the Government of Bombay propose to pursue in regard to the land revenue administration of certain districts of Gujerat. The Government of India observe with satisfaction that, while the local Government propose to adopt strong measures in regard to the non-payment of land revenue when this is connected with the civil disobedience movement, it is their intention to deal generously with cases in which the failure to make payment is due to economic distress. They also approve of the policy of proceeding with caution in the first instance and of restricting forfeiture and sale of lands at the outset to selected and exemplary cases.

"2. The Government of Bombay request the concurrence of the Government of India in the use in these districts of the powers of forfeiture and sale of land in cases of contumacious default to pay land revenue, and an assurance that they will support hereafter, if necessary, the local Government in refusing to yield to any agitation which may arise for the restoration of the forfeited lands. The Government of Bombay also ask for the concurrence of the Government of India in the policy to be pursued in regard to village officers who have resigned their rights and appointments in the course of the civil disobedience campaign, in accordance with which discretion will be given to Collectors to take certain action described in paragraph 9 of the letter under reply on the clear understanding that the action will be final and that Government will not subsequently consider proposals to bring pressure on those who have filled the vacant posts to resign in favour of the original holders. The Government of India have no doubt that the Bombay Government will, if they consider it desirable, have warnings given to the village officers concerned, either generally or individually, before their posts are filled, of the consequences of not resuming their duties."

"3. I am to say that the Government of India attach the utmost importance to the pursuit of a firm and consistent policy in order to defeat the attempts that are being made by the organisers of the civil disobedience movement to paralyse the revenue administration in Gujerat. They fully concur in the measures which it is proposed to take, and they have no hesitation in giving the assurances for which the Government of Bombay ask."

RESOLUTION.—Copies of the letter from the Government of India and of the letter to which it is a reply should be forwarded to the officers concerned fo. information and guidance.

By order of the Governor in Council,

G. K. JOSHI,

Under Secretary to the Government of Bombay.

G. R., R. D., No. 5387/28-Confl., dated the 22nd July 1930.

To

The Commissioner, Northern Division,
The Commissioners, Central and Southern Divisions,
The Collector of Ahmedabad,
The Collector of Kaira,
The Collector of Broach,
The Collector of Surat,
The Settlement Commissioner and Director of Land Records,
The Finance Department,
The Home Department.

No. of 1930.

Copy forwarded for information and guidance to

Document 16: Court Order sentencing Dadubhai to five months rigorous imprisonment, 13 October 1930

In the Court of M.A. Faruqui F.C. S.D. Magistrate N.D.
Kaira.

[illegible] vs. Dadubhai [illegible]urshottamdas Desai.

The case against Mr. Dadubhai is under section 17(1) of the Criminal Law Amendment Act of 1906 (xiv of 1908) in that he was and continues to be a member and president of the Kaira Jilla Samiti with its head office at Nadiad. He is popularly known as the Sar Mukhtar or dictator . Act XIV of 1908 is extended to Bombay Presidency under Government of India Notification No. P. .L. 15 of 4-1-10 . Under their Notification No. S.D. 4471 dated 10-10-1930 the Government of Bombay have declared the Kaira Jilla Samiti as an unlawful associaition (Exh. 2-4). Mr. Dadubhai by reason of being its member and president and continuing as such becomes guilty of the offence under section 17(1) of Act XIV of 1908. Mr. Dadubhai declines to take any part in the proceedings . The evidence offered by prosecution is adequate to bring home the guilt to Mr. Dadubhai . It is not denied he is its member and President [illegible] Kaira Jilla Samiti has been declared an Unlawful Associaition and being its member is made an offence. The offence against Mr. Dadubhai is clear and I hold it proved. I convict him under section 17(1) of the Act and sentence him to a term of 6 months' rigorous imprisonment and a fine of Rs. 500 , in default of fine he shall undergo rigorous imprisonment for a month and a half. Mr. Dadubhai [illegible] Zamindar — a [illegible] of respectable family and an [illegible]. I therefore class him as " A."

The fine to be recovered under section 386 C.P.C.

Na[illegible]
13-[illegible].

Sd. M.A. Faruqu i.
S.D.M.N.D.

Document 17: Charotar Patidar's Marriage Circles (Gols)

In 1697 the leader of Charotar Patidars, Vir Vasandas, named Nadiad, Sojitra and Vaso as the top Kulin villages. All the other villages were considered lower than the above three. To these three were added the small population of the Desais of Savli which is south of the River Mahi. Immediately below these three and a half villages came the ten villages of Bhadran, Dharmaj, Karamsad, Nar, Od, Pij, Sunav, Tarapur, Uttarsanda and Virsad. Later, in the nineteenth century, Bhadran, Dharmaj and Karamsad experienced relative prosperity. Thus they were able to join the top three to form the now famous Chhagam. While Tarapur and Virsad broke away and have remained separate. In 1901 Nar, Od, Pij, Sunav and Uttarsanda formed their own gol. The present grouping is of 182 Patidar (Patel) villages divided into 10 gols. In the list of village groupings the name of the Taluka is shown in brackets. Most villages are shown on the two maps which follow after the document.

A grouping of so many inter-connected villages provided a formidable phalanx against any outside power. This was the might and muscle behind the leaders of Gujarat (which included Mahatma Gandhi).

(Courtesy of David Hardiman).

1. *The Chhagam*
   1. Bhadran
   2. Dharmaj (Petlad)
   3. Karamsad (Anand)
   4. Nadiad
   5. Sojitra (Petlad)
   6. Vaso (Petlad)

2. *The Five Villages*
   1. Nar (Petlad)
   2. Od (Anand)
   3. Pij (Petlad)
   4. Sunav (Borsad)
   5. Uttarsanda (Nadiad)

3. *The Nine Villages*

The original group of nine expanded in the early twentieth century to twenty-two by 1930. Now there are twenty-seven villages in this gol.

1. Chikhodra (Anand)
2. Jharola (Bhadran)
3. Khambholaj (Anand)
4. Ras (Borsad)
5. Rudel (Bhadran)
6. Saipur (Borsad)
7. Sarsa (Anand)
8. Vadod (Anand)
9. Vasad (Anand)

+

10. Adas (Anand)
11. Amod (Borsad)
12. Bhurakui (Petlad)
13. Bochason (Borsad)

14. Gana (Anand)
15. Isnav (Borsad)
16. Kanisa (Bhadran)
17. Navli (Anand)
18. Pandoli (Borsad)
19. Ranoli (Petlad)
20. Runaj (Petlad)
21. Sinjivada (Matar)
22. Sisva (Bhadran)

4. *The Twenty-seven Villages*

This gol was founded around 1900 by a Patidar of Chakalashi. Originally, there were twenty-seven villages, but by 1930 it had expanded to thirty-four. I only managed to find out the names of five of these extra seven villages. Now there are fifty-six villages in this gol

1. Alindra (Matar)
2. Alindra (Nadiad)
3. Anand
4. Bakrol (Petlad)
5. Bandhani (Petlad)
6. Boriavi (Anand)
7. Chakalashi (Nadiad)
8. Changa (Petlad)
9. Dabhan (Nadiad)
10. Dabhou (Petlad)
11. Demol (Petlad)
12. Deva (Petlad)
13. Gada (Petlad)
14. Kanjri (Nadiad)
15. Khandali (Matar)
16. Mahelav (Petlad)
17. Maholel (Nadiad)
18. Mahudha (Nadiad)
19. Malataj (Petlad)
20. Napad (Anand)
21. Narsanda (Nadiad)
22. Palana (Petlad)
23. Piplav (Borsad)
24. Ramol (Petlad)
25. Salun (Nadiad)
26. Sanjaya (Petlad)
27. Thamna (Anand)

+

28. Mogari (Petlad)

29. Napa (Borsad)
30. Palaj (Borsad)
31. Valvod (Bhadran)
32. Vanthvali (Mehmedabad)
33. ?
34. ?

5. The Twenty-one Villages of Borsad

This gol was founded in 1859–60 with an original group of four villages. It expanded within a few years to nine villages. By 1930, there were twenty-one, and today there are twenty-four.

1. Agas (Petlad)
2. Anklav (Borsad)
3. Ashi (Borsad)
4. Bodal (Borsad)
5. Boria (Petlad)
6. Borsad
7. Dabhashi (Borsad)
8. Dantali (Petlad)
9. Davol (Borsad)
10. Dedarda (Borsad)
11. Dhundakuva (Borsad)
12. Ghunteli (Petlad)
13. Joshikuva (Bhadran)
14. Kavitha (Petlad)
15. Sandesar (Anand)
16. Sihol (Petlad)
17. Simarda (Petlad)
18. Surkuva (Borsad)
19. Vahera (Borsad)
20. Vasna (Borsad)
21. Virol (Borsad)

6. The Twenty-two villages of Nadiad

This gol was founded in 1876 by a Patidar of Bhumel. There were eight villages originally. By the early twentieth century, the number had increased to twenty-two villages.

1. Akhdol (Nadiad)
2. Bhumel (Nadiad)
3. Bilodra (Nadiad)
4. Davda (Nadiad)
5. Dumral (Nadiad)
6. Gutal (Nadiad)
7. Kaloli (Petlad)

8. Kanjoda (Nadiad)
9. Keriavi (Nadiad)
10. Manjipura (Nadiad)
11. Mitral (Nadiad)
12. Padgol (Petlad)
13. Petli (Petlad)
14. Piplata (Nadiad)
15. Porda (Borsad)
16. Sandhana (Matar)
17. Thalendi (Petlad)
18. Undhela (Matar)
19. Vadtal (Nadiad)
20. Valasan (Anand)
21. Valetva (Nadiad)
22. Valla (Nadiad)

7. The Twenty-seven villages of Anand

I have not managed to get good information about this gol. In Kunjarao, I was told that the gol was strong in the early twentieth century, but the organization is very weak today. The list of villages is incomplete.

1. Bhalej (Anand)
2. Bharoda (Anand)
3. Gamdi (Anand)
4. Jitodia (Anand)
5. Kasor (Anand)

7. Kunjarao (Anand)
8. Lambhvel (Anand)
9. Lingada (Anand)
10. Marida (Nadiad)
11. Parvata (Anand)
12. Rasnol (Anand)
13. Ratanpura (Anand)
14. Samarkha (Anand)
15. Shili (Anand)
16. Surasamal (Nadiad)
17. Tranol (Anand)
18. Vaghasi (Anand)
19. Vansol (Anand)

8. The Fourteen Villages of Borsad

This gol is about a hundred years old.

1. Bhatial (Petlad)
2. Bhavanipura (Borsad)

3. Davalpura (Borsad)
4. Phagani (Cambay)
5. Golel (Borsad)
6. Israma (Borsad)
7. Jesarva (Borsad)
8. Naman (Borsad)
9. Rangaipura (Borsad)
10. Rupiapura (Borsad)
11. Santokpura (Borsad)
12. Shahpur (Cambay)
13. Vadeli (Borsad)
14. Vishrampura (Petlad)

9. The Sixteen Villages of Borsad

The gol was founded in 1923 with sixteen villages and has taken in no new members since then.

1. Alarsa (Borsad)
2. Ambav (Borsad)
3. Anklav (Borsad)
4. Asodar (Borsad)
5. Bhetasi (Borsad)
6. Dahemi (Borsad)
7. Haldari (Borsad)
8. Kantharia (Borsad)
9. Khadol (Borsad)
10. Kinkhalod (Bhadran)
11. Lalpura (Bhadran)
12. Nisraya (Borsad)
13. Pamol (Borsad)
14. Pipli (Bhadran)
15. Singlav (Borsad)
16. Umlav (Borsad)

10. The Sixteen Villages of Petlad

This gol was formed in 1900 with four villages. By 1925, it had expanded to sixteen. At present, there are eighteen villages in the gol.

1. Danteli (Borsad)
2. Devataj (Matar)
3. Jalsan (Bhadran)
4. Jalundh (Bhadran)
5. Jantral (Borsad)
6. Kanjhat (Bhadran)
7. Khadana (Borsad)
8. Khotavi (Petlad)

9. Limbali (Petlad)
10. Manaj (Petlad)
11. Piploi (Petlad)
12. Sansej (Petlad)
13. Sayma (Cambay)
14. Sundra (Petlad)
15. Vatra (Borsad)
16. Vasna (Borsad)

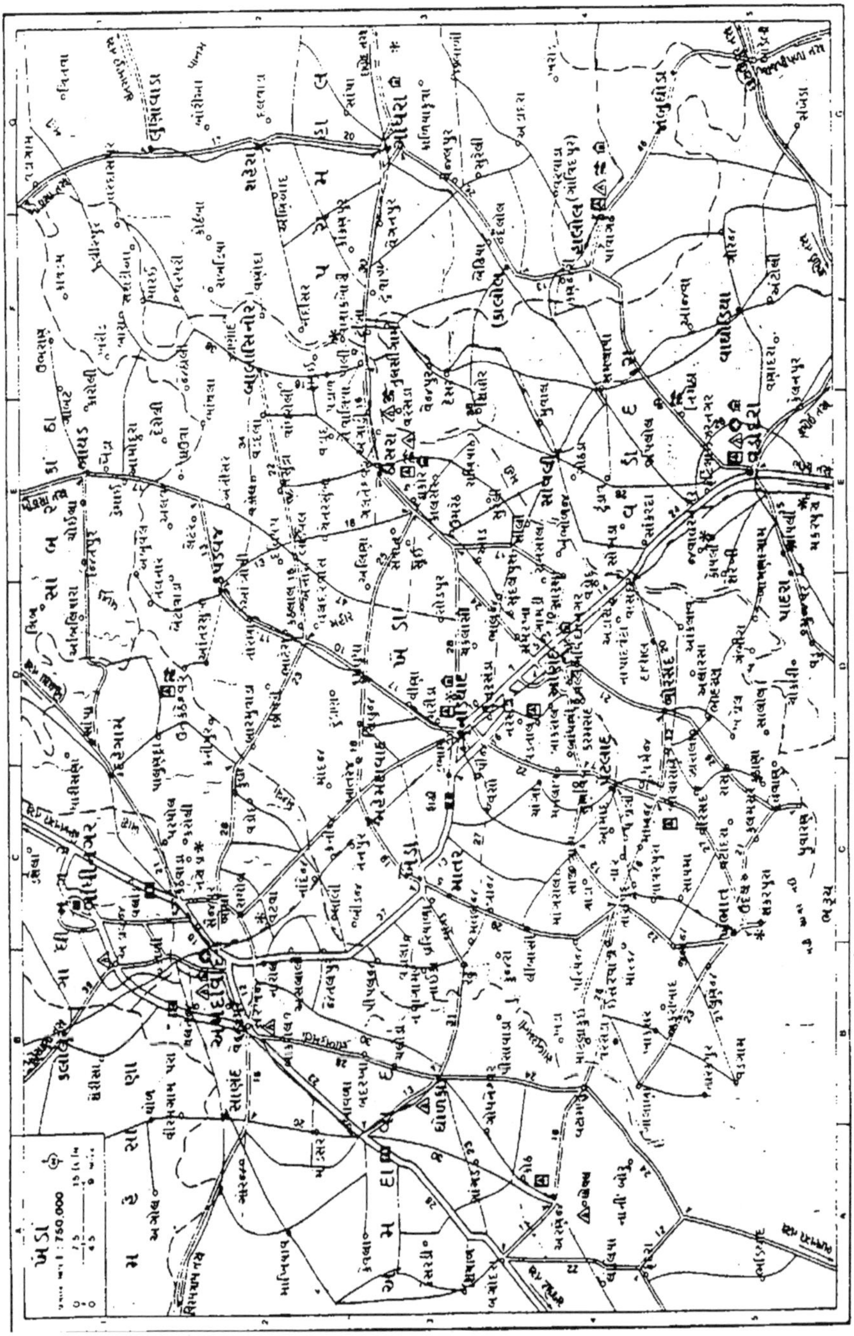

Kaira and Ahmedabad

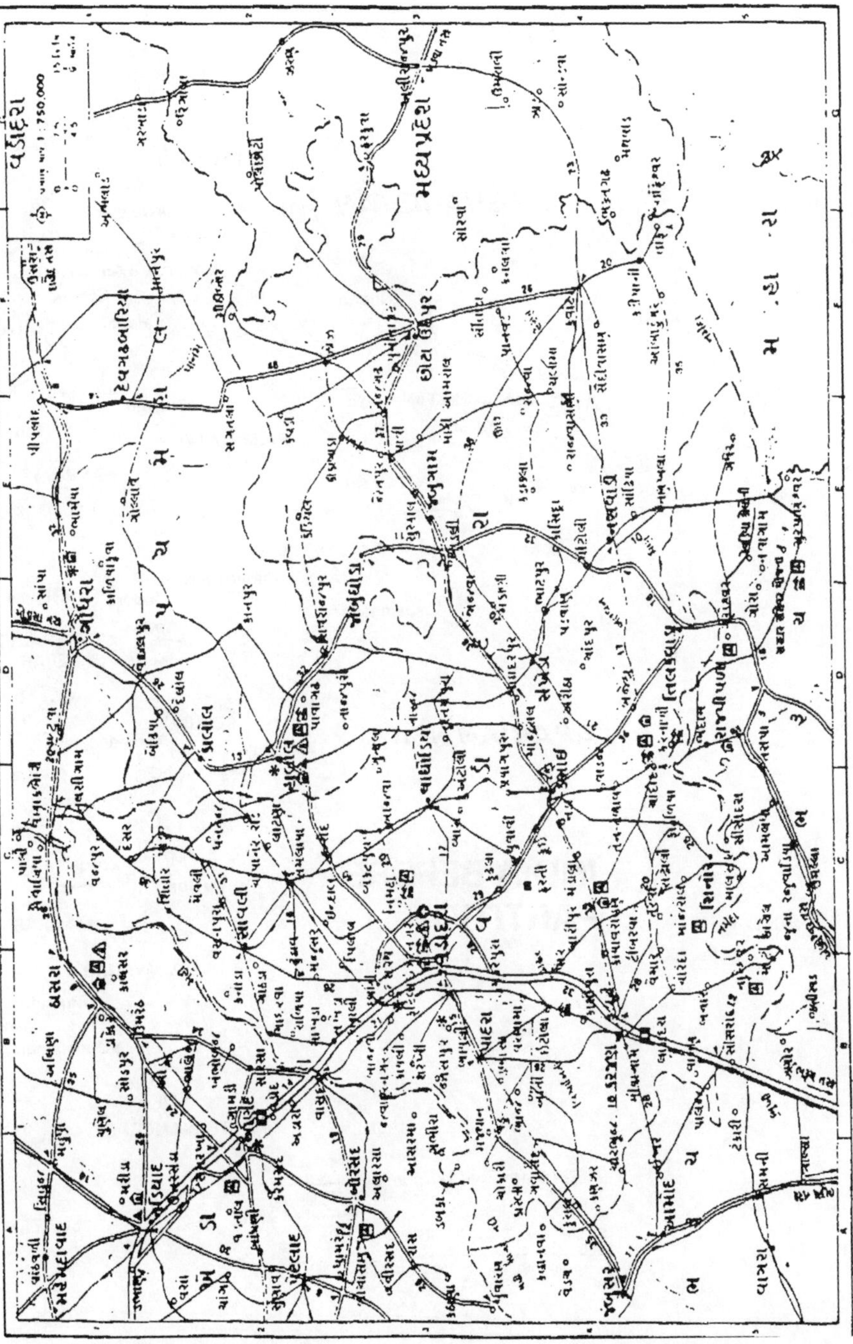

Kaira and Bardoli

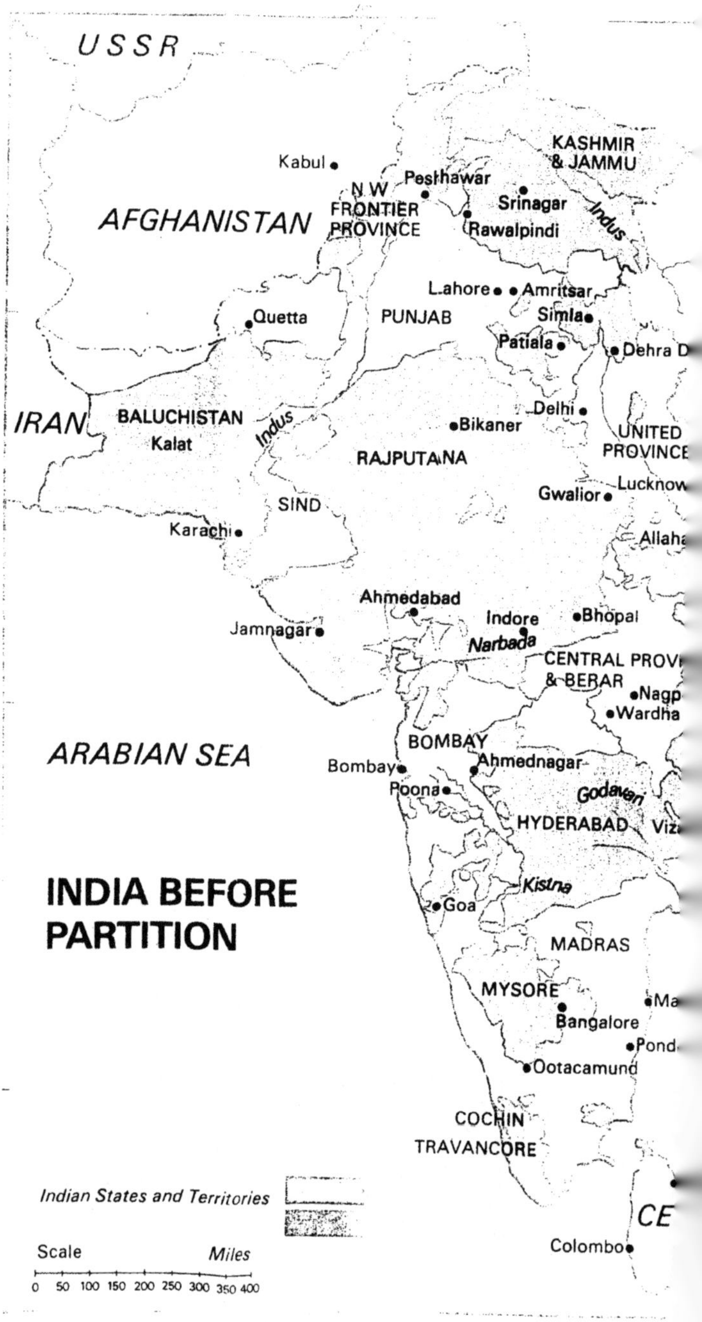
USSR
Kabul
KASHMIR & JAMMU
N.W. FRONTIER PROVINCE
Pesthawar
Srinagar
Rawalpindi
Indus
AFGHANISTAN
Lahore
Amritsar
Simla
Quetta
PUNJAB
Patiala
Dehra D
IRAN
BALUCHISTAN
Kalat
Indus
Delhi
Bikaner
UNITED PROVINCE
RAJPUTANA
Gwalior
Lucknow
SIND
Karachi
Allaha
Ahmedabad
Indore
Bhopal
Jamnagar
Narbada
CENTRAL PROV
& BERAR
Nagp
Wardha
ARABIAN SEA
BOMBAY
Bombay
Ahmednagar
Poona
Godaveri
HYDERABAD
Viz
INDIA BEFORE PARTITION
Kistna
Goa
MADRAS
MYSORE
Ma
Bangalore
Pond
Ootacamund
COCHIN
TRAVANCORE
Indian States and Territories
CE
Scale
Miles
0 50 100 150 200 250 300 350 400
Colombo

CHINA
TIBET
Brahmaputra
EPAL
SIKKIM
BHUTAN
Gorakhpur
Brahmaputra
ASSAM
Patna
Ganges
Shillong
Benares
Imphal (Manipur)
BIHAR
BENGAL
Dacca
Midnapore
Calcutta
Chittagong
Mandalay
BURMA
Cuttack
ORISSA
BAY OF
BENGAL
Rangoon
ANDAMAN
ISLANDS
NICOBAR
ISLANDS

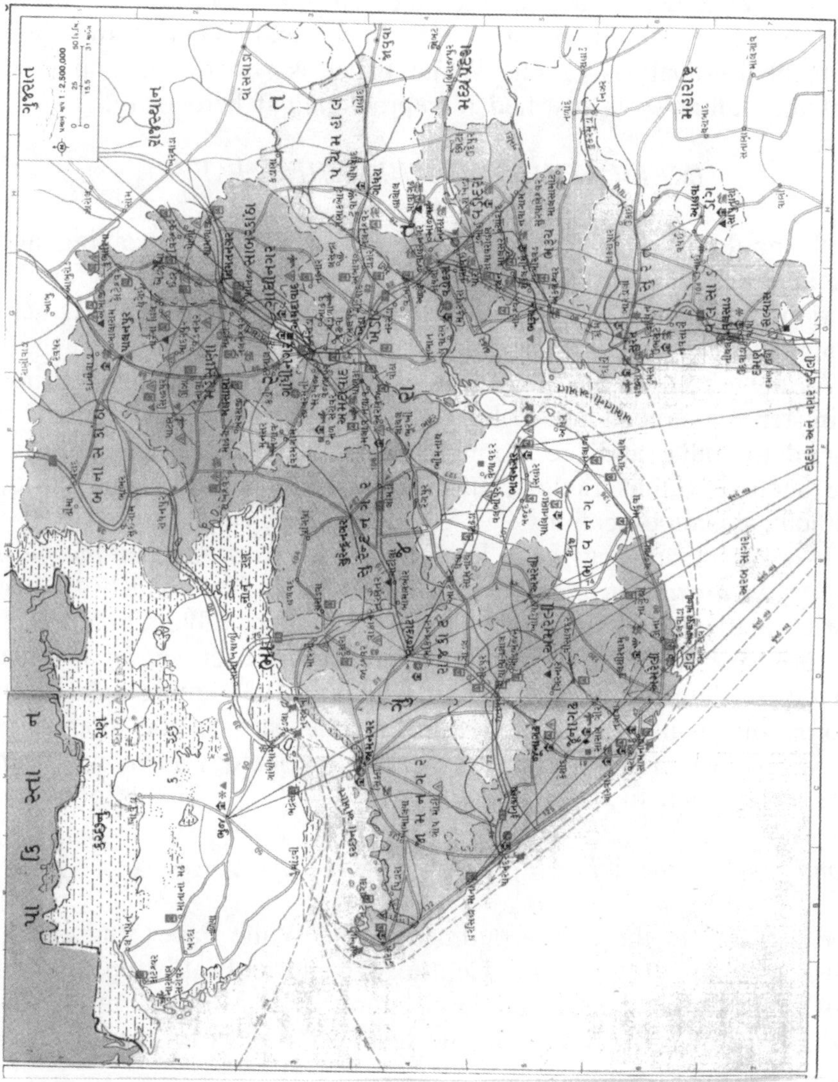

Gujarat

Document 18: Vithalbhai's Statement on the Failure of the Second Round Table Conference

On the 28th of December, 1931, eight days before he left for Vienna, Vithalbhai had issued a statement on the results of Second R.T.C., as contained in the White Paper, published at the time. Vithalbhai's analysis of this White Paper is so brilliant and lucid that the author feels justified in reproducing it here in full:

IMPLICATIONS OF THE WHITE PAPER

"I should like, in the first place, to explain the meaning and implications of the White Paper, and next to state how far the National demands as embodied in the resolution of the Karachi Congress have been conceded.

At the close of the First Round Table Conference, the Prime Minister announced the policy of His Majesty's Government in regard to India, and the White Paper now issued at the close of the Second Round Table Conference merely reaffirms that policy without any modifications.

It is significant that the White Paper *ignores altogether the most important document, namely the Gandhi-Irwin Pact*, which secured the co-operation of the Congress to the Round Table Conference.

Those who maintained that the Gandhi-Irwin Pact was an advance on the declaration of the 10th of January 1931, must have been thoroughly disillusioned. The words in the pact 'in the interest of India' by which Congressmen swore till yesterday have not been even mentioned in the White Paper.

Conditions in the White Paper.

According to the policy outlined in the White Paper, India is to have responsibility at the Centre, if, and only if, the Central Government and the Central Legislature are constituted on an All-India Federal Basis. Even so, the responsibility is to be subject to the following conditions:

(1) Defence and external affairs are to be reserved to the Governor-General.

(2) Control over finance is to be subject to such conditions as would secure the fulfilment of the obligations incurred under the

authority of the Secretary of State, and the maintenance unimpaired of the financial stability and credit of India.

(3) The relations of the Princes to the British Government are to remain with the Crown.

(4) There must be no unfair economic or commercial discrimination against the British trader.

(5) The Governor-General must be granted the necessary power to enable him to fulfil his responsibility for securing the observance of the constitutional rights of the minorities. He must also have the power to enable him to fulfill his responsibility for ultimately maintaining the tranquility of the State.

It is true that conditions No. 3 and No. 4 have not been expressed in the White Paper; but the speech of Sir Samuel Hoare, Secretary of State for India, in the House of Commons makes specific mention of them. Mr. Baldwin, leader of the Conservative Party, in his speech, also made it clear that there was no difference of any kind between what Sir Samuel Hoare said and what was contained in the White Paper, and the Secretary of State's speech was the White Paper and the White Paper was his speech.

Mr. Baldwin further explained that Mr. MacDonald spoke for 20 minutes and Sir Samuel Hoare for 40 minutes, and therefore the former could not have covered all the ground, the latter had done.

Reading the two declarations together with the debate in the House and the report of the Federal Structure Committee, there can be no doubt whatever that the principle of control at the Centre foreshadowed in the White Paper is subject to all the conditions I have just briefly enumerated.

White Paper rejects Congress Demands.

I now state the National demands, as embodied in the Karachi Congress resolution. They are:

1. Complete Independence, and, in particular—
2. Complete control of defence.
3. Complete control of external affairs.
4. Complete control of finances.
5. India's right to secede at will.
6. Examination of the debt position of India by an impartial tribunal to ascertain how much of it is justly chargeable to

the new Government of India, and how much must be shouldered by the British Government.

The Congress mandate also gave power to its delegate at the R.T.C. to accept such adjustments as 'may be demonstrably proved to be in the interests of India.'

I have no doubt that any impartial reader of the White Paper and the Congress resolution will come to no other conclusion than that the White Paper rejects every demand made by the Congress.

Reservations of National defence and external affairs in the hands of the Governor-General means the rejection of the Congress demand for complete independence even in that limited interpretation of the phrase, namely, 'voluntary partnership with Britain.'

Insult Added to Injury.

In his speech in the House of Commons, the Prime Minister goes further and adds insult to injury when in answer to some interruptions, he more than once declares that there is no intention to give independence, and that India does not want it, in that it agrees to the reservations regarding defence and external affairs.

In the opinion of the Prime Minister, therefore, the Congress demand for the control of defence and external affairs, is not a National demand, but the view expressed by some other British-Indian delegates that in the present circumstances the two subjects should not be entrusted to a Minister responsible to the Indian Legislature, represents India's demand. The mentality underlying this statement explains why the Conference has failed to consider the demands of the Congress seriously.

Throughout the deliberations of the Conference, the Congress was regarded as one of the many parties representing India, and it was never recognized, or perhaps conveniently forgotten, that the Congress represented an overwhelming majority of the people of India.

Control of Finances Illusory.

With defence as a reserved subject, the control of finances, apart from other conditions sought to be imposed by the White Paper, becomes illusory, inasmuch as 45 per cent. of the central revenue is expended on the military.

If we add to this, the huge amount representing the salaries and pensions of persons appointed by the Secretary of State together with interest on debt, and similar charges, very little indeed would be left for the Legislature to vote upon. Even so the White Paper, by imposing two other conditions, namely that suitable provision should be made in the Constitution as would effectively insure the fulfilment of the obligations incurred by the authority of the Secretary of State, and the maintenance unimpaired of the financial stability and credit of India, renders even that limited control of finance still more farcical.

What self-respecting Indian would be prepared to hold the portfolio of Finance under the new Government with these humiliating limitations? It is, therefore, quite clear that the Congress demand for the control of finances has been rejected.

Examination of Debt Position.

The next demand of the Congress for the examination of the debt position of India, was not even discussed at the Conference. But there can be no doubt that the White Paper, by imposing a condition that the obligations incurred under the authority of the Secretary of State are to be effectively guaranteed, rejects this claim.

India's Right to Secede.

The last and the most important claim of the Congress is India's right to secede. This was not and could not be raised, as India's claim to be admitted into partnership with Britain was not discussed.

As if these conditions, which reject every demand made by the Congress, were insufficient, the White Paper imposes other conditions before His Majesty's Government would be prepared to recognize the principle of responsibility at the Centre.

Nationals and Non-Nationals.

I should like to refer to one of them at this stage. The first R.T.C. decided upon the following formula at the suggestion of the British delegates in regard to India's right to discriminate between nationals and non-nationals.

"At the instance of the British commercial community, the principle was generally agreed to, that there should be no discrimination between the rights of the British commercial community, firms and companies, trading in India, and the rights of Indian-born subjects and that an appropriate convention based upon reciprocity should be entered into for the purpose of guaranteeing these rights."

Public opinion in India strongly protested against this serious curtailment of the right of India's future Parliament, and Mahatma Gandhi made it clear on behalf of the Congress that any Constitution which in any way impaired the power of the future Legislature of India to discriminate against non-nationals, when it considered it necessary to do so in the National interest, was not worth having, and would not be acceptable to the Congress

Some Indian members of the R.T.C., in defending their attitude, relied upon the word, 'generally' in the formula and contended that this word left it open to the Legislature to discriminate in exceptional cases.

The second R.T.C. extended the scope and purpose of this recommendation in a variety of ways. The improved recommendation dropped the word 'generally', gave protection not only to the British traders, but to all subjects of the Crown; not only against legislative discrimination, but also against administrative discrimination, not only in regard to trade, but also in regard to taxation, holding of property and a host of other matters.

In order to avoid any misunderstanding, I shall quote the words of that recommendation:

"The Committee are of opinion that no subject of the Crown who may be ordinarily resident or carrying on trade or business in British India, should be subject to any disability or discrimination, legislative or administrative, by reason of his age, descent, religion or place of birth in respect to taxation, the holding of property, the carrying on of any trade, profession or business, or in respect of residence or travel."

I hardly need add that the new Constitution is to make provision vesting in the Governor-General the power to take such measures as he may consider necessary to maintain the peace and tranquillity of the country.

Transition Period.

We have been told that, after all the so-called reservations and safeguards are meant to apply only during the period of transition, and that a few years are nothing in the lifetime of a nation. Neither in the White Paper nor in the report of the Federal Structure Committee do we find the period of transition specified. Heaven only knows whether it is going to be five years or fifty years.

Mr. Baldwin, in his speech in the House, in reply to a query from Mr. Wardlaw Milne, stated that nobody could say how long the transitional period would last. He further added that it would last as long as it was the will of the Parliament that it should last, and if and when the Constitution was set up, nothing in that Constitution would be relaxed without the assent of Parliament.

It is thus clear that all talk that the new Constitution would automatically lead India to its cherished goal, or that the period of transition would be brief, is mere moonshine.

Viceroy's Extraordinary Powers.

It has also been argued that the extraordinary powers to be vested in the Governor-General would by convention fall into disuse, as has been found to be the case in Self-governing Dominions. This is not the view of the British Government, and we know to our cost that such extraordinary powers have been and are exercised by the Governor-General in India.

I have endeavoured to show that the second R.T.C. has failed. A third conference has no doubt been promised and several Committees will shortly be set up to work out some of the details of the scheme. But neither the third conference nor any of the Committees will be entitled to override the express terms of the declaration. They will be bound to work within the four corners of those terms, and can have no power, for instance, to recommend the transfer of control of defence or foreign affairs or the grant of any other demand of the Congress, which have been categorically refused by the declaration.

Series of Insults.

I repeat that the Conference has failed, and that British diplomacy has, at any rate for the time being, triumphed all along the line since the Gandhi-Irwin Pact, which, in my opinion, was the masterstroke of that diplomacy. From the day of that truce up to the present, it has been one long and painful chapter of a series of insults and humiliations for the Congress and Congressmen, both in India and in England.

Whilst the authorities in India have all along treated the truce as a scrap of paper, as can be demonstrated by instances too numerous to mention, the Congress and its leaders have consistently and earnestly endeavoured to secure the strict observance of its terms by the people.

Impression created in the International World

At the R.T.C. the British Government played their cards so well that our delegates were drawn into a discussion of the communal problem and other details before the Conference could come to grips with fundamentals. As a result of this clever manoeuvring, to which, unfortunately, our delegates were willing victims, the impression created in the international world has been that the British Government is all willing to give freedom to India; but India's people are so hopelessly divided amongst themselves that they do not know what they want, and therefore the continuance of British rule is all the more necessary in their own interest.

Mahatma Gandhi, no doubt with the best of intentions and in the larger interests of the country, pocketed insults and humiliations hurled at him from various quarters, and continued to serve on the Conference. He had gone to London with a firm determination to make every endeavour to turn the truce into a permanent settlement, and in order perhaps, to create an atmosphere for that purpose, he sometimes made statements, both in and outside the Conference, tantamount to substantial concessions to Princes, Britishers and others. In fact, I often felt that Mahatmaji's attitude in this respect was hardly consistent with the spirit of the Congress mandate. The British statesmen interpreted this attitude of Mahatmaji as weakness on the part of the Congress, and the Conference failed.

Premature Truce.

The fact is that the truce was premature. It did not recognise the Congress claim to speak and negotiate on behalf of the whole of India. Its terms were vague and indefinite. Even so, the words, 'safeguards and reservations in the interests of India' were definite enough if the British Government seriously intended to act upon them and turn the truce into a permanent settlement.

The truce was an agreement between the Congress on the one hand, and the British Government on the other, and though no express provision was made as to what was to happen in case the two parties did not agree on the question whether a particular safeguard was in the interests of India or not, neither party could claim that its own view shall prevail; and that the matter must by common consent be referred to an impartial tribunal. If this procedure had been adopted, there was a reasonable chance of a settlement. But the truth is that, having induced the Congress to give up its campaign of Civil Disobedience, the boycott of British goods, etc., the Government felt themselves safe and secure.

Perhaps this is all to the good of the country. On this occasion it looked, to the great mortification of the youth of the country, as if India was too anxious to be admitted into equal partnership with Britain and Britain unceremoniously rejected that claim. Next time the position would be reversed. England would be too anxious to have India as a partner and India would be unwilling to accept that position.

On this occasion, India was represented by the nominees of the British Government. Next time their places would be occupied by delegates chosen by the Indian people. On this occasion, the venue of the Conference was London. The next time it would be Delhi.

Real Issue Complicated and Side-tracked.

I would like to say a few words on some features of the proposed Federal Executive and the Federal Legislature. To my mind, the Federation of the Princes and the Commoners is unthinkable. Even so, it would take years for such a Federation to materialize. In the meantime, forces in favour of the introduction of provincial autonomy are bound to make headway. The Prime Minister has already hinted that the decision for a comprehensive scheme dealing with both the Central and Provincial responsibility is not irrevocable. A Parliamentary Bill for the introduction of some sort of Provincial Autonomy relegating the comprehensive scheme to the background is, therefore, not outside the range of possibility.

I have always maintained, since the idea of Federation was first mooted, that we should have a Constitution for British India alone to start with, leaving the door open for the Indian States to come in, if and when they choose to do so.

Those who initiated the idea of Federation have successfully complicated and sidetracked the issues confronting the country and have made their solution almost impossible. The British Indian delegates, in their anxiety to start some sort of Constitution going, have made compromises and concessions to the Princes, with the result that the Constitution of the Federal Legislature, as finally recommended by the Committee, is ten times worse than the Constitution under which the present Assembly has been working. Even if complete control of defence, external affairs and finance is conceded, I am certain that the Legislature so constituted would not be in a position to carry into effect any of the progressive ideas the Congress has in view.

Does Mahatma Gandhi really think that he can get that Legislature to repeal the Salt Tax or reduce the military expenditure to any appreciable extent? Is such a Legislature likely to vote in favour of a reduction of troops, either British or Indian, or of the pay and pension of high officers of the Government?

If, therefore, the expenditure of the Central Government could not be reduced, how are we, with full Provincial Autonomy, going to carry into effect our ideas of prohibition and of reducing the land revenue to half?

Indications are not wanting to show that India is fast heading towards agrarian revolution, and the only way to save the situation is to invest the starving workers and peasants with responsibility for carrying on the administration of the country as best they can. Instead, the Round-Tablers, by agreeing to a Constitution which provides for 80 out of 200 seats to the nominees of the Princes in the Upper House, and 100 out of 300, in the Popular Assembly, besides special representation for zamindars, trade, commerce, etc., would virtually hand over the administration of the country to a combination of Princes, zamindars and their capitalist allies.

If I had a choice, I would any day prefer the present Assembly being invested with further power than agree to have a Constitution such as is now proposed. No wonder, therefore, that in addressing the House of Commons the other day Sir Samuel Hoare stated: "Indeed, I go so far as to say that I believe that a Government set up under such condition as I mentioned might very well be a stronger Government than the Government we have got in India at the present time."

If the Princes, however, agree to have the fundamental rights of their people embodied in the Constitution, and to the establishment of a Supreme Court for the enforcement of those rights and to the representation of the people on the Federal Legislature, under the same franchise as the people of British India, one might be inclined to consider the idea of Federation.

The fact, however, remains that the Princes are not yet in a mood, for reasons into which it is unnecessary to enter, to do anything of the kind. The sooner we give up the idea of federating with the Princes and go ahead with British India, the better for all concerned. But the British Government would not have it. Apart from other conditions and limitations, His Majesty's Government are not prepared, the White Paper declares, to recognise the principle of responsibility at the Centre unless and until the Central Government and the Central Legislature are constituted on an all-India Federal basis.

Britain's Attitude.

I am not in favour of exploring any further avenue for negotiation with the Government. If personal entreaties by Mahatmaji in Downing Street and at St James's Palace did not avail, no further appeals by him, however earnest, from a distance of 6,000 miles, can do any good.

In spite of what Mahatmaji says, I venture to think that *the Gandhi-Irwin Pact was a blunder and has sufficiently harmed our cause.*

Gandhiji's presence and activities in England have hardly enhanced the prestige of the Congress. On the contrary, the proceedings of the R.T.C. have left the world wondering whether there is any substance in the claim hitherto made by the Indian National Congress that it represents an overwhelming majority of the people of India, and that at its bidding millions of people are ready to suffer and sacrifice for the freedom of the country.

We must regain this lost ground in world opinion. Let us wait and see what lead the Congress gives to the country.

In view of what has happened at the last Conference, the Congress might perhaps consider it advisable to devote its attention exclusively to the solution of the communal problem before launching a fresh campaign. The morale of our people is splendid and they are awaiting the orders of the Congress."

REFERENCES

Part One

Chapter 1

1. Kerr's 'Voyages', IX 126
2. Mandelslo's 'Voyages', 73
3. Thevenot's 'Travels', V 97
4. Forbes' Oriental Memoirs. 1813, II 88
5. Heber's 'Travels', II 146
6. Transactions, Bombay Geological Society, VII 107
7. Brigg's 'Cities of Gujarashtra', p. 359
8. Bombay Gazetteer, Chapter XIV, p. 175c; I.O.L. (India Office Library).RR.DG.Bom.36
9. 'Peasant Nationalists of Gujarat' David Hardiman, p. 71; Oxford University Press 1981

Chapter 2

1. 'Representative Men of the Bombay Presidency', John Huston; The Historical Publishing Company, Philadelphia, USA, 1887, pp. 90–1
2. Journal of the UP Historical Society, Vol 1, pp. 169–170
3. Mirat (India Office; Manuscript III, Folio 605)
4. Document in Urdu 1686, with the seal of the Emperor (from Family archives)
5. Bombay Government R.D., Conference Serial No. 8 of No. 181 Conference, 9243, I.O.R. P/8036

Chapter 3

1. Vincent A. Smith 'Akbar the Great Moghal' 1917 p. 377
2. I.O.L.RR.DG.Bom36, Bombay Gazetteer Land Administration, Chapter VIII, pp. 90–1

3. I.O.R. (India Office Records) W2076 p. 743, 28 May 1817
4. Bombay Revenue Selections. Revenue letter from Bombay to Court of Directors, London, 17 April 1816. Subject: Introduction of Amani Management into Neriad; I.O.R.W2076, p. 732, para. 77
5. Ibid p. 738, paras. 9 and 13, I.O.R.W.2076
6. Ibid pp. 738–9, para. 14, I.O.R.W2076

Chapter 4

1. I.O.R.DG.BOM.36, Chapter XIII Nadiad pp. 152–3

Chapter 5

1. 'History of the Marathas', James Grant Duff, 2 vols, 1921
2. 'The Golden Book of India', Sir Roper Lethbridge KGIE
3. 'Treaties, Engagements and Sanads' Sir Charles U. Aitchison; I.O.L.W2076, p. 743; 28 May 1817
4. Ibid No. VII, I.O.L. V6651
5. Ibid No. VII, I.O.L. V6651 pp. 337–9
6. 'England – A Social and Economic History', E.H.Spalding
7. 'British Historical Facts', Chris Cook and John Stevenson; Macmillan Press

Chapter 6

1. 'Battle of Arras', James Forbes, I.O.L. Mss Eur B3, 1775. Extensively quoted throughout
2. 'The Golden Book of India', Sir Roper Lethbridge, Macmillan & Co, London 1893; pp. 63–4
3. Aitchison's 'Treaties, Engagements and Sanads', Vol VI, Baroda No. 11, p. 306
4. 'India, A History', John Keay, Harper Collins 2000

Chapter 8

1. Aitchison 'Treaties, Engagements and Sanads', V6651, No. XII, pp. 340–47, number of articles 57
2. Ibid p. 340, No. XII
3. M.S.A. (Maharastra State Archives) – Robert Drummond, 'Journal of Mission to Mowassi Villages'
4. M.S.A., R.D.D.91, 1676 of 1 June 1806
5. I.O.R. (India Office Records) W2076, 28 May 1817, p. 734

Chapter 9

1. I.O.L.W2076, Bombay Revenue Collections, p. 734
2. I.O.R. P/380/61, Entry No. 973, Wutton Commission Report
3. M.S.A. Secret and Political, D.S., 195; 10372; Holford to Duncan 22 December 1806

Chapter 10

1. M.S.A. J.D.D. 77:1890–2 Letter to Rowles from Purbhodass Soonderdas
2. M.S.A. J.D.D. 77:1882 Ironside to Warden, 25 September 1815
3. M.S.A., R.D.D. 102:2583–84 Robertson to Warden, 25 September 1815
4. M.S.A., J.D.D. 77; 1882, Ironside to Warden 25 September 1815; M.S.A., R.D.D. 102: 2583–4, Robertson to Warden 25 September 1815
5. M.S.A., R.D.D. 102: 2597; Robertson to Barnwall
6. M.S.A., R.D.D. 102: 2602/3; Robertson to Barnwall
7. M.S.A., R.D.D. 102: 2602; Robertson to Barnwall
8. M.S.A., R.D.D. 102: 2597; Robertson to Barnwall
9. M.S.A., R.D.D. 108: 1717; Barnwall to Robertson
10. M.S.A., R.D.D. 108: 1725–27; Barnwall to Rowles 1 August 1816
11. M.S.A., R.D.D. 108: 1729; Barnwall to Rowles
12. M.S.A. Judicial Department, letter from Bombay to Court of Directors 5:212, 19 February 1819
13. I.O.R. Judicial Letters to Bombay 1:264; Court of Directors to Bombay, 19 February 1819
14. I.O.R. Judicial Letters to Bombay 1:265–66 and 1:269–70, 19 February 1819
15. I.O.R. P/367/71 of 1 November 1819, p. 3678
16. I.O.R. P/367/71 of 1 November 1819, p. 3677

Chapter 11

1. M.S.A., R.D.D. 108: 1711, 1718; Barnwall to Rowles 1 August 1816
2. M.S.A., R.D.D. 108: 1704–07; Rowles to Warden 16 August 1816
3. I.O. Revenue Letters from Bombay to Court of Directors, 3:409–10, 28 May 1817

4. I.O. Revenue Letters from Court of Directors to Bombay, 2:168–69, 14 July 1817
5. M.S.A., R.D.D. Robertson to Warden 135:5494 30 November 1818 M.S.A., R.D.D. minutes of Government 135:5495 11 December 1818
6. M.S.A, Revenue Department Comp., 166:405–6, Parish to Williamson, 23 November 1827
7. East.India.Co. – selection of papers 3:704, minutes of Prendergast 29 June 1821
8. Ibid, 1:685. minutes of Elphinstone 6 April 1821
9. Forbes – Ras Mala pp. 591–2.
10. Karl Marx 'The Future of British Rule in India', mesw 1:352. Quoted by David McLellan in 'Karl Marx', Macmillan 1973
11. Deputy Collector's Report, Kheda District 1897–98, B.A., R.D. 1899 Volume 24 Compilation 1128
12. B.A. R.D. 1914 Compilation 764

Chapter 12

1. I.O.R. P/367–71 of 1 November 1819; B.A. Bombay Castle pp. 3677–3685, Collector A. Robertson
2. I.O.R. R/1215 of 24 February 1914, Bombay Revenue Department No. 4289 – serial No. 217 Bombay Castle 7 May 1914. pp. 961–4
3. I.O.R. P/9619 p. 964 C.W.A.Turner 5 May 1914, telegram to Collector Kheda No. 4215
4. Collector's Report, Kheda District 1916–17, B.A., R.D. 1918, compilation 511, Part II
5. Collector's Report, Kheda District 1913–14, B.A., R.D. 1915, compilation 511, Part III

Chapter 13

1. I.O.R. P/9351 Revenue Department, 1 August 1913
2. 'Peasant Nationalists of Gujarat' David Hardiman p. 266 Oxford University Press 1981
3. Ibid pp. 49–50

Chapter 14

1. B.A. (Bombay Administration), G.D. 1915 Compilation 829

2. B.A., G.D. 1914 Compilation 764
3. B.A., G.D. 1916 Compilation 876
4. 'Peasant Nationalists of Gujarat', David Hardiman p. 75 Oxford University Press 1981

Chapter 15

1. Revenue Department, Revenue Survey and Assessment Kaira, I.O.R., P/9619 Serial No. 237 20 May 1914
2. Revenue Department, No. 1667/45 Confl. of 1911, I.O.R. P/8850, 18 February 1911

Part Two

Chapter 16

1. 'Vithalbhai Patel, Life and Times', Gordhanbhai J Patel, Shree Laxmi Narayan Press, Bombay 1950, pp. 385 and 424
2. Ibid, p. 426
3. 'The Indian Struggle 1920–1942', Subhas Chandra Bose, Asia Publishing House, London 1964, p. 357
4. Vithalbhai's letter to Dadubhai from Vienna, 11 May 1933 (Desai Family Archives, see Appendix 4)
5. 'The Peasantry and Nationalism', Shirin Mehta 1924, p. 96, Manohar Publications, New Delhi
6. Ibid, p. 97
7. Narhari Parikh, 'Bardoli na Kheduto', Ahmedabad 1927, p. 44
8. 'The Peasantry and Nationalism', Shirin Mehta, p. 99
9. Oriental and India Office Collections, The British Library, P/11402, pp. 589–590; Revenue Department Government of Bombay No. L.C./157-B, Bombay Castle 28 June 1924
10. 'Peasant Nationalists of Gujarat', David Hardiman, Oxford University Press, pp. 183–4
11. *Indian Daily Mail*, 5 March 1927; *Indian National Herald*, 8 March 1927
12. *Bombay Chronicle*, 1 June 1927
13. 'The Story of Bardoli', Mahadev Desai, Navjivan Press 1929. p. 40
14. 'The Peasantry and Nationalism', Shirin Mehta, p. 102

15. Ibid, p. 104
16. 'The Story of Bardoli' Mahadev Desai, Navjivan Press 1929, p. 44; also present Author's interview with Dadubhai
17. Ibid, pp. 49–50, I.L.O. T/28590
18. Ibid, p. 44
19. Ibid, p. 44
20. Ibid, p. 46
21. Ibid, p. 47
22. Ibid, p. 50
23. Ibid, pp. 53–4
24. Ibid, pp. 52–3
25. Ibid, p. 108
26. Ibid, p. 110
27. Ibid, p. 111
28. Ibid, p. 40
29. *The Times of India* (Bombay), 23 May 1928
30. *The Times of India* (Bombay), 23 May 1928, also 'The Peasantry and Nationalism', Shirin Mehta, p. 133
31. Ibid
32. Government of India, Home Department (Political), Fortnightly Report of the first half of May 1928, File No. 1/28, secret nos SD 456; National Archives of India, New Delhi
33. Wilson to Irwin 23 April 1928, Lord Irwin's Papers Mss EUR C152/22, NBt No. 282, p. 389
34. Ibid, p. 151; Irwin to Wilson
35. Ibid, p. 38; Wilson's reply
36. Ibid, V J Patel to Wilson, 17 May 1928, No. 386, p. 441
37. Ibid, Wilson to V J Patel, 20 May 1928, p. 457
38. Ibid, Wilson to Irwin, 22 May 1928, No. 345, p. 453
39. Ibid, telegram from Irwin to Wilson, 31 May 1928, No. 321, p. 225
40. Ibid, telegram from Wilson to Irwin, 31 May 1928
41. Ibid, Wilson to Irwin, 1 June 1928, No. 369, p. 493
42. Ibid, Wilson to Irwin, 2 June 1928, No. 374, p. 496
43. Ibid, Irwin to Wilson, 25 June 1928, No. 391a, p. 264a
44. Ibid. Wilson to Irwin, 14 June 1928, No. 419 p. 547
45. *Bombay Chronicle*, 12 June 1928, Wilson to Munshi
46. Purushottamdas Thakurdas to Chunilal C. Mehta, 2 June 1928; Purushottamdas Thakurdas Papers II, Nehru Memorial Museum and Library, New Delhi

47. Mss EUR C152/22, Wilson to Irwin, 26 June 1928, N448a, p. 582
48. *Bombay Chronicle* 4 July 1928
49. Mss EUR C152/22, Irwin to Birkenhead, 6 July 1928, N214, p. 111
50. 'The Story of Bardoli', Mahadev Desai, p. 154.
51. Government of India, Home Department (Political), 1928 Fortnightly Report, the second half of May 1928, File 1/28, Secret No. SD595, National Archives of India, New Delhi
52. Mss EUR C152/22 Wilson to Irwin, 26 June 1928, No. 448, p. 582
53. Ibid, Wilson to Irwin, 2 July 1928, No. 462, p. 599
54. *Times of India*, 3 July 1928
55. U.K. Commons Parliamentary Debates, Series 5, Volume 128, pp. 979–80, 5–22 June 1928
56. Mss EUR C152/22 Wilson to Irwin, 26 June 1928, No. 448a, p. 582
57. Mss EUR C152/22 Wilson to Irwin, 19 July 1928, No. 502a, p. 365
58. Birkenhead to Governor of Bombay, telegram No. 1992, 19 July 1928, p. 639, Mss EUR C152/22
59. Wilson to Birkenhead, telegram 1992, 19 July 1928, pp. 639–40, Mss EUR C132/22
60. Wilson's report to Birkenhead, 19 July 1928, pp. 632, 637–9
61. Ibid, Wilson to Irwin, 24 July 1928, No. 514, p. 647–9
62. Notes of J.H. Garrett, the Collector of Surat, 'Measures to Deal with the Agitators in the Non-payment of Land Revenue assessment campaign', File 584-E, Part VIII
63. 'The Story of Bardoli', Mahadev Desai, p. 253
64. Ibid, p. 256
65. Ibid, pp. 260–1
66. Ibid, Appendix II, The Settlement Documents, 6 August 1928, pp. 336–8
67. Ibid, p. 156
68. Ibid, p. 159
69. Ibid, p. 159
70. 'The Indian Struggle', Subhas Chandra Bose, Asia Publishing House, London 1964, p. 152
71. 'Autobiography', Pandit Jawaharlal Nehru, The Bodley Head, London 1936, p. 171

72. 'A Centenary History of the Indian National Congress', B.N. Pande, released by Rajiv Gandhi, published by All India Congress Committee 1985, p. 206
73. I.O.L. Mss EUR C152/1, Halifax letters to the King No. 50, 18 July 1928
74. Lord Birkenhead to Irwin 12 July 1928, Lord Birkenhead Collections, National Archives of India, New Delhi
75. Ibid, Lord Irwin's letter to the King No. 51; Mss EUR e152/1
76. I.O.R. Mss EUR e152/22; Letter No. 533b of 6 September 1928 and Letter No. 645 of 29 October 1928
77. Lord Irwin to Viscount Peel, 1 May 1929, No. 24
78. Vallabhbhai's letter to Dadubhai, 16 January 1930 (Desai Family Archives)
79. 'History of the Indian National Congress', Pattabhai Sitaramaya, p. 558, published by the Congress Working Committee 1935
80. Ibid, p. 588.
81. 'The Indian Struggle', Subhas Chandra Bose pp. 168–9, Asia Publishing House, London 1964. I.O.L. Mss EUR C152/1, letter No. 100, 5 February 1931, Halifax letter to the King
82. I.O.L. Mss EUR C152/1, Halifax letter to the King No. 100, 5 February 1931
83. 'History of the Congress', Pattabhai Sitaramaya, p. 767
84. 'The Indian Struggle', Subhas Chandra Bose, p. 170
85. 'Autobiography', Pandit Jawaharlal Nehru, p. 194

Chapter 17

1. Wilson to Irwin 15 August 1929; I.O.L. Mss C152
2. Irwin to Provincial Governors 6 September 1928; Mss Eur 152, Volume 22
3. 'Peasant Nationalists of Gujarat', Hardiman, p. 3
4. Ibid, p. 10
5. See Map of Bardoli Taluka at end of Chapter 16
6. Desai Family Archives, 201–2 Vallabhbhai to Dadubhai 16 January 1930 and 20 January 1930 (see Appendix 4)
7. I.O.L. P/11245, Bill to amend Salt Act 1890, Bill No. XVIII of 22 September 1922, & Lord Reading's letter to Viscount Peel (see Appendix 5)
8. 'The Lyttons in India', Mary Lutyens, pp. 555–6

9. Proceedings of the Legislative Department, 7 December 1922, Pro No. 13 The Bombay Salt Amendment Act 1922 No. 95 – a Bill to further amend the Bombay Salt Act 1890 (Bill No. XVIII of 1922)
10. Mss EUR E238/25, Viceroy to Governors' telegram No. 237, 25 March 1923, p. 50; also Governor of Bombay to Viceroy telegram No. 126, 25 March 1923, p.151
11. Bombay Government Secret Abstracts 1923, p. 254; also *Bombay Chronicle* 12 and 14 November 1923
12. 'Two Centuries of Change', Book II, p. 57, Hutchins and Stephens; Blackie and Sons, London, 1941
13. Ibid, p. 68
14. 'History of Congress', Pattabhi Sitaramaya, pp. 624–5
15. Vithalbhai's letter to Dadubhai, 6 March 1930
16. 'History of Congress', Pattabhi Sitaramaya, p. 638
17. J. Nehru's 'Autobiography', p. 210
18. 'History of Congress', Pattabhi Sitaramaya, pp. 648–9
19. *Bombay Chronicle* 13 March 1930

Chapter 18

1. Birkenhead Papers 'Halifax', pp. 281–2
2. Vallabhbhai's letters to Dadubhai 14/1/1930 and 20/1/30, DPA No 201/2 (from Family Archives)
3. Hardiman, 'Peasant Nationalists of Gujarat', pp. 192–3
4. *Bombay Chronicle* 9 and 11/3/1930 and Bombay Secret Abstracts 1930, p. 369
5. Mahadev Desai to Dadubhai 21/3/1930, DFAL No. 203
6. Kheda Jilla Samachar, 20/6/1930; also 'Peasant Nationalists of Gujarat', Hardiman, p. 203
7. 'The Press and Society', R D Parikh, Bombay 1965, p. 101
8. 'Peasant Nationalists of Gujarat', David Hardiman, p. 194
9. Ibid, pp. 194–5; Navjivan & Bombay Source Material Vol III, Pt III, p. 11
10. M K Gandhi's Autobiography, Phoenix MCM XLIX
11. Haridas Mazumdar of *Bombay Chronicle* April 1930, quoted by Hardiman p. 195
12. 'Peasant Nationalists of Gujarat', Hardiman p. 195
13. Ibid, p. 196
14. 'History of the Congress', Pattabhi Sitaramaya. pp. 656–7

15. ‘Autobiography’ Nehru, published by John Lane The Bodley Head, London 1936, p. 212
16. Halifax Papers I.O.R. Mss EUR 152/25; Nehru’s letter to Gandhiji from Almoda jail (censored mail)
17. ‘The Indian Struggle 1920–1942’, Subhas Chandra Bose, Asia Publishing House, London 1964, p. 186
18. Ibid, p. 186
19. ‘Birkenhead Papers’, Birkenhead to Halifax, p. 282
20. ‘History of the Congress’, Pattabhi Sitaramaya, pp. 661–3
21. Ibid
22. Mss EUR C152/1, p. 112, Letter 75, Halifax Papers I.O.R.
23. Manilal Gandhi to the Author, 24 November 1953, from Phoenix, Natal; now authenticated by I.O.R. P/Conf/78 Confidential, Serial 33, No. CNJP, 438 III, 28 May 1930 Home Department, Government of Bombay
24. ‘War Council’ as described by Dadubhai to the Author and I.O.R. P/Conf/78, Home Department, Government of Bombay
25. ‘Mahatma Gandhi’, Robert Payne, p. 394
26. I.O.R. P/Conf/78, Home Department, Government of Bombay, Conf serial 33, No. CNJP, 438 III, 28 May 1930, p. 143
27. Ibid, P6, p. 143–4; I.O.R. P/Conf/78
28. I.O.R. P/Conf/78, p. 6, Confidential serial No. 33, 28 May 1930
29. ‘I Found No Peace’, Webb Miller, pp. 192–6
30. ‘Gandhi, His Message to the World’, Luis Fisher, 1962
31. ‘Gandhi and Civil Disobedience’, Judith Brown, p. XIII
32. ‘Halifax’, Birkenhead, p. 284
33. ‘Mahatma Gandhi’, Robert Payne, p. 396
34. ‘Gandhi and the Empire’, Mazumdar, p. 112
35. The Annual Register 1931, Government of India, Volume 1, p. 127
36. Mss EUR C152/1, letter No. 75, p. 112
37. ‘The History of Congress’, Pattabhi Sitaramaya, pp. 732–3
38. ‘Collected Works of Mahatma Gandhi’, Navajivan, p. 132
39. Government of India, Political Department, S.481/31
40. ‘Peasant Nationalists of Gujarat’, David Hardiman, Oxford, p. 236.

Chapter 19

1. Two letters from Vallabhbhai to Dadubhai, January 1930

2. Letter of V.J. Patel to Lord Irwin, 20 April 1930, pp. 1120–22; Vithalbhai Book 2 by Gordhanbhai J. Patel 1950
3. Lord Irwin letter to the King, Mss EUR e152/25, p. 626a
4. Letter from Nehru to Gandhi, Naini gaol 28 July 1930
5. Letters from Vithalbhai to Dadubhai from Vienna, 9 March 1932 and 11 May 1933
6. Bombay Government Revenue Department, Secret Abstracts 1930, p. 110
7. *Bombay Chronicle* 15 January 1930
8. *Bombay Chronicle* 3 February 1930. Quoted by Hardiman in 'Peasant Nationalists of Gujarat', p. 192
9. I.O.L. Mss EUR c152; Irwin to all Provincial Governors 6 September 1928; No. 533b p. 391a and No. 645 p. 489 29 October 1928
10. I.O.L. Mss EUR 152/1, Irwin's letter to the King, No. 71 of 11 March 1930
11. Letter from Vithalbhai to Dadubhai 3 December 1929, Delhi
12. Mahadev Desai to Dadubhai at Nadiad, 21 March 1930
13. *Bombay Chronicle* 8 April 1930
14. Ravjibhai Patel to Jivanna Jharna, Vol 1, pp. 331–4
15. 'Satyagraha Chaavni Borsad Patrika', Lalloobhai Laxmidas Patel 30 April 1930 and letter from Shivabhai Ashabat Patel 30 April 1930
16. Oriental and India Office P/Conf 78, Home Department Government of Bombay 5 June 1930 also *Bombay Chronicle* 2 June 1930
17. 'History of Congress', B.N. Pande, Volume 2, p. 239.
18. I.O.R. P/Conf/78 Government of Bombay Home Department, No. O-B 17 June 1930, resolution 5387/28-Conf
19. Government of India H.D., Political No. D – 4166/30, 3 July 1930
20. *Young India*, edited by Mahatma Gandhi, 26 June 1930
21. *Bombay Chronicle* 13 and 24 October 1930
22. *Bombay Chronicle* 18 November 1930
23. Vallabhbhai Sardar released from gaol 26 June 1930
24. Kheda Jilla Patrika 10 June 1930 and 11 January 1931 (the detailed names of villages are shown in Appendix 5)
25. *Bombay Chronicle* 11 November 1930
26. 'Peasant Nationalists of Gujarat', David Hardiman
27. *Bombay Chronicle* 27 December 1930

28. *Bombay Chronicle* 18 October 1930 and Judgement Order on Dadubhai Desai's sentence 13 October 1930
29. Bombay Secret Abstracts 1930, pp. 1525–6, Kheda Police Report 13 September 1930
30. Borsad Satyagraha Samachar, 21 September 1930
31. Borsad Satyagraha Samachar, 7 December 1930
32. Court Order sentencing Dadubhai to 5 months in prison
33. Baroda Hazur Political Department, Section 38, File 5
34. Ibid File 43 and Borsad Satyagraha Samachar 7 December 1930
35. *Bombay Chronicle* 10 and 20 November 1930
36. Gandhi Smarak Sangralaya, Document 21415 and NAI H-Pol 1931, File 33, Part 3
37. 'Peasant Nationalists of Gujarat', David Hardiman, Oxford University Press 1981, pp. 233–4
38. CWMG Vol 45, pp. 428–9
39. Ibid Vol 45, p. 193
40. Ibid Vol 45, p. 245
41. 'Peasant Nationalists of Gujarat', David Hardiman, p. 234
42. CWMG Vol 5, p. 241
43. Government of India, H.D. Political, No. D–4166/30, 3 July 1930
44. 'The India Struggle', Subhas Bose pp. 201–2, Asia Publishing House, London
45. Ibid p. 210
46. Ibid p. 210
47. 'Vithalbhai', Gordhanbhai Patel, pp. 1171–2

Chapter 20

1. Mehta, S., 'The Peasantry and Nationalism', Manohar Publications, New Delhi 1984
2. British Library I.O.R. P/Conf/78; Government of Bombay, Home Department, Conf. Serial 33, ND, CNJP 438 111; 28 May 1930

Part Three

Chapter 21

1. Vallabhbhai letter to Dadubhai, 1 July 1948, Desai Archives
2. Vallabhbhai letter to Dadubhai 25 July 1948, Desai Archives

3. I.O.R. Parliamentary Papers Vol. XLII, The Report of the Royal Commission on Opium with Annexes
4. Report on the Miscellaneous Old Records at the India Office by Sir G. Brownwood, p. 36 Report of the Royal Commission on Opium. I.O.R. Parliamentary Papers Volume XL2
5. Hastings' minutes 18 January 1775, p. 39. Royal Commission on Opium
6. Patna Council's letter 27 March 1775, in Bengal Rev. Cons. 3 May 1775
7. Minutes of May 1775, Bengal Rev. Cons.
8. Letter from Governor General in Bengal to Council in London, Royal Opium Commission
9. Letter from Court of Directors in London to the Governor and Council, 23 December 1778
10. Minutes by Sir John Macpherson, Governor General, and Council to Court of Directors 29 April 1785; I.O.R. Parliamentary Papers Vol. XLII
11. 'Gandhi and Civil Disobedience' Judith Brown p. 63
12. Vivekananda's letter to Haridas September 1894
13. Vivekananda's letter of 2 March 1896 from 223 W 22nd Street, New York

Chapter 22

1. Revenue Department, confidential serial No. 5-No. 1667/45 conf of 1911, I.O.R. p/8850, pp. 21–22. Some suggestions by Purushottamdas V Desai, Nadiad 24 May 1910
2. 'Peasant Nationalists of Gujarat', David Hardiman, Oxford University Press 1951, Introduction p. 1
3. Gandhiji's speech, CWMG Vol. 14, p. 55
4. Speech at Ajarapura, CWMG Vol. 14, p. 361
5. Speech at Federal Structure Committee of the Second Round Table Conference London, CWMG Vol. 68, p. 16
6. Revenue Survey and Assessment, Kaira No. 4697, serial No. 237, p. 1033, I.O.R. p/9619 of 20 May 1914
7. Patidar Yovak Mandal – 'Suvarna Jayanti Ank', N6, Section IV, p. 15.
8. Ibid, N6, Section II, p. 15.

Chapter 23

1. Agreement of 17 January 1906 between Ganpatidas Purushottamdas Desai and Krishna Rao Ambalal Desai (Desai Family Archives)
2. Government of Bombay Revenue Department Proceedings, August 1913. Petition No. 1531 of 12 April 1913, Memorandum 2659 5 July 1913 from Commissioner N.D. (I.O.R. P/9351)
3. BA, RD Compilation 511, Part III, Kheda Collector's Report
4. 'Peasant Nationalists of Gujarat' David Hardiman, Oxford University Press pp. 26–7
5. Bombay Administration Judicial Department 1911, Volume 120, Compilation 2331
6. Government of Bombay Revenue Department, Confidential Proceedings July 1913, Memorandum 6434–164 Conf. (I.O.R. P/9552)

Chapter 24

1. See Desai's dynastic family tree following the Foreword
2. Gandhiji to Devdas Gandhi 12 April 1918, CWMG Vol 14 p. 333
3. M.K. Gandhi 'An Autobiography', p. 423
4. Select Correspondence, Sardar Patel, edited by V. Shankar pp. 570–1
5. 'India Wins Freedom', Maulana Abul Kalam Azad p. 162
6. Ibid, p. 165
7. Maulana Azad 'Autobiography', p. 170
8. 'Wavell's Diary', 19 January 1946
9. Sardar's letter to the writer's Father, Simla, 9 May 1946
10. 'Wavell', edited by Moon Penderel pp. 258–9; Oxford University Press
11. Letters to Pethwick-Lawrence quoted by Gopal in 'Jawaharlal Nehru' p. 317
12. Maulana Azad 'Autobiography', p. 166
13. Select correspondence of Sardar Patel, edited by V. Shankar pp. 510–3
14. Ibid, p. 513
15. Ibid, p. 514
16. Ibid, p. 536
17. Ibid, p. 503
18. Ibid, p. 508

19. Parikh Narhari 'Sardar Vallabhbhai Patel' Navajivan Press p. 329
20. Bardoli Satyagraha Patrika 4 April 1928
21. Ibid, 30 March 1928

Chapter 25

1. 'Vithalbhai – Life & Times', Pravin Shah; Manibhai D. Desai, Nadiad 1976 p. 71, in Gujarati
2. 'Vithalbhai Patel', G.I. Patel, 1950, p. 818
3. Ibid, pp. 818–9
4. Ibid, pp. 820–822
5. Halifax Papers. Mss EUR C152, p. 51, letter no. 88
6. 'The Indian Struggle', Subhas Bose, p. 213
7. 'Vithalbhai Patel', G.I. Patel; publisher the same

Chapter 26

1. 'The History of Congress', Pattabhi Sitaramaya, p. 299
2. Ibid, p. 422
3. Ibid, p. 429
4. Ibid, p. 431
5. Ibid, p. 432
6. Ibid, p. 492
7. Ibid, p. 498
8. Ibid, p. 529
9. Ibid, p. 541
10. Ibid, p. 543
11. Ibid, p. 552
12. Ibid, p. 556
13. Ibid, pp. 560–1
14. Ibid, p. 565
15. 'The Indian Struggle', Subhas Bose, p. 264
16. 'Mother India', Katherine Mayo, 1927
17. 'The History of Congress', Pattabhi Sitaramaya, pp. 588–9
18. 'A Centenary History of the Indian National Congress 1885–1985', p. 179; volumes released by Shri Rajiv Gandhi, jointly published by A.I.C.C. and Vikas Publishing House, New Delhi 1995
19. 'The Indian Struggle 1920–1942', Subhas Chandra Bose, Asia Publishing House, London 1964, p, 170
20. 'An Autobiography', Jawaharlal Nehru, published by John Lane, the Bodley Head, London 1936, preface pp. vii–viii

21. This whole Section is drawn from 'Book 2 Vithalbhai Patel', Gordhanbhai Patel
22. 'The Indian Struggle 1920–42' Bose Subhas, Asia Publishing House, London p. 160
23. Ibid, p. 168
24. Ibid, p. 177
25. Ibid, p. 190
26. Sardar's letter to Dadubhai, 7 November 1947, from 1 Aurangzeb Road, New Delhi
27. Author's interview with V. Shankar, Permanent Secretary, Ministry of Home Affairs and with Dr. Nagendra Singh, Secretary Ministry of Transport and Shipping
28. 'India Wins Freedom', Maulana Azad, p. 166 onwards
29. 'India from Curzon to Nehru'; Kripalani to Durgadas, quoted by the latter, p. 230
30. Patel Maniben's remarks in Durgadas (Ed) 'Sardar Patel's Correspondence', 10 volumes, Navajivan Ahmedabad p. xxxviii
31. Entry in Maniben Patel's diary 16 September 1948
32. Kripalani's 'Gandhi, his Life and Thoughts', Government of India, Publications Division, 1970
33. 'India Wins Freedom', Maulana Abul Kalam Azad, p. 162, Orient Longman Ltd., Madras 1988
34. Ibid, p. 162
35. Selected correspondence of Sardar Patel 1945–50, Volume 2 (1977), edited by V. Shankar, Navajivan Publishing House, Ahmedabad 380 014
36. 'Reminiscences of the Nehru Age', M.D. Mathai, Vikas Publishing House 1978, p. 241
37. Ibid, p. 242
38. 'India Wins Freedom', Maulana Azad, p. 180
39. *The Times*, 14 May 2004, Editorial
40. Ibid, 15 May 2004 Ben Macintyre

APPENDIX 1

1. I.O.R. P/367/71

APPENDIX 3

1 I.O.R. P/368/9

BIBLIOGRAPHY

Adams, W.H.D., *The Makers of British India*, 1902
Aligarh Muslim University, *Mediaeval India – A Miscellany*, Asia Publishing House, London, 1972
Anderson, P., *The English in Western India*, 1854
Aober, P., *Rise and Progress of British Power in India*, 1837
Arnold, Sir Edwin, *India Revisited*, 1886
Ashton, T., *The Industrial Revolution 1760–1830*, Oxford University Press, 1947
Azad, M.A.K., *India Wins Freedom*, Orient Longman, Madras, 1988
Baden-Powell, B.H., *The Land System of British India*, 1892
Barva, P., *Military Developments in India, 1750–1850*, 1994
Basham, A.L., *The Wonder that was India*, Sidgwick and Jackson, 1967
Bayley, C.A., *Indian Society and the Making of the British Empire*, 1988
Beale, T.W., *An Oriental Biographical Dictionary*, 1894
Birkenhead, Earl, F.E., *The Life of F.E. Smith, First Earl of Birkenhead*, 1959
Blacker, V., *Operations of the British Army in India during Maratha War of 1817–1819*, 1821
Bose, S.C., *The Indian Struggle 1920–42*, Asia Publishing House, London, 1964
Briggs A., *The Age of Improvement 1780–1867*, 1959
Brown, J., *Gandhi and Civil Disobedience*, Cambridge, 1977
Brown, J., *Modern India*, OUP 1994
Buckland, C.E., *Dictionary of Indian Biography*, Bloomsbury, London, 1906
Carrington, C.E., *The British Overseas*, Cambridge University Press, 1950

Court, W.H.B., *British Economic History 1870–1914*, 1965
Duff, J.G., *History of the Marathas*, 1921
Elphinstone, H, *History of India*, 1915
Elphinstone, M., *Selections from the Minutes of*, 1884
Erikson, S., *Gandhi's Truth*, London, 1969
Forbes, D., *Sketch of the Early Life of*, 1859
Forbes, J., *Battle of Arras*, 1775
Forbes, J., *Oriental Memoirs*, 1813
Ford, P. & G., *A Breviate of Parliamentary Papers 1917–1939*, 1951
Forrest, G.W., *Administration of Warren Hastings*, 1892
Forrest, G.W., *Cities of India*, 1903
Foster, W., *The English Factories in India*, Oxford, 1906
Gandhi, M.K., *An Autobiography*, Navajivan Trust, 1927
Gandhi, R., *Patel – A Life*, Navajivan Publishing House, Ahmedabad, 1991
Ghosal, U.N., *Hindu Revenue System*, Calcutta, 1919
Hamer, D.A., *John Morley: Liberal Intellectual in Politics*, 1968
Hamilton, W., *Geographical, Statistical, etc., Account of Hindustan*, 1820
Hardiman, D., *Peasant Nationalists of Gujarat*, Oxford University Press, Bombay, 1981
Hobsbawn, E.J., *On History*, Abacus, 1997
Hobsbawn, E.J., *Industry and Empire*, 1968
Hough, W., *Political and Military Events in British India 1756–1849*, 1853
Huston, J., *Representative Men of the Bombay Presidency*, Historical Publishing Company, 1887
Hutchings and Stephens, *Two Centuries of Change*, Blackie and Son, 1941
Hyde, M., *Lord Reading*, 1967
Imperial Gazetteer of India, new edition, 26 volumes
Jackson, S., *Rufus Isaacs*, 1936
Judd, D., *Lord Reading*, Weidenfeld and Nicolson, 1982
Keay, J., *The Honourable Company*, Macmillan, New York, 1991
Keay, J., *India – A History*, HarperCollins, London, 2000
Kendell, P., *India and the British*
Khan, A.M., *Mirat-I-Ahmadi*, Bombay, 1889 (English translation, British Library, I.O.R.)
Lethbridge, R., *The Golden Book of India*, Macmillan, 1893

Macpherson, J., *East India Company – History and Management of, from its Origin in 1600 to 1799*
Majundar, M.R., *Cultural History of Gujarat*, Bombay 1965
Mandelslo, J.A de., *Voyages and Travels into the East Indies*, London, 1669
Marx, K., *The Future of British Rule in India*
Mathai, J., *Village Government in British India*, London, 1913
Mathai, M.D., *Reminiscences of the Nehru Age*, Vikas Publishing, 1978
Mayo, K., *Mother India*, 1927
Medieval India – A Miscellany, Aligarh Muslim University, Asia Publishing House, London, 1972
Meghani, J., *Mansaina Diva*, Bhavnagar, 1967
Mehta, S., *The Peasantry and Nationalism*, Manohar Publications, New Delhi, 1984
Menon, V.P., *Integration of the Indian States*, Orient Longman, Hyderabad, 1956
Menon, V.P., *The Transfer of Power*, Orient Longman, Hyderabad, 1957
Mitchell, B.R and Deane P., *Abstract of British Historical Statistics*, 1962
Muller, F.M., *India, What it Can Teach Us*, 1892
Muller, F.M., *Indian Philosophy*, 1899
Nehru, J., *An Autobiography*, Bodley Head, London, 1936
Newark, T., *Turning the Tide of War*, Hamlyn, 2001
Pande, B.N. (Ed.), *A Centenary History of the Indian National Congress*, Vikas/A.I.C.C., 1985
Parikh, R.D., *The Press and Society*, 1965
Patel, G.I., *Vithalbhai Patel – Life and Times*, Narayan Press, 1950
Payne, R., *The Life and Death of Mahatma Gandhi*, Koneck and Konelly, New York, 1969
Pechel, S., *Bombay – an Historical Account of the Settlement and Possession of by the East India Company*, 1781
Pocock, D., *Kanbi and Patidar*, Oxford University Press, 1972
Reports of the Committee of Secrecy, Appointed by Parliament to Investigate the Affairs of E.I. Co's, 1773
Roe, T. Sir, *Embassy to the Court of Emperor Jehangir, 1615–16*, Hakluyt Society, 1926
Saran, P., *The Provincial Government of the Mughals 1526–1658*, Asia Publishing House, London, 1941

Sarkar, J., *India of Aurangzeb*, 1901
Shankar, V. (Ed.), *Sardar Patel, Select Correspondence 1945–1950*, Navajivan Publishing House, Ahmedabad 1976
Sitaramaya, P., *History of the Indian National Congress*, Congress Working Committee, 1935
Smith, V.A., *Akbar the Great Moghal*, 1917
Stokes, E., *The Peasant and the Raj*, Cambridge, 1978
Taylor, A.J.P., *English History 1914–1945*, 1965
Thomas, E., *Revenue Resources of the Mughal Empire*, London, 1871

GLOSSARY

(Spelling of the Indian names is not always consistent, particularly in early documents. The original spellings have been left throughout the book.)

Ashram – a hermitage, a resting place
Bardoli – a small town in Gujarat
Beega/Bigha – a sub-division of an acre
Collector – a government official who collects revenue and also the district magistrate
Cos – a measurement of distance, about $1\frac{1}{2}$ miles
Crore – ten million
Dacoit – a bandit
Desaigiri – authorisation of collecting land revenue and maintaining law and order in all villages of a Taluka or Purganna
Dewan/Diwan – Prime Minister of a princely state
Fozdar – police inspector
Girnar – mountain range in the State of Saurashtra
Gol – a marriage circle of a few villages
Hartal – strike
Hijrati – people who move across a state border
Inam – present, tip, baksheesh
Khaddar – hand spun cloth
Lakh – one hundred thousand
Lathi – a thick bamboo stick
Maharajah – the ruler of a state
Mahatma – great or elevated soul, a saint
Mal – an area in Kaira district, semi-arid
Mamlatdar – an officer below the grade of Collector who computes land revenue

Mandal – society
Nadiad/Nariad/Neriad/Naryad/Neryad – alternative spellings for the name of this town
Pandit – a religious expert
Paraganah/Pergunnah/Purganna – a cluster of villages
Patels – a close-knit community in Gujarat
Patidar – a community in Gujarat State, mainly Desais, Patels and Amins
Patrika – a giveaway pamphlet
Peon – a person who carries messages, a 'gofer'
Sardar – a commanding leader
Satyagraha – a strategy of non-violent non-cooperation with the Government administration or a strategy to spread the truth
Shri – a polite address to a gentleman
Sjt – a very polite address to a gentleman, abridged version of 'Shriyut'
Swaraj – Sanskrit for independence
Talati/Tullatee – an official appointed to keep village account books and a check on the village Patels
Taluka – a sub-division of a district

INDEX